institute of
financial services

MARKETING MANAGEMENT

Helen Meek
& Richard Meek

Institute of Financial Services
IFS House
4-9 Burgate Lane
Canterbury
Kent
CT1 2XJ

T   01227 818649
F   01227 479641
E   editorial@ifslearning.com

Institute of Financial Services publications are published by The Chartered Institute of Bankers, a non-profit making registered educational charity.

Typeset by Kevin O'Connor

Printed by Antony Rowe Ltd, Wiltshire

© The Chartered Institute of Bankers 2001

Reprinted 2004

ISBN 0-85297-570-8

CONTENTS

Contents

INTRODUCTION

The Concept of this Book

This study text has been written for students of The Chartered Institute of Bankers' ACIB/ BSc subject Marketing Management and for practitioners in financial services who are looking for a practical refresher.

Each chapter is divided into sections and contains learning objectives and clear, concise topic-by-topic coverage.

Syllabus

The key sections of the Marketing Management syllabus are:

- Corporate Strategy;
- Marketing Strategy;
- Marketing Management and Planning;
- Marketing Services;
- Buyer Behaviour;
- Marketing Information;
- Segmentation, Targeting and Positioning;
- Product Management;
- Pricing;
- Channel Management;
- Communications.

Your contribution

Although this study text is designed to stand alone, as with most topics certain aspects of this subject are constantly changing. Therefore it is very important that you keep up-to-date with these key areas. For example, you should read the quality press and financial journals and look out for relevant websites.

We anticipate that you will study this course for one session (six months), reading through and studying approximately one unit every week. However, note that as topics vary in size and as knowledge tends not to fall into uniform chunks, some units are unavoidably longer than others.

Study plan

If you are a distance-learning student and have not received your study plan by the beginning of the session, please contact the CIB Tuition Department.

Tel: 01227 818637

Fax: 01227 453547

e-mail: tuition@cib.org.uk

Part One

MARKETING MANAGEMENT OVERVIEW

1

CORPORATE STRATEGY

Learning Objectives

After reading this chapter students should:

● Understand the nature of strategy and of strategic decisions;

● Understand the hierarchy of planning levels and how this influences objectives;

● Know and understand the influences of different stakeholder groups on an organization;

● Know and understand the different elements of environmental and internal analysis;

● Understand the factors influencing the management of change in an organization.

Figure 1.1: Chapter Map

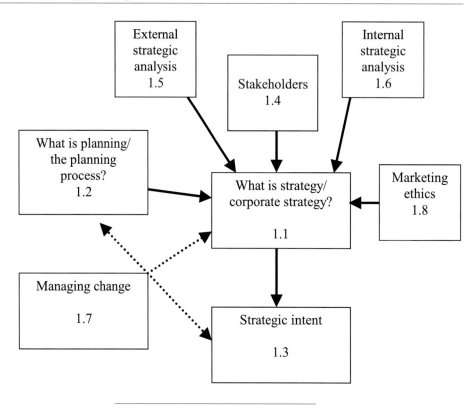

Introduction

In considering the processes, details and differences between strategy and planning, and their application to business, an important starting point is to decide what organization entity you are working with. Students often become confused by these subjects, simply because they have no clear idea of the organizational entity that is the focus of their study. Readers could work for the following types of organization:

- a private corporation (e.g. a public limited company) which is owned by shareholders;

- a small to medium-sized enterprise which is owned by a few or many shareholders;

- self-employed in a partnership or as a sole trader;

- public sector with a national, regional or local remit,

- state-controlled, stand-alone, business entity.

In considering the ideas of this chapter we shall think of the hypothetical structure typical for many multinational businesses and which is presented in Figure 1.2.

Further confusion of the meaning of 'strategy' arises from the difficulty of defining strategy in any but the most general of ways – i.e. as an approach for achieving an objective. Where a manager works within an organization affects whether the work is strategic or tactical. The context of strategy is discussed.

There are many influences on the setting of corporate objectives. A useful approach for understanding this is the 'stakeholder' concept. Each stakeholder group has different objectives and these may be specified very differently. It is important to understand the relative influence of these various, often competing, groups if a more detailed insight into corporate behaviour is to be achieved.

The highly competitive, dynamic marketplace has resulted in a much more rapid rate of change in the business environment. Change must be managed for both the individual and the organization to remain competitive.

Figure 1.2: Hypothetical Structure for a Multinational Corporation

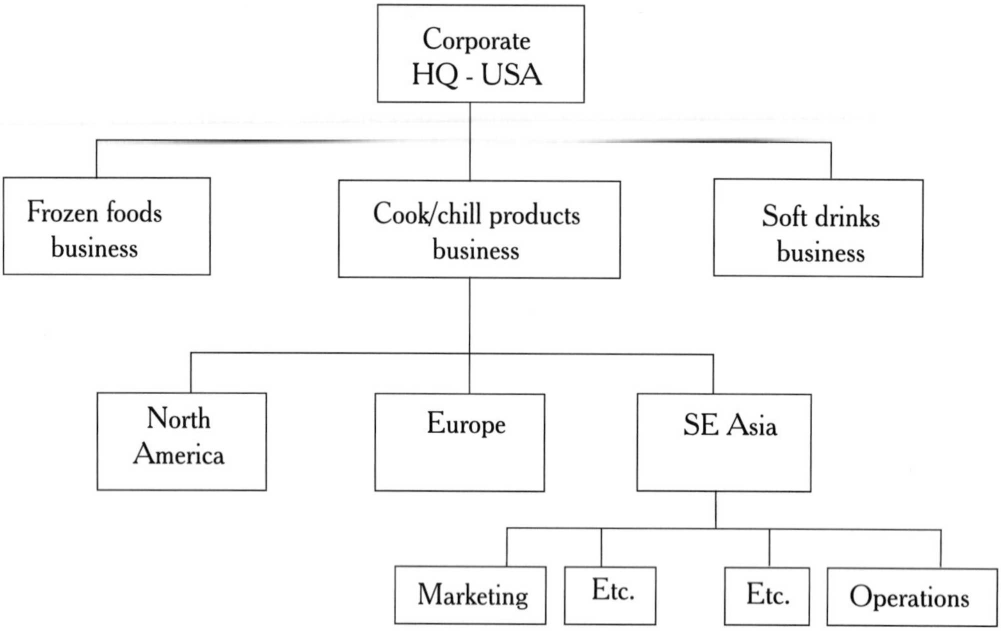

1.1   What is Strategy/Corporate Strategy?

Strategy versus tactics

Strategy is 'a course of action, specifying the resources required to achieve a given objective': i.e., how we intend to achieve our objectives, for example by adopting an attacking strategy on the football field or by using a sales-push strategy in the marketplace.

Tactics are the details of the plan, indicating the deployment of resources in the agreed strategy; for example we will substitute defender Y with attacker X after 25 minutes or we will increase our sales push with a telesales campaign, operated by an agency and targeted at 6,000 client leads over three months from January.

What is strategic and what is tactical depends on the level at which the decision is taken and the perspective involved.

Characteristics of strategy

In practice 'strategic' may refer to 'broad', 'general' and 'long-term'. Johnson and Scholes (1999) identify the characteristics of strategic decisions in organizations as follows:

Scope   Strategic decisions are concerned with the *scope* of the organization's activities.

Environment	Strategy involves relating an organization's activities to the *environment* in which it operates.
Resource capability	Strategy also involves the matching of an organization's activities to its *resource capability*
Resource allocation	Strategic decisions therefore involve major decisions about the *allocation* or *reallocation of resources.*
Affected by three main types of influences	Strategic decisions will be affected not just by (1) environmental considerations and (2) resource availability, but also by (3) the *values and expectations* of the people in power within the organization.
Long-term business direction	Strategic decisions are likely to affect the *long-term direction* that the organization takes.
Major driver of change	Strategic decisions have implications for change throughout the organization, and so are likely to be *complex in nature.*

Corporate and functional strategies

Corporate strategy is the most general level of strategy in an organization. In the words of Johnson and Scholes (1999), corporate strategy 'is concerned with what types of business the company as a whole should be in and is therefore concerned with decisions of scope'. Corporate strategy involves issues such as:

- diversifying or limiting the activities of the business;

- investing in existing units, or buying new businesses;

- surviving.

Business strategy relates to how an organization approaches a particular market, or the activity of a particular business unit. For example, this can involve decisions as to whether, in principle, a company should:

- segment the market and specialize in particularly profitable areas;

- compete by offering a wider range of products.

An example of a business strategy is the recent decision by *Mercedes-Benz* to expand its product range to include four-wheel drive vehicles and a small-car model.

Operational and functional strategies involve decisions of strategic importance, but which are made or determined at operational levels. These decisions include product pricing, investment in plant (e.g. timing), personnel policy and so forth. The contributions of these different functions determine the success of the strategy because, effectively, a strategy is implemented only at this level.

1.2   What is Planning/the Planning Process?

Planning is basically a way of coping with the uncertainty and risk of the future, in a way that will allow the organization's objectives to be achieved. This involves:

1.   deciding what the organization, and units within it, should achieve (objective-setting);

2.   anticipating, as far as possible, the opportunities and threats that are likely to be offered by the future (forecasting); and

3.   making decisions about:

- what to do;
- how to do it;
- when to do it; and
- who should do it.

The future cannot be foreseen with certainty, and even the best-laid plans will go wrong to a greater or lesser degree. Nevertheless, plans give direction and predictability (to an extent) to the work of the organization, and enable it to adapt to environmental changes without crisis.

Planning is an all-embracing activity of the organization, from the determination of its overall 'direction' ('what business are we in?'), right down to the details of how the organization fulfils its day-to-day operational tasks.

An organization does not have just one plan to 'cover' all of its activities but many plans which cover each level of hierarchy and each functional activity.

1.3   Strategic Intent

Introduction

Strategic intent is the vision that the business has of where it wants to be at some stage in the future. This is the overall guiding influence on the strategic direction of the business, on which a whole hierarchy of planning activity is based.

Planning hierarchy

Figure 1.3: Planning Hierarchy

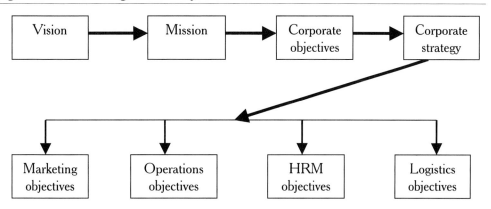

Business vision

A coherent and exceptional statement of where the business should be in the future, often in ten years' time.

Business mission

Defines the business domain(s) in terms of products, technologies, customers or a combination of these. They are long-lasting statements which are not quantified. Mission statements determine the nature and direction of an organization and say what its area of interest is (i.e., what it is about). Mission statements focus on:

● What business are we in?

● Who is to be served?

● What benefits are to be delivered?

● How are consumers to be satisfied?

The mission statement outlines the present view of the organization's purpose without restricting future possible development. For example, a computer company may wish to emphasize its width of possible work: it is not simply concerned with computer hardware or solving problems in information technology. To meet the criteria provided for a good mission statement the business may focus on customer segments where it will use computers to solve business problems. Similarly a publisher of music CDs may state that it is in the entertainment business. Good mission statements are invaluable because they provide some boundaries to management thinking which guide the business in core competencies, but do not constrain manager ingenuity and freethinking to an excessively narrow extent.

Corporate objectives

Quantified statements should be 'SMART' (specific, measurable, actionable, realistic with a timescale). Objective setting is not an isolated process and there should be a clear link with performance measures. Kaplan & Norton (1992) developed the concept of the balanced scorecard to highlight the fact that the business should be viewed from a four different perspectives and not purely from a financial perspective. This framework can help to identify objectives and link them with performance measures.

- *Financial perspective* – This is of obvious importance for all companies but should not be viewed in isolation. This highlights the business from the shareholder's perspective.

- *Customer perspective* – How customers view the business is key to business success. They will be concerned with factors such as quality and level of customer service.

- *Internal* – Internal processes are important to external customer satisfaction, such as manufacturing, logistics and marketing.

- *Innovation and learning* – The ability of a company to maintain its competitive advantage is clearly linked to its ability to continually innovate and learn, i.e. the concept of the learning organization.

The balanced scorecard encourages managers to consider the business from a variety of viewpoints rather than just financial. It also encourages managers to develop objectives that are consistent with one another.

More detailed coverage of corporate objectives is provided in section 1.4, where stakeholder interests are discussed.

Corporate strategy

How the objectives will be achieved.

Functional objectives

Marketing, operations, HRM, logistics etc. must each specify its own functional objectives which each, separately, support the achievement of the overall corporate objective. As for corporate objectives, functional objectives must be 'SMART'. Marketing objectives focus on products and markets.

MARKETING IN PRACTICE
McDonalds Mission

To be the family restaurant that people enjoy more. This will be achieved through five strategies: Development, **Our People**, **Restaurant Excellence**, Operating Structure, and **The Brand**.

- *Our People:* Achieve a competitive advantage through people who are high-calibre, effective, well motivated and feel part of the McDonald's team in delivering the company's goals.

- *Restaurant Excellence:* Focus on consistent delivery of quality, service and cleanliness through excellence in our restaurants.

> ● *The Brand:* Continue to build the relationship between McDonalds and our customers in order to be a genuine part of the fabric of British society.

The UK leading grocery supermarket group Tesco does not compartmentalize its specification of mission statement. Instead, it effectively combines mission statements with strategy statements. The company does not use textbook terminology and this practice by companies in general can confuse students. Tesco's statements for customer service and for pricing are presented. Here they use the term 'objective', which is in fact a strategy statement rather than a 'SMART' objective.

MARKETING IN PRACTICE

Tesco

Customer Service

Objective (**Strategy**): provide customers with outstanding, naturally delivered personal service

Examples: Customer Assistants, No Quibble Money Back Guarantee, 'One in Front' queuing policy and Baby-Changing Facilities

Pricing

Objective (**Strategy**): to be competitive even on the basics (i.e. basic grocery products)
Examples: Value Lines and consistently low prices on key brands and own-brand products

Source: www.tesco.com

1.4   Stakeholders

Stakeholders

An organization pursues goals and objectives in the light of environmental pressures and the demands of its own managers. In fact, there are many stakeholders in an organization, who can be identified as follows:

● Internal stakeholders (employees, management);

● Connected stakeholders (shareholders, customers, suppliers, financiers);

● External stakeholders (the community, government, pressure groups).

Internal stakeholders

Employees and management (which includes the chairman and the board of directors) are so intimately connected with the company that their objectives are likely to have a strong and immediate influence on how it is run. They are interested in the following issues:

1. The *organization's continuation and growth*. Management and employees have a special interest in the organization's continued existence. This interest may not be held by

shareholders. For example, if the organization has surplus funds, the management might try to invest them in new projects, whereas the shareholders might prefer these funds to be returned to them as dividends;

2. Managers and employees have *individual interests* and goals which, it is hoped, can be harnessed, in part at least, to the goals of the organization. Managers and employees look to the organization for:

    -   security of income

    -   increases in income

    -   a safe and comfortable working environment

    -   a sense of community

    -   interesting work

    -   skills and career development

    -   a sense of doing something worthwhile.

Connected stakeholders

These include the following:

1. *Shareholders*. Shareholders own the business, however their prime interest is a return on their investment, whether in the short or long term. Shareholders are now being asked to take a more involved interest in a company's affairs. There are many types of shareholder:

    -   If you have a few shares in, say, a privatized utility, you can be classified as a personal investor. British Gas has many millions of investors;

    -   Many individuals who wish to invest in the stock market choose to pool the amounts they invest with other investors, in order to buy a mix of shares. Unit trusts are widely used for this purpose;

    -   There are many other financial institutions that invest in shares, such as life insurance companies and pension funds. A pension fund acts to channel long-term savings to provide investors with a pension.

2. *Bankers* are also interested in a firm's overall condition from the point of view of the security of the capital advanced and interest payments.

3. *Customers* want products and services. Customers might be powerful (e.g. a retail chain buying from a supplier) and can have a significant influence over prices and procedures.

4. *Suppliers* will expect to be paid and will be interested in future business.

External stakeholders

External stakeholder groups – the government, local authorities, pressure groups, the community at large and professional bodies – are likely to have quite diverse objectives and have a varying ability to ensure that the company meets them.

1.   The government has an interest in:

     -   tax revenue (corporation tax, VAT) or other revenue;

     -   compliance with legislation (e.g. on health and safety);

     -   statistics;

     -   regional development (because companies are employers and wealth creators).

2.   Local authorities are also interested, because companies:

     -   can bring local employment;

     -   can affect the local environment (e.g. by increasing road traffic);

     -   professional bodies are interested to ensure that members who work for companies comply with professional ethics and standards;

     -   pressure groups will have an interest in particular issues.

3.   Pressure groups have a range of influences on a business, depending on the type of pressure group and especially whether it is a single-issue or multiple-issue pressure group. The single-issue fuel tax protests in Europe in the summer of 2000 resulted in an easing of the tax burden partly for general motorists, but also for high fuel-using groups, such as the transport industry. Support for this intense but relatively short-lived group resulted in an adjustment to governement taxation policy and constrained the leeway of oil companies to increase prices following large rises in the price of crude oil.

Stakeholder interests

For a business, the owners are considered to be the most important stakeholders. After all, that is why the business exists – as a business – at all, which is to increase (over the long term) the owners' wealth. This is the primary corporate objective.

Businesses have to do lots of other things too, such as satisfying their customers, obeying the law and motivating employees, but these are all secondary or subsidiary objectives that serve to ensure the achievement of the primary objective. How do we measure the primary corporate objective? The primary objective for a company is a financial objective based on shareholders' wealth, but there are different ways of expressing such an objective in quantitative terms for practical purposes. Various financial objectives include the following:

(a)   Profitability;

(b)   Return on investment (ROI) or return on capital employed (ROCE);

(c)   Share price, earnings per share, dividends;

(d)   Growth;

(e)   Survival;

(f)   Multiple objectives.

(a)   *Profitability*

Profitability (profits as a percentage of revenue) *on its own* is not satisfactory as an overall long-term corporate objective.

-    It fails to allow for the size of the capital investment required to make the profit.

-    Since capital is often in restricted supply, profitability must be measured in terms of the limiting factor, i.e. in terms of the scarce financial resources that a company will have at its disposal. Therefore, return on capital employed would be a more appropriate objective.

-    Shareholders, as a group, should be interested in maximizing profits over time. In order to maximize profits over time, costs will have to be incurred today in order to generate returns in the future, and so a profit-maximizing firm will seek to make investments, spending money now to realize benefits in future.

Profitability, despite its shortcomings, must remain a yardstick for managerial performance, provided that profit targets are stated in acceptable and consistent terms.

(b)   *Return on capital employed (ROCE)*

Some companies use ROCE (profits as a percentage of capital invested) as a primary objective, but there are drawbacks to its use.

-    Capital employed is suspect as a financial measure, because a book value in the balance sheet probably bears little or no comparison with the 'true' value of the assets.

-    If ROCE were used, there would be some difficulty in balancing short-term results against long-term requirements.

-    The choice of ROCE as an objective also ignores the *risk* of investments. High-risk projects might promise a high return if they succeed, but it may be safer to opt for a project with a lower return but a greater guarantee of success. For example, a company in a low-risk business might be satisfied with a return of, say, 15%, whereas in a comparable high-risk business the required return might be a minimum of 25%.

It has been suggested that return on shareholders' capital (ROSC) (i.e. ROCE, but ignoring long-term borrowings and interest payments) is the prime corporate objective, but adds the following:

—   There is a *minimum* return that shareholders will accept, allowing for the *risk* of the investment;

– The target return *must* exceed the minimum, but *may* be satisfactory or even excellent if events turn out well. Shareholders seek an investment that stands a good chance of yielding a high rate of return and at the same time a very low risk of achieving a poor rate of return.

Risk can occur from many sources. Here are some examples:

– *Physical risk*. This has been highlighted by earthquakes in the past few years in the USA and Japan. Other physical risks include fire, flooding, and equipment breakdown;

– *Economic risk*. The strategy might be based on assumptions as to the economy, which might turn out to be wrong;

– *Financial risk*. This relates to the type of financial arrangement in the decision. A firm that borrows heavily suffers if interest rates are raised. Share capital gives the firm more flexibility because dividends are paid at the directors' discretion;

– *Business risk*. These risks relate to commercial and industry factors. In other words, there is the possibility that the strategy will fail;

– *Political risk*. This includes nationalization, sanctions, civil war and political instability, if these have an impact on the business. This is sometimes called country risk;

– *Exchange risk*. This is the risk that changes in exchange rates will affect the value of a transaction in a currency, or how it is reported.

(c) *Share price, earnings and dividends*

Earnings per share (EPS) or *dividend payments* may be used as a basis of establishing corporate objectives. They are both measures that recognize that a company is owned by its shareholder-investors and the purpose of a company is held to be the provision of a satisfactory return for its owners.

Failure to provide a satisfactory EPS or dividend would presumably lead the shareholders to sell their shares or, in extreme circumstances, to wind up the company. When earnings and dividends are low, the market value of shares will also be depressed unless there is a strong prospect of dividend growth in the future.

Shareholders are concerned with the size of the return they get, but also with the size of the investment they must make to achieve the return. To overcome this problem, earnings and dividend growth could be expressed as:

– Dividends received; plus

– Capital growth in market value expressed as a percentage of market value at the start of the period under review.

(d) *Growth*

It is arguable that a company should make growth its prime objective – growth in EPS, growth in profits, growth in ROCE or growth in dividends per share. There are some difficulties, however, in accepting growth as an overall objective.

Growth of what? If we suppose that the aim is *balanced growth* – i.e. a commensurate growth in profits, sales, assets, number of employees etc. – such a policy might be applicable in the short term, but in the long run some elements must be expected to grow faster than others because of the dynamics of the business environment.

In the long run, growth might lead to diseconomies of scale so that inefficiencies will occur and the growth pattern will inevitably stagnate. The idea that a company must grow to survive is no longer widely accepted.

There is little reason why in theory companies should not pay all their earnings as dividends, and have no growth. A consequence of such a policy would be that if no money were reinvested in the business, it would be overtaken by competitors.

Growth is, however, in the interests of management, as stakeholders, because it provides them with a career. Growth is likely to be a prime objective for the following types of company:

– *Smaller companies*, because these will usually have a greater potential for significant rates of growth.

– *Larger companies* which are seeking to achieve a size that will enable them to compete with other multinationals in world markets.

(e) *Survival*

Drucker (1973) suggested that the prime objective of a company is not simply financial, but is one of survival. He argued that there are five major areas in which to decide objectives for survival:

1. There is a need to anticipate the social climate and economic policy in those areas where the company operates and sells. A business must organize its behaviour in such a way as to survive in respect to both.

2. A business is a human organization and must be designed for joint performance by everyone in it.

3. Survival also depends on the supply of an economic product or service.

4. A business must *innovate*, because the economy and markets are continually changing.

5. Inevitably, a business must be *profitable* to survive.

The needs and opportunities in each of these five areas in turn affect performance and results in the others. Survival is not widely accepted as a corporate objective. Argenti, for example, has argued that the owners of a company might choose, in some circumstances, to wind up their business or sell out to another company in a takeover bid, and so their objectives would obviously be better served by not surviving. Survival is perhaps more important to employees and managers than to investors.

(f)   *Multiple objectives*

A firm can identify several objectives. For example, a target increase in:

- Share price

- In % ROI

- In % profitability.

All objectives may be linked but not in a perfect way. For example, while a rise in profitability will result in an increase in ROI, the magnitude of the rise in share price can not be determined with any certainty.

A firm should be concerned with its risk posture, and that its objectives should therefore have regard to its financial risk, expressed as its debt/equity ratio. It is suggested that there is a 'golden mean', or optimum combination, of the following.

- Scope for growth and enhanced corporate wealth, through a suitable balance between equity and debt finance.

- Maintaining a policy of paying attractive but not overgenerous dividends.

- Maintaining an acceptable, but flexible, gearing ratio. The acceptable norm will vary from industry to industry.

The Time Horizon

Strategic decisions are typically concerned with the long term, however the firm must reach basic minimum targets in the short term to get to the long term.

Thus, objectives may be long-term and short-term.

- A company that is suffering from a recession in its core industries and making losses in the short term might continue to have a primary objective in the long term of achieving a steady growth in earnings or profits, but in the short term its primary objective might switch to *survival*.

- For example, a company's primary objective might be to increase its earnings per share from 30p to 50p in the next five years. Strategies for achieving the objective might be selected to include the following:

    - increasing profitability in the next 12 months by cutting expenditure

    - increasing export sales over the next three years

    - developing a successful new product for the domestic market within five years.

- Secondary objectives might then be reassessed to include the following:

    - the objective of improving manpower productivity by 10% within 12 months.

    - improving customer service in export markets with the objective of doubling the number of overseas sales outlets in selected countries within the next three years;

- investing more in product market research and development, with the objective of bringing at least three new products to the market within five years.

Factors affecting the time horizon of planning are various.

● In the oil industry, firms have to plan for decades ahead to ensure they have enough capacity to satisfy demand. Oil fields involve long-term research. Demand for oil will not vanish overnight – people will still drive cars.

● In information technology on the other hand, developments move quicker. In the past decade new computer chips, offering significant performance improvements, have been launched at least bi-annually.

● Different markets change at varying rates driven by the speed of change in customer needs and wants. For some products, such as those in the clothing industry, needs and wants change rapidly, depending on fashion. In other markets, e.g. current banking accounts, customer needs and wants change at a very low pace.

1.5   External Strategic Analysis

Environmental analysis

Any business organization has competitors. Organizations need to identify who their competitors are. In the UK market over ten years ago, four large clearing banks regarded *each other* as 'the competition'. However, building societies invested heavily in automation and some now rival the banks and many have now become banks. These competitive changes forced the original large four banks to improve their service, including, for example, extended opening hours and extension of their ATM networks.

In April 1996, the supermarket firm Tesco announced that it was going to compete with the High Street banks by offering an 'own-label' deposit account and credit card via its existing Clubcard scheme. Marks and Spencer at that time already offered pensions. This was only the beginning of the rush of non-traditional institutions into financial services. The original large four clearing banks were therefore guilty of defining their 'industry' and their competitors too narrowly.

Environmental Issues in Outline

Detailed discussion of the environment is covered in Chapter 3, but we can flag some key strategic issues that strategic marketing planners have to cope with. Crystal-ball gazing, however, is always a hazardous exercise.

Key trends are these:

● *Globalization:* this means that national barriers are breaking down. For example, the World Trade Organization has more power to promote free trade than GATT, the organization which it replaced. There is increasing political will to improve the freedom of trade in financial services. Most of the major firms operating London's financial markets are owned by non-British companies. (This is discussed further at the end of this section.)

● There is increasing pressure for changes in the law both at national and at EU level. For example, since early 1996 the EU's Investment Services Directive has been in operation, enabling freer trade within the EU.

Restructuring in the financial services sector will lead to two types of business developing:

– global, wholesale retailers of financial services;

– specialist providers, in the domestic market.

● The distinctions between banks, building societies and other financial institutions will fade, and other High Street retailers (e.g. Marks & Spencer) will continue to develop their financial products, integrating financial and non-financial products. Virgin is promoting itself as a financial brand.

● People will need to increase their savings, as a result of reduced state benefits and demographic changes. There will be increased demand for pensions and health care savings products. People will prefer financial assets to physical property (such as houses, real estate).

● There will be new sources of finance in the global financial system, as developing countries invest their wealth.

● The use of derivative products (e.g. futures) will increase.

● Telecommunications will support the increasing sophistication and volume of information between users.

● The cost of IT will continue to fall. Effective implementation of IT systems will be a vital component of competitive advantage.

● Fraud and systems hackers will continue to create problems. Financial service providers must assure customers of the integrity of systems if they are to continue to trade.

● The decline in the use of cheques will continue.

Trends and market opportunities

Few commentators see purely technological issues as barriers to progress. In fact extensive changes and the delivery of financial services in the retail sector will be made possible by:

1. Improved telecommunications;

2. The falling costs of computer power;

3. The widespread use of multimedia systems;

4. The growth of computer literacy;

5. Secure communication.

Five Forces

Michael Porter (1985) provided a more analytical framework for the external environment. He hypothesized that there were 'five forces' that influenced the nature of competitive behaviour in any industry sector, namely:

1. The threat of new entrants
2. Barriers to entry
3. The threat from substitute products
4. The bargaining power of customers
5. The rivalry among current competitors.

1. *The threat of new entrants.* Is it easy for other firms to enter the industry, or are there *barriers to entry?* Barriers to entry are:

   - economies of scale (the bigger the better, or small is beautiful?);
   - product differentiation;
   - requirements for capital investment (e.g. to spend on IT systems);
   - switching costs (i.e. the cost and inconvenience that customers would experience by changing supplier);
   - access to distribution channels;
   - others such as patents, experience and know-how, government subsidies etc.

   Entry barriers can be raised by increasing the perceived riskiness of the industry to a potential new entrant.

2. *The threat from substitute products.* Crudely, substitute products are produced by two or more industries, but satisfy the same customer need. (For example, people who wish to go from London to Paris without driving can fly or take the Eurostar Channel Tunnel rail service.) Substitutes limit the price an industry can charge but this depends on the degree of substitutability.

3. *The bargaining power of customers.* Customers are in a strong position to exert pressure on suppliers for lower prices and/or more product features (which reduce the profitability of an industry) if:

   - the customer buys a large proportion of the output;
   - the customer can easily find other sources of supply;
   - there are low switching costs;
   - the customer makes low profits;
   - the customer can take over sources of supply.

4. *The bargaining power of suppliers.* This is a mirror image of the bargaining power of customers.

● Can suppliers easily find other customers?

● How important are the suppliers' products?

● Switching costs (e.g. the cost or inconvenience of changing bank accounts);

● Number of suppliers – few suppliers mean little choice.

5. *The rivalry among current competitors* will affect the industry as a whole.

● How many are there? A few dominant firms?

● Is the market growing as a whole, or declining?

● Can customers switch easily between suppliers?

● Is it easy to leave the industry or are there high exit barriers?

● High strategic stakes? If the industry is a key industry for some competitors then they will act highly aggressively in response to action by other firms in the industry.

● Capacity and unit costs?

● Fixed costs (high fixed costs imply a high breakeven point, and the need for economies of scale).

Globalization

The profound influence of globalization requires particular discussion within the external environment, but what is 'globalization'?

Global companies, i.e. multinational corporations (MNCs), allocate their resources to serve global markets. Such companies source worldwide to supply markets spread across the globe. Globalization is the trend for MNCs to take a greater share in national, regional and world markets.

What has encouraged this trend towards globalization?

There has been pressure to reduce trade barriers in the world. Since the late 1940s the GATT was the most active forum for this. The World Trade Organization (WTO), successor to GATT, has greater powers to reduce trading barriers further. In addition there has been a growth in the number of regional trading groups, such as the European Union (EU), North American Free Trade Association (NAFTA) and Association of South East Asian Nations (ASEAN). Against a global background of reducing trade barriers, these regional groups have sought to reduce barriers at a much greater rate at the regional level.

The impact of such activity is well demonstrated in the EU, which is at the forefront of regional elimination of trade barriers as an economic and, to some degree, political union. As barriers have been removed, the 'domestic' market suddenly becomes one of 15 nations, stretching from the Arctic Circle to the Mediterranean. Organizational structures, and size, formed to serve single domestic markets suddenly become inadequate for such a large single market. The response is to grow bigger through mergers and acquisitions. There has been an explosion in growth in the number of pan-European business since the formation of the single European market in January 1993. In all markets, fewer, large businesses now operate within Europe.

While the European experience is being repeated throughout the world, the globalization of activity has been particularly strong in the Triad economies (i.e. NAFTA, EU and Japan). Large businesses have for decades tried to organize to operate successfully, simultaneously within all three regions. Events in the last decade, such as the demise of communism and of apartheid as economic and political systems and the explosive growth of the Tiger economies, has spread intense global activity beyond the Triad region.

There are potential benefits and problems connected with globalization. Some benefits and problems are presented, however the key issues of concern are the size of the potential benefits and the extent to which potential benefits are shared in comparison with the potential negative impact of globalization.

Potential benefits from globalization

- The potential for large economies of scale and for greater efficiency are maximized where companies source and supply on a global basis.

- Everyone gains from access to cheaper goods and services.

- Large resources within MNCs result in much greater innovation for the benefit of consumers.

- Remote, or less developed countries gain access to world markets through MNCs. Without MNCs they would not gain access to markets and would remain in a less developed state.

Potential dangers from globalization

- Relatively few very large MNCs control the world economy. They may abuse this power for the benefit of their shareholders and to the detriment of everyone else. Some studies have suggested that over two-thirds of world trade is controlled by the leading 500 MNCs, including intra-firm movement of funds (i.e. transfer payments) and over three-quarters of international investment.

- MNCs are not committed to each company or region from which they source their supplies. As soon as wages become too high in a location, MNCs will move to another country. This can have a highly destabilizing effect on countries.

- The world becomes a less interesting place as the same goods are supplied to most markets of the world.

- Not only does choice and variety decline, but variation in world culture is diminished by the globalization of the 'North American dream' from McDonalds to Microsoft.

- Sourcing supplies from all over the globe to supply global markets is highly inefficient, especially in terms of energy use. It is far better to produce locally and supply locally. Transport costs and times are minimized. Also, suppliers and customers are more likely to commit to one another for the long term if they live as well as work in the same community.

- MNCs are staffed by unelected people who are accountable only to their shareholders. Large MNCs become uncontrollable, especially by governments in smaller countries. Today the leading ten MNCs each have an annual turnover which exceeds national output of the poorest 50 countries.

Competitor Analysis

In order to gain a sustainable competitive advantage it is imperative that companies know their competitors and develop effective competitor information systems to monitor their activity. Kotler (1999) proposes that in order to evaluate competitors companies need to undertake the following:

- **Identify competitors** – This may seem obvious but there are many different levels at which you can identify your competitors. For example, direct competitors such as two car manufacturers but also indirect, for example holidays competing with a new conservatory. It is also important that companies consider not only current competitors but also potential competitors. For example, the entrance of companies such as Virgin into their market threatened traditional banks.

- **Determine competitor's objectives** – What is the likely future direction of the competitor, is it achieving its objectives? For example, some would argue that when BA established Go its main objective was to try and put other budget airlines out of business. Other objectives may include market share, survival, short-term profitability.

- **Identify competitors' strategies (past and current)** – Identification of the current markets, or market segments within which the competitor operates. A comparison of current and past strategies can provide useful insight into the direction the competitor is moving. It can also highlight strategies that have been unsuccessful in the past.

- **Assessing competitors' strengths and weaknesses (capabilities)** – What are their strengths and weaknesses? As assessment of competitors' capabilities allows a judgement to be made about how well equipped they are able to address the market. Areas of capabilities include management and marketing capabilities, ability to innovate, and production and financial capabilities.

- **Estimating competitors' reaction patterns** – Are they likely to respond to your attack? Kotler (1999) identifies four types of competitive reaction:

  - Laid back – does not respond

  - Selective – responds only to certain types of attack

- Tiger – reacts to any attack

- Stochastic – unpredictable

● **Select those companies to attack and those to avoid** – Must decide which competitors to attack and those to avoid.

Strategic groups

Once competitors have been identified it is virtually impossible for companies to monitor all competitors. Therefore, it is often useful to segment competitors into clusters according to various criteria and to identify those key competitors that are operating in similar sectors. These 'strategic groups' can be identified by a variety of factors such as geographic area covered, company size, markets served, product quality, scope of operation. Figure 1. 4 illustrates the strategic groups in the financial service industry.

Figure 1.4: Strategic Groups in the Financial Service Industry

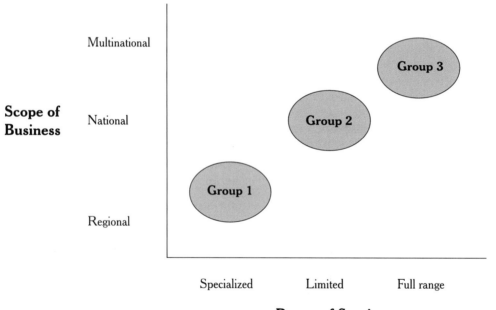

Group 1 – Local Building Societies, e.g. Cumberland Building Society.

Group 2 – National Building Societies, e.g. Nationwide.

Group 3 – Multinational Financial Service Institutions, e.g. HSBC.

1.6 Internal Strategic Analysis

Resources, assets and competencies

The purpose of internal strategic analysis is to assess how the firm can capitalize on internal strengths and overcome internal weaknesses to compete successfully in selected markets. There are several alternative perspective which may be used in an internal assessment. These respectively view the firm as possessing resources, assets and competencies.

Porter's concept of business value added includes five primary business activities (inbound logistics, operations, outbound logistics, marketing and sales, and service) and four support activities (procurement, technology, human resource management and firm infrastructure). Businesses should decide what their core competencies are and ensure that they lead in this area if they are to maximize value added. This business model, which deconstructed the business, led to management thinking on outsourcing. If the business did not have a core competence in a specific area, why not subcontract the work to specialists who did. That way unit costs could be reduced, although the issue of strategic interdependency had to be considered before proceeding.

Figure 1.5: Porter's Value Chain (1985)

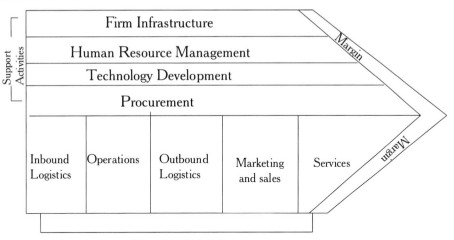

PRIMARY ACTIVITIES

A resource-based view is that the performance of any firm is dependent on its historical deployment of resources. How good the firm is in marshalling its resources determines its competitive success. Resources contain firstly assets, i.e. land, capital, human resources and systems, and, secondly, the 'competency' of the firm in management and entrepreneurial activity. Competitive success therefore concerns selecting and developing the ideal resource mix and deploying this effectively in the marketplace. This resource-based approach attempts to develop the ideas propounded by Porter in his value chain model.

1.7   Managing Change

Introduction

This is a potentially vast topic. The main problem is to decide where to set the limits of interest in this subject. In this context we are considering the corporate business in a constant state of change. Even if the business is not changing, which is highly unlikely, its position relative to its competitors will change because some or all of them are in a constant state of flux. Ultimately, the key impact on the business of 'change' is its relative success in the markets in which it operates and the relative success of each product marketed.

The factors that influence change and how it is managed include:

- The magnitude of change required – profound organizational change requires substantial alterations to organizational behaviour, in contrast to minor change.

- The type of change required depends on the reason for change.

- The degree of stability in the markets and products in which it competes.

- Existing organization structure and the new structure that is considered to be appropriate.

- Centralizing versus decentralizing tendencies – affects the configuration of organization structure. Centralized decision making will focus on hierarchical command and control structures.

- The approach to managing people through change. This depends on the type and frequency of resistance to change.

Breaking hierarchies – creating fewer levels of hierarchy and providing line management with greater authority and budgetary control

Self-managing teams – tends to operate in conjunction with the setting up of self-managed teams who have not simply accountability but authority, and *resources*, to act.

Re-engineering – critical organizations processes are radically restructured to reduce cost and increase speed, e.g. creating a web-based site results in major re-engineering of the order fulfilment process and its links with manufacturing as well as of the marketing-customer interface and how this is managed.

Learning organizations – because change is the only certainty, organizations require continual updating/upgrading of skills and of the corporate knowledge base. Many organizations think of web-based strategy simply as creating a web page!

The magnitude of change

Minor changes in corporate behaviour are a regular occurrence. These may range from slight changes in reporting structures to the annual modification in corporate objectives and strategy. These types of change are relatively modest in comparison to drastic levels of change required in response to predicted or actual changes in the basis of the competitive advantage of the business. Perhaps the most celebrated example of response failure is when IBM failed to respond to the new markets created by the rapid development of desk-top computer technology. Johnson and Scholes (1999, page 497) describe this type of situation as requiring 'transformational change', where the current business 'paradigm and organizational routines' must be altered. This implies that the way the business views the world must be altered and manifested in more appropriate business structures and processes.

One such paradigm shift that has gained much support is the concept of the 'learning organization'. The basis of interest in this business model is the impossibility of maintaining a competitive advantage (for example as the lowest-cost producer, the company with the leading-edge technology, or with the best customer service). Very few businesses are able to maintain a leading industry position for more than a few years. Consequently, if defending a position is untenable, it is argued that the only other approach is to become the quickest at responding to the business environment. This can be achieved only where the organization is considered as an organism that is continually learning from the environment and responding appropriately. Such a concept has been made possible by information technology, which supports knowledge-sharing across the organization. However, much more difficult than simply adopting facilitating technology is the need for the business to change the very culture of the organization. This may be regarded as highly 'transformational' because it requires employees to change the way they think about their role in the organization.

Figure 1.6: Paradigm Shift from the Traditional to the Learning Organization

Traditional business organization	**Learning organization**
Knowledge is the basis for individual power, therefore 'key' knowledge must be closely guarded to maintain influence and job security.	Knowledge is the basis of corporate power. By sharing knowledge the business increases its competitive strength, prevents unnecessary and wasteful duplication, individuals are able to develop more rapidly, to have more interesting job experience and in addition, therefore, job security increases.

Individuals may find the transitional stage between the traditional and learning organization to be disturbing. This may include accepting the loss of symbols of power, such as personal secretaries as well as other perceived 'demotions' including, for example: reduction in budget allocation, increased accountability, increased cooperation and contact with staff previously considered as too junior. Various authors have suggested phases of personal change through which corporate staff evolve when they experience organizational change. A simplified scheme is presented in Figure 1.7.

Figure 1.7: Individual Reaction to Organizational Change

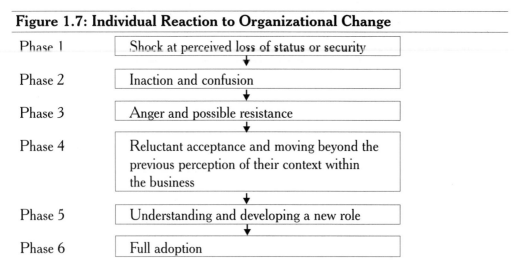

Phase 1	Shock at perceived loss of status or security
Phase 2	Inaction and confusion
Phase 3	Anger and possible resistance
Phase 4	Reluctant acceptance and moving beyond the previous perception of their context within the business
Phase 5	Understanding and developing a new role
Phase 6	Full adoption

The impact of change must be managed effectively if members of staff are not to progress beyond phases 2 or 3.

Organizational structure and culture

An important strategic choice is the *organization structure*. This is the way in which the activities of an organization, and the people within it, are given direction and their work is controlled. The basic structure might be illustrated in an organization chart. Organization structure is reinforced by *controls* and *operating mechanisms* (e.g. a procedures manual).

Structure determines how work is allocated, and who is responsible for what. It enables the organization's goals to be translated into performance. It covers such general issues as:

● formalization (documentation v. informal communication);

● job specialization (narrow range?);

● standardization of work and behaviour;

● hierarchy of authority and span of control (unit size);

● complexity, number of departments (unit grouping);

● centralization or delegation, planning and control systems;

● professionalism, training;

● liaison and communication devices;

● deployment of employees to different activities.

An organization's structure is bound up with goals, the culture in which employees are indoctrinated and its management practices (e.g. motivation, leadership style).

Mintzberg (1994) identified an approach to organization structure that considers the organization as comprising five components:

- The *operating core* is where the work is done (e.g. factory and warehouse, bank dealing room); its members perform work directly related to goods and services (primary activities, perhaps, to use value-chain terminology);

- The *strategic apex* ensures that the organization serves its mission in the wider environment. If an organization has owners or is controlled from the outside, the strategic apex is where this control is exercised;

- The *middle line* connects the strategic apex to the operating core, through middle manager ranks, team leaders etc.;

- The *technostructure* contains analysts who plan the work of others, by designing standardized work processes. Arguably the technostructure exercises functional authority;

- *Support staff* are those not directly involved with operations (e.g. public relations), and have no control or authority over the operating core.

The relationships between these components, the type of power they possess and the work they do result in a *structural configuration*.

Some of the influences on organization structure are as follows:

- The organization's age;

- The organization's size;

- Degree of automation;

- Power of external stakeholders;

- The industry's age;

- Environmental dynamism/complexity;

- Diversity of markets.

Each component part exerts its own pull towards a particular *structural configuration*.

Figure 1.8: Structural Configuration

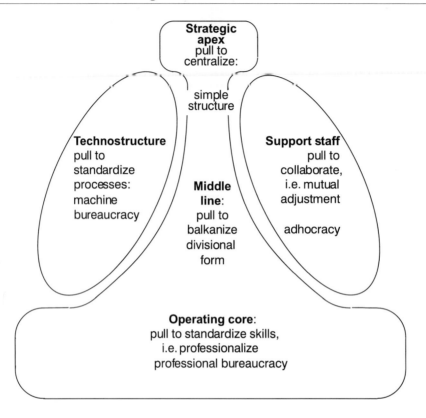

The *simple structure* achieves coordination by direct supervision, with little middle line and technostructure between the operating core and the strategic apex.

● This is characteristic of small businesses (owners set strategic direction and cannot escape the 'nitty-gritty').

● It is suitable in fast-moving environments, where standardization is cumbersome.

The *machine bureaucracy* achieves coordination by standardized work processes, procedures, form filling etc. There is a strong emphasis on task specialization (division of labour) and control. The technostructure has a powerful influence over work processes, and there is an elaborate, if controlled, middle line. Machine bureaucracies:

● are designed for specialist purposes, and are good at integrating routine specialized tasks;

● flourish in stable environments, and find it hard to adapt.

The *professional bureaucracy* minimizes the influence of administrators, whether in the technostructure or the middle line, over the operating core. For example, teachers' work in the classroom is not directly supervised. Coordination is achieved largely by skills standardization, which might be controlled by an external agency. Work processes are too complex to be standardized by a technostructure.

The *divisional form* splits a business into autonomous regions or *strategic business units (SBU)*, most of which are configured as machine bureaucracies, although the relationship between the strategic apex and each SBU is based on standardization of outputs. The SBUs are probably more 'bureaucratic' than they would be if they functioned as independent companies.

The *adhocracy* is where the support staff predominate. Coordination is not formalized and is based on a *mix* of skills rather than on standardized skills. Decision-making power does not depend on the level in the hierarchy. The apex does not formulate strategies but is a battleground where strategic choices are made. The adhocracy:

● is unsuitable for standardized works;

● is suited to dynamic and complex environments.

In the past many of the *clearing banks* had the features of the machine bureaucracy. It processed millions of routine transactions, efficiently. A High Street insurance broker might have had the features of a *simple structure*.

You can see that the type of business a firm is in has a powerful influence on the structural configuration. Many banks might have features of the divisional form, if they have different divisions covering, say, corporate and domestic customers.

Drivers of change

● Entry into new markets

● Withdrawal from existing markets

● Arrival of new competitors (current/anticipated)

● Decline in competitiveness of the business

Staff problems resulting from organizational change

Problems that staff may encounter in a changing organizational environment are:

● Feeling of insecurity;

● Disruption of the social structure of the working environment and the relationships developed between staff;

● Not understanding the reasons for change.

Successful change management practices

● Support from all levels of management including senior management

● Planning the process of change and providing staff with pre-implementation training

- Ensuring personnel changes to support the new organization

- Open and consistent communications

Frequent communication is an essential aspect of securing successful change. Rather than using one communication channel, management will obtain greater impact by employing a selection of channels which can include.

- face-to-face communications;

- e-mail updates;

- internal organization newsletters;

- management team updates by the project team responsible for the 'change' project;

- CEO or senior manager presentations.

Depending on the size and scope of the project, successful communication must be undertaken at least weekly.

1.8   Marketing Ethics

The place of 'ethics' has risen on the agenda for business and marketing. One of many explanations for this is the increasing difficulty which organizations have in differentiating on the basic product or service offer. The emphasis on the individual, and on the achievement of high levels of individual consumption, was popular in the 1980s and early 1990s. Ethics represents a development in response to this and in addition has been encouraged by the rise in importance of relationship marketing. Here the consumer is regarded as a long-term 'friend' rather than as a faceless statistic from which a single transaction was desired. Consequently, the parameters of business conduct and behaviour, which establish the relationship between the organization and the individual, become increasingly similar to those employed between individuals.

The basis for considering ethical behaviour as a 'development' may be regarded as valid if one employs Maslow's hierarchical view of behaviour (see Chapter 5). Using the framework provided by Maslow, marketers have evolved their activity initially differentiating on rational aspects, through emotional appeal and now increasingly on ethical/spiritual appeal. Ethics are increasingly used, most notably Anita Roddick's Body Shop or more recently (mid-1990s) through the UK Co-operative Bank, to make the firm the most favoured supplier of a service to an 'ethically sensitive' target market segment.

Absolute ethical positions are extremely difficult to define. Problems of definition arise not simply with regard to magnitude, but in terms of the type of ethics the organization wishes to focus on, e.g. environmental, social responsibility etc. In addition, while a company may strive for the 'higher' ethical ground, in practice it may not be perceived as adopting such a policy by consumers. One of the most celebrated examples of this, namely Shell and its oil platform disposal policy in the North Sea, provides a salutary lesson for all companies, including those providing financial services. Shell followed an 'ethical' policy, consulting government and deciding on land disposal as the most environmentally 'friendly' approach, after considerable analysis of the options. However, it initially lost the corporate ethical communications battle and was perceived unjustly in an unethical light, a situation encouraged by an environmental pressure group. The ethical credentials of the organization, with regard to their environmental policy in the North Sea, eventually gained the attention of some of the public, but this was by no means inevitable and for many the 'ethical' credentials of the company have been severely damaged. Having an ethical policy, communicating it effectively and having contingency plans to deal with counterclaims and action, are all essential in maintaining an organization's 'ethical' credentials.

MARKETING IN PRACTICE
Ethics and Legal and General

Legal and General launched the first ethical individual savings account (ISA) in 1999 to meet the growing demand for ethical investing. The criteria that L & G employed, with regard to ethical investment, was to *exclude* companies involved in one of 14 activities, for example including the military, human rights abuses, tobacco, animal testing and gambling. It is a fund which was planned, in principle, to track the UK FTSE 350 Index, using the above criteria to exclude companies. The selected 14 criteria originally resulted in the exclusion of companies such as Nat West, BP Amoco and Cadbury Schweppes.

Codes of ethics

These cover a wide range of topics and are most usually presented within annual reports. Further versions of ethical policies may be obtained from company web sites. The example of 'marketing in practice' for HSBC has been selected 'at random', to exemplify current practice.

MARKETING IN PRACTICE

HSBC

HSBC declares five business principles and 12 Key Business Values, many of which have an ethical focus.

Staff in the organization are expected to operate according to certain 'Key Business Values' including:

- the highest personal standards of integrity at all levels; commitment to truth and fair dealing;

- hands-on management at all levels;

- openly esteemed commitment to quality and competence;

- a minimum of bureaucracy;

- fast decisions and implementation;
- putting the Group's interests ahead of the individual's;
- the appropriate delegation of authority with accountability;
- fair and objective employment practices;
- a merit approach to recruitment/selection/promotion;
- a commitment to complying with the spirit and letter of all laws and regulations wherever we conduct our business;
- the promotion of good environmental practice and sustainable development and commitment to the welfare and development of each local community.

HSBC's reputation is founded on adherence to these principles and values. All actions taken by a member of HSBC, or staff member on behalf of a Group company, should conform with them.

The group also has codes of conduct for staff. These include strict rules against staff accepting gifts or favours and a policy of actively discouraging customers from offering them – a bold policy given that there are several parts of the world where this runs counter to common practice.

Source: HSBC website - http://www.hsbcgroup.com

Manifest ethical behaviour?

The traditional UK financial sector, in particular retail banks and building societies, were accused of unethical behaviour in their pursuit of lower cost bases between 1999 and 2000. They were accused of closing branches in non-profitable districts and charging penal rates for counter transactions (for example those announced in the UK in the summer of 1999 by Abbey National). Banks, in particular, are accused of discriminating against low-income and disabled groups who do not have the same level of access to remote banking technology as the general population. The change in bank charging practice encouraged the UK government to monitor the closure of branches and bank policy towards branch automation from 1999.

Two popular measures of the 'ethical' credentials of and organization: 'consumer friendly' and 'environmental'

Organizations are increasingly using their websites to declare their 'ethical' credentials. It is therefore unsurprising that the Halifax, a UK bank with solid ethical foundations, includes these two topics within its 'ethical' policy pronouncements. Their environmental policy is presented in 'Marketing in Practice' to exemplify the Halifax approach.

MARKETING IN PRACTICE

Halifax Environmental Policy

'Halifax recognizes that its business activities have both direct and indirect environmental impacts. We will identify adverse impacts and seek to minimize them through good management, aiming for continuous improvements in our environmental performance.'

Our policy is to:

- Take environmental considerations into account throughout our operations and when choosing suppliers.

- Measure our environmental impacts wherever possible, set realistic targets for improvements and monitor our progress.

- Use energy and natural resources wisely and minimizing waste and recycling whenever it is sensible to do so.

- Encourage new home buyers particularly and customers generally to adopt sound environmental principles.

- Set targets for the delivery of the programme including cost savings which can be subjected to a formal audit.

- Ensure that our staff have a sound understanding of environmental issues and provide appropriate training for those with particular responsibilities.

- Publish information on environmental performance for the benefit of our stakeholders.

HALIFAX AND THE ENVIRONMENT

Every business has an impact on the environment and the Halifax is no exception. We recognize that we cannot resolve environmental issues in isolation. Both nationally and globally governments, businesses and communities need to work together if the environmental issues which face us all are to be successfully addressed.

At the Halifax we believe that our large customer base puts us in an ideal position to maximize our contribution to protecting the environment. We can do this by encouraging staff, suppliers and customers – in particular new home buyers – to adopt sound environmental principles.

Source: Halifax web site

The UK Co-operative Bank is an organization that has adopted a differentiation policy in the UK based on ethics for a considerable period of time. Rather than provide extracts here, students are encouraged to visit the bank's web site (http://www.co-operativebank.co.uk).

Ethics can be highly evident in marketing strategy with regard to corporate communications. Some corporate brands, such as the Co-operative Bank in the UK, major on the ethical dimension. Other corporate brands simply include ethics as one dimension of corporate branding, for example one dimension of the credit card launched in the UK by a utility (British Gas) included a brand attribute of 'honest'.

Cause related marketing

The linkage of a brand to a social cause or issue is termed 'Cause Related Marketing'. This approach is employed to increase the level of consumer involvement in purchasing of services (including financial) and products and attempts to engage the consumer at the highest levels of Maslow's hierarchy of needs (see Chapter 5). The UK insurance firm Norwich Union, for example, formed a link with St John's Ambulance and first aid training. In recent years many service companies have created a link between expenditure on their products and donations to stated charities, or to specific programmes run by charities. This policy has been embraced by professional associations where, for example in the UK, Royal Institute of British Architects members have provided a 'free' consultation in return for a donation to the homeless charity 'Shelter'. The charity gains revenue and association members obtain additional client leads from a segment which may otherwise not approach architects.

Summary

The meaning of 'strategy' depends on the context of its use. Generally it concerns the achievement of objectives. Its specific meaning depends on the level of hierarchy in the organization at which it is used as well as on organizational structure, especially where more than one product area is marketed.

The concept of 'stakeholders' entered popular language a few years ago. In a business context it embraces the idea that interest groups in a business can be very broad, not simply confined to staff, suppliers and customers. Each interest group (stakeholder) has its own agenda for a business and this is manifested in a wide variety of business objectives, strategies, tactics and business policy. The interplay of different stakeholders ultimately determines business policy, depending on their relative strengths.

The PEST or SLEPT (social, legal, economic, political and technological) acronyms provide only a thematic structure to the vast external environment. Porter provided a tool to facilitate strategic business analysis, Porter's five major forces model. He suggested that five main forces operate on the business and the interplay of these forces determines the ultimate competitive success of the business. Strategic analysis of the internal dimension of the business also requires a tool and this has been provided by Porter's value chain model. This perceives the business as engaging in nine key activities that are used to add value. Any one or some of these activities can be the basis for competitive advantage.

Change is one business certainty. It is logical for management thinking to consider that this should be managed proactively rather than reactively. All aspects of the organization must be considered as managing change. This ranges from organizational structure and management hierarchies, human resource management (ranging from supporting staff uncertainty, insecurity and fostering cooperative and ultimately creative working practices) and implementing facilitating technologies to create a 'learning organization'.

Many economies have moved beyond the industrialized stage. As consumer affluence has increased, their interests have moved beyond simply satisfying basic needs. Interest in ethical issues has grown in the way consumers live their lives and this is applied increasingly as an important dimension in their perception of organizations from which they buy products and services.

References

Drucker P F (1973) *Management: Tasks and Responsibilities and Practices*, New York: Harper and Row

Johnson G & Scholes K (1999) *Exploring Corporate Strategy*, 5th edition, Prentice Hall Europe

Kaplan R S & Norton D P (1992) The balanced scorecard: Measures that drive performance, *Harvard Business Review*, Vol. 70, No. 1, pp 71-79.

Kotler P, Armstrong G, Saunders J, & Wong V (1999) *Principles of Marketing*, 2nd European edition, Prentice Hall Europe

Mintzberg H (1994) The fall and rise of strategic planning, *Harvard Business Review*, 72 (1) pp 107-14

Porter M E (1985) *Competitive Advantage*, New York, The Free Press

2

STRATEGIC MARKETING

Learning Objectives

After studying this chapter students should:

- Be able to define strategic marketing and explain the difference between strategic and operational marketing;

- Understand the concept of market orientation and the characteristics of market-orientated companies;

- Appreciate the relationship between corporate and marketing strategy;

- Understand and be able to explain portfolio analysis;

- Be able to describe Porter's three generic strategies;

- Be able to explain and apply Ansoff's matrix;

- Understand the importance of market position in marketing strategy;

- Be able to explain the methods available for evaluating strategic options.

Figure 2.1: Chapter Map

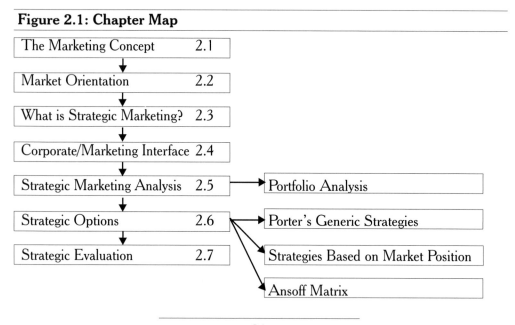

The Marketing Concept	2.1
Market Orientation	2.2
What is Strategic Marketing?	2.3
Corporate/Marketing Interface	2.4
Strategic Marketing Analysis	2.5	→ Portfolio Analysis
Strategic Options	2.6	→ Porter's Generic Strategies
Strategic Evaluation	2.7	Strategies Based on Market Position
	Ansoff Matrix

Introduction

The essence of strategic marketing lies in the ability of a company to meet the changing needs of markets and to match potential opportunities with company capabilities. This chapter seeks to define strategic marketing, explore the relationship between corporate and marketing strategy, explain how strategic marketing differs from operational marketing and outline techniques available for strategic analysis and models for formulating strategy. In order to explain strategic marketing it is essential to firstly set the scene by exploring the marketing concept and market orientation.

2.1 The Marketing Concept

The term 'marketing' is one that is widely used and often misunderstood. To some it has an image of glamorous and exciting careers; to others it concerns the cynical exploitation of consumers using a variety of means of persuasion. Certain marketing activities such as selling and advertising are highly visible and often form the central components of many people's understanding of marketing. In practice, though, marketing as a business activity is much broader than just these activities; it is not always glamorous and rarely does it involve persuading consumers to buy what they do not actually want.

There are at least as many definitions of marketing as there are books on the subject – and probably more. The Chartered Institute of Marketing defines marketing as:

> *The management process responsible for identifying, anticipating and satisfying consumer requirements profitably.*

This definition highlights the importance of satisfying customer needs while at the same time achieving organizational goals in the form of profit. However, this definition is in some respects rather too narrow, i.e. not all organizations are profit-driven. In 1985 The American Marketing Association reviewed more that twenty-five definitions and then developed the following definition:

> *Marketing is the process of planning and executing the conception, pricing, planning and distribution of ideas, goods and services to create exchanges that satisfy individual and organizational objectives.*

This definition focuses on marketing as a process within an organization and highlights the importance of 'exchange' in this process while also acknowledging that organizational goals may not only be profit. This definition of marketing can therefore be applied to all types of organizations – commercial, not-for-profit organizations such as charities and trusts, and service-based companies such as banking.

Crosier (1975) reviewed more than fifty definitions of marketing and concluded that definitions of marketing could be classified into three distinct groups:

- The *marketing process*, which is concerned with connecting the supplier and the customer;

- The *marketing concept* (philosophy), which suggests that marketing is concerned with exchange between willing parties;

- The *marketing orientation*, which is the phenomenon that makes the marketing process and the marketing concept achievable.

It is clear that there is no one definitive definition of marketing. However, it is clear that marketing can be discussed from two different perspectives. Firstly marketing can be seen as a functional activity that is concerned with the operational aspects of marketing such as promotion, pricing, product development, distribution, market research etc. However, it can also be seen in the wider context as a business philosophy that seeks to put the customer at the centre of an organization's activities. This philosophy is often referred to as 'market orientation'. A company that is market orientated all departments, not just the marketing department, would be customer focused and the aim of providing superior customer value would be seen as everybody's responsibility.

2.2   Market Orientation

A number of business philosophies/orientations have been identified and these can be traced historically. These business philosophies define an organization's stance towards the customers of its products and/or services. Table 2.1 outlines the development of these orientations.

Table 2.1: Business Orientations

STAGE	PHILOSOPHY	EMPHASIS
1. Demand exceeds supply – a seller's market	**Production Orientation** Managers are centred on needs of operations.	The organization could be more successful by producing more, so managers concentrate on processes, operations, seeking ways to make more effective use of inputs: an inward-looking focus.
2. Output and new competitors increase. Demand and supply become more equal.	**Sales Orientation** Managers seek to ensure their output is taken up by available customers.	Production is now fine – but there are fewer unsatisfied customers. Managers turn their attention to advertising and selling to 'push' finished goods at customers.

Table 2.1: Business Orientations (continued)

STAGE	PHILOSOPHY	EMPHASIS
3. Output continues to grow. Supply exceeds demand – a buyer's market.	**Market Orientation** To survive managers must satisfy customer needs.	Emphasis on market research to identify and anticipate customer needs before putting scarce resources into production. The customer now comes before the production process. Managers are now externally focused.
4. Environmental and quality concerns. Emphasis on quality not quantity and the wider interests of society not just the satisfaction of the individual.	**Societal Marketing Orientation** Legal and consumer pressures force firms to consider the long-term interests of customers not just the short-term mutually profitable exchange.	Emphasis becomes broader, encompassing environmental issues and the ethics of business activities. Now managers have the needs of society and the customer to satisfy.

This comparison of the various business philosophies highlights the differences between a company that is sales orientated and a truly market-orientated one. The sales concept is concerned with the idea that customers will not buy sufficient quantities of a company's product unless it is actively sold. This philosophy takes an 'inside out' perspective and focuses very much on generating short-term sales and creating profit through sales volume. The market orientation in contrast takes an 'outside in' perspective and starts with the market and customer needs and focuses on generating profit through customer satisfaction. The sales orientation is very much focused on achieving one-off sales while the market orientation is concerned with building loyalty and repeat purchases. The sales perspective is rather short-sighted in that most dissatisfied customers do not buy again. In addition, research has shown satisfied customers will tell three other people about their experiences whereas dissatisfied customers will, on average, tell ten people about their dissatisfaction (Farber & Wycoff 1991).

Focusing on the products themselves can lead a business into the '*marketing myopia*' trap as identified by Theodore Levitt in his seminal paper in 1960. Levitt attributes the decline of the railway companies in America to the management's narrow-minded belief that railways were their business. Whereas in fact, they were in the transportation business and the recognition that they operated to service these particular needs might have provided them with a sounder base for future development.

Hence, in the case of a bank's lending products for example, management should not see their function as simply providing car loans or home improvement loans – these are only the range of products that are currently employed to fulfil consumer needs. By focusing on the needs the bank is satisfying, the business could perhaps more appropriately be seen as one of providing customers with the ability to make purchases at an earlier date than might otherwise have been possible. In other words: the company sells *products* but the customer buys *satisfactions*.

Adopting and implementing a market orientation also makes an organization competitive because the business that is most successful at meeting the needs of its customers in a cost-effective way will be placed in a strong position in relation to its competitors. Ultimately, it may not matter in absolute terms whether products marketed are a very good match to consumer needs or a very poor match. What is more important is whether the organization is able to meet customer needs more or less effectively than its competitors.

In current business environments, marketing is arguably far too important to be left solely to marketing departments. It is an approach to business and an attitude to customers that must permeate the structure of an organization. The successful marketing-orientated company will be successful only if the philosophy underlies all activities, not just at senior management level but also among employees at all levels.

Much research has been undertaken to try to identify the key characteristic of market-orientated companies and to identify a link between market orientation and superior performance (Narver & Slater 1990 and Jaworski & Kohli 1993). The key elements of market orientation as identified by Narver and Slater (1990) are shown in Table 2.2.

Table 2.2: Key Elements of Market Orientation (Narver & Slater 1990)

Elements	Implication
Customer orientation	Understanding customers throughout the company in order to create superior value.
Competitor orientation	Knowledge and understanding of the short- and long-term capabilities of competitors.
Interfunctional coordination	All areas of business use resources to focus on creating value for target customers.
Organizational culture	Staff's behaviour is linked to customer satisfaction.
Long-term profit	Focus on a long-term perspective rather than short-term.

Despite much discussion of the key component of market orientation companies still struggle to become market orientated. There are many barriers to achieving market orientation, such as cultural and political factors. These barriers often cause problems at the implementation stage of marketing strategy. These barriers along with possible solutions will be discussed in Chapter 3 as part of the implementation stage of the marketing plan.

2.3   What is Strategic Marketing?

Marketing strategy aims to transform corporate objectives into a competitive market position. The main role is to differentiate our products/services from that of our competitors by meeting the needs of our customers more effectively. Marketing strategy therefore addresses three key areas: assessing the external environment and identifying customer needs, matching customer needs with internal competencies and implementing programmes that achieve a superior competitive advantage. The essence of marketing strategy lies in a company's ability to effectively segment the market, target the most appropriate segments and then position itself in a superior position to that of competitors. The three key aspects of marketing strategy are customers, competitors and internal organizational factors. Ohmae's strategic triangle (1982) as illustrated in Figure 2.2 highlights the relationship between these three key factors: company, customers and competitors.

Figure 2.2: Ohmae's Strategic Triangle (1982)

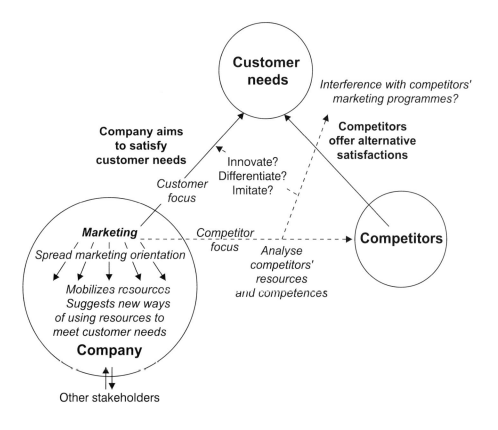

Strategic marketing as opposed to tactical marketing is concerned with questions such as:

- What markets should we be in?

- What is our distinct competitive advantage?

- Where do we want to be in 10 years time?

- Do we have the necessary resources, skills, competencies and assets?

- Who are our current and future competitors and what are their strategies?

These are strategic issues because they are relevant to the whole organization and focus on the future. Operational or tactical marketing is concerned with the more practical aspects of marketing such as the deployment of the marketing mix. It is becoming increasingly evident that marketing is not simply a short-term tactical component of business. The elements of the marketing mix are of undoubted importance, but their simple manipulation will provide little in the way of long-term solutions to an organization's marketing problems. The marketing mix will be discussed in section 3 of the text. Effective marketing is dependent on the organization's taking a strategic view and considering marketing as an integrated and driving force in its strategy and planning.

The terms strategy and tactics are often used and even confused at times. The difference between the two is not black and white and can be seen on a continuum. Weitz and Wensley (1988) have identified eight ways to distinguish between strategy and tactics, and these are illustrated in table 2.3.

Table 2.3: Differences Between Strategy and Tactics (Weitz & Wensley 1988)

	Strategy	**Tactics**
Importance	More important	Less important
Level at which conducted	Senior managers	Junior management
Time horizons	Long	Short
Regularity	Continuous	Periodic
Nature of problem	Unstructured and often unique involving considerable risk and uncertainty	More structured and repetitive with risks easier to assess
Information needed	Require large amounts of external information much of which is subjective and futuristic	Depend more on internally generated accounting and marketing research information
Detail	Broad	Narrow and specific

Table 2.3: Differences Between Strategy and Tactics (continued)

Ease of evaluation	Decisions are more difficult to make and evaluate	Decisions are easier to make and evaluate

2.4   Corporate/Marketing Interface

There is often much confusion as to the similarities and differences between corporate and marketing strategy. In Chapter 1 the overall corporate planning process was described and the relationship between corporate planning and other business functions was discussed. This section will focus on the relationship between marketing and corporate planning. In a company that is truly market driven marketing will be the driving force for corporate strategy. This may partly explain some of the confusion that arises when comparing and contrasting corporate and marketing strategy.

From the office junior to the managing director, everyone plans his or her work and decides how best to allocate resources (possibly only time) to achieve the objectives that have been set. As a result people at all levels of the organization will talk about their objectives, strategy and tactics. To avoid confusion it is necessary to clarify the level in the organization at which the individual is working. Imagine a flight of stairs: as a person steps down from one level to another, the tactics of the higher level becomes the strategy of the lower one. Figure 2.3 illustrates the relationship between corporate and marketing planning. This model highlights the importance of developing objectives that are consistent with the objectives at a higher level within an organization. Objectives, strategy and tactics are key elements of planning at all levels; it is just the focus of the planning that is different. For example, corporate strategy will be concerned with the deployment of resources between the various business units, the portfolio of activities across the whole organization, specifying the organization's mission, and defining organizational objectives, while marketing strategy is primarily concerned with selecting markets and segments, products and determining the marketing mix.

Figure 2.3: Relationship Between Corporate and Marketing Planning

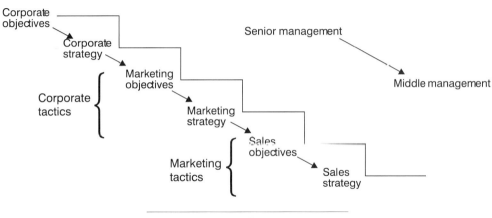

Table 2.4 contrasts corporate and marketing strategy and objectives for a hypothetical bank.

Table 2.4: Objectives and Strategies for a Hypothetical Bank

	Objectives	Strategy
Corporate	To increase gross operating profit by 25 % within 5 years.	To increase corporate activity in the pensions market.
Marketing	To gain a 15% share of the stakeholder pensions' market in the UK within 5 years.	By launching a low-cost stakeholder pension via the Internet.
Marketing mix Promotion (for example)	To achieve an awareness of 50% within our target market within 1 year that we offer a stakeholder pension.	By using an integrated communications strategy that will include television and press advertising, in-store point-of-sale materials, banner advertising on related internet sites, direct marketing and various public relations activities.
Public relations	To generate at least 6 'positive' news stories within 1 year.	By sending out press releases to target media such as Money Management, The Money Programme and MoneyBox Live.

Figure 2.4: Corporate Planning Integration

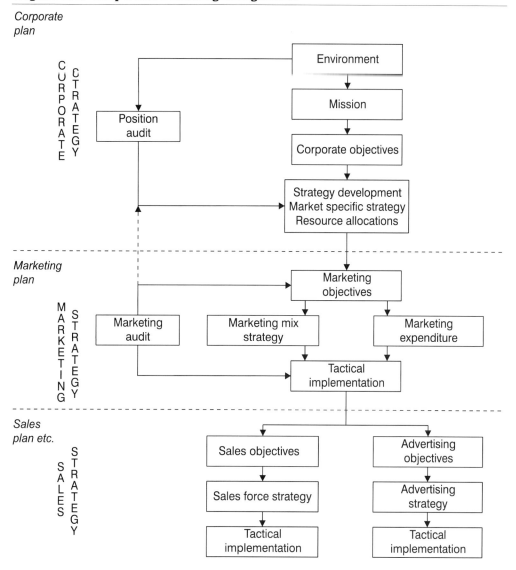

It is difficult to relate marketing objectives clearly to corporate objectives and even more difficult to distinguish clearly marketing objectives from corporate objectives. There can be no corporate plan that does not involve products/services and customers. Figure 2.4 clearly expresses the interactive two-way relationship between marketing plans and strategic business planning. Of the various aspects of the corporate plan, the marketing plan is uniquely concerned with products and markets. These are typically stated in terms of market share, sales volume, levels of distribution and profitability. Decisions might be taken as to the type of products sold to particular customer groups.

Figure 2.5: Relationship Between Marketing and Corporate Planning

The relationship between corporate and marketing strategy is crucial to the success of marketing plans. However, marketing's relationship with other functional areas can also have a major impact on the effectiveness of marketing planning.

- The marketing plan is mainly concerned with markets and the products sold in them or, more precisely, the total set of benefits that the firm can offer the market.

- The production plan deals with purchasing, acquiring resources and forming them into products/services the firm can offer.

- Human resources deal with obtaining the right number of employees at the right level of skills – but this is vital in service industries.

- Finance deals with the need to remain profitable, raising and distributing money and maintaining a healthy cash flow.

- In addition, there may be other functional plans relevant to various aspects of the organization.

- Some firms have a separate research and development function, independent of either production or marketing.

- In firms where information technology is a key resource, there might be separate plans and strategies for IT. Financial services firms such as banks pay particular attention to IT.

Table 2.5 shows potential conflicts that can arise with other departments in the organization. Again this can only be a typical list and is intended as a warning of potential dangers. The top management of the organization needs to take a strong line on any conflicts which arise and to ensure that departmental heads have clear instructions as to the organization's priorities.

Table 2.5: Summary of Organizational Conflicts Between Marketing and Other Departments

Other Departments	Their emphasis	Emphasis of marketing
Engineering	Long design lead time Functional features Few models with standard components	Short design lead time Sales features Many models with custom components
Purchasing	Standard parts Price of material Economic lot sizes Purchasing at infrequent intervals	Non-standard parts Quality of material Large lot sizes to avoid stockouts Immediate purchasing for customer needs
Production	Long order lead times and inflexible production schedules Long runs with few models No model changes Standard orders Ease of fabrication Average quality control Tight quality control	Short order lead times and flexible schedules to meet emergency orders Short runs with many models Frequent model changes Custom orders Aesthetic appearance
Inventory management	Fast-moving items Narrow product line Economic levels of stock	Broad product line Large levels of stock
Finance	Strict rationales for spending Hard and fast budgets Pricing to cover costs	Intuitive arguments for spending Flexible budgets to meet changing needs Pricing to further market development
Accounting	Standard transactions Few reports	Special terms and discounts Many reports

Table 2.5: Summary of Organizational Conflicts Between Marketing and Other Departments (continued)

Other departments	Their emphasis	Emphasis of marketing
Credit	Full financial disclosures by customers	Minimum credit examination – customers
	Lower credit risks	Medium credit risks
	Tough credit terms	Easy credit terms
	Tough collection procedures	Easy collection procedures

Source: Philip Kotler, 'Diagnosing the marketing takeover', Harvard Business Review, Nov-Dec 1965 (70-72)

2.5   Strategic Marketing Analysis

In Chapter 1 the various tools available for strategic analysis in a corporate setting were discussed in terms of both external and internal analysis. These tools of strategic analysis are just as appropriate at a marketing level and are an integral part of the strategic marketing planning process. This section will concentrate on the use of portfolio planning in strategic analysis.

Portfolio Analysis

Portfolio analysis methods may be used either at the level of corporate strategy or for planning the management of the product portfolio.

At the level of corporate strategy, this technique may be used to determine the relative positions of businesses and to identify strategies for resource allocation between them. Thus, for example, a bank might apply such a technique to evaluate the relative position and profitability of its corporate division vis-a-vis that of its international division or merchant banking division etc.

However, the same techniques are equally valuable when considering products and the management of the product portfolio. Each product may be plotted and the portfolio planning tool used to assess the degree of balance in the product portfolio.

The two most widely used approaches are the Boston Consulting Group's (BCG) growth-share matrix and the General Electric (GE) multi-factor portfolio matrix.

The Boston Consulting Group Matrix (BCG)

The BCG matrix, which is illustrated below, works by classifying products (or businesses) on the basis of their market share relative to that of the largest competitor and according to the rate of growth in the market as a whole. The split on the horizontal axis is based on a market share identical to that of the firm's nearest competitor, while the precise location of the split on the vertical axis will depend on the rate of growth in the market. Products are positioned in the matrix as circles with a diameter proportional to their sales revenue. The underlying assumption in the growth-share matrix is that a larger market share will enable the business to benefit from economies of scale, lower costs per unit and thus higher margins.

Figure 2.6: The Boston Consulting Group Growth/Share Matrix

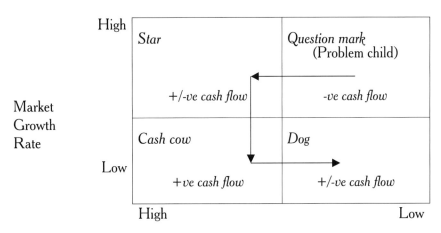

Note: Arrows indicate progression of a product from initial launch to final decline.

Each product can then fall into one of four broad categories.

A **question mark** (or *problem child*) has a small market share but in a high-growth market industry. The generic product is clearly popular, but customer support for the specific company version is limited. A small market share implies that competitors are apparently in a strong position and that if the product is to be successful it will require a substantial injection of funds, particularly on the marketing side. The organization should either invest in a 'build' strategy for promising products, or consider withdrawing the product.

A **star** is a product with a high market share in a high-growth market. By implication, the star has potential for generating significant earnings currently and in the future. However, certainly initially, it may still require substantial marketing expenditures to 'maintain' its position.

A **cash cow** has a high market share but in a comparatively mature and slower growing market. Typically, it is a well-established product with a high degree of consumer loyalty. Product development costs are typically low and the marketing campaign is well established. The cash cow will normally make a substantial contribution to overall profitability. The appropriate strategy will vary according to the precise position of the cash cow. If market growth is reasonably strong then a 'holding' strategy will be appropriate, but if growth and/ or share are weakening, then a harvesting strategy may be more sensible – cut back on marketing expenditure and maximize short-term cash flow.

A *dog* is a product characterized by low market share and low growth – again typically a well-established product, but one that is apparently losing consumer support and may have cost disadvantages. The usual strategy would be to consider divestment unless cash flow position is strong, in which case the product would be harvested in the short term prior to deletion from the product range.

Progression of products around the matrix
The suggestion that most products will move through each of the stages of the BCG (see arrows in Figure 2.6) does not weaken the argument for the role of marketing – on the contrary, it strengthens it, since poor marketing may mean that a product moves from being a 'problem child' to a 'dog' without making any substantial contribution to the profitability. Equally, good marketing may enable the firm to prolong the 'star' and 'cash cow' phases, thus maximizing cash flow from the product.

The framework provided by the matrix can offer guidance in terms of developing appropriate strategies for products and in maintaining a balanced product portfolio – ensuring that there are enough cash-generating products to match the cash-using products.

However, there are a number of criticisms of the BCG.

1) The BCG matrix oversimplifies product analysis. It concentrates on only two dimensions of product markets – namely size and market share – and therefore may encourage marketing management to pay too little attention to other market features.

2) It is not always clear what is meant by the terms 'relative market share' and 'rate of market growth'. Not all banks and not all products will be designed for market leadership, in which case describing performance in terms of relative market share may be of limited relevance. Many firms undertaking this approach have found that all their products were technically 'dogs' and yet were still very profitable, so saw no need to divest. Firms following a market niching strategy will commonly find this occurring because they are looking to appeal to only a limited segment of the market.

3) A further problem lies in how we define market share because this may have a major implication on a product's position. How do we define the market, the share of what market? For example, a small regional building society may have a large share of the local market for savings accounts but on a national level this may only equate to an insignificant share.

4) The validity of the matrix depends on the notion of a relationship between profitability and market share. There is empirical evidence for this in many industries, but it may not always be the case, particularly in situations were there is demand for more customized products. Moreover, market share might be purchased at the expense of profitability, especially in the short term.

5) The BCG analyses products or SBUs in isolation and does not consider any interrelationships or synergies created between two or more products or SBUs. For example a bank may classify its current accounts as 'dogs' but they are an essential part of its portfolio because with them these customers may purchase more 'profitable' services such as ISAs and credit cards.

6) The basic approach may oversimplify the nature of products in large diversified firms with many divisions. In these cases, each division may contain products that fit into several of the categories. Despite these criticisms, the BCG matrix can offer guidance in achieving a balanced portfolio. However given the difficulty of generalizing such an approach to deal with all product and market situations, its recommendations should be interpreted with care.

The General Electric (GE) multi-factor portfolio model

The GE approach is more comprehensive than the BCG approach which uses only two factors, market share and market growth rate. The approach leaves the selection of relevant factors to managers conducting the analysis, although there are several factors which tend to be assessed in most cases. The results are analysed on a two-dimensional grid and this requires all factors to be divided into two groups.

The approach considers, independently, two dimensions of the marketing environment. These include the inherent *attractiveness* of the market (irrespective of the business's strength to compete in the market). For example, fast-growing, profitable markets are highly attractive. *Business strength* is examined separately in terms of its level of competitiveness in the market that is being assessed.

Factors commonly assessed under these two main headings are presented:

Industry attractiveness
Market size, market growth, industry profitability, competitive climate, stability of demand, ease of market entry, industry capacity, levels of investment, nature of regulation, etc.

Business strength (Competitive position)

Market position, relative market share, company image, production capacity, production costs, financial strengths, relative product quality, distribution systems, control over prices/margins, benefits of patent protection, experience curve effect, etc.

How is this information used?

1. The analyst decides on the number of factors that will be used in the assessment.

2. Each factor is given a weighting to reflect its relative importance. All weighting factors must add up to 1.00. For example if two factors only are assessed and each is of equal importance, they will each be weighted at 0.5.

3. Each factor is then assessed on a scale of 1 to 5 (5 very good, 1 very poor). A very fast-growing market would be assessed at 5 on this scale.

4. The raw score must be multiplied by the weighting factor to reflect the relative importance of the factor. A good score for an important factor should produce a higher rating than a good score for an unimportant factor.

5. Adding up the weighted scores will produce a calculated number in the range of 1 to 5. It is this number that is used as one of the two points to plot the position on the matrix.

If the above assessment was undertaken for 'industry attractiveness' then it must be repeated, separately, for 'business strength' to provide a second number in the range of 1 to 5. The process is summarized in Table 2.6.

Table 2.6: Industry Attractiveness Assessment Using the GE Planning Approach

Measure	Weight	Raw Score 1 to 5	Weighted Score
Market size	0.6	4	2.4
Growth rate	0.2	3	0.6
Industry profitability	0.1	2	0.2
Level of competition	0.05	1	0.05
Entry barriers	0.05	2	0.1
TOTAL	1.00	32	3.35

This assessment may have been undertaken for industry attractiveness, e.g. of financial service provision to the small/medium business (SMEs) market in a particular country. A second, separate assessment must be undertaken examining the strength of the business to compete in this market, using selected criteria. It is not necessary to use the same criteria that were employed in assessing industry attractiveness. In fact many of these criteria may not be relevant in assessing business strength.

Assume that in addition to the industry attractiveness rating of 3.35, business strength is calculated at 2.00 a business. This must be allocated to one of nine cells in a GE planning matrix. This particular value is entered.

Figure 2.7: GE Portfolio Planning Matrix

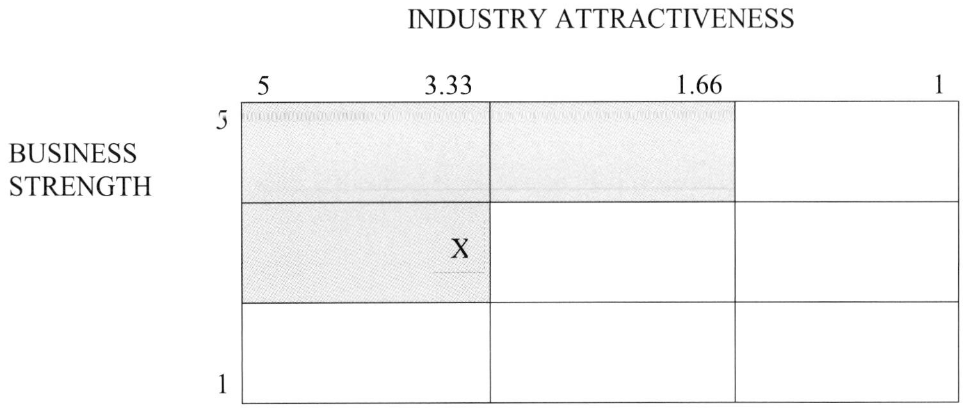

INDUSTRY ATTRACTIVENESS

Three main planning zones may be considered. Products in the

- Non-shaded zone should be deleted or sold

- Most heavily shaded zone should be supported strongly with resources

- Critical decisions must be taken for products in the lightly shaded zone. Management should decide whether these products fit within the organization's product portfolio, or not. If products do fit, then substantial investment of time and/or resources must be made, otherwise the product should be deleted. One approach to moving the product towards the most favourable zone is to narrow the focus of the segments served. In doing this the organization may focus on the most attractive parts of the industry, while a narrower range of business strengths may be required for this narrower target segment(s).

The GE matrix, because of its broader approach, places emphasis on the notion of trying to match distinctive competencies within the company to conditions within the marketplace. However, the difficulties associated with measurement and classification mean that again the results of such an exercise should be interpreted with care and not seen as an immediate prescription for expanding or divesting particular products.

Integration and application of models

The product life cycle and Boston Consulting Group matrix are linked, although there is not a perfect connection between the two. The 'problem child' is typically a newly introduced product, the 'star' is a product in its growth phase, the 'cash cow' one that has reached maturity and the 'dog' is typically a product in the decline phase.

The product life cycle model and the two portfolio planning models presented allow a marketing manager to assess whether the product portfolio is balanced. The firm requires a spread of products across the PLC and BCG models because both these models represent the life of a product. Obviously an organization requires sufficient new products (at the 'development' and 'growth' stage of the PLC or as 'question marks' in the BCG) to be available eventually to replace older products (at the 'maturity' or 'decline' stage of the PLC or the 'dog' stage of the BCG).

Apart from the intuitive appeal of requiring a balanced portfolio, the argument for balance is driven by harsh financial reality. Products at each stage of these two models typically have different net cash flow positions. If all products are at the new stage of either model then the organization would have a highly negative cash flow. Balance is therefore another means of achieving long-term business viability.

Product Portfolio Planning

Managing the product portfolio goes beyond the simple extension or reduction of a bank's product range. It also raises broad issues such as what role a product should play, how resources should be allocated between products and what should be expected from each product. Of particular importance is the notion of maintaining some balance between well-established and new products, between cash-generating and cash-using products and between growing and declining products. This process of managing the product portfolio is thus a key component of marketing.

- If products are not suitable for the market or not profitable, then attempts to achieve corporate objectives will be jeopardized and the marketing function will be failing to fulfil its stated goals.

- Equally, if potentially profitable products are ignored or not given sufficient support, then crucial marketing opportunities may be lost.

2.6   Strategic Options

One of the greatest challenges for any organization is to develop a coherent, appropriate strategy that will provide a distinct competitive advantage. Competitive advantage is the process of identifying a unique and sustainable basis from which to compete. There are a number of generic frameworks that companies can use to identify the strategic options available to them. This section will discuss Porter's generic strategies, which are based on market position, and the Ansoff matrix.

Porter's Generic Strategies

Porter (1980) identifies three generic strategies that can provide organizations with a competitive advantage: cost leadership, differentiation and focus strategies. These generic strategies, it can be argued, underpin all strategic activities and are discussed in turn below. Figure 2.8 illustrates the alternative sources of competitive advantage and highlights the decisions facing companies in terms of defining their source of strategic advantage and the competitive scope, i.e. targeting a narrow or broad range of customers.

Figure 2.8: Alternative Sources of Competitive Advantage (Porter 1980)

Competitive Advantage

	Lower Cost	Differentiation
Broad target	**Cost Leader**	**Differentiation**
Narrow target	**Cost Focus**	**Differentiation Focus**

Competitive scope

Cost leadership

One potential source of competitive advantage lies in an organization's ability to be the overall cost leader within an industry. Low-cost producers would typically focus on maintaining or reducing their cost structure. This would be achievable via policies such as economies of scale, cost reductions and controlling overheads, global sourcing and the application of new technologies. Typically, the product is undifferentiated, although differentiation cannot be ignored, because the cost savings for the consumer must compensate for the loss of product features, while the discount offered by the firm should not be so high as to offset cost advantages. Prior to deregulation, cost leadership was a common strategy in many areas of financial services with organizations concentrating on a narrow product range. Low-cost producers are not necessarily the lowest price and may use the additional revenue generated to plough back into research and development in order to continue to reduce costs.

It is often difficult to sustain a cost leadership strategy in the long term due to the threat of competitors that have significantly lower cost structures. For example, the UK-based discount retailer Kwik Save was threatened by the entry of German-based Netto and Aldi into the low-cost retail market.

Differentiation

This strategy is to offer products that can be regarded as unique in areas which are highly valued by the consumer. It is the product's uniqueness and the associated customer loyalty that protects the firm from competition. However, the price premium received must outweigh the costs of supplying the differentiated product for this strategy to be successful; at the same time, the customer must feel that the extra features more than compensate for the price premium. As a consequence of deregulation, suppliers of financial services are moving increasingly towards a differentiated approach to their markets and, as a result, competition is increasing.

MARKETING IN PRACTICE

Marks & Spencer

Marks & Spencer has always differentiated on 'quality' and in the past customers were prepared to pay a premium to buy the M&S brand. However, as competitors' product offerings have also increased in quality levels M&S has lost its differentiating factor and customers have no reason to pay the price premium that M&S is charging. M&S is currently striving to identify its new differentiating factor.

Focus

This strategy uses either costs or differentiation but rather than serving the entire market, the organization looks to operate only in particularly attractive or suitable segments or niches.

Differentiation focus is the most common form of focus strategy and implies producing highly customized products for very specific consumer groups. There are already many examples of this in the financial sector, particularly from smaller building societies offering specialized savings products.

The use of a *cost focus* strategy is probably less common, but may be of use where markets are segmented geographically, as has been observed with some of the small regional banks in certain continental European countries.

Inconsistent strategy

Porter (1980) believes that companies must adopt a consistent approach to their generic strategy and that to mix the above strategies within a defined market may result in companies becoming 'stuck in the middle', as shown in Figure 2.9.

Figure 2.9: 'Stuck in the Middle' (Porter 1980)

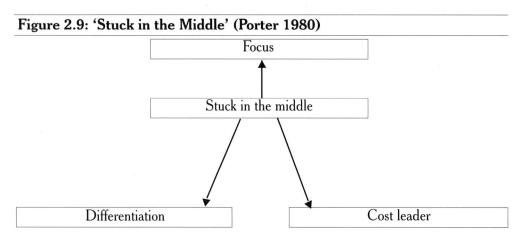

Strategies Based On Market Position

The position that a company holds in a particular industry is going to influence the means by which it is going to gain a competitive advantage. For example, the strategies that are available and appropriate for a multinational bank are not necessarily going to be appropriate for a regional building society. Kotler and Singh (1981) developed a framework for classifying competitors according to their position in the marketplace and identified four distinct categories: market leaders, market challengers, market followers and nichers. This framework draws heavily on military strategy where marketing strategies are paralleled with military strategies and the competitors are regarded as the enemies and where we are fighting not in the battlefield but in the marketplace.

Market Leaders

Market leaders are characterized as being dominant forces in a particular market or segment. This leadership is usually due to domination in market-share terms. The means by which the market is defined has important implications for identification of market leaders. Market leaders are faced with the challenge of maintaining their market leader position, often while under attack from aggressive competitors. There are a number of options open to market leaders:

- Expand the total market – identify new users or uses and this will expand the market for everybody and the market leader will have the same amount of share but of a bigger market.

- Adopt defensive strategies

    - Position defence

    - Flank defence

    - Pre-emptive defence

    - Counter-defence

    - Mobile defence

    - Contraction defence

These defensive strategies are illustrated in Figure 2.10 and are discussed below.

Figure 2.10: Defence Strategies (Kotler & Singh 1981)

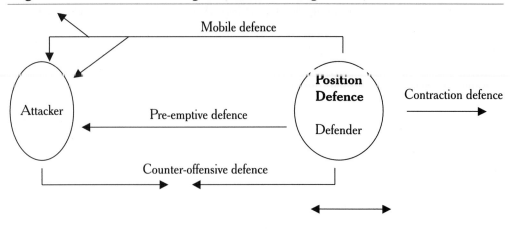

Position defence

This strategy involves strengthening the current position and trying to block out competitors. It will be necessary for companies to adopt a process of continuous improvement to ensure that they continue to meet customer needs more effectively than competitors. Gillette is adopting a position defence strategy in light of increased competition from Wilkinson Sword.

Flank defence

It is often not sufficient to defend the main areas of business, and companies should be concerned with non-core business. Flank defence is associated with protecting the 'weak spots'. For example, the Co-operative Bank recognized its weakness in the area of remote access banking and launched Smile.

Pre-emptive defence

Pre-emptive defence is concerned with attacking competitors before they attack you. This may involve using any of the attacking strategies detailed below. For example, electricity-generating companies started retailing gas after the market was de-regulated.

Counter-defence

When attacked most companies will respond with a counterattack. Counter-defence strategies are largely reactive rather than proactive. WH Smith launched an Internet sales operation in response to Amazon.com.

Mobile defence

This involves adopting a flexible approach to competitor attacks by moving into new areas of business to reduce the reliance on one market sector. For example, a financial services' market leader may launch a stakeholder pension.

Contraction defence

It may not be possible for a market leader to maintain its position in all areas and it may decide to withdraw from particular markets. This will enable companies to concentrate on their core business. For example, Royal and Sun Alliance sold off its Italian life assurance operations in an attempt to consolidate existing business.

Market Challengers

Market challengers often adopt aggressive strategies to challenge the market leader in the hope of securing the market leader position and the assumed associated benefits such as economies of scale, status and power. They seek to achieve market leadership through offensive marketing strategies. There a number of options available to market challengers:

Adopt offensive strategy:

- Frontal attack
- Flank attack
- Encirclement attack
- Bypass attack
- Guerilla attack

Each of these strategies is illustrated in figure 2.11 and explained below.

Figure 2.11: Offensive Strategies (Kotler & Singh 1981)

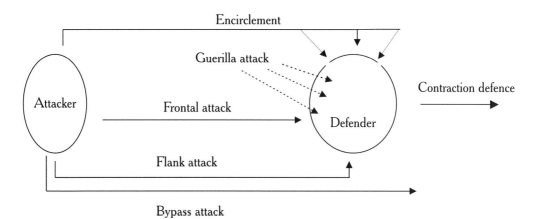

Frontal attack

This involves a direct and head-on attack of competitors. In order to sustain such an attack on competitors the market challenger must have sufficient resources to survive the potential short-term losses that this strategy may incur. Virgin has taken on BA head to head in Business Class on transatlantic flights.

Flank attack
This attack strategy relies on the identification of weak spots in the competitors 'armoury' and concentrating efforts in these areas. For example, Ford acquired Land Rover to protect its flanks.

Encirclement attack
Competitors adopting an encirclement strategy would attempt to surround competitors by attacking them on all sides by serving multiple segments. However, the disadvantage of this strategy may be the additional costs incurred by offering a diverse product range. For example, the Volkswagen group offers a diverse product range in the form of Skoda, Seat, Audi and Volkswagen, etc.

Bypass attack
This strategy relies on the capabilities of companies to identify areas that their competitors are not present in. This may be achieved through technological leapfrogging, identifying new market segments or even new geographical markets. Royal and Sun Alliance have moved into new markets such as China.

Guerilla attack
Guerilla attack as the name suggests are intermittent and random attacks that the competitors cannot anticipate. Tactical marketing initiatives such as price cuts or sales promotions are used to achieve short-term gain which will hopefully erode market share in the longer term. This is a strategy often adopted by supermarket retailers.

Market Follower

Market followers are companies that may be positioned third, fourth or fifth in the market and often copy the strategies of the market leader. The degree to which the follower copies the activities of the market leader may vary from cloning through to adaptation. Sony, a long-established innovator in consumer electronics, is often followed by rival Japanese competitors.

Market Nichers

Market nichers are those companies that focus on a specific market segment and specialize their product offering to meet the needs of a narrow segment. They seek competitive advantage not through economies of scale but through specialization.

Ansoff

Ansoff (1957) developed a matrix that provides a useful framework for identifying alternative strategies in terms of products and markets. The Ansoff matrix (figure 2.12) identifies four alternative growth strategies that are based around 'new and existing markets' and 'new and existing products'. The further an organization moves away from its existing customers and products the higher the level of risk involved. Therefore, diversification is the most risky strategy and market penetration the least risky.

Figure 2.12: Ansoff's Matrix (1957)

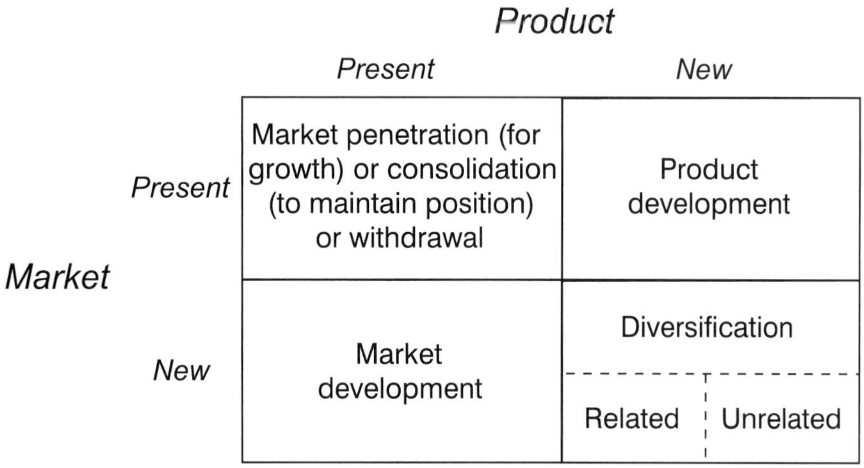

| | | *Product* | |
		Present	New
Market	*Present*	Market penetration (for growth) or consolidation (to maintain position) or withdrawal	Product development
	New	Market development	Diversification Related ¦ Unrelated

Market penetration

This involves selling more of the existing products in existing markets. Possible options are as follows.

● Persuading existing users to use more (increase credit card use by offering higher credit limits or gifts based on expenditure).

● Persuade non-users to use (offering gifts with new accounts or new insurance policies).

● Attracting customers from competitors. For example Cahoot, the Internet bank of Abbey National, is offering new customers the opportunity to reduce their last credit card bill by 5% if they transfer their account to Cahoot.

Market penetration will, in general, be a viable strategy only where the market is not saturated, and there is unsatisfied demand.

Market Development

This entails expanding into new markets with existing products. These may be new markets geographically or new market segments. The use of new distribution channels may open up new markets such as Internet banking. With globalization, the opportunities for market development are likely to increase significantly in some (although not all) areas of financial services. As a strategy, it requires effective and imaginative promotion, but it can be profitable if markets are changing rapidly. For example, some UK building societies have tried to extend their mortgage-lending activities to continental Europe.

MARKETING IN PRACTICE

Royal and Sun Alliance

Royal and Sun Alliance adopted a market development strategy when they moved into India by forming a non-life insurance joint venture in India with Sundaram Finance, an Indian financial services group. This opportunity arose when the Indian Government amended rules to allow foreign companies to enter the country's insurance sector.

Product Development

This approach requires the organization to operate in its existing markets but to develop modified versions of its existing products to appeal to those markets.

Recent developments in the mortgage market provide a good example of product development because the traditional standardized mortgage account is rapidly being supplemented by variants which offer lower starting rates, special terms for particular types of customer, particular mixes of fixed and flexible repayment rates etc.

A strategy of this nature relies on good service design, packaging and promotion and often plays on company reputation to attract consumers to the new product. The benefits are that by tailoring the products more specifically to the needs of some existing consumers and some new consumers the organization can strengthen its competitive position.

Diversification

Diversification is often a high-risk strategy because the organization is moving into areas in which it has little or no experience. The level of risk will be associated with the extent to which the activities are related or unrelated to existing business. The move of Virgin into the financial services industry is an example of unrelated diversification. Diversification into unrelated activities can be very high risk and is often pursued via joint ventures or acquisition; an example of this is illustrated below.

MARKETING IN PRACTICE

Lego Car

The Danish toy manufacturer Lego is currently discussing with a number of car makers the possibility of launching the 'ultimate family vehicle'. Lego is diversifying into this unrelated market but is seeking a partner to reduce the level of risk associated with this new venture. The car will build on Lego's goal of becoming a leading family brand. The car will be designed with the family at the centre of the concept with features such as removable rubbish bins, a paper towel dispenser and a system to monitor children in the back seat without the driver having to turn round. It is expected that the car will be launched in Europe by the end of 2004.

2.7   Strategic Evaluation

Once an organization has identified the various strategic options open to it, it is then necessary to evaluate them in order to identify the most appropriate strategy that will gain the best source of competitive advantage. In reality many companies do not adopt formal processes to evaluate strategic options and rely on gut feeling. However, this is a key element of the strategic marketing planning process and a number of approaches have been developed in order to assess strategies.

Criteria

Johnson & Scholes (1999, p355) developed a list of criteria which they suggest companies should use to evaluate alternative strategies.

- Suitability – does it:
    - Exploit strengths and competencies?
    - Rectify weaknesses?
    - Deflect threats?
    - Seize opportunities?
- Feasibility – can it be implemented?
    - Sufficient finances?
    - Deliver the goods?
    - Deal with competitor's response?
    - Access to technology etc.?
    - Time?
- Acceptability
    - To stakeholders?
    - Legislation and environmental impact?

Aaker (1998) p30 provides a slightly different list of criteria to that of Johnson & Scholes and in particular highlights the importance of how the proposed strategy fits with existing strategies.

- Consider in the context of environmental opportunities and threats
- Sustainable competitive advantage?
    - Exploit strengths or competitors' weaknesses?
    - Neutralize weaknesses or competitors' strengths?
- Consistent with vision/objectives?

- – Achieve long-term ROI?
- – Compatible with vision?
- ● Be feasible
  - – Need only available resources
  - – Be compatible with the internal organization
- ● Relationship with other strategies
  - – Balanced portfolio?
  - – Consider flexibility?
  - – Exploit synergy?

Use of Portfolio Analysis in Strategy Evaluation

The role of portfolio analysis in strategic analysis has been discussed earlier in this chapter. In addition to being a useful tool in strategic analysis, portfolio analysis can be adapted to evaluate alternative strategies. Instead of plotting existing strategic business units or products on the matrix, it is possible to plot the alternative strategies. For example, the General Electric (GE) matrix could be used where the two axes are market attractiveness and competitive strength. The process for plotting the alternative strategies would be the same as for strategic business units/products and this is outlined in Chapter 3. The resulting matrix would illustrate those strategies that would be the most attractive to pursue and those which a company should avoid.

Summary

Marketing strategy is concerned with the means by which organizations match their assets and capabilities with market opportunities and transform corporate objectives into a sustainable competitive market position. Marketing can be viewed from two different perspectives: (1) as an operational activity concerned with functions such as new product development, promotion, pricing and market research and (2) as a business philosophy that permeates the whole organization, where the customer is central to all activities. Strategic marketing focuses on a longer time horizon and is concerned with issues such as what markets should we be in and what is our competitive advantage?

Many companies strive to become market orientated but this is not an easy task. Companies will only become market orientated if this philosophy underlies all activities at all levels within an organization, not just at senior management level.

Strategic analysis is a key part of any marketing strategy. Portfolio analysis plays an important role in evaluating a company's product portfolio. Portfolio planning can be applied at both a corporate level and for the management of individual products. The Boston Consulting Group Matrix classifies products according to relative market share and market growth rate and is a useful diagnostic tool for evaluating a product portfolio. This model has been criticized for being over-simplistic and multi-factor portfolio matrices, such as the General Electric matrix, have been developed to overcome some of these weaknesses. These multi-factor matrices are more comprehensive and enable managers to evaluate a range of factors contributing to market attractiveness and business strength.

In terms of strategic options companies can adopt one of three broad strategies. Firstly that of cost leadership where companies can strive to gain a cost advantage over their competitors. Secondly, they can pursue a strategy of differentiation where customers are willing to pay a higher price for something different or better from that of competitors. The final generic strategy is a focus strategy where companies opt to focus their attention on one specific segment in the market.

The Ansoff matrix is a valuable framework that helps companies to identify the alternative growth strategies open to them. Growth can be achieved through market penetration, market development, product development or diversification, either related or unrelated.

The position that a company occupies in the market – leader, challenger, follower or nicher – can have a major impact on the alternative strategies it employs. This chapter outlines the various strategies open to each of these players.

Once organizations have identified the alternative strategies open to them they need to have some means of evaluating which are the most appropriate. Portfolio analysis can be used in this context to plot alternative strategies and identify the most attractive that match with organizational assets and resources.

References

Aaker D A (1998) *Strategic Market Management*, 5th edition, John Wiley, New York

American Marketing Association (1985) cited in Brassington F & Pettitt S (2000) *Principles of Marketing*, 2nd edition, FT Prentice Hall, Harlow

Ansoff H I (1957) Strategic diversification, *Harvard Business Review*, 25 (5) pp113-125

Chartered Institute of Marketing cited in Brassington F & Pettitt S (2000) *Principles of Marketing*, 2nd edition, FT Prentice Hall, Harlow

Crosier K (1975) What exactly is marketing? *Quarterly Review of Marketing*, Winter

Farber B & Wycoff J (1991) Customer service: evolution and revolution. *Sales and Marketing Management*, May p47.

Jaworski B J & Kohli A K (1993) Market Orientation: Antecedents and consequences, *Journal of Marketing*, 57, July, 53-70

Johnson G & Scholes K (1999) *Exploring Corporate Strategy*, 5th edition, Prentice Hall Europe

Kotler P (1965) Diagnosing the marketing takeover, *Harvard Business Review*, Nov-Dec, pp70-72

Kotler P & Singh R (1981) Marketing warfare in the 1980s, *Journal of Business Strategy* (3) 30-41

Kotler P, Armstrong G, Saunders J & Wong V (1999) *Principles of Marketing*, 2nd European edition, Prentice Hall Europe

Levitt T (1960) Marketing myopia, *Harvard Business Review*, July-August pp45-56

Narver J C & Slater S F (1990) cited in Hooley G J, Saunders J A & Piercy N F (1998) *Marketing Strategy and Competitive Positioning*, Prentice Hall Europe

O'hmae K (1983) *The Mind of the Strategist*, Penguin, London

Porter M E (1980) *Competitive Strategy*, Free Press, New York

Weitz B A & Wensley R (1988) *Readings in Strategic Marketing*, Dryden, New York

3

MARKETING MANAGEMENT AND PLANNING

Learning Objectives

After studying this chapter students should:

- Understand and be able to describe the planning process;

- Appreciate the importance of developing plans;

- Be able to describe the marketing planning process and write an outline marketing plan;

- Be able to undertake a marketing audit and develop a comprehensive SWOT;

- Be able to develop realistic marketing objectives, marketing strategies and marketing programmes;

- Understand the importance of budgeting and resource allocation;

- Be able to identify barriers to the effective implementation of marketing plans and be able to discuss various methods for ensuring successful implementation;

- Be able to explain the various ways in which the marketing function can be organized.

Introduction

The first section of this text is concerned with the contribution that marketing makes to corporate strategy and to the overall process of matching organizational capabilities with environmental opportunities. Chapter 2 introduced strategic marketing, the role of portfolio analysis in strategic analysis and outlined a variety of strategic options, namely growth options, developing a competitive position and competitive strategies based on market position. This chapter will examine the implementation of marketing through the planning process. The first part of the chapter discusses the planning process and how marketing planning relates to corporate planning. The chapter then goes onto outline the various stages of the marketing planning process, the components of a marketing plan and finally discusses the various ways in which the marketing function can be organized to support marketing planning.

Figure 3.1: Chapter Map

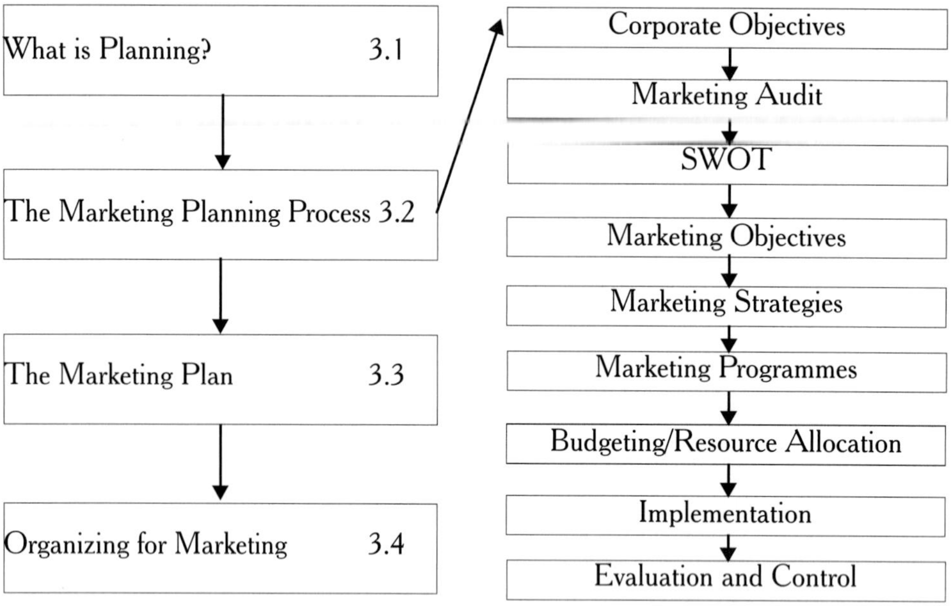

What is Planning? 3.1	Corporate Objectives
The Marketing Planning Process 3.2	Marketing Audit
The Marketing Plan 3.3	SWOT
Organizing for Marketing 3.4	Marketing Objectives
	Marketing Strategies
	Marketing Programmes
	Budgeting/Resource Allocation
	Implementation
	Evaluation and Control

3.1   What is Planning?

Planning is a fundamental part of all managers' roles and it helps to drive organizations forwards by coordinating resources and channelling them towards the achievement of pre-determined goals. The future is uncertain, however planning can help to provide a framework for considering the future, appraising the various options and developing strategies to meet their objectives. Too often people in organizations are too concerned with the immediate day-to-day tasks to think about the often more important long-term tasks. Planning encourages people to consider the future and to realize that change is inevitable in a rapidly developing world. Without planning both strategic and operational activities would be uncoordinated and lacking in focus. Organizations may be highly reactive and fail to identify threats in the form of competitor activity even to the extent that they are not commercially viable to continue. The steps involved in planning are the same whether we are discussing corporate, marketing or advertising planning and are illustrated in Figure 3.2. It is the focus of the plan that will differ.

Figure 3.2: Planning Process

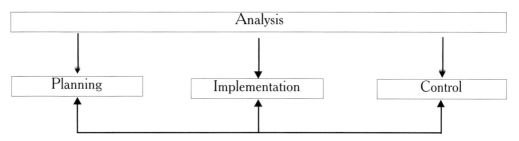

Analysis

It is essential that we understand the current situation before identifying the direction in which we want to go. The analysis stage involves a complete review of the external and internal environment in order to identify opportunities. The information generated from this exercise will help to define the future strategy and will be utilized at all stages of the planning process.

Planning

Planning is concerned with objectives and the strategies to help to achieve these objectives. In a marketing planning context we would be concerned with marketing product or brand plans.

Implementation

Implementation is concerned with turning the plans into action and involves decisions relating to resources such as people and finance. Companies often overlook implementation and it is at this stage that many plans fail – not because they were poor strategies but because they were poorly implemented. This will be discussed in greater detail in section 3.2.

Control

A key element of the planning process is the evaluation of the plan – i.e. the control mechanisms. These are necessary to measure the success of the plan and to take corrective action if necessary.

It is important to differentiate between planning and a plan. Plans are the outcome of the planning process and act as a vehicle for communicating the objectives and strategy to all involved people.

There are many barriers to planning in organizations, such as lack of time, fear of change, lack of expertise and lack of robust marketing information. Companies need to seek solutions to try to overcome these barriers so that they can remain forward thinking. Planning is an essential organizational function; however, there are problems associated with planning. The resultant plans are only as good as the planning process and sometimes companies can fall into the trap of seeing planning as highly mechanistic and technique-orientated without actually considering the key issues. A further problem may surface because some organizations set up dedicated planning organizations that may become divorced from reality and – more importantly – divorced from those tasked with the implementation.

The main benefit of planning is to provide a coherent and coordinated approach for organizations. However, the planning process and the resulting plan must be fully integrated so that the plans are viable and acceptable.

3.2   The Marketing Planning Process

The marketing planning process will vary considerably from organization to organization depending partly on whether it is focusing on strategic or operational plans. The strategic marketing plan and operational plan differ in two respects according to Abell (1982). The strategic marketing plan is concerned with the total strategy in terms of customers, competitors and organizational capability whereas the operational marketing plan deals with the marketing mix. Secondly, strategic marketing plans are focused at an SBU or company level whereas operational marketing plans are more concerned with products or market segments. Figure 3.3 illustrates the major stages in the planning process. The early stages are associated with strategic marketing planning while the marketing mix programmes deal with the more operational aspects of marketing planning.

Figure 3.3: Major Stages in the Planning Process

Corporate objectives/strategic intent

↓

Marketing audit

↓

SWOT analysis

↓

Marketing objectives

↓

Marketing strategies

↓

Marketing programmes

↓

Budgets/resource allocation

↓

Implementation

↓

Evaluation and control

Corporate objectives/strategic intent

Corporate objectives are central to the planning process. They provide the organization with a sense of direction and guide marketing planning. Corporate objectives relate to the whole organization and are often expressed as a quantifiable financial target such as return on investment. These should be SMART (specific, measurable, actionable, and realistic with a timescale). In reality objectives often have to be prepared with a number of trade-offs in mind. Table 3.1 outlines a number of such trade-offs, identified by Weinberg (1969), that companies have to manage.

Table 3.1 Strategic Direction Trade-offs (Weinberg 1969)

Short-term profit v. long-term growth
Profit margin v. market positioning
Direct sales effort v. market development
Penetrating existing markets v. developing new ones
Profit v. non-profit goals
Growth v. stability
Change v. stability
Low-risk v. high-risk investment

Objectives that are more qualitative in nature are often expressed in the form of a mission statement. A mission statement should provide a vision of where the company is today and where it wants to be in the future. It is intended to provide all stakeholders with a sense of purpose, communicate the distinctive and key values of the company and provide a view of the company's strategic intent. Day (1990) outlines four key characteristics of successful mission statements:

- Future orientated – not purely focused on old successes;
- Reflecting the values and orientation of the leader;
- Stating strategic purpose – in terms of strategy, markets and competitors;
- Enabling – provide clear guidelines to staff as to how they may contribute to the organization.

Strategic intent is also discussed in Chapter 1.

The Marketing Audit

The term audit is used in many contexts but is usually associated with undertaking a review of current activities. It can be applied at a corporate level or a functional level such as finance or marketing. This section will discuss the role of the audit in a marketing context as a means of reviewing the current status of marketing activity. It helps to answer the question 'where are we now?'

> A *marketing audit is a* comprehensive, systematic, independent and periodic *examination of a company's environment, objectives, strategies and activities to determine problem areas and opportunities, and to recommend a plan of action to improve the company's marketing performance.*
>
> *(Kotler et al. 1999, p111)*

The marketing audit involves a critical analysis of both the external and internal marketing environment and will form the basis of marketing planning. A marketing audit should consider the following:

- The external macro environment (discussed in Chapter 1)
- The external micro environment (customers, competitors and markets, intermediaries)
- Internal environment
- Marketing strategy
- Marketing mix
- Marketing organizational structure
- Marketing systems (such as MKIS)
- Marketing productivity

> *(Adapted from Kotler 1996, pp780-781)*

This review should identify the external opportunities and threats, and the internal strengths, in terms of assets and competencies, and weaknesses. A key aspect of the marketing audit is that it is undertaken objectively, which is sometimes difficult when the auditors are too close to the situation. The use of external consultants can help to overcome this problem.

SWOT Analysis

The marketing audit is often a time-consuming process that generates a huge amount of data and information that needs to be analysed in an attempt to identify the key issues that will form the basis of the marketing strategy. SWOT (strengths, weaknesses, opportunities and threats) analysis is a valuable tool for structuring the information generated from the audit.

- An *opportunity* is simply any feature of the external environment that creates conditions which are advantageous to the firm in relation to a particular objective or set of objectives.

- By contrast, a *threat* is any environmental development that will present problems and may hinder the achievement of organizational objectives. What constitutes an opportunity to some firms will almost invariably constitute a threat to others. An increased presence in domestic financial markets by overseas banks might be regarded by them as the pursuit of an opportunity but will be perceived as a threat by domestic banks.

- A *strength* can be thought of as a particular skill or distinctive competence that the organization possesses and which will aid it in achieving its stated objectives. These may relate to experience in specific types of markets or specific skills possessed by employees. A strength may also refer to factors such as a firm's reputation for quality or customer service.

- A *weakness* is simply any aspect of the company that may hinder the achievement of specific objectives such as limited experience of certain markets/technologies, or the extent of financial resources available. The lack of experience within building societies of money transmission facilities could be regarded as a weakness when considering the development of current accounts, whereas banks may consider their experience in wholesale money markets to be a strength in relation to the development of mortgage services.

This information would typically be presented as a matrix of strengths, weaknesses, opportunities and threats. There are several points to note about presentation and interpretation. Effective SWOT analysis does not simply require a categorization of information, it also requires some *evaluation* of the *relative importance* of the various factors under consideration. These features are of relevance only if they are perceived to exist by the consumers. Listing corporate features that internal personnel regard as strengths/weaknesses is of little relevance if the organization's consumers do not perceive them as such. Strengths can be related to a firm's distinctive competence. Threats and opportunities are conditions presented by the external environment and they should be independent of the firm.

Having constructed a matrix of strengths, weaknesses, opportunities and threats with some evaluation attached to them, it then becomes feasible to make use of that matrix in guiding strategy formulation. The two major strategic options are as follows.

Figure 3.4: SWOT Analysis

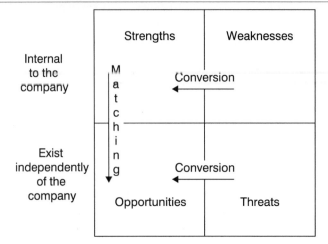

Matching. This entails finding, where possible, a match between the strengths of the organization and the opportunities presented by the market. Strengths that do not match any available opportunity are of limited use while opportunities that do not have any matching strengths are of little immediate value from a strategic perspective.

Conversion. This requires the development of strategies that will convert weaknesses into strengths in order to take advantage of some particular opportunity, or converting threats into opportunities that can then be matched by existing strengths.

To summarize the marketing SWOT:

Strengths and Weaknesses
These are internal factors controllable by marketing managers.

Opportunities and Threats
These are external uncontrollable factors related to an appraisal of changing product/market position.

Marketing objectives

Without a lead on strategy from senior management, middle managers could be faced with a corporate objective of increasing profitability by x% over three years. In pursuit of this, *operations* could cut costs, reduce stockholdings and trim back production levels. *Marketing* could be implementing strategies to increase revenue, through higher sales. These two departments would clearly be working *against each other,* although both aiming to contribute to the stated corporate goal.

Armed with clear, quantified corporate objectives and the coordinating influence of a corporate strategy, the unit managers can develop their own functional plans, as we have seen, but the first step is to generate unit objectives. In essence this requires translating the corporate objectives and strategy into terms that have a meaning to those working within the department, in this case marketing.

Marketing objectives are often expressed in sales terms, for example, market share or revenue or sales volume. For example, A Ltd wishes to increase market share to 45% by 2002. This objective can then be further developed by the sales manager who can forecast that 45% in 2002 will equal 1 million cases. In turn the sales manager can then develop the next level of objectives into terms which mean something to those in the sales team: to sell 1,000 more cases per month by 2002.

Note that the individual sales targets or objectives can be set from this. With a salesforce of 20, each salesperson needs to be selling 50 extra cases per month by 2002.

Sub-objectives for elements of the marketing mix can also be set to help to achieve the overall marketing objectives. Of course, many of them require the cooperation of other departments.

Product. Although 'marketing' deals with products and markets, marketing objectives for products require the cooperation of the production department and R&D. Marketing can suggest that a percentage (e.g. 15%) of revenue should come from new products launched within the last 3 years. 3M has such an objective.

Pricing has market share implications (e.g. penetration or skimming pricing).

Distribution. An objective might be to reduce the time from when the order is received to when the goods are delivered.: 'By March 2002, reduce delivery lead times from 5 to 3 days'.

Promotion. Advertising and promotion objectives aim to shape customer awareness and expectations of the product as well as to generate sales leads.

- Recall: How many remember an ad?
- Awareness
- Interest (e.g. % of people replying to a mailshot
- Share of voice (compared to other promotions)

There are other issues to consider.

Objectives for elements of the service marketing mix (*people* – staff training; *processes* – efficiency; *physical evidence* – cleanliness of sites).

Pursuit of Market Share and PIMS Research

Many marketing objectives are expressed in market share terms. Why is it that many companies are preoccupied with market share? Economies of scale and the experience curve suggest that being the biggest will be the most cost effective and therefore many companies pursue market share objectives. There are many reasons as to why achieving high market share is desirable. A large market share can give companies more bargaining power with their suppliers.

Being the number one in the market can also give the feeling of apparent security among groups of stakeholders such as financiers and employees. It also provides companies with the opportunity to determine the basis of competition if they are the market leader. Finally there is a great deal of status associated with being the number one in the market.

The benefits of pursuing market share objectives are also supported by the PIMS (profit impact of market strategy) research. This research programme has built a database of information on the success and failure of more that 3000 SBUs. The aim of the research was to identify the most significant determinants of profitability. Research findings showed that market share was a key factor in profitability. In general terms it was found that profits will increase in line with relative market share (see Figure 3.5). This relationship has prompted actions at increasing market share as a route to profitability. For example, the study has shown that organizations with a market share of more than 40% will achieve ROIs of 30%, three times that of companies with market share of under 10%.

Figure 3.5: Profit and Market Share Relationship – PIMS Research

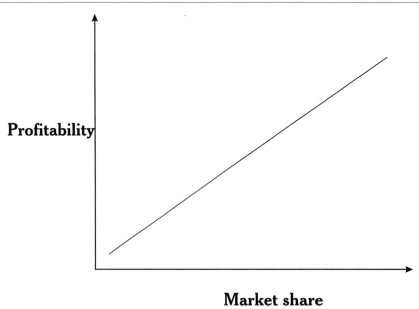

Profitability

Market share

There have been a number of criticisms targeted at the PIMS research and its findings regarding the link between market share and profitability. The difficulty in analysing market share is defining the market within which a company is operating. For example, Mercedes Benz – do we define the market as the total car market or the luxury car market? In addition, there is evidence of many successful low-share businesses.

In some industries there is evidence of a V-shaped curve rather than the accepted linear relationship between market share and profitability (see Figure 3.6). Small niche players and large dominant players are successful whereas the medium sized companies are 'stuck in the middle' and see their profits falling.

Figure 3.6: V-shaped Relationship between Market Share and Profitability

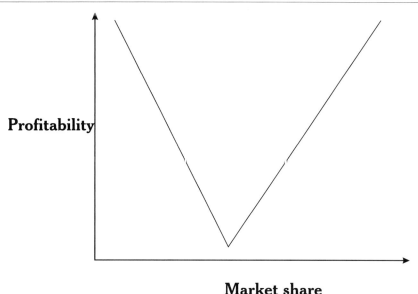

The conclusion is that market share does not automatically bring with it profitability. This will also depend on the company's overall strategy, level of maturity in the market, effect on other areas of the company's activities, level of customer loyalty and likely competitive reactions.

Marketing Strategies

A *marketing strategy* may be defined as a plan to achieve the organization's marketing objectives. The main focus of the marketing strategy will relate to the target market and the deployment of the marketing mix. It will also involve the allocation of resources required and the structure and allocation of responsibilities. Segmentation, targeting and positioning are key elements of marketing strategy and this is discussed in detail in Chapter 7. The choice of target market will be influenced by the competitive nature of the market and in turn links with generic competitive strategies as discussed in Chapter 2.

Marketing Programmes

Marketing programmes specify detailed actions, responsibilites and time scales and link the formulation and the implementation of marketing strategy. The strategy focuses on the interdependency between the elements of the mix. The marketing programmes are concerned with translating the strategy into action for each element of the mix. The planning process can then be applied to each aspect of the mix in turn, i.e. audit, objectives, strategy, programmes and controls. The marketing mix is addressed in Part 3.

Budgets/allocating resources

A key element of the planning process is the allocation of budgets and other resources such as human and physical resources. Budgeting for sales revenue and selling costs is plagued with uncertainty. The variables are so many and so difficult to estimate, even within a wide tolerance (largely because of competitive action and changing consumer habits and tastes), that both setting budgets and budgetary control on the marketing side are different from the more 'mechanical' approach that can be adopted with other budgets.

It is unsatisfactory to engage in minute cost-control systems in production, and then hope that all other costs (such as research, distribution, and sales) will look after themselves. A sales and marketing budget is necessary for the following reasons:

- It is an element of the overall strategic plan of the business (the master budget) which brings together all the activities of the business.

- Where sales and other non-production costs are a large part of total costs, it is financially prudent to forecast, plan and control them.

- The very uncertain nature of factors that influence selling makes the need for good forecasts and plans greater, and it can be argued that if budgets are to be used for control, the more uncertain the budget estimates are, the more budgetary control is necessary.

Implementation

Marketing planning can fail not because it is based on a poor strategy but because it has been poorly implemented. Too often implementation is bolted onto the end of the planning process with very little thought. Marketing implementation failure may occur because planning has become separated from management and those that have been tasked with implementation may not have 'bought into the plan' and may be resistant to change in which they were not involved. Successful strategies are dependent on two key factors. Firstly the appropriateness of the strategy and secondly how well it is executed. Figure 3.7 illustrates the various outcomes that may arise in a four different situations.

Figure 3.7: Success versus Failure Matrix (Bonoma 1984)

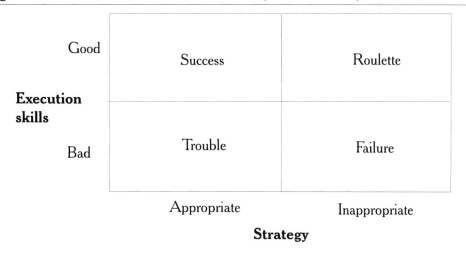

As can be seen from the matrix it is not enough to have an appropriate strategy; it must also be effectively implemented. In fact the matrix suggests that an inappropriate but effectively executed strategy may have more chance of success than an appropriate strategy that is ineffectively executed. This illustrates the importance of developing an implementation plan alongside the marketing plan. Piercy (1997) p593 addresses the issue of implementation problems and suggest that for successful implementation the following must be considered:

● Gaining support of key decision makers;

● Changing attitudes and behaviour of employees and managers;

● Winning commitment to making the plan work and ownership of the key problem solving tasks;

● Managing incremental changes in the culture.

It has been suggested that to increase the likelihood of successful implementation the practices of external marketing should be applied to the internal marketplace. This is known as internal marketing (which is also discussed in Chapters 4 and 14). Employees should be regarded as internal customers and marketing plans need to be 'marketed' internally to gain acceptance and to ensure that employees understand the rationale behind the plans, can see how they can contribute to the success of the plan and, importantly, 'buy into' the plan. The internal marketing plan would take the same format as an external marketing plan with objectives, strategy and market segmentation, marketing mix programmes and evaluation. Internal customers could be segmented on a variety of bases such as work function, extent to which they will support change, geographical location etc. Marketing programmes would then be designed to target the most appropriate segments. For example, opinion leaders could be targeted in the hope that they will influence others' opinions. The internal marketing mix could consist of the following:

- *Product* – the plan itself and its associated benefits;

- *Price* – the price the internal customers will have to pay to accept the marketing plan, e.g. change of role, fear of change etc.;

- *Promotion* – the message and the media by which the plan will be communicated. Obviously two-way communication is more effective than one-way;

- *Place* – the places where the product is delivered, e.g. use of the company intranet, presentations, workshops, meetings etc.

It is essential to monitor the success of the internal marketing plan. This is not an easy task but various methods can be adopted. For example, a regular staff survey can monitor staff attitudes or alternatively you can measure the extent to which the plan has been implemented in the external marketplace by measuring customer satisfaction.

Evaluation and Control

It is essential that marketing plans are monitored, controlled and evaluated to ensure that the objectives are being met. If objectives are not being met any problems can be identified and corrective action taken if necessary. Marketing planning is not just a linear process; it is cyclical and information regarding the effectiveness of the plan can be used in future planning. Control measures should relate to the objectives and should cover both effectiveness – 'doing the right things' – and efficiency – 'doing things right' measures. Too often companies focus on measuring the efficiency of activities without actually questioning whether they are doing the right things. It is often easier to measure efficiency as opposed to effectiveness. For example, a retail bank operates a call centre to deal with customer service and it wants to establish measurements to monitor the staff's performance. It is far easier to develop efficiency measures such as number of calls dealt with in an hour, number of new leads generated, length of call etc. However, this tells us nothing about the effectiveness of the staff and the customer's experience of the service. It is much more difficult to develop effectiveness measures relating to customer satisfaction.

An increasingly popular evaluation technique is benchmarking. This is concerned with comparing key performance indicators with competitors, recognized industry leaders and even companies in different sectors that are regarded as market leaders. Comparisons can also be made internally over time-to-track development. A limitation of benchmarking is that it is focused on competitors rather than customers. Companies should set targets that customers value.

3.3   The Marketing Plan

The marketing plan is a physical document that is responsible for communicating the strategic marketing planning process. Kotler (1999) p112 provides a useful framework on which to base one's marketing plan:

- *Executive summary.* This is a summary of the main goals and recommendations in the plan;

- *Current situation.* This consists of the marketing audit and SWOT analysis;

- *Objectives and issues.* What the organization is hoping to achieve, or needs to achieve, perhaps in terms of market share or 'bottom-line' profits and returns;

- *Marketing strategy.* This considers the selection of target markets, the marketing mix and marketing expenditure levels;

- *Action programme.* This sets out how these various strategies are going to be achieved;

- *Budgets* are developed from the action programme;

- *Controls.* These will be set up to monitor the progress of the plan and the budget.

3.4   Organizing for Marketing

It is clear that marketing can be viewed from two different perspectives, as discussed in Chapter 2. Firstly marketing is an activity that is concerned with functions such as market research, advertising, pricing and new product development. Marketing professionals are employed to undertake these roles. However, marketing is not just the responsibility of professional marketers; it should be regarded as the concern of everybody from the most junior employee to the Chief Executive. In this respect marketing is a business philosophy that puts the customer at the centre of the organization's activities. The importance of every employee being involved in 'marketing', regardless of his or her function, has resulted in the term 'part-time' marketer. This term recognizes the role that all employees play in delivering high-quality products and services. This is particularly important in high customer contact situations such as financial services. Due to the intangibility of the service, any contact the customer has with the organization will influence his or her perception of the service and the service provider. Therefore, any employees working at the interface with the customer must be aware of the importance of their role and the impact they may have on customer's experiences. The easyJet case study at the end of Part 1 highlights the importance of 'part-time marketers' and the role they play in delivering high-quality services.

The next section is concerned with how the marketing function may be organized.

The organizational role and form of marketing departments continues to vary. There is no one format that can be described as 'best' or 'most effective'. The existing organizational structure, patterns of management and the spread of the firm's product and geographical interests will all play a part in determining how it develops. Whatever the format, the marketing department must take responsibility for four key areas:

- functions (promotion, pricing etc.);

- geographical areas;

- products;

- markets.

These four areas of responsibility will provide insight into how the different forms of marketing department may arise.

Functional organization

The department is headed by a marketing director who is responsible for the overall co ordination of the marketing effort. A number of functional specialists such as a market research manager and a sales manager are found in the second tier of management and they take responsibility for all related activities across all products and markets. This format has the benefit of great simplicity and administrative directness. It allows individuals to develop their particular specialisms, but also imposes a burden on the marketing director who has to coordinate and arbitrate activities to ensure the development of a coherent marketing mix for elements of the product range.

With a limited product portfolio, the burden on the marketing director may not be a problem. As the range of products and markets expands, however, it will tend to become less efficient. There is always the danger that a particular product or market may be neglected because it is only one of many being handled by a single manager who will find it difficult to play a specialist role for all products.

Geographical organization

This is an extension of the functional organization. Responsibility for some or all functional activities is devolved to a regional level, through a national functional manager. This type of organization is more common in firms operating internationally where the various functional activities need to be broken down for each national market or group of national markets.

Product-based organization

Product managers are responsible for specific products or groups of products. This type of approach is likely to be particularly appropriate for organizations with very diverse product assortments or with a very extensive range of products.

The individual product manager develops plans for specific products and ensures that products remain competitive, drawing on the experience and guidance of functional managers. The product manager is effectively responsible for all the marketing activities relating to a particular product group and consequently needs skills in promotion, pricing and distribution. This approach allows the individual product managers to develop considerable experience and understanding of particular product groups and as such may be effective within a rapidly changing competitive environment. Because they have to undertake a variety of functional activities, the danger is that they will become 'jacks of all trades and masters of none'. In spite of this, the product-based approach is becoming increasingly important because the benefits of managers with expertise related to specific product groups is seen to outweigh the costs associated with a loss of functional specialization.

Market management

This is a variant on the product management structure. Instead of individual managers taking responsibility for particular products they instead take responsibility for particular markets. When an organization sells a variety of different products into particular markets, the understanding of the product is perceived to be slightly less important than the understanding of the market. So managers with knowledge and experience of a particular market are more valuable.

Matrix management

Matrix management can be thought of as an integration of the product and market management approaches. In an organization dealing with a variety of products in a variety of markets the product-based approach requires managers to be familiar with a wide variety of different markets, whereas the market-based approach requires managers to be familiar with a wide variety of products. In either case, however, expertise may not be fully or efficiently utilized. The matrix-based system combines the two. A series of managers deal with markets and a further series deal with products. The market managers take responsibility for the development and maintenance of profitable markets while the product manager focuses on product performance and profitability. The system involves these being interlinked. Each product manager deals with a variety of market managers and each market manager deals with a variety of product managers.

Although this system may seem to resolve the dilemma of choosing the best form of organization for a marketing department, it presents certain problems. It is extremely costly, employing large numbers of managers. There are also possible conflicts between product and market managers to consider and, particularly, the issue of who should take responsibility for certain activities. Should the sales force be product- or market-based and who should take responsibility for pricing?

Divisional marketing organization

As well as the organization of marketing within a unitary organization, of course there are many organizations where the larger product groups are developed into separate divisions (what is often called a multi-divisional or 'M' form organization). These divisions have a high degree of autonomy, but ultimately are responsible to a head office. Here, marketing activity is often devolved to divisional level although this is not invariable because some marketing decisions naturally remain the responsibility of corporate headquarters. The extent of corporate involvement can vary from none at all to extensive. No particular level of corporate involvement is more desirable than another; however, it is often suggested that corporate involvement tends to be more extensive in the early stages of the organization's development when the divisions are individually quite weak, but as divisions strengthen, corporate involvement in marketing begins to decline.

Summary

Marketing planning is concerned with developing objectives, strategies and tactics that take advantage of opportunities in the marketplace and reduce the impact of external threats. The planning process is similar whether we are concerned with corporate marketing or advertising planning. It involves analysing the current situation, developing objectives and strategies, turning these plans into action and finally measuring them as a method of control. Planning encourages people to consider the future and to develop a means of driving their organization forwards by coordinating resources and channelling them towards pre-determined goals.

Marketing plans can be either strategic or operational. The stages in the planning process of either plan will be the same, but the focus will be different, e.g. developing a five-year marketing plan versus a one-year advertising plan. The marketing plan is the output of the marketing planning process and is a vehicle for communicating information and a means of coordinating resources.

The marketing audit is an invaluable tool for undertaking a review of current marketing activities. It helps to answer the question – Where are we now? The marketing audit is often a time-consuming exercise and can generate a wealth of information. It is essential that this information is analysed in an attempt to identify key issues that will form the basis of marketing strategy. SWOT analysis is a valuable tool for evaluating the information generated from the audit. Strengths and weaknesses are concerned with internal issues and opportunities and threat with factors that are external to the company.

Marketing planning can sometimes fail, not because of a poor strategy, but because it has been poorly implemented. Many companies are now recognizing that they need to develop a separate implementation plan to ensure that staff 'buy into' the marketing plan. Internal marketing can play a key role in gaining acceptance of plans among staff.

There are a number of ways in which organizations can manage their marketing activity. Companies can choose either to structure according to function, geography, product, market or alternatively to use a matrix structure. How the marketing department is structured will depend on a number of factors, such as historical developments, cultural issues and company size.

References

Abell, D F (1982) 'Metamorphosis in Market Planning' in KK Cox and V J McGinnis (eds), *Strategic Market Decisions*, Prentice-Hall.

Bonoma T V (1994) Making your marketing strategy work, *Harvard Business Review*, Vol. 62, No. 2 pp68-76.

Day G S (1990) *Market-driven Strategy*, Free Press

Kotler P, Armstrong G, Saunders J & Wong V (1999) *Principles of Marketing*, Second European Edition, Prentice-Hall.

Piercy N (1997) *Market-led Strategic Change*, Butterworth-Heinemann, Oxford.

Weinberg R (1969) *Developing Market Strategies for Short-term Profits and Long-term Growth*, Paper presented at Advanced Management Research Inc. Seminar, New York.

4

SERVICE MARKETING MANAGEMENT

Learning Objectives

Students after reading this chapter should:

- Know the characteristics of services and understand the types of issues that these raise for marketers;

- Understand one concept of service quality and how this may be used as the basis for delivering service quality improvements;

- Understand the meaning of 'customer satisfaction' and know how this may be measured;

- Understand the key issues that marketing managers must address in managing services.

Figure 4.1: Chapter Map

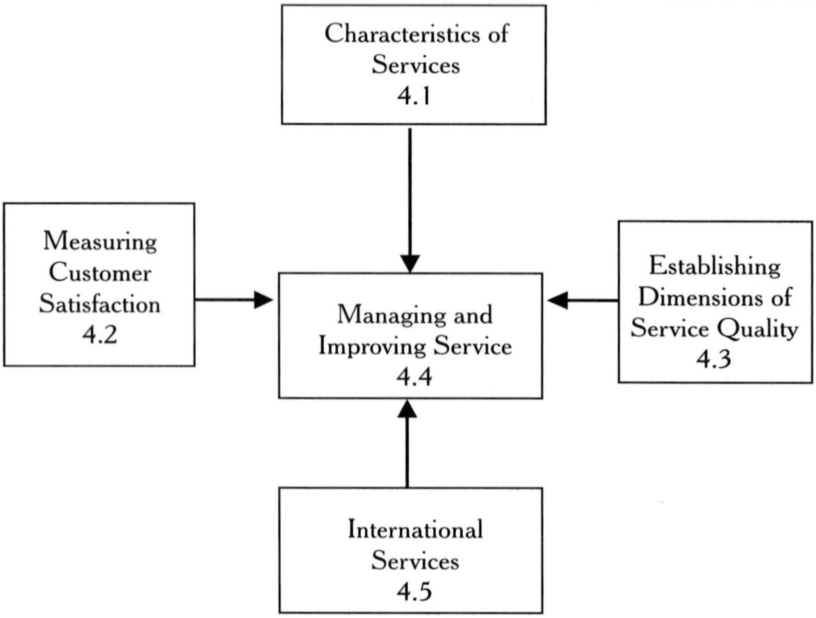

```
                    ┌─────────────────┐
                    │ Characteristics of │
                    │    Services       │
                    │      4.1          │
                    └─────────┬─────────┘
                              │
                              ▼
┌─────────────┐     ┌─────────────────┐     ┌─────────────────┐
│  Measuring  │     │                 │     │  Establishing   │
│  Customer   │────▶│  Managing and   │◀────│  Dimensions of  │
│ Satisfaction│     │ Improving Service│     │ Service Quality │
│    4.2      │     │      4.4        │     │      4.3        │
└─────────────┘     └────────▲────────┘     └─────────────────┘
                              │
                    ┌─────────┴─────────┐
                    │  International    │
                    │    Services       │
                    │      4.5          │
                    └───────────────────┘
```

Introduction

In the EU, almost 1.3 million new jobs per year were created in the service sector between 1980 and 1992. This was twice that of the average for the European economy as a whole (Eurostat 1995). The service sector has replaced manufacturing as the most substantial element of the economy in the leading industrialized countries. In Great Britain, for example, 76% of employees in 1998 were employed in the service sector (Office for National Statistics 1999).

Service marketing management shares many problems and issues with product management. However, there are additional problems with regard to the management of services, due to their 'intangibility', 'inseparability', 'heterogeneity', 'persishability' and difficulty of defining ownership. Approaches for addressing these issues are discussed.

Two key elements for successful service marketing management are defining and measuring customer satisfaction and service quality. Techniques for measuring these two elements are discussed and approaches for managing and improving service quality presented.

4.1   Characteristics of Services

There are many possible definitions of a service. Kotler *et al.* (1999) p646 defines a service as:

> *Any activity or benefit that one party can offer to another which is essentially intangible and does not result in the ownership of anything.*

Many definitions focus on the intangibility of a service. This is to distinguish services from products. It is increasingly more difficult to make a distinction between products and services because products include intangible service elements and services include tangible product elements (Table 4.1). Many product markets are now mature. There is little scope for product innovation and so to gain competitive advantage companies have developed the service component of the product offer. Competition in product markets takes place at the augmented product level (see Chapter 9). Similarly, for pure services, sustainable competitive advantage cannot be maintained and this has led service marketers to offer tangibility to their services. Services and products now compete in the 'zone of competitive advantage' (shown by the rectangle in Figure 4.2) and this increasingly makes it difficult to distinguish full product offers from full service offers.

The successful entry of Daewoo cars into the European car market focused heavily on the service elements of the product offer to overcome the traditional 'me too' approach to marketing cars.

Table 4.1: Tangible and Intangible Elements of Classic Products (Cars) and Services (Haircuts)

	Tangible product elements	Intangible service elements
Car	THE PRODUCT	
	●The car	●Delivered to your home
		●Free car tax
		●Free insurance
		●3-year warranty
		●3-year free service
	●Courtesy car provided while the car is being serviced	●Courtesy car provided while the car is being serviced
Hair cut in a 'salon'		THE SERVICE
	●Free coffee	
	●Free biscuits	●The haircut
	●Product 'give aways'	●Relaxing environment
	●Salon card or leaflet	●Magazines
		●MTV (Music TV)

Figure 4.2: Zone of Competitive Advantage in the Service-Product Offer

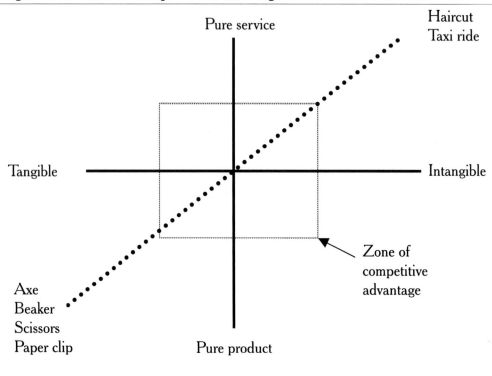

Marketing difficulties inherent in service marketing

The intangibility of the service means that the consumer may forget:

- The 'true' quality of the service provided;

- Who provided the service.

Product sellers have developed services to add to their product offer as a means of gaining competitive advantage. In contrast, service firms, concerned at the marketing difficulties that are created by the intangibility of services, have tried to give the service greater tangibility in their attempt to gain competitive advantage.

Various strategies can be employed to build in tangibility into the service offering such as producing freephone numbers, corporate brochures and sponsorship. For example, sponsorship of the English Football League by the Nationwide Building Society helped to give their brand tangibility and build their corporate image.

Basic service characteristics

Services exhibit several unique characteristics that differentiate them from products. Service companies must consider these characteristics when devising marketing programmes. The unique characteristics of services are:

- Intangibility

- Inseparability

- Heterogeneity (variability)

- Perishability

- Lack of ownership.

Intangibility

Prior to services being purchased, they cannot be seen or felt, in complete contrast to products. Services gain tangibility as they are experienced as the five senses (touch, sight, smell, hearing and taste) can be used in their assessment. Dealing with intangibility involves the following:

Increasing the level of tangibility. When dealing with the customer, staff can use physical or conceptual representations/illustrations to make the customer feel more confident as to what it is that the service is delivering.

Focusing the attention of the customer on the principal benefits of consumption. This could take the form of communicating the benefits of purchasing the service so that the customer visualizes its appropriateness to the usage requirements within which the principal benefit is sought. Promotion and sales material could provide images or records of previous customers' experience.

Differentiating the service and reputation-building: This could involve enhancing perceptions of customer service and customer value by offering excellence in the delivery of the service and promoting values of quality, service reliability and value for money. These must be attached as values to brands, which must then be managed to secure and enhance their market position.

Inseparability

Services are produced by the service providers at the same time as they are consumed by customers (i.e. service provision is coterminous with consumption). This is in contrast with products that may be produced and sold at a later date.

Provision of the service may not be separable from the person or personality of the seller. Consequently increasing importance is attached to the quality of service provision by service staff because customers tend not make a distinction between service staff and the company that employs them.

Heterogeneity (Variability)

Services are provided by people, and in large organizations services may be provided all over the world, by people from all over the world. Many services therefore face the problem of maintaining consistency in the standard of output. In contrast, products may be produced with quality controlled by accurate, automated control mechanisms which measure tolerances of product specification.

Perishability

Services cannot be stored. Once a film has been shown in a cinema the opportunity to sell the seat to view the film has gone. It is critical, therefore, for service firms to mange differences between supply and demand, for example through price variations that encourage off-peak demand and promotions to stimulate off-peak demand.

Demand management. As for the provision of products, service firms may alter their output to cope with fluctuations in demand. More staff can be recruited, and/or existing staff may be asked to work overtime. Companies planned for the (non-existent) threat of the millennium bug through the use of IT staff on short-term contracts while existing company staff worked long hours to make systems millennium-bug proof.

Supply management. In addition to coping with service, supply companies must manage demand and this is most frequently achieved through the use of price incentives. Non-peak travel fairs and low-season holidays are classic examples of companies managing the heterogeneity of service demand.

Lack of Ownership

Services are ephemeral and cannot be owned. The user experiences the services and may subsequently forget the service offer and its relative merits. This is obviously undesirable for a firm wanting repeat business.

The nearest to ownership that a service purchaser comes to is the purchase of a service over a given amount of time. The consumer therefore 'owns' the service for a specified, or implied, amount of time. Time may be specified in the service purchase, e.g. a one-hour tennis lesson, or it may be implied by the service purchase. Purchasers of haircuts, or of a 'round of golf', will have an idea of the amount of time these particular services will take. They may even use this concept of time in their assessment of the price they are prepared to pay for a given service.

Various marketing approaches to the non-ownership serices are possible.

1. *Promote the advantages of non-ownership.* This can be done by emphasizing, in promotion, the time and cost savings and performance benefits of paid-for maintenance. For example, service contracts to supply an organization with computers releases staff time from the administration that this entails.

2. *Make available a tangible symbol or representation of ownership* (certificate, membership of professional association). This can come to embody the benefits enjoyed.

3. *Increasing the chances or opportunity of ownership*, for example, time-shares or shares in the organization for regular customers.

MARKETING IN PRACTICE
Launch of Egg

Prudential launched their innovative Egg banking operation in October 1998. Egg offered customers a savings rate of 8% and the opportunity to conduct all their transactions via the Internet or eventually digital television with the telephone and postal system as back up. The instant access savings account rate was 0.75 of a point higher than base rate and several points above the rates offered by most competitors.

The challenge facing Egg was how to communicate the benefits of this highly intangible service to their target customers. This was achieved by using high-profile celebrities from the media (Zoe Ball) and from sport (Linford Christie) to endorse their service and to build a strong brand image.

However, despite overcoming the problem of intangibility Egg had problems overcoming the issue of perishability. The Prudential was inundated with enquiries because of their 8% savings rate and their systems were unable to cope.

It was reported that customers were warned that it may take up to 28 days to open their Egg account. However, Prudential claimed that it was only 3-4 days to open new accounts. This is an example of how Prudential managed customer expectations. By stating that it may take up to 28 days to open a new account, and in reality it was only 3-4 days, customers were not dissatisfied.

The fact that customers were queuing up to open Egg accounts in itself was a positive public relations story!

Issues for service marketers

The five service characteristics (intangibility, inseparability, perishability, heterogeneity and lack of ownership) create marketing problems that are additional to those encountered by 'pure product' marketers. The implications for marketing managers are summarized in Table 4.2.

Table 4.2: Service Issues for Marketers

	Implications for marketing
Intangibility	Create tangibility through deployment of the marketing mix.
Inseparability	Invest in systems and staff training to achieve a target level of quality and to maintain that level. In addition, try to separate production from consumption to drive down costs and maintain quality standards. Examples of this include ATMs and pre-packed sandwiches in self-service restaurants.
Perishability	Invest in systems to manage the flow of customer demand. Deploy the marketing mix, especially promotions and pricing, to operate the service at near to capacity levels through 'managing' demand.
Heterogeneity (variability)	As for 'inseparability'.
Lack of Ownership	This creates two potential problems. ● Lack of payment for the service – it is frequently not possible to repossess a service that has not been paid for: financial planning advice or the unblocking of a blocked drain are difficult to undo subsequently. Need to ensure pre-payment (cinema, theatre, theme park attractions) or payment immediately after the service is experienced (dentist). ● Consumers may forget who provided the service and/or the 'true' service quality provided. Marketing communications must support the solution of problems in this area.

The challenge of the financial service marketer is to develop marketing programmes to overcome some of the problems caused by these characteristics and to turn them into opportunities. This is achieved through the deployment of the marketing mix. However, for service marketers there are three marketing mix elements which are additional to the four marketing mix elements for products. These are:

● People
● Process

● Physical location.

These additional service mix elements are discussed in Chapter 13 on the extended marketing mix.

4.2   Measuring Customer Satisfaction

What is satisfaction?

Consumer satisfaction is an abstract concept that is difficult to define precisely. It is all the more difficult to define in service marketing, compared with the marketing of products. Consider a consumer purchasing a set of golf clubs. Here the consumer can pick up the club and in many situations actually hit a golf ball. The consumer gets to 'test drive' the product offer. It would be a somewhat foolish consumer who purchased these clubs if s/he was dissatisfied with them. In contrast, it is not possible for a consumer to similarly 'test drive' a service, for example a meal offered by a restaurant. In order for the consumer to be satisfied with the visit to a restaurant, the consumer needs to have an idea of what this experience should offer. This assessment, perhaps of the level of service, the level of decoration, the friendliness of the staff etc., is based on the standard that the restaurant should achieve on a range of restaurant attributes. This particular example may be generalized into the following two conjectures:

1.   Consumer satisfaction is assessed by consumers in relation to the expectation that they have of a service.

2.   Expectations are assessed on a range of attributes which:

    –   vary from one product area to another;

    –   vary from one consumer to another;

    –   consumers give different relative emphasis to.

The general conclusion is that as long as organizations equal or exceed expectation, then consumers will be satisfied.

In undertaking comparative satisfaction studies it is critical to ensure that 'similar' services are being assessed. For example, that a cheap and simple motel hotel room is not compared with a more expensive product, e.g. the Hilton hotel. Strange results may arise, for example dissatisfaction with the Hilton hotel and satisfaction with the motel room. The consumer may have no experience of a motel and have excessively low expectations that are surpassed. Similarly, the consumer, with much experience of the Hilton hotel, may have become bored with the service offer and register this as dissatisfaction.

How do you measure satisfaction?

Satisfaction may be measured by analysing sources of information that are readily accessible using company databases, i.e.:

- Customer database, including complaints received as well as using the customer database for specific customer research;

- Employee database for specific internal research.

In addition, the company may use a variety of techniques to assess existing and potential customer attitudes and the performance of employees.

Analysis of complaints

This is frequently overlooked as an information resource. Simply logging complaints received reveals basic information. By tracking complaints received over time, the company can at the very least establish a baseline level of complaint. Any sudden rise is instantly apparent and must be investigated further.

Complaints may also support internal views on how services should be developed, by revealing flaws in the current service offer. However managers are left with many unknowns. Is the given level of complaints acceptable? Are the complaints unreasonable, i.e. are they from professional complainers (customers who are frequent complainers) or do complaints received either represent the views of a particular customer segment or of most customers?

Employee research

Investigating employees' perceptions of service delivery is an important input into understanding the actual level of service delivery and therefore, by implication, the level of customer satisfaction. Employee research may be cross-checked against customer research to establish any significant divergence of views. For example, where employee research concludes that service delivery quality is high but in contrast customer research concludes that it is low, then one, or both, of the following may be the cause:

- Employees are following company strategy and tactics but this is inappropriate for the customer segments which are targeted;

- Employees are misinterpreting company policy.

If it is option (a) then company strategy must be changed, and for option (b) internal marketing and training must be implemented.

It is important not to confine employee research to staff that have contact with customers. All staff have an influence on the level of service delivery and subsequently on customer perception of the quality of service received.

Approaches to employee research include: staff suggestion boxes, focus groups, staff seminars, staff appraisals, feedback from operational managers and formal staff surveys.

Regular customer surveys

Two main approaches may be followed: customer surveys or customer panels. Customer surveys include ad hoc questionnaires, or constant customer surveys where questionnaires are permanently available for customers to fill in. The latter approach has been favoured by many family restaurant chains.

The second approach, customer panels, is favoured by research agencies for product groups. Individual companies select a group of customers as a 'type of non-statistical representative sample' (according to their profile of product use or type of business), in order to track their perceptions over time, or to assess their perceptions of particular product and service offers. Panels may comprise the same customers, or a policy of rotating panel members may be followed.

Transaction analysis

This is a variant of customer research where the objective is to assess the current level of service provision in terms of customer perception. Information is collected on customer perception of the quality of service, on the staff providing the service and on the physical environment. Results from this type of research provide information for managers to alter service delivery immediately.

Mystery 'shopping'

This is a form of observation research where researchers experience the service as ordinary customers. Company staff are not informed when this research takes place. However, many companies inform staff that mystery shopping research is undertaken by the company. In some cases companies directly link the outcome of this research to the annual payment of bonuses.

This form of research is undertaken both on the commissioning company's services and on those of competitors. Key service criteria are specified which are then assessed by researchers. Examples of generally important service criteria researched using this technique include:

- time to be served (queuing times);

- friendliness of staff;

- staff knowledge (e.g. airline check-in staff could be asked about arranging a self-drive car at the destination airport, a bank clerk could be asked about how to get advice on long-term investments).

4.3 Establishing Dimensions of Service Quality

One of the main methods by which service organizations can differentiate themselves from competitors is by delivering higher levels of service quality. It is essential that financial service companies understand the meaning of service quality before they can manage and improve it.

Quality is an extremely difficult concept to define and to measure. One of the most authoritative attempts at defining service quality is that provided by Grönroos (1984), who considered it to comprise two main elements:

Technical service quality

Easily 'measured' by the consumer, i.e. the consumer is able to quantify this service element. For example:

- **Waiting times** (for a phone enquiry, to be served in a store, to get your car exhaust replaced etc.)

- **Timely start and end times** where these are known in advance (for transport by air, sea, train, bus; to see a doctor or dentist; for a hospital operation etc.)

Functional service quality

How the 'measurable' aspect of the service is delivered.

- **Waiting time**

  Did the call-handling system tell you how long it would be before someone spoke to you, how frequently were you informed, how pleasant was the music?

  Was there a clear queuing system in the store (i.e. did you have to jostle with other customers to keep your place?). Did the staff deal with customers ahead of you in the queue efficiently and courteously or did you think they took an excessive amount of time to do their job?

  Were you provided with a clean room to sit in with some tea and coffee, a newspaper and/or television, or did you have to stand around a dirty, oily, smoky garage in a draught?

- **Timely start and end times**

  Was the driver or guard helpful and friendly?

  Was the doctor or dentist sympathetic and suitably comforting?

  Did the hospital keep you informed about confirming the start and end times, what to expect, who would look after you, visiting hours etc.? Were they reassuring, sensitive and comforting?

Consumers evaluate both the technological and functional quality of a service. The functional quality cannot be evaluated as objectively as the technical quality. These two main elements may be considered as an attempt to describe the objective aspect of service quality. However, consumers bring to their assessment of a service their prior views of the company, of its service or of the generic form of the service (e.g. of banking customer service in general rather than for a particular bank). In other words the assessment of the service may not, in an extreme case, be influenced by how well the service was performed (on technical and functional aspects) but on consumer perception of how the service should be performed, based on expectation. **Expectation** is the third, and perhaps most difficult aspect of service quality for the company to manage.

Figure 4.3 The Triangle of Service Quality Perception

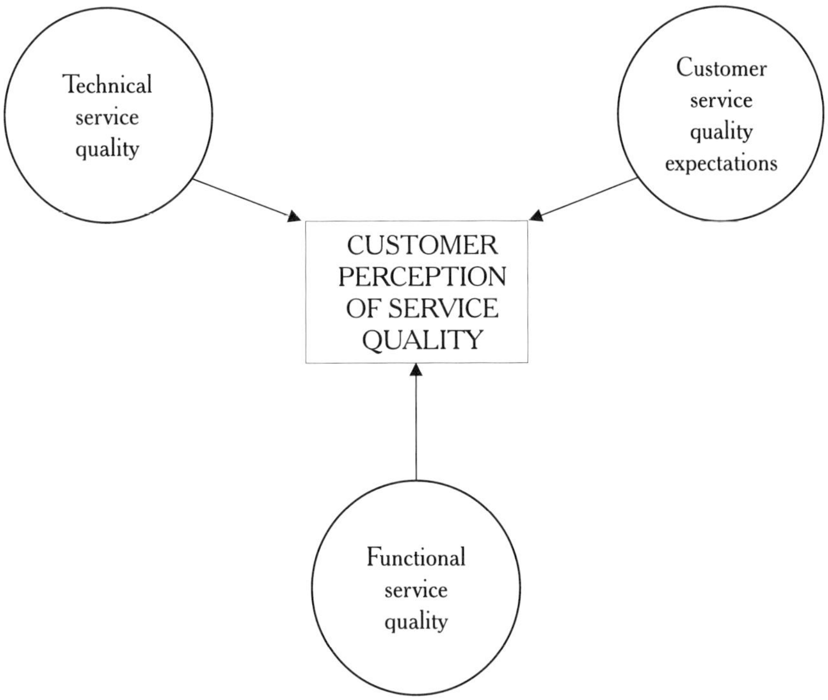

Source: Based on Grönroos (1984)

4.4   Managing and Improving Service Quality

Companies must manage service quality and they may do this by controlling the three elements of the triangle of service quality perception (see Figure 4.3). Chapter 13 on the 'Extended marketing mix' discusses how the technical and functional elements of service quality are handled by marketers. Here we shall focus on managing service expectations and quality improvements.

In brief, consumers come to the service with expectation about what they should experience based on some or all of the following: their previous experience of the service, their experience of a competitor's service, or simply from general communications from which a view has been established. The service is judged to be of high quality if expectations are exceeded and of low quality if expectations are not reached (Figure 4.4).

Figure 4.4: Factors Influencing Perception of Service Quality

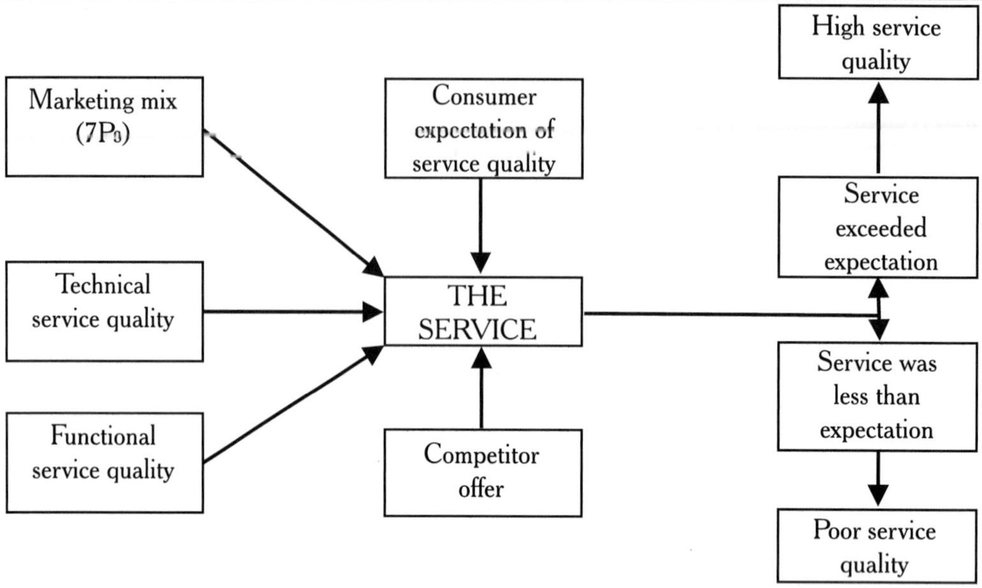

Parasuraman *et al.* (1985, 88, 93) produced the SERVQUAL model which was designed to measure and manage service quality.

The model centres on the difference between customer expectation of a service in a particular industry and their evaluation of that service. There are five 'SERVQUAL' components identified by Parasuraman and colleagues and for each of these components 4 or 5 items are used to assess a firm's service quality (Table 4.3).

Table 4.3: The Components of SERVQUAL

SERVQUAL component	Definition	Number of items used to rate this component
Reliability	The ability to perform the promised service dependably and accurately	4
Tangibles	The physical evidence of the service, including appearance of staff	5
Responsiveness	The willingness to help customers and to provide prompt service	4
Assurance	The knowledge and courtesy of employees and their ability to convey trust and confidence	5
Empathy	The provision of caring, individualized attention to customers	4

Source: Parasuraman et al. *(1991)*

The authors claimed that service quality could be deficient in one of 5 areas and this led to the model being described as the 'gaps' model (Figure 4.5). Service quality could be improved if the gaps could be reduced.

Figure 4.5: Quality Gaps in the Service System

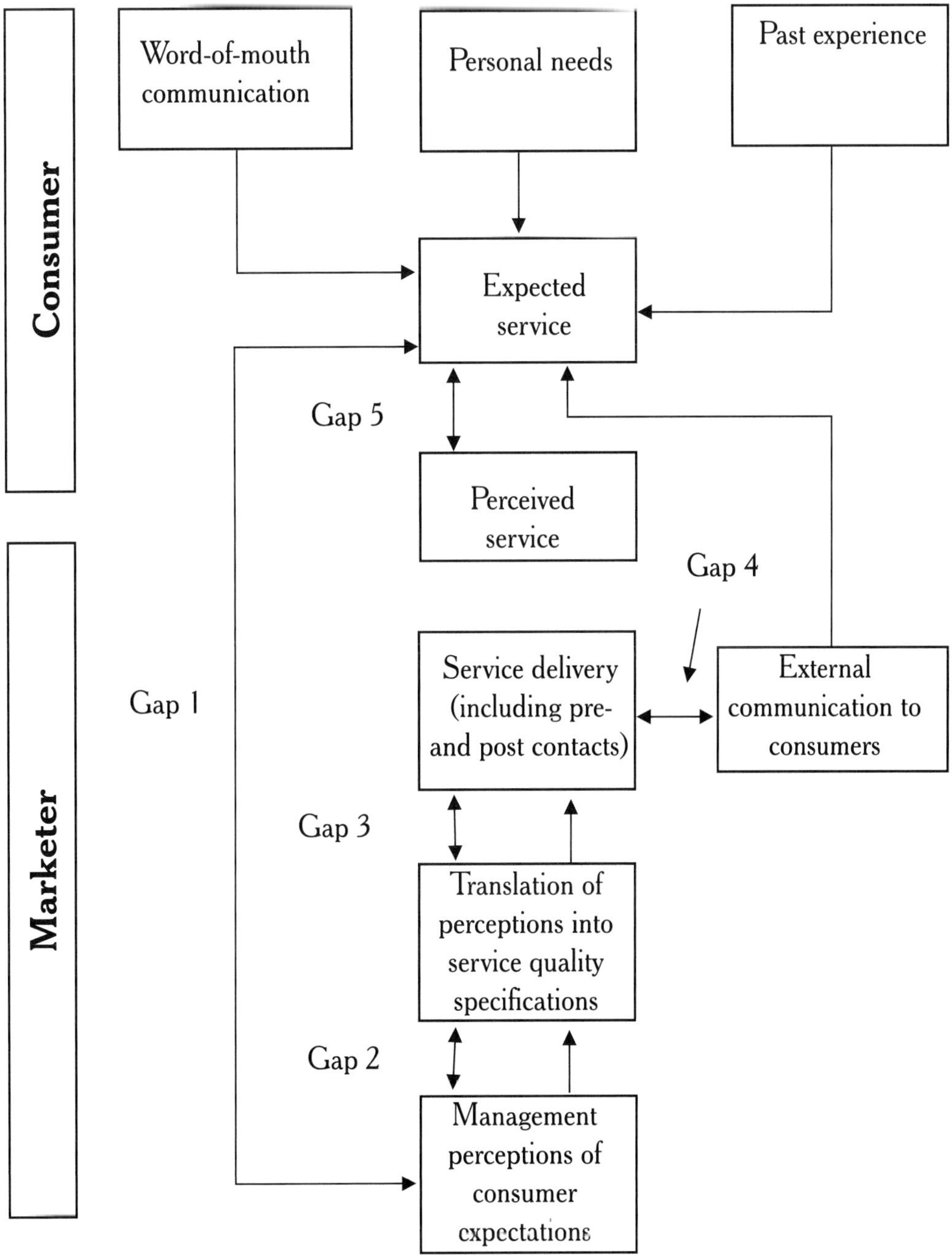

Source: *Parasuraman et al. (1993)*

A summary explanation of the gaps in the 'gaps model' is presented in Table 4.4.

Table 4.4: Summary Explanation of the 'Gaps' Model

GAP	THE GAP BETWEEN:	SUGGESTED IMPACT ON:
1	Consumer expectations and management perceptions of those expectations	Consumer's evaluation of service quality
2	Management perceptions of consumer expectations and the firm's service quality specifications	Consumer's perception of service quality
3	Service quality specifications and actual service delivery	Consumer's perception of service quality
4	Actual service delivery and external communications about the service	Consumer's perception of service quality
5	The perceived service and expected service AND the magnitude of this gap, which is based on one or more of the above gaps	Consumer's perception of service quality

Source: Parasuraman et al. (1993)

Queuing time
One aspect of service, because of its commonality among most services, deserves particular attention, and that is queuing time. Maister (1986) identified eight propositions relating to the gap between customers' perception of waiting time and actual waiting time. Jones and Peppiatt (1996) modified these ideas on perception of waiting time according to whether users were frequent or infrequent users of the service.

All users
- the more valuable the service, the longer people will wait
- solo waiting feels longer than group waiting
- unoccupied time feels longer than occupied time
- unfair waits feel longer than equitable waits
- uncomfortable waits feel longer than comfortable waits
- new or infrequent users feel they wait longer than frequent users.

Propositions affecting frequent users
- unexplained delays seem longer than explained delays.

Propositions affecting infrequent users

● anxiety makes waits feel longer

● uncertain waits seem longer than certain waits

● unexplained waits seem longer than explained waits

● pre-process waits feel longer than in-process waits.

Fast-service restaurants recognize the importance of user experience in their perception of queuing time, and consequently of customer evaluation of the service. Inexperienced customers require different customer information and care to experienced customers. For example, TGI Fridays asks customers whether they have eaten in the restaurant before. Customer service is then tailored according to their response.

Internal marketing

> *Coordinating internal exchanges between a firm and its employees to achieve successful external exchanges between the company and its customers.*

> Source: Dibb et al. (1997, page 717)

Internal marketing is a vital element in an organization achieving planned levels of service quality. As employees are an essential part of delivering appropriate service quality levels they must understand fully what and how the organization wishes to achieve such planned levels.

In order to do this it is important to develop an internal marketing plan with objectives, internal customers, internal marketing mix and control mechanisms. Internal marketing is of particular importance to financial services because success of marketing activities relies to a large extent on the cooperation of staff.

MARKETING IN PRACTICE

Internal Marketing – 'A Better Buy'

This case study highlights the importance of internal marketing in helping to achieve organizational goals.

Results of a major survey exploring levels of staff understanding and commitment to organizational goals provides business leaders with valuable benchmarks for staff 'buy-in'.

A survey conducted by MORI in the autumn of 1998 involved 350 face-to-face interviews. This was a nationally representative quota sample of managers and staff working in British organizations with 1,000 or more employees, from a cross-section of industry sectors. The results show that British organizations face a critical challenge in aligning their people with the business vision and direction. Currently, less than half of staff say their overall awareness and understanding of key business goals is high, and just two in five strongly agree that they know what they need to do as individuals to support business goals. Even more worrying is

---

that managers in large British companies show no greater grasp of the business picture than do non-managers.

First National worked with MCA to benchmark itself against the national survey, and discovered that its communication work is already making a difference. In contrast to the national survey, 63% of First National staff surveyed feel strongly committed, and no one felt uncommitted.

According to the national benchmarking survey, only 15% of people have full confidence in their organization's leadership or their vision for the future. By contrast, more than double that percentage feel strongly confident in the leadership of First National. One respondent commented, 'I've been with the company for 12 years now and this level of commitment from the top has never been seen before'. This may reflect in part on the many ways First National has begun to listen to staff views as part of its communication work and is involving staff in business goals. In the national survey, less than one in ten strongly agrees that their organization values their views and participation.

Perhaps the most important finding from this benchmarking survey is that people who buy-in both intellectually and emotionally to organizational goals consistently say it improves their job performance. They are also a third more likely to act as advocates for their organization by recommending it to customers, recruits and other stakeholders.

The survey shows an important link between good communication and strong buy-in. Those who score the effectiveness of their organization's communication highly also show higher levels of buy-in. In fact, increasing the effectiveness of communication from a six to an eight out of ten can potentially double levels of buy-in.

Source: 'A better buy' Financial World May 1999 p25

4.5   International Services

International service organizations are presented with additional marketing problems, both compared with an international product marketer and a domestic marketer. To be successful they have to be particularly skilled in using the service marketing mix to overcome the problems presented by the five service characteristics. Successful organizations have been particularly skilled in their use of two of the service Ps, namely 'process' and 'people'. Consider some of the leading international service organizations, for example McDonalds, Disney, many banks and international retailers. Standardizing 'process' and 'people' has allowed their rapid expansion.

Cultural differences create particular problems for international service marketers. McDonalds, for example, could not offer Indian Hindus burgers produced from beef as cattle are held to be sacred, while in Japan it was necessary to offer a fish dish in a country where fish consumption exceeded that of red meat. Disney when setting up 'Euro Disney' in Paris insisted on an alcohol-free theme park, which was corporate policy. However this was not regarded as acceptable in a country in which alcohol consumption is an integral aspect of every day life. Disney had to change to accommodate local demands.

There are many problems presented by the internationalization of services. The product aspect of service is relatively easy to resolve. Ensuring that the service offer will succeed in the international market is somewhat more difficult, even where the organization employs service quality assessment in support of marketing management, for example using the methods suggested by Grönroos. Such organizations may not be using appropriate service attributes in every country in which they operate. In a study of the use of hotels in Hong Kong, Choi & Chu (2000) compared Western and Asian travellers. They found seven attributes to be significant (the leading five were staff service quality; room quality; general amenities; business services; value) out of 33 tested. For Asian travellers they found the most important factor was 'value for money'. Factors used to explain 'value' included hotel food and beverages, the accommodation, being part of a reputable chain, and having a comfortable ambience. In contrast Western travellers considered room quality to be most important in determining their overall satisfaction with hotels in Hong Kong.

The service offer had to be altered to account for variations in cultural background. Even where international segments appear to have similar demographic characteristics, consumption behaviour may be very different. It is poor international marketing practice to assume, automatically, that services can be exported without modification, i.e. to offer a standardized service.

Summary

Tangibility has often been used to explain the difference between products and services. It is increasingly less useful for this purpose as product marketers have added services to extend the product offer and service marketers have added products to give tangibility to their service offers. The distinction between products and services is increasingly less evident on the service characteristic of 'tangibility'. Services have four other characteristics, in addition to tangibility. These are 'inseparability', 'perishability', 'heterogeneity' and 'lack of ownership'. The five characteristics may be used to assess the implications for marketing a particular service. Service marketers, as well as using the four Ps of the marketing mix, additionally emphasise the three 'Ps' of the service marketing mix ('people', 'place' and 'physical evidence') in their marketing activity.

Services contrast substantially with a considerable number of products, which have many tangible dimensions that are amenable to measurement and to quality control. In addition, services are often purchased less frequently than products: e.g. holidays, travel, theatre, special event meals, insurance etc. Service marketers have been provided with several research tools to measure 'satisfaction' and perception of service quality, both by the customer and the employee. These range from 'mystery shopping' to 'employee research'. But what influences customer service quality perception? Grönroos defines this as the difference between 'total delivered service quality' and 'service quality expectations'. Delivered service quality may be subdivided into technical and functional service quality.

Grönroos developed the five-component SERVQUAL framework as a means of measuring and managing service quality. One important dimension of his work was the creation of the 'gaps' model which marketers could employ in attempting to improve service quality. In this model there are five main components of service quality.

References

(1999) A better buy, *Financial World* May p25

Choi T Y, Chu R (2000) Levels of satisfaction among Asian and Western travellers, *International Journal of Quality & Reliability Management*, vol. 17, issue 2 ISSN 0265-671 X

Dibb S, Simkin L, Pride W M & Ferrell O C (1997) *Marketing Concepts and Strategies*, 3rd European edition, Houghton Mifflin

Grönroos (1984) *Strategic Management and Marketing in the Service Sector*, London: Chartwell-Brace

Jobber D (1998) *Principles and Practices of Marketing*, 2nd edition, McGraw Hill, Maidenhead

Jones P & Peppiatt E (1996) Managing perceptions and waiting times of service queues, *International Journal of Services Industry Management*, vol. 7, no. 5, pp47-61

Kotler P, Armstrong G, Saunders J & Wong V (1999) *Principles of Marketing*, 2nd European edition, Prentice Hall Europe

Maister D H (1986) *The Psychology of Waiting Lines in the Service Encounter* Czepiel J A, Solomon M R & Suprenant C F, Lexington M A: Lexington Books/DC Heath, pp113-123

Parasuraman A, Zeithaml V A & Berry L L (1985) A conceptual model of service quality and its implications for future research, *Journal of Marketing*, vol. 49, Fall, pp41-50

Parasuraman A, Zeithaml V A & Berry L L (1988) SERVQUAL: A multiple item scale for measuring customer perceptions of services quality, *Journal of Retailing*, 64 (1) 14-40

Parasuraman A, Zeithaml V A & Berry L L (1994) Reassessment of expectations as a comparison standard in measuring service quality: implication for further research, *Journal of Marketing* 58 (1), 111-124

Part 1

CASE STUDIES

Boots

How far can they stretch the health and beauty brand?

INTRODUCTION

Boots has been well known as a 'High Street chemist' for many years. However, the Boots Company is now recognizing that to stand still is in fact to go backwards and is developing marketing strategies that take advantage of the changes in the external environment and build on their core business of 'pharmacy'. The Boots Company states its goal as 'to become the global leader in health and beauty by drawing on our knowledge and experience to offer excellent products and services through a wide variety of channels to consumers around the world'. The Boots Company may be famous as a High Street chemist but it is now stretching its brand into a number of related service markets – optometry, dental health and chiropody. All these new business opportunities build on Boots' core business of health and beauty. New technology is providing Boots with even more ways to reach its target customers and to develop closer relationships with them. Boots states that its objective is to 'maximize the value of the company for the benefit of its shareholders. While vigorously pursuing our commercial interests at all times we seek to enhance our reputation as a well-managed ethical and socially responsible company'.

STRATEGIC BUSINESS UNITS

The Boots Company comprises eight separate strategic business units. Each business operates independently for the majority of the time and is managed by an executive board and management team. The eight businesses are as follows:

Boots the Chemist (BTC)

Boots the Chemist is the UK's leading retailer of health and beauty products with over 1,400 stores and 63,000 employees. One in three people visits a Boots store every week to buy products ranging from cosmetics to medicines. Over half of these products are Boots own brand. There are over 11 million Advantage Cards (the Boots loyalty card) in use that use Smart technology and provide valuable customer information. BTC offers a wide range of products and services including healthcare dispensary, vitamins and minerals, beauty products, gifts, photographic equipment, food, baby and related products and services. BTC is in a mature market and is facing increasing competition from other retailers such as Superdrug and more recently supermarkets, and in particular from Wal-Mart's Asda.

In order to take on the on-line competitors Boots has relaunched its website boots.co.uk that sells a range of products. It has also launched a men's health site boots-men.co.uk and more recently an online photo shop through a partnership with Yahoo.

A further development is the new joint credit card venture with Egg. Boots' Advantage cardholders will be offered the opportunity to take out an Advantage credit card which will combine a credit facility with the existing loyalty scheme. This strategy can be seen as a further step to build up a range of channels through which Boots can talk to its customers and tailor its offering to meet individual needs.

The latest and probably most radical strategy to be launched is a new in-store health and beauty 'experience'. This is being trialed in two stores and offers a range of conventional and alternative therapies such as osteopathy and reflexology.

Boots Opticians (BO)

Boots is now becoming one of the leading UK chains of opticians with approximately 300 stores. BO provides eye examinations, contact lens fitting, optical laboratories and spectacle dispensing.

Boots Healthcare International (BHI)

BHI is a market leader in the development and marketing of innovative consumer healthcare brands. These brands have international presence and are sold in over 130 countries. Household brand such as Strepsils, E45 and Nurofen are all brands developed by BHI. The portfolio of products is based on three categories of products – skincare, analgesics and cough and cold remedies. BHI not only develops its own home-grown brands but it is also pursuing a strategy of growth via acquisition. BHI has recently acquired Proctor and Gamble's 50-year old Clearasil brand. It is believed that this acquisition will also open up the US market for the first time.

handbag.com

handbag.com is a joint venture between The Boots Company and Hollinger International. It is positioned as the most useful location on-line for British women. The website provides a portal for access to fashion, beauty, entertainment and news. handbag.com employs its own team of editors and expert writers and is attempting to provide information on health and beauty.

Halfords

Halfords has 410 stores in the UK and is the leading retailer of car parts and accessories, cycles and cycle accessories and is also developing its car repair and servicing business in conjunction with Daewoo.

Boots Contract Manufacturing (BCM)

BCM is the largest contract manufacturer in its field in Europe and develops and manufactures a wide portfolio of cosmetics, healthcare and toiletry products in both private and contract markets. Two-thirds of sales are to customers within the Boots Group and a third to external customers.

Boots Retail International (BRI)

The objective of BRI is to expand Boots internationally. There are over 70 Boots stores in four countries outside the UK – Thailand, Japan, the Netherlands and the latest opening in Taiwan.

Boots Properties (BP)

BP manages the freeholds and leaseholds on over 800 Boots' stores. In addition BP also applies property development and management skills in the wider retail property market.

BOOTS AND GRANADA MEDIA JOINT VENTURE

The latest development in the Boots portfolio is to launch a combined TV, Internet and broad-based health and beauty company with Granada Media. A transactional website and an ITV channel is planned for February 2001. It is to be positioned as Britain's leading e-business for health, beauty and well being. This company will build on the strengths of both Boots and Granada to provide an extensive range of health and beauty products combined with information and advice from a team of leading experts.

The future

Boots is pursing a strategy that builds on its High Street stores and yet provides an on-line presence: a 'clicks and mortar' strategy. Strategic wear-out is a danger facing any company that may become complacent. In an attempt to innovate and to stay ahead of the competitors the Boots Company has developed The Activist Centre whose role is to 'think outside the box' and maintain a broad strategic perspective. This group is given the responsibility of looking beyond their natural horizons and to focus on the interfaces between businesses, in order to avoid suffering from what Levitt (1960) describes as 'marketing myopia'.

(Source: adapted from information at www.hoovers.com)

- Think about to what extent the Boots Company has a balanced portfolio of businesses. Use the Boston Consulting Group Matrix to illustrate the relevant position of each strategic business unit.

- Using the Ansoff Matrix classify the various strategies that Boots has pursued and comment on their appropriateness in light of their core values of health and beauty.

- Select one of the eight strategic business units and undertake an analysis of the competition using Porters generic strategies model.

easyJet – easyMoney?

Within five years of launching its low-cost flights easyJet has become a household name and has successfully expanded into new markets on the back of the 'easy' brand name. Stelios Haji-Ionnou, son of a Greek shipping tycoon, founded easyJet and on 10 November 1995; the inaugural flight took place between London Luton and Glasgow. The organization is based at Luton airport and serves 18 European destinations from Luton and Liverpool airports. easyJet's mission statement is:

> 'To provide our customers with safe, good value, point-to-point air services. To effect and to offer a consistent and reliable product and fares appealing to leisure and business markets on a range of European routes. To achieve this we will develop our people and establish lasting relationships with our suppliers.'

easyJet's strategy was based on the belief that they could develop their business not just by taking market share away from the existing operators but by expanding the total market. The discounted fares would encourage people to fly who previously had not been able to afford to or alternatively to encourage customers to fly more often. The location of Luton and Liverpool airports has been central to the success of easyJet's strategy. Both airports are easily accessible by motorway. London Luton airport is 15 minutes from the M25 and approximately half an hour from North London by road. In addition, Luton is only 30 minutes from London by train and connecting services are provided to transport people to the airport. easyJet does not offer any connecting flights and therefore it is possible to operate out of these secondary airports because passengers are not making connections. It also simplifies the booking process.

Booking for the flights was initially available only over the telephone. By dealing direct with customers easyJet eliminated the cost of intermediaries and combined with ticket-less flights helped to keep costs down – and there are no seat allocations. This speeds up the embarkation process because passengers are not searching for pre-allocated seats. This also means that the time spent on the tarmac is reduced and leads to reduced airport fees. There are no business seats available which enables easyJet to offer 148 seats on a Boeing 737-300 as compared with airlines with business class that have significantly fewer. easyJet has stripped away many of the processes that increase costs and has targeted customers who are looking for value for money. For example, meals are not provided as part of the flight and customers can choose to purchase refreshments if they wish. This has enabled the airline to operate with fewer cabin staff. Despite this streamlining of the business, safety is still regarded as paramount. Companies are targeted in addition to individuals. easyJet has realized that many companies are keen to control their travel budgets and have seen this as an opportunity.

In April 1999 easyJet launched its on-line booking arm and within a few months this accounted for approximately 30% of all sales. By October 2000 this figure had increased to 80% of the 5.5 million customers and it is expected that this trend will continue until all sales will be sold by the Internet and the existing call centre will become a dedicated customer support centre. In 2000 easyJet's turnover was £263 million and it now employs 1,400 people.

There has been a great deal of activity in the budget airlines market, with companies such as RyanAir, Debonair (subsequently went out of business), and Go (subsidiary of British Airways that has been put up for sale). These companies have also located at secondary airports to help to minimize costs, for example Go operates out of Stansted airport.

easyJet has expanded its business by adding new routes to its portfolio. It is now possible to fly via 31 routes to 18 European destinations and from January 2001 it was also possible to fly to Amsterdam from Edinburgh, Belfast and Nice. It is likely that easyJet will continue to expand its business by moving out of Europe. It has been suggested that China is a potential market due to its high population density and according to Stelio Haji-Ioannou there are a billion people in need of budget flights.

The profile of easyJet has been raised significantly through the televising of a prime-time series featuring the airline and its staff dealing with passengers. easyJet has won several awards, for example the readers of *Business Traveller* magazine voted easyJet the best low-cost airline for the second year running.

easyJet realizes that it has built a very strong brand and that there are other opportunities in different but related markets to build on the easy brand. A spokesperson from easyJet gave an indication as to the types of markets that it might enter. 'easyGroup is looking at classic innovations where, traditionally, there are lots of middlemen and high overheads'. easyJet has diversified into cyber cafes and car rental and is currently planning the launch of a cyber bank, a web-based e-mail system and an on-line price comparator. These new ventures, outlined below, build on easyJet's core capabilities of dealing directly with customers and offering customers' value for money.

easyEverything was launched in September 1999 and has now become one of the world's largest Internet cafes. It is estimated that by 2001 easyEverything will have 60 branches, including 11 new operations in Britain and 40 in key European cities such as Paris, Rome and Brussels. In December 2000 a branch opened in New York which will provide an entry into the US market. It is likely this will be followed by a move into the Far East.

easyMoney – keen to exploit the opportunity for electronic financial services the easyGroup is planning to launch an on-line bank sometime in 2001. The aim is to eliminate costs and thus undercut traditional High Street banks. This venture is dependent on the easyGroup securing agreement from the banking ombudsmen and also finding a suitable partner to act as the underwriter.

easyRentacar was launched in 2000 and offers people the opportunity to hire cars on-line from as little as £9 a day from easyJet destinations. This is a joint venture with Mercedes which is leasing its A class cars to easyRentacar.

www.easy.com is a free private web-based e-mail system due to be launched soon.

easyValue.com is due to be launched imminently and consists of an on-line price comparison site that will search for the most competitive prices on the Internet.

In November 2000 easyJet floated on the stock market in order to raise cash to fund new planes and expand their Scottish business. Stelios Haji-Ioannou and his family will continue to retain majority control after the floatation.

Sources: www.hoovers.com and www.easyjet.com

Prepare an outline marketing plan for the launch of easyMoney. Your plan should include:

- Situation analysis;
- Objectives and goals;
- Marketing strategy (target markets and positioning);
- Action programme (marketing mix);
- Budgets (make realistic assumptions based on the information contained in the case study);
- Controls (including timescales).

Part Two

UNDERSTANDING CUSTOMERS AND MARKETS

5

CONSUMER BUYER BEHAVIOUR

Learning Objectives

After reading this chapter students should:

- Understand a range of influences affecting consumer buyer behaviour;

- Know and understand at least one model of consumer buying behaviour;

- Know the stages in the decision-making process and the implications of these for marketing activity.

Figure 5.1: Chapter Map

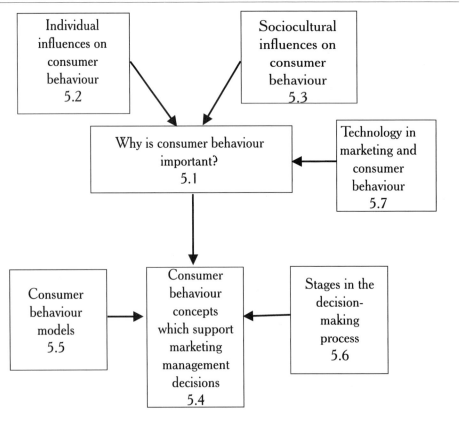

Introduction

Consumer behaviour is the name marketers give to the decision process individuals engage in when evaluating, acquiring, using and assessing (after purchase) goods and services.

The initial reason for studying consumer behaviour was to enable marketers to predict how consumers would react to promotional messages, and to understand why they made the purchasing decisions they did. It was first thought that marketing was simply applied economics and that the assumptions of economics would be sufficient to allow behaviour to be predicted.

Researchers soon realized that consumers were not always consciously aware of why they made the decisions they did. An attempt was made to develop techniques to uncover the hidden motivations of consumers. Between the end of the 1930s and late 1950s, the use of Freudian psychoanalytical techniques were developed in an approach known as 'motivational research' and this gave a large impetus to consumer behaviour research.

There are many factors influencing consumer response, rather than purely factors which help to explain the individual's personal motivation. These factors may be allocated to one of three groups:

1. The individual consumer

2. Environmental influences

3. Consumer decision making

   the process of perceiving and evaluating brand information, considering how brand alternatives meet the consumers needs and deciding on a brand.

5.1 Why is Consumer Behaviour Important?

Customers are the reason for any business's existence because without customers to sell to, a business cannot operate. Meeting the needs of those customers more effectively than competitors do is the key to continued profitable existence for any business.

It is important that each customer who deals with an organization is left with a feeling of satisfaction. This outcome is important because it can lead to increased sales and/or a willingness to pay higher prices and thus to higher profits. If customers are satisfied they may:

- buy again from the same supplier;

- buy more of the same item or more expensive items;

- advise their friends to buy from the supplier.

Loyal customers will stay with their supplier when competitors try to lure them away with special offers. In addition, it is possible to build a rapport with loyal customers which helps the supplier understand customer needs more fully, thus allowing the position to be reinforced.

Customer dissatisfaction is the reverse of customer loyalty in that it may dissipate established goodwill and can adversely affect the company image. The added complication is that bad news travels faster than good news.

5.2   Individual Influences on Consumer Behaviour

Personality

Individuals are unique. In order to explain, describe and identify the differences between people, psychologists use the concept of *personality*. This is a term that is used in common speech as well as in psychology, and the assumptions behind its use in a given context must be clearly understood. Personality has been defined as 'the total pattern of characteristic ways of thinking, feeling and behaving that constitute the individual's distinctive method of relating to the environment'.

There are four main personality theories used to describe consumer behaviour:

● Psychoanalytical theory

● Social cultural theory

● Trait theory

● Self-concept (self-image) theory.

1   Freud's Psychoanalytic Theory

Sigmund Freud conceived of three elements of the individual:

(a) The *id*, which he regarded as the original system of personality and the source of its primary energy and drive (which Freud took to be the libido, or sexual energy, although other psychologists have disagreed with this). The id operates for pleasure and to avoid pain.

(b) The *super-ego* is the internal representative of the values, rules and ideals of society, as learned from social interaction and institutions, i.e. a sociomoral influence. It restrains the id by punishing inappropriate behaviour through the creation of guilt.

(c) The *ego* manages the conflicting demands of the id and the super-ego. It does this by redirecting the impulses of the id so that they can be gratified in the real world. It is the 'executive' of the personality, integrating the demands of the id, super-ego and external environment, for the psychological health of the individual. Where demands are not integrated, guilt can result.

2   Social Cultural Theory

This focuses on the cultural and social context of the individual. Ideas from this branch of theory are included in the main section on sociocultural influences.

3 Traite Theory

Traite-type theories of personality divide people into *categories*, which are defined as possessing common behaviour patterns. The trouble with 'types' is that they are too general, and do not do justice to the complexity and subtlety of individual personality.

Eysenck *et al.* (1975) explanation of personality and individual differences is one of the most influential current theories. He suggests that individuals who possess one particular trait are likely to possess certain other 'compatible' traits. Eysenck has identified two major areas in which variations in individual personality can occur.

The 'E' dimension. Human beings are divided into two types (the terms for which were coined by the German psychologist Carl Jung):

i)   Extrovert: Traits: expressiveness, impulsiveness, risk-taking, sociability, practicality, irresponsibility, activity;

ii)   Introvert: Traits: inactivity, carefulness, responsibility, control, reflectiveness, unsociability, inhibition.

Most people lie somewhere on the line or continuum between these two extremes.

The 'N' dimension. There is a similar continuum between:

i)   Neuroticism: Traits: anxiety, guilt, obsessiveness, hypochondriasis (imaginary illness), unhappiness, lack of autonomy, low self-esteem;

ii)   Stability: Traits: calm, freedom from guilt, casualness, sense of health, happiness, autonomy, self-esteem.

4 Self-Concept (Self-Image) Theory

This focuses on how an individual's self-image affects his of her purchasing behaviour.

It holds that individuals have a concept of self based on who they think they are (actual self) and a concept of who they think they would like to be (ideal self).

Actual self: self-image that varies with an individual's role (e.g. husband, worker, friend). Consumers achieve self-consistency by buying products they perceive to be similar to self-image. There is a high-level relationship between brand image and self-image. However this position is complicated by the fact that consumers change their self-image in different situations.

Ideal self: the greater the difference between the actual and ideal the lower the self-esteem. Consumers make purchases to compensate for low self-esteem.

Extended self: What you own reflects your personality. Consumers buy products for their symbolic meaning.

Motivation

Much motivation theory explains how people are motivated and is applied in human resource management as well as in marketing.

Motives sit between needs and action. Motives are derived from needs: a need motivates a person to take action. The difference between needs and motives is as follows:

- Motives activate behaviour. Being thirsty (need) causes (motivates) us to buy a drink (action). If the need is sufficiently intense, we are motivated to act;

- Motives are directional. Needs are general but motives specify behavioural action. A need to belong may lead to a motivation to join a badminton club;

- Motives serve to reduce tension. Essentially an individual aims to be in a state of equilibrium. This aim is known as the concept of homeostasis. If we are too cold, we are motivated to reduce the tension in our bodies that this causes by seeking a source of warmth. If we are not accepted by those we regard as important, we aim to reduce the tension this causes by seeking to change our behaviour so as to gain acceptance by those we value. This tension is also known as dissonance. When it exists, we aim to reduce it.

For example, *dissonance* may arise when an item is purchased which does not give satisfaction. The buyer may feel that he has not 'done the right thing'. This tension has to be reduced. Buyers may seek to convince themselves that they have bought the right thing by rereading the sales brochure or revisiting the salespeople who sold the product to them. Alternatively they may get rid of the item and reduce the tension in this way. Importantly, what remains is likely to be a negative image of the supplier.

Thus motives arise form needs and can lead to purchasing actions. However, motives do not tell us how consumers choose from the options available to satisfy needs. Other influences are clearly at work.

Maslow's hierarchy of needs
Maslow (1954) formulated a widely popular theory of universal human needs ranked in a 'hierarchy of relative *pre-potency*' (overriding force). According this theory, the lowest 'level' or need which is unsatisfied is dominant. Once it is satisfied, the next level 'up' becomes the dominant motivating impulse, until it in turn is satisfied – or until a lower-level need becomes dominant again, through renewed deprivation.

Because no need is ever completely satisfied, the levels overlap in practice, and more than one level of need may operate at the same time. However, the prime motivator – the dominant impulse within the individual at a given time – is said to be the lowest level of need that is substantially unsatisfied.

Figure 5.2: Maslow's Hierarchy of Needs (1954)

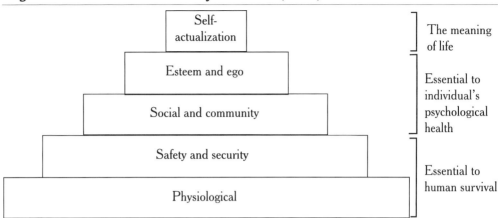

Maslow's need categories are:

a) physiological needs — food, water, air, shelter, sex

b) safety and security needs — freedom from threat, health, but also security, order, predictability, 'knowing where you are with people'

c) social or companionship needs — for friendships, affection, sense of belonging

d) esteem or ego needs — for self-respect and self-confidence, competence, achievement, independence, prestige and their reflection in the perception of others

e) self-actualization needs — for the fulfilment of personal potential: 'the desire to become more and more what one is, to become everything that one is capable of becoming'

There is a certain intuitive appeal to Maslow's theory. After all, you are unlikely to be concerned with status or recognition while you are hungry or thirsty. Unfortunately, research does not bear out the proposition that needs become less powerful as they are satisfied, except at the very primitive level of 'primary' needs like hunger and thirst.

There are various problems associated with Maslow's theory:

● Empirical verification for the hierarchy is hard to come by;

● It is difficult to *predict* behaviour using the hierarchy: the theory is too vague;

● Self-actualization, in particular, is difficult to offer in practice: it depends on what we perceive to be our personal potential, which in turn depends largely on social values, beliefs, ideals and customs. People's perception of their own worth and potential is bound up with the expectations and roles imposed on them by their culture;

● The 'ethnocentricity' of Maslow's hierarchy has also been noted. It does seem broadly applicable to Western English-speaking cultures, but is less relevant elsewhere.

However, the hierarchy offers a simple and readily understood model of motivation for marketers in the broadly Western cultures to which it is most applicable. Physiological needs are met by food and drink, houses and clothes; safety needs by insurance, job training, double glazing and seatbelts; social needs by cosmetics, personal hygiene products and pets; esteem or ego needs by luxury items, bigger cars and designer clothes; self-actualization needs by education and training services, health-club membership and career consultancy.

Freud's psychoanalytical theory and motivation
Psychologists believe that the id and super-ego operate to create motives for purchases which are unconscious. Because the individual is unaware of his or her own motives, special techniques are required to establish the basis of such purchasing motives. Direct questioning is inappropriate, so two indirect approaches tend to be used: projective techniques and in-depth interviews.

Learning

Learning involves many aspects of individual behaviour, particularly perception, motivation, and social interaction and cultural influences. Learning can be defined as the process of acquiring, through experience, knowledge that leads to changed behaviour. The common factors of any learning situation are motivation, association and reinforcement.

Several learning theories have been proposed. Stimulus response/behaviourist theory states that where an association is established between a given behaviour and positive reinforcement, the individual is more likely to respond in that way in future. If every time you choose Brand X you get good results, you will tend to choose Brand X in future. If every time you wear a certain outfit you get the praise and approval of your friends, you will feel confident about wearing it again. If every time you reach your sales targets, you get a financial reward, you will work equally hard to do the same again. Negative reinforcement works in the same way. If a product lets you down, you say: 'I'll know better than to use that next time'.

Probably the best-known learning theory is the classical/respondent conditioning theory of Pavlov. The Russian physiologist Ivan Pavlov formulated the theory that behaviour which is associated with one stimulus can be 'attached' to another stimulus by conditioning: the behaviour is the same, but has been redirected. He was able to condition dogs to salivate when they heard a bell, by initially showing them some meat and at the same time ringing a bell. Advertisers sometimes try to achieve similar results by associating a product in an ad with a happy image (the chocolate bar 'Crunchie' was associated with the 'happy Friday feeling'). The idea was that when consumers saw the bar in the absence of the advert they would still get the happy feeling and so would buy the product to obtain the feeling. This is a conditioned stimulus, i.e. stimulus not naturally associated with the product.

5.3   Sociocultural Influences on Consumer Behaviour

Groups

A group is a collection of individuals that acts as a unit. Groups provide a sense of belonging, 'solidarity' and strength to individuals. This can help them where unpleasant and risky decisions need to be taken. It will also tend to strengthen group attitudes – whether positive or negative.

Reference groups

Reference group theory was formulated to describe the way in which an individual uses groups as a point of comparison or 'reference' for his or her own judgements, beliefs and behaviour. Groups can serve as a benchmark for:

- general behavioural norms; and/or

- specific attitudes or behaviour – such as 'fashionable' product purchases.

An individual may be influenced by a non-contractual or secondary group, as well as a primary one with which he or she is intimately in contact. Note, too, that the individual does not need to be a member of a group in order to measure behaviour by it.

- An aspirational group can impel an individual to act as it does, or to wear the same 'badges', in order to feel closer to attaining actual membership;

- A dissociative group can impel an individual to disown any behaviour or object associated with it.

The power of the group depends on its ability to impose sanctions – whether positive or negative – to encourage conformity. In fact, few individuals wish to be complete conformists, and there is usually a range of acceptable alternatives within given norms: in consumer terms, for example, the group might dictate the product (a personal organizer, say) or even the brand (Filofax), but the sense of independence will be maintained by the choice of size, colour and so on.

Reference groups influence a buying decision by making the individual aware of a product or brand, allowing the individual to compare his or her attitude with that of the group, encouraging the individual to adopt an attitude consistent with the group, and then reinforcing and legitimizing the individual's decision to conform.

It has been suggested that we adopt different reference groups for different areas of our lives and consumer choices. For example, the peer group of adolescent girls may be most influential in the choice of clothes and books, while in more important matters, such as the choice of school, parents' opinions may be more valued. Reference groups may even conflict: the member of a shop-floor work team who also aspires to managerial status and lifestyle may face a dilemma over the kind of behaviour that will gain acceptance in either circle or both.

Consumer-relevant groups

Some reference groups or groupings are particularly relevant to marketers in their influence on consumer behaviour.

- The *family* is the main primary group for most individuals, involving the most frequent contact and the greatest significance or perceived importance to the individual. Family norms and influences on all behaviour are particularly strong.

- *Work groups* are also primary, if only because of the sheer amount of time people spend at work. The opinion of colleagues can be an important factor, especially if they are also part of informal friendship groups in the workplace. 'Politics' at work also influences the choice of products that enhance status and image.

- *Friendship* groups are an important influence on buyer behaviour, because the desire to form and maintain friendly relationships is one of Man's basic motivations, and since people trust their friends to advise them in their best interests – particularly those friends whom they perceive to share their values and goals. Marketers frequently depict product choice, in advertising, in the context of friendly sharing, advice and encouragement.

- *Interest or action groups.* Membership of a particular interest or 'pressure' group may have an influence on purchase behaviour. A 'consumer action' or 'consumerist' group, for example, may address directly consumer-relevant issues by boycotting a product that is thought to be dangerous or deceptive. Other groups – animal rights, anti-fur, anti-apartheid or whatever – may include in their programmes purchase-oriented behaviour.

- Any group (including an aspirational or symbolic group) that serves as a 'frame of reference' for an individual's behaviour, and may therefore influence that behaviour, is called a reference group.

The Family

The family is perhaps the most important primary group for any individual, although its structure, behaviour and influence will vary greatly from society to society, and even according to individual circumstance. Such questions as who looks after children, how and for how long, are vital to understanding the family unit.

A family has traditionally been defined as a number of people who are related by blood, marriage or adoption – and who usually reside together. Such a family unit may be:

- a married couple who have not yet 'started a family' (had children – a reflection of the child-oriented nature of the family unit) or who have already raised children and seen them leave home.

- a nuclear family, consisting of a couple or single parent plus one or more children, living together; or

- an extended family, consisting of the parents, children and other relatives (grandparents, aunts and uncles, in-laws etc.). Since increased mobility in industrialized nations has tended to separate parents from their adult offspring, and siblings from each other, the extended family is less common than it was in such cultures, and the nuclear family has become the main decision-making unit for consumption activity.

- In addition there is the pseudo-family unit, the household. A household – or number of people sharing a residence and its consumption decisions – may be a family, but may also be a number of unrelated people living together: boarders/lodgers, house/flat sharers, unmarried couples and so on.

Family decision-making roles

Multi-individual decision making involves several decision-making roles. It is obviously of relevance to marketers whether the woman or man in the household is the buyer or decision-maker, or whether it is the parents or children; who usually finds out first about products and brands; who in the family has the power to persuade the buyer to make a particular brand choice and purchase. This kind of information determines the product's positioning (masculine/feminine, youthful/mature image?) distribution and promotion pattern, and target audience for information. Marketers must also be aware how the shifting pattern of family roles (with financial independence for working women, the acceptance of household tasks by men, and the earlier age at which children expect their own independence) is changing the composition of traditional target markets.

Family consumption roles

Initiator	suggests the idea of buying a particular product
Influencer	provides information about a product/service to other members
Gatekeeper	controls the flow of information about a product/service into the family (for example by 'giving the gist' of a consumer article, or selecting the advertising message that is relayed to the family).
Decider	has the power to determine whether to purchase a specific product/service
Buyer	makes the purchase of the product/service
Preparer	makes the product into a form suitable for family consumption (by preparing food, say, or assembling DIY furniture)
User	consumes or utilizes a particular product/service
Maintainer	services or repairs a product so that it continues to satisfy
Disposer	initiates or performs the disposal or termination of the product/service.

Within a family group as a decision-making unit various members may occupy these roles. See Table 5.1.

Table 5.1: Example of Family Consumption Roles

Toy		Car	
Initiator:	Child	Initiator:	Parents
Influencer:	Parents	Influencer:	Mother
	Playgroup staff		Family
	Friends		Friends/colleagues
	Salesperson		Salesperson
Decider:	Parents	Decider:	Joint parental decision
Buyer:	Mother	Buyer:	Joint purchase
User:	Child	User:	Parents

Marketers will be interested in reaching each of these roles: to make the product attractive to the initiator (if it is not a product automatically bought), influencer and decider in particular. They would need to make the product readily available for the purchaser, and satisfying enough for the user to initiate future repurchase. The family life cycle (Table 5.2) is a useful model for assessing family buying activity.

Cultural Influences

'Culture' is a much broader concept than the sense in which it is most often used by people – to refer to classical aesthetic or artistic pursuits. The term is used by sociologists and anthropologists to encompass the sum total of the learned beliefs, values, customs, artefacts and rituals of a society or group.

As suggested by the definition above, 'culture' embraces the following aspects of social life:

Beliefs are perceived states of knowing, or cognition: we feel that we know about 'things' on the basis of objective and subjective information.

Customs are modes of behaviour that represent culturally approved ways of responding to given situations: usual and acceptable ways of behaving.

A *ritual* is a type of activity that takes on symbolic meaning, consisting of a fixed sequence of behaviour repeated over time. Ritualized behaviour tends to be public, elaborate, formal and ceremonial – like marriage ceremonies. Ritualistic behaviour, however, is any behaviour a person makes a ritual out of (performing certain superstitious acts on the morning of an exam, for example). Rituals commonly require ritual artefacts (representing, for the marketer, products): think of the 'accessories' that are associated with a wedding.

The different *languages* of different cultures is an obvious means of distinguishing large groups of people. Language can present a problem to cross-cultural marketers, as we shall see.

Table 5.2: The Family Life Cycle

I	II	III	IV	V	VI	VII	VIII	IX
Bachelor stage	Newly married couples	Full nest I	Full nest II	Full nest III	Empty nest I	Empty nest II	Solitary survivor in labour force	Solitary survivor(s) retired
Younger single people not living at home	Young no children	Youngest child under six	Youngest child six or over	Older married couples with dependent children	Older married couples, no children living with them, head of family in labour force	Older married couples, no children living at home, head of family retired		
Few financial burdens	Better off financially than they will be in the near future.	Home purchasing at peak.	Financial position better.	Financial position still better.	Home ownership peak.	Significant cut in income.	Income still adequate but likely to sell family home and purchase smaller accommodation.	Significant cut in income.
Fashion/opinion leader led	High levels of purchase of homes and consumer durable goods.	Liquid assets/savings low.	Some wives return to work.	More wives work.	More satisfied with financial position and money saved.	Keep home.		Additional medical requirements.
Recreation orientated		Dissatisfied with financial position and amount of money saved.	Child-dominated household.	School and examination dominated household.	Interested in travel, recreation, self-education.	Buy medical appliances or medical care products which aid health, sleep and digestion.	Concern with level of savings and pension.	Special need for attention, affection and security.
		Reliance of credit finance, credit cards, overdrafts etc.		Some children get first jobs; others in further/higher education.	Make financial gifts and contributions.	Assist children.		May seek sheltered accommodation.
		Child-dominated household.		Expenditure to support children's further/higher education.	Children gain qualifications: move to Stage I.	Concern with level of savings and pension.	Some expenditure on hobbies and pastimes.	Possible dependence on others for personal financial management and control.
Buy: Basic kitchen equipment, basic furniture, cars, equipment for the mating game, holidays	Buy: Cars, fridges, cookers, life assurance, durable furniture, holidays.	Buy necessities: washers, dryers, baby food and clothes, vitamins, toys, books etc.	Buy necessities: foods, cleaning materials, clothes, bicycles, sports gear, music lessons, pianos, holidays etc.	Buy: new, more tasteful furniture, non-necessary appliances, boats etc., holidays.	Buy: luxuries, home improvements, e.g. fitted kitchens etc.	Some expenditure hobbies and pastimes.	Worries about security and dependence.	
Experiments with patterns of personal financial management and control	Establish patterns of personal financial management and control.							

Symbols are an important aspect of language and culture: the symbolic nature of human language sets it apart from animal communication. Each symbol may carry a number of different meanings and associations for different people, and some of these meanings are learned as part of a society's culture. The advertiser using slang words or pictorial images must take care that they are valid for the people he or she wants to reach – and up-to-date.

Culture embraces all the physical 'tools' or *artefacts* used by people for their physical and psychological well-being. In our modern society, the *technology* we use has a very great impact on the way we live our lives, and new technologies accelerate the rate of social change.

- *Appearance and dress*. Cultures vary widely on what is accepted and desirable in the way of apparel and general appearance. In Muslim countries, for example, females cover themselves while in Western societies, depending to some extent on the ebb and flow of fashion, female semi-nudity is accepted. Obviously this has a great impact on marketing; for instance, the market in the UK for ties is much larger than in Australia where 'dressing down' even in a business context is the norm.

- *Food and eating habits*. Different cultures have different attitudes to food and eating together, with some cultures embracing the idea of convenience food (the USA, UK) while others devote a great deal of time and effort to food preparation (France, Japan).

- *Gender roles*. In different cultures the expectations and rules governing male and female behaviour vary widely. Increasingly the extent to which women have broken away from the traditional role of nurturer in Western society has been reflected in advertising campaigns, while in other societies the male/breadwinner-female/homemaker imagery persists.

- *Mental processing and learning styles*. In Western societies, a great deal of store is set by rationality and logic when it comes to business and other commercial decisions. This is often in stark contrast to the more intuitive and political decision making that goes on in Eastern countries.

- *Time and time consciousness*. Time horizons vary considerably across cultures, ranging from time-pressured societies, e.g. USA and Japan, to societies that are not 'time conscious'.

The transfer of cultural meaning

Some consumer researchers talk about the 'transfer of cultural meaning' at different stages of the marketing process. The 'culturally constituted world' produces products that are invested with cultural meaning or significance by advertising and 'fashion'. Those consumer goods, symbolic of cultural values, are then sold to individual consumers, who thus absorb the cultural values. Meanwhile, by using the products in rituals of possession, exchange, grooming or whatever, the consumer adds further cultural meaning to the goods.

Micro-culture

A micro-culture is a distinct and identifiable cultural group within society as a whole: it will have certain beliefs, values, customs and rituals that set it apart – while still sharing the dominant beliefs, values, customs and rituals of the whole society or 'mainstream' culture.

Cross-cultural issues

Cultural segmentation must be considered particularly carefully in international (or cross-cultural) marketing. The marketer would need to understand the beliefs, values, customs and rituals of the countries in which a product is being marketed, in order to alter or reformulate the product to appeal to local needs and tastes, and reformulate the promotional message to be intelligible and attractive to other cultures.

● Legal and regulatory provisions with regard to advertising vary from country to country: the showing of cigarettes in ads, for example, the use of comparative advertising, or the use of children in advertising.

● Products are positioned as exotic imports with the specific appeal of their country of origin (Australian lager, Italian pizza, French mineral water) – while in the domestic market they are sold on familiarity and cultural loyalty.

There are two ways of looking at cross-cultural marketing:

● *Localized marketing strategy* stresses the diversity and uniqueness of consumers in different national cultures;

● *Global marketing strategy* stresses the similarity and shared nature of consumers worldwide.

Lifestyle and Social Class

Social class is one of the oldest approaches to grouping consumer behaviour. The UK JICNARs six-class classification of social class has been updated with a new nine-class system for the 2001 UK population census (Table 5.3).

Table 5.3: The Proposed Nine-Class System for the 2001 UK Census

Social class	Occupations	Examples
1	Higher managerial and professional occupations	
1.1	Employers and managers in larger organizations	Company directors
1.2	Higher professional	Doctors, lawyers, dentists, academics, teachers, librarians.

Table 5.3: The Proposed Nine-Class System for the 2001 UK Census (cont.)

Social class	Occupations	Examples
2	Lower managerial and professional	Police officers, fire-fighters, nurses, physiotherapists, journalists, actors, musicians.
3	Intermediate occupations	Secretaries, driving instructors, airline flight attendants, clerical workers.
4	Small employers and own account workers	
5	Lower supervisory, craft and related occupations	Electricians, car mechanics, train drivers.
6	Semi-routine occupations	Drivers, hairdressers, bricklayers, welders, cooks, shop assistants, supermarket check-out operators.
7	Routine occupations	Cleaners, road workers, refuse collectors, road sweepers.

Source: Adapted from Rose & O'Reilly (1999)

Such classifications are based on specific demographic factors:

Objective measures of social class consist of selected demographic – mainly socioeconomic – variables: income, education and occupation are the most common. (These can then be combined with geodemographic data about social class location and distribution, to offer useful information for market segmentation.) Other variables sometimes added – to supplement the limited value of a pure 'amount of income' measurement – include value/ quality of residence or residential area, source of income (e.g. earned, inherited, assisted), and possessions in the home.

From a marketer's point of view, it is possible to infer shared values, attitudes and behaviour within a social class, as distinct from those of a higher or lower class.

5.4   Consumer Behaviour Concepts that Support Marketing Management Decisions

The Purchase Decision: Involvement Levels

Not all consumers behave in the same way. The decision processes involved in a major purchase such as a car are very different from the decision processes involved in the purchase of chocolate confectionery. Assael (1998) presents a typology of consumer decision making based on two main dimensions:

a)   The extent of decision making;

b)   The degree of involvement in the purchase.

Figure 5.3: Four Types of Consumer Behaviour

Level of decision making

	Low	High
High	Classical conditioning	Cognitive learning theory
Low	Passive learning theory	Instrumental Conditioning

Level of involvement

Cognitive learning theory: consumers 'think before they act'. They develop brand attitudes and evaluate brand alternatives in detail – example a new car.

Passive learning theory: generally a repetitive purchase that requires little cognitive thought, e.g. toilet cleaner or the usual packet of mints. However, sometimes a low-involvement product requires some decision making, e.g. as a result of (1) introduction of a new product (2) a desire for a change for something new, probably the result of the consumer subconsciously remembering marketing communications advertising some new desirable feature (e.g. super-absorbent nappy). Here the consumer has responded passively, i.e. has not actively sought information on new product attributes.

Instrumental conditioning: strong satisfaction with the performance of the brand results in a commitment to the brand (positive reinforcement based on satisfaction results in repetitive behaviour). The store where shirts or blouses are bought for the office. High involvement as it affects self-image, however low level of decision making as the purchase source represents a 'safe' solution.

Classical conditioning: consumers have no interest in adverts for low-involvement products. However they passively and subconsciously store this information. Any evaluation of the brand takes place after the purchase. They remain with the brand so long as it meets minimum levels of satisfaction set by consumers. Household insurance is in this category. Advertising tries to suggest that the advertised product demonstrates the failings in existing policies because of the new features which are being introduced for lower cost.

It is suggested that consumer behaviour is affected by the level of consumer involvement and the complexity of the decision-making process. This results in four types of consumer behaviour (Table 5.4).

Table 5.4: Types of Consumer Behaviour

	High involvement	Low involvement
Decision making (information search, consideration of brand alternatives)	Complex decision making	Limited decision making
Habit (little or no information search, consideration of only one brand)	Brand loyalty	Inertia

Decision making to *habit* represent opposite ends of a scale. 'Decision making' equates to the cognitive process of information search and the evaluation of brand alternatives. Habit is the opposite of this.

High-involvement purchases are those that are important to the customer in some way; for example, they may be closely tied to the customer's ego and self-image. Such purchases involve risk. *Low-involvement purchases* are not as important to the customer and therefore the level of risk is lessened. With such purchases it may not be worth the customer's while to engage in the search for information about competing brands and evaluate a wide range of alternatives, and therefore a limited process of decision making usually occurs.

5.5 Consumer Behaviour Models

The process of consumer buying behaviour described in the previous section is inevitably very simplified and there are a number of external cultural, social, personal and psychological factors influencing the decision. Given the complexity of the factors influencing the process of consumer buying behaviour, models can be of use in simplifying the process to make it more manageable for marketers, bearing in mind that their ultimate objective is to build repeat purchasing patterns on an ongoing basis.

One of the major ways in which models may help the marketer is to put some form of framework on the thought processes that the consumer goes through when buying. If the marketer understands these thought processes he or she is more likely to be able to develop communication activities that will effectively influence the consumer to buy a particular brand. A number of different types of simple models have been put forward by way of explanation. These simple models can be classified into three major types – response hierarchy models, black box models and personal variable models.

Response Hierarchy Models

Response hierarchy models attempt to predict the sequence of mental stages that the consumer passes through on the way to a purchase. Some of the major response hierarchy models are given in the diagram on the following page. These models are useful in the sense that they attempt to prioritize the communication objectives at various stages of the buying process.

These objectives can be classified into three main areas – cognitive, affective or behavioural.

1. Cognitive objectives are concerned with creating knowledge or awareness in the mind of the consumer.

2. Affective objectives are concerned with changing the consumer's attitude to the product as a whole or a specific aspect of the product.

3. Behavioural objectives are concerned with getting the consumer to act in some way (buy the product).

Figure 5.4: Response Hierarchy Models

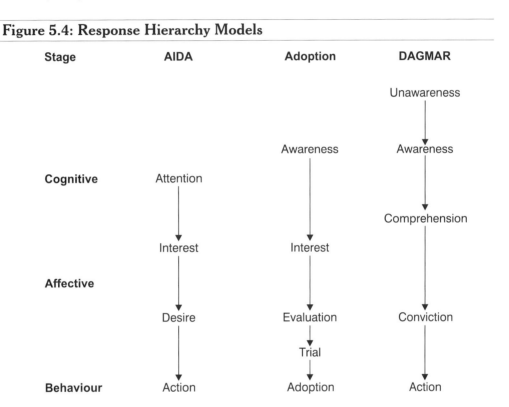

These models have some drawbacks, as identified by Smith (1993). As has been said, the core model of buying behaviour is most applicable to complex buying behaviour. In other situations the consumer may not go through the staged process of information search and evaluation of objectives before the purchase decision. Indeed, some of the stages might occur simultaneously, as in the case of an impulse purchase. Buyers may also bypass the hierarchy of stages. For example, during the evaluation stage a buyer may go back to the information search stage in order to obtain more information before making the decision to buy.

Black Box Models

These models are concerned with how people respond to stimuli, and as a result are often referred to as stimulus-response models. Such models do not attempt to explain the complexities of the customer's thought processes and the mind of the consumer is likened to a 'black box' which cannot be penetrated to find out what is inside. Therefore the intervening variables described in the previous section are ignored and the models focus on the input or stimulus (for example, advertising) and the response or output (purchase behaviour). The next diagram shows a simple black box model with an indication of examples of 'input' and 'output'.

Figure 5.5: 'Black Box' Model

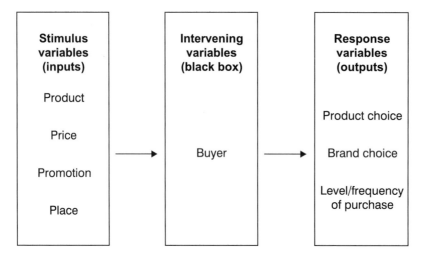

Personal Variable Models

These models attempt to penetrate the black box, but they consider only a few variables such as beliefs, attitudes and intentions. The three main types of personal variable models are linear additive models, threshold models and trade-off models (Smith 1993).

Linear additive models are based on an estimation of the number of attributes that a particular product has, multiplied by the score each attribute is perceived to have, multiplied by the weighting that each attribute is perceived to have. Such models attempt to deconstruct attitudes by indicating which attributes are important to consumers and their relative weighting by consumers. Although attitudes are not always translated into buying behaviour, such models can be used to determine marketing strategies based on the understanding of consumer beliefs about products.

Threshold models have cut-off points or thresholds beyond which the buyer will not venture. These thresholds may be related to price, or some other particular feature that the product must have if it is to be considered by the customer. These models state that the buyer undergoes a selection process that screens and accepts those products or services within the threshold for further analysis or immediate purchase. Those outside the threshold are not considered any further.

Trade-off models put forward the viewpoint that because buyers have such a wide array of choices no one product will be the best on all product attributes, therefore the buyer will undertake some kind of trade-off, accepting a product that is lacking in one attribute but is strong in another.

Complex models of buyer behaviour (also known as 'comprehensive' models or 'grand' models) attempt to take both personal and environmental variables into account in order to produce models that explain the totality of the buying behaviour process. The three most commonly used comprehensive models are those put forward by Engel, Blackwell and Miniard (1990), Howard and Sheth (1969) and Nicosia (1966). Each will be considered in turn.

Engel, Blackwell and Miniard model

This model was originally developed in 1968 by Engel, Kollat and Blackwell but has since undergone several revisions. The 1990 version considered here is the most recent. This is represented in the diagram below.

Figure 5.6: The Engel-Blackwell-Miniard Model (1990)

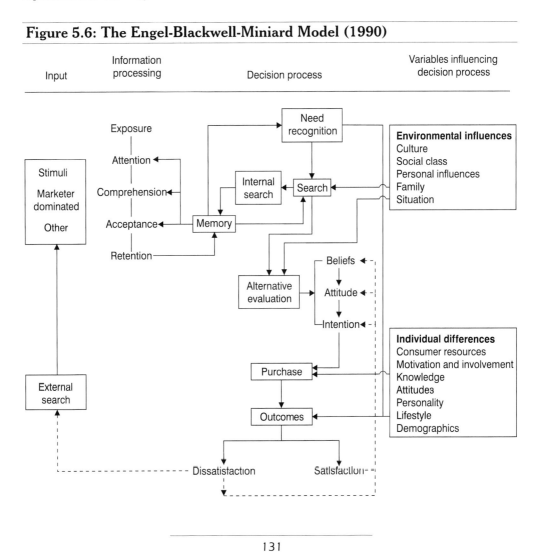

The basis of the Engel-Blackwell-Miniard model takes the simple process of consumer behaviour described above as its basis. Behaviour is depicted as a decision process comprising five major *activities* occurring over time:

a)   Need recognition

b)   Search for information

c)   Alternative evaluation

d)   Purchase

e)   Outcome.

The *influencing variables* are divided into four main categories:

a)   Stimulus inputs

b)   Information processing

c)   Decision process

d)   Variables influencing the decision process.

The starting point of the process is the customer's perception of a want or a problem that must be satisfied. This stimulates the start of the next stage, information search, which can be divided into two further stages. First, the customer searches his internal memory to ascertain what is known about potential solutions to the problem. If insufficient information is found through this course of action, the customer will begin the process of external search. The likelihood of external search is also affected by environmental factors, such as the urgency of the need, and also the individual characteristics of the customer. For example, individuals who are low risk takers will tend to seek more information before making a decision.

This search process identifies the various ways in which the problem can be solved. Those various ways are then evaluated. The *alternative evaluation* stage involves comparing the alternative brands against evaluative criteria, which are 'product judging standards that have been stored in the permanent memory' (Loudon and Della Bitta, 1993). This evaluation process may lead to changes in beliefs regarding the brands, which, in turn, leads to changes in attitudes and intentions to purchase.

The process of alternative evaluation leads to an intention to make a purchase of the most favourably evaluated brand. This intention will be translated into action unless unforeseen circumstances intervene to postpone or prevent the purchase. Once purchased, the customer will use the product and will continue to evaluate the product by comparing performance against expectations. If the product chosen does not meet expectations, the result is dissatisfaction and this may lead to further search for information about the brand and/or changes in beliefs. The overall process can, therefore, be seen as a continuous one.

Loudon and Della Bitta (1993) have evaluated this model, stating that it has proved to be a popular representation of the buying behaviour process. Like most comprehensive models it lends itself most readily to an explanation of the process of complex decision making described earlier. However, the flow of this model is quite flexible and the authors recognize that in numerous purchase decisions many of the steps are passed through very quickly or are bypassed altogether, such as in limited problem solving.

Loudon and Della Bitta state that the major drawback with this model is the vagueness regarding the role of some of the variables. For example, the influence of environmental variables is noted, but their role in influencing the process is not well specified. The role of motives in influencing behaviour is also quite vague.

Howard-Sheth model

The Howard-Sheth model attempts to pull together a disparate set of variables that influence the buying process.

Figure 5.7: The Howard-Sheth Model (1969)

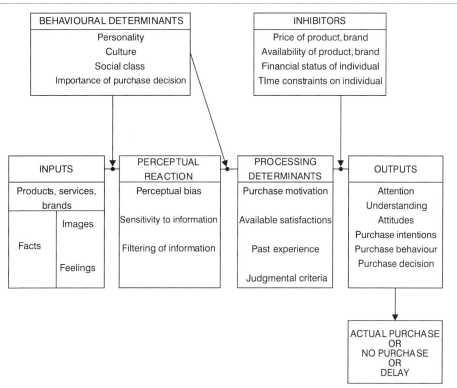

Source: Adapted from Howard J & Sheth N (1969) Theory of Buyer Behaviour

Inputs. Information inputs about the alternative services available include both rational and emotional elements. Thus, the interest-rate structure information for a particular type of savings account at a bank or building society (rational or factual data) can be an input, as can the customer's reaction to the organization's logo (emotional or irrational factor).

Behavioural determinants. These elements include the existing predispositions of the purchaser which have been influenced by culture, socioeconomic group, family and personality factors, among others. This element will have a larger role for big or otherwise significant purchase decisions.

Perceptual reaction. Information from inputs is not accepted at face value but interpreted. For example, an individual is likely to value information more highly if it has been actively sought than if it has been passively received (from TV advertisements, for example). The credibility of information varies according to the credibility of the source, perceived authority and content of the information. The customer will filter out information that is thought to be unimportant or lacks credibility.

Processing determinants. These are the factors affecting how the information gathered is evaluated. They include motivation (based on perceived needs), the available satisfactions relevant to the purchase motivation and the individual's past experience of the supplier's services. The individual will also have some judgmental criteria with which to evaluate the alternatives. These personal criteria are clearly vital in the process. Organizations can use market research methods to try to identify these criteria so as to try to influence the individual.

Inhibitors. There are external constraints on actual or potential purchase behaviour. For example, for the purchase of a car, constraints could include:

- the rate of interest charged for a loan;
- legal constraints on credit terms;
- the price of petrol and performance criteria of different models of car;
- time constraints, such as the duration of a special offer.

Outputs. The outcome of the complex process of interacting elements may be a purchase decision, a decision not to buy or a decision to delay buying.

The Howard-Sheth model has a number of advantages over other models:

- It has been validated for practical examples of purchases;
- It indicates the complex nature of the buying process;
- It emphasizes the need for marketing managers to analyse the satisfactions which customers seek in relation to the purchase of goods or services;
- It emphasizes the need to gain a clear understanding of individual purchase motivations;
- It points to the importance of external constraints on the process;
- It suggests that customer satisfactions occur on a number of levels and in a number of forms at the same time. For example, both rational and emotional satisfactions are likely to be sought.

Thus the Howard-Sheth model can help the marketing manager to obtain useful and practical insights into customer behaviour. The Howard-Sheth model places more emphasis on perception, attitudes and learning processes than does the Engel-Blackwell-Miniard model, and as such has been described as 'a significant contribution to understanding consumer behaviour' (Loudon and Della Bitta) by virtue of its attempts to detail how the influencing variables interact with each other. However, it does have limitations in that it does not make sharp distinctions between exogenous and other variables, and that some of the variables are not well defined and are difficult to measure.

Problems with Buyer Behaviour Models

While these complex models of consumer buying behaviour have their uses in extending knowledge of the processes of consumer buying behaviour, their use has not been without criticism. This criticism mainly reflects the fact that, by their very nature, models can provide only a simplification of complex issues. Various criticisms of these models have been raised by Foxall as follows:

- The models assume an unrealistic degree of consumer rationality;

- Observed behaviour often differs significantly from what is described;

- The implied decision process is too simplistic and sequential;

- Insufficient recognition is given to the relative importance of different types of decisions – each decision is treated by comprehensive models as significant and of high involvement, but the reality is very different and by far the vast majority of decisions made by consumers are relatively insignificant and of low involvement;

- The models assume consumers have a seemingly infinite capacity for receiving and ordering information – in practice, consumers ignore, forget, distort, misunderstand and make far less use than this of the information with which they are presented;

- Attitudes towards low-involvement products are often very weak and emerge only after the purchase, not before as comprehensive models suggest;

- Many purchases seem not to be preceded by a decision process;

- Strong brand attitudes often fail to emerge even when products have been bought on a number of occasions;

- Consumers often drastically limit their search for information, even for consumer durables;

- When brands are similar in terms of their basic attributes, consumers seemingly do not discriminate between them but instead select from a repertoire of brands.

The results of attempts to test comprehensive models have proved disappointing. However, this should not detract from their use as a first base analysis of a very complex issue.

5.6 Stages in the Decision-making Process

The decision-making stages in the buying process have been identified by Kotler *et al.* (1999) as follows:

- Need recognition
- Information search
- Evaluation of alternatives
- Purchase decision
- Post-purchase evaluation.

Need Recognition

The process begins when the buyer recognizes a need or problem. This can be triggered by internal stimuli, such as hunger or thirst, or external stimuli, such as social esteem. If the need rises to a threshold level it will become a drive, and, from previous experience, the buyer will know how to satisfy this drive through the purchase of a particular type of product. Kotler states that the task for the marketer is to identify the circumstances and/or stimuli that trigger a particular need and use this knowledge to develop marketing strategies that trigger consumer interest.

Information Search

Once aroused the customer will search for more information about the products that will satisfy the need. The information search stage can be divided into two levels. The first is 'heightened attention', where the customer simply becomes more receptive to information about the particular product category. The second stage is 'active information search'. The extent of active search will depend on the strength of the drive, the amount of information initially available, the ease of obtaining additional information and the satisfaction obtained from the search. The amount of search will increase as the customer moves from limited decision making to complex decision making.

The task for the marketer is to decide which are the major information sources that the customer will use and to analyse its relative importance. According to Kotler consumer information sources fall into four groups:

- *Personal sources*: family, friends, neighbours, work colleagues;
- *Commercial sources*: advertising, salespeople, packaging, displays;
- *Public sources*: mass media, consumer rating organizations;
- *Experiential sources*: handling, examining, using the product.

A consumer will generally receive the most information exposure from commercial sources, but the most effective information exposure comes from personal sources.

Through this information-gathering process the consumer will learn about competing brands and their relative pros and cons. This will enable the consumer to narrow down the range of alternatives to those brands that will best meet his or her particular needs – what has been called the 'choice set'. The marketer's task is to get his brand into the customer's 'choice set'.

Evaluation of Alternatives

There is no generally accepted, single evaluation process. Most current models of evaluation are *cognitively* oriented – in other words they take the view that the customer forms judgements largely on a conscious and rational basis.

Kotler states that, as the consumer is trying to satisfy some need with the buying process, he or she will be looking for certain benefits from the product chosen and each product will be seen as a 'bundle of attributes' with varying capabilities of delivering the benefits sought and hence satisfying the need. The composition and the relative importance of the components of this bundle of attributes will differ between customers, and therefore the marketer should determine what importance the customer attaches to each attribute.

In order to ensure that the brand has the best chance of being chosen by the consumer, the marketer has a range of options for action, including the following:

1. *Modifying the brand.* Redesigning the product so that it offers more of the attributes that the buyer desires.

2. *Altering beliefs about the brand.* Kotler recommends that this course of action be pursued if the consumer underestimates the qualities of the brand, and calls it 'psychological repositioning'.

3. *Altering beliefs about competitors' brands.* This course of action would be appropriate if the consumer mistakenly believes that a competitor's brand has more quality than it actually has, and can be referred to as 'competitive repositioning'.

4. *Altering the importance weights of attributes.* The marketer would try to persuade consumers to attach more importance to the product attribute in which the brand excels.

5. *Calling attention to neglected attributes*, particularly if the brand excels in these attributes. ('Have you forgotten how good they taste?')

6. *Shifting the buyer's ideals.* The marketer would try to persuade consumers to change their ideal levels for one or more attributes.

Purchase Decision

Having evaluated the range of brand choices the consumer may have formed a purchase intention to buy the most preferred brand. However, some factors could intervene between the purchase intention and the purchase decision. The first factor is the attitude of others. If, for example, a friend or relative of the consumer expresses a strong negative opinion regarding the brand choice, this may influence the consumer to change his or her mind. Purchase intention is also influenced by unanticipated situational factors that may intervene between purchase intention and decision. Such factors could include a change in financial circumstances such as redundancy, or circumstances in which some other purchase becomes more urgent.

Post-Purchase Evaluation

Having purchased the brand the consumer will experience some level of satisfaction or dissatisfaction, depending on the closeness between the consumer's product expectations and the product's perceived performance. These feelings will influence whether the consumer buys the brand again and also whether the consumer talks favourably or unfavourably about the brand to others. Some firms, such as Volvo, have focused their marketing communications on reassuring the consumer that they made the correct purchase, i.e. to minimize post-purchase dissatisfaction or cognitive dissonance.

5.7   Technology in Marketing and Consumer Behaviour

Developments in datamining, database management, customer relationship management and in the application of technology to marketing research have been at the forefront in the application of technology. Technology, in particular utilizing the Internet, has enabled companies to get closer to their customers, providing support and enabling them to track buyer behaviour. Technology is now transforming the way organizations handle information on consumers and the very basis in which organizations operate within new markets. The transformation includes:

- How organizations trawl for new prospects;

- The way information is collected and cross-referenced on prospects who have registered an interest in the organization and its products and services as well as in clients;

- How organizations develop their relationship with clients;

- How organizations establish a presence in a new market, including the systems required to develop that presence.

Xelector is an example of an organization that is pushing back the boundaries of marketing business, with systems which apply understanding of consumer behaviour. The company markets itself as possessing a unique B2B2C (business-to-business-to-consumer) model and as such is highly innovative in its application of technology. The website is not yet fully operational (winter 2000/1). However presenting *company information* on its intended activity is at the very least highly illuminating on the potential application of the new technology.

MARKETING IN PRACTICE

Xelector – a unique B2B2C model?

Xelector is building a digital marketplace for consumers to compare, select and buy financial services and utilities products. With its unique B2B2C (business-to-business-to-consumer) model, Xelector enables every product provider and Web site partner to find the right consumer – and every consumer to find the right product.

Xelector provides unique and powerful benefits to everyone:

- **Consumers** at last have what they demand: choice.

- **Financial services providers** gain eIntelligence and value, maximizing the Internet's capabilities to generate new customers, new markets and new products.

- **Web site partners** brand Xelector's comparison shopping experience as their own, enhancing their site's stickiness and maximizing revenues.

Consumers

Xelector is soon to become a powerful and easy new way for consumers to compare and buy financial products, such as motor insurance, credit cards and personal loans.

Xelector will be easy to access and available via web sites in the UK that brand Xelector's services as their own. The service allows consumers to apply online, confident in the knowledge that the transaction will be carried out smoothly and safely

Financial services providers

Xelector's platform provides the ability to maximise the Internet's capabilities to generate new customers, new markets for products and new products.

New customers: with Xelector's Internet marketplace, financial service providers will be able to gain rapid access to new customers in the UK from one platform. Xelector's multiple Web site partners offer higher market penetration than a single Web site.

New markets: with minimal cost, financial service providers gain a powerful e-commerce strategy, leapfrogging into the Internet age *and* tapping into new business opportunities on an unprecedented scale. Xelector effectively delivers a cohesive, powerful Web strategy without the investment required to go it alone. Xelector's data permits providers to market 'virtually' and price precisely via multiple Web sites in the UK.

New products: Xelector enables financial service providers to achieve a strong understanding of customer value and deliver lasting customer satisfaction through its award-winning *eIntelligence* solutions. Xelector instantly collects important demographic information and preferences from consumers. Consumer trends and patterns are tracked and analysed in real time, based on solid market information.

Xelector provides a testing ground for new products on a very controlled basis before full rollout decisions are undertaken. With access to Xelector's *eIntelligence* solutions, financial service providers are able to create highly targeted products and deploy them efficiently and quickly – with low development costs.

Measure product performance: Through Xelector's eMarket reports, providers can view the amount of new business generated and see how this varies across time. In addition to information about purchased products, the number of product inquiries, requests for product quotes, the value of applications, etc. can also be accessed.

Track consumer trends and patterns: By charting transactional and behavioural data in real time, based on up-to-the-minute market activity, financial service providers are provided with information on what products customers looked at, what products they chose and what drove them to make those choices.

Build richer customer relationships: By instantly collecting important demo- and psycho-graphic information and preferences from all its users, Xelector's sophisticated 'Analysis Reports' can provide financial services providers with unprecedented marketing opportunities and web site partners with invaluable customer insight.

Costs: the service is free to financial service providers. Xelector makes commission on the products sold.

> *Source: information presented was obtained from the company website at:*
> *http://www.xelector.com/*

Summary

Consumers are the ultimate customers of business. For some businesses (business-to-business markets) they are indirect customers, but non-the-less customers. An understanding of consumer behaviour (the subject of the popular abbreviation B2C marketing) is therefore vital in understanding how to influence their purchasing decisions.

Current thinking suggests that consumer behaviour can best be understood from two perspectives. These are (1) the influence of the individual on behaviour (which includes four main categories of personality theory to explain behaviour) and (2) the influence of society. Sociocultural factors (or the influence of society) have been applied more commonly to consumer segmentation.

Consumer behaviour research is based on one of two fundamental principles. One view is that the drivers of human behaviour are deeply rooted within the human mind, while the opposing view suggests that society, and particular social groups, have a profound influence on individual behaviour through mechanisms of social conformity and socialization. A practical application of these theories, which is rooted in both perspectives, concerns the classification of consumers by the level of decision making and by the level of involvement in the purchase. This results in a four-category model. Consumers in each category will behave in a different way and will require the marketing mix to be adapted for each segment. An additional consumer behaviour concept, which has been useful in applied marketing, is the consumer 'decision-making process' model. Consumers, in general, move through a series of stages in making a purchase. Understanding these stages allows marketers to influence the final purchase decision.

Consumer behaviour theorists have generated several models to explain consumer behaviour. One of the most influential for marketing communications has been the response hierarchy category of models (e.g. AIDA) which hypothesize that consumers go through a series of different states of mind as they move towards the purchase decision. More comprehensive, all-inclusive models have been produced, e.g. Howard-Sheth. However their practical application has been questioned. Some prefer to employ the general principles on which parts of such models are constructed, namely consumer decision-making stages. This, for example, breaks down consumer decision making into discrete stages, each of which may be used as the basis for deploying the marketing mix, especially the communications mix.

References

Assael H (1998) *Consumer Behaviour and Marketing Action*, 6th edition, South Western College Publishing, Cincinnati

Engel J F, Blackwell R D & Miniard P (1990) *Consumer Behaviour*, 6th edition, Hinsdale IL: The Dryden Press

Eysenck H J & Eysenck S B G (1975) *Manual of the Eysenck Personality Questionnaire*, Hodder and Stoughton

Foxall G (2000) Consumer decision-making: process, investment and style cited in Baker M (2000) *The Marketing Book*, Butterworth-Heineman, Oxford

Howard J A & Sheth J N (1969) *The Theory of Buyer Behaviour*, New York: Wiley

Kotler P, Armstrong G, Saunders J and Wong V (1999) *Principles of Marketing*, 2nd European Edition, Prentice Hall Europe

Loudon D & Bitta A J D (1993) *Consumer Behaviour, Concepts and Applications*

Maslow A (1954) *Motivation and Personality*, New York Harper and Row, pp80-106

Nicosia F M (1969) *Consumer Decision Processes*, Englewoods Cliffs N J: Prentice Hall

Pavlov I cited in Shrimp T A (1991) Neo-Pavlonian conditioning and its implication for consumer research in Robertson T S and Kassarjian H H (eds.) *Handbook of Consumer Behaviour*, Englewood Cliff, N J Prentice-Hall, pp162-87

Rose D & O'Reilly K (eds.) (1999) *Constructing Classes: Towards a New Social Classification for the UK*, ESRC/ONS.

Smith P (1993) *Marketing Communications: An Integrated Approach*, Kogan Page

6

ORGANIZATION BUYING BEHAVIOUR

Learning Objectives

After reading this chapter students should:

- Know the different types of organizational buying;

- Understand the greater number of influences on organizational buyer behaviour and how this results in its greater complexity over consumer buying behaviour;

- Know the stages in the business-to-business buying process;

- Know and understand at least one model of the decision-making unit for business-to-business buying.

Figure 6.1: Chapter Map

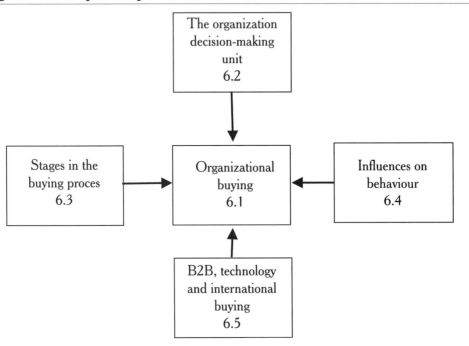

Introduction

Business-to-business buying behaviour is more complicated than consumer buying behaviour, because the buying is affected by additional variables. These include the business environment and the organizational context within which buying takes place. Buying is also influenced by the complexity of the buying situation and the extent to which the buying situation has changed, from the perspective of the organization. One model in particular is presented that illustrates the complex influences on buying behaviour.

Business-to-business buying is more usually undertaken in a group context. There are various roles that individuals undertake and this has led to the development of various buyer decision-making unit models which are used to explain business-to-business buying. Whether buying takes place in groups or by solitary individuals, the decision-making unit goes through a series of stages and these are presented.

6.1   Organizational Buying

Comparison with consumer buying

Ultimately all organizational buying decisions are made by individuals, or groups of individuals, each of whom is subjected to the same types of influences as they are in making their own personal buying decisions. There are, however, some differences between personal and corporate buying-decision processes.

- Organizations buy because the products/services are needed to meet wider objectives, for instance to help them to meet more closely their customers' needs. That is to say, organizations buy to fulfil organizational requirements whereas personal customers buy in order to fulfil their own needs.

- A number of individuals are involved in the typical organizational buying decision, typically more individuals than for consumer buying decisions.

- The decision process may take longer for corporate decisions; the use of feasibility studies, for example, can prolong the decision process. Tendering processes in government buying also have this effect.

- Organizations buy a complex total offering which can involve a high level of technical support, staff training, delivery scheduling, finance arrangements etc.

- Organizations are more likely to employ buying experts in the process.

- In organizational buying an intermediary is often involved in the process, acting like a broker, thereby adding to the complexity of the process.

- The customer can often account for a substantial proportion of total sales. For marketing purposes the relationship between the supplier and the large customer needs to be managed well.

Examples of the complexities of organizational buying

UK food buyers

The potential complexity of the relationship between suppliers and their organizational customers can be illustrated by two simple examples. A study of head-office buyers for a major UK food product produced the following list of customer service elements that were considered important by organizational buyers.

1 Product availability

2 Prompt quotation

3 Representation

4 Order status

5 Distribution system

6 Delivery time

7 Pricing

8 Merchandising

9 Product positioning

10 Invoice accuracy

11 New product introductions

12 Advertising

Choice of lead bank by US and European Multinational Corporations (MNCs)

An alternative example concerns the factors that influence the choice of lead bank by MCNs in the USA and in Europe. The rankings applied to a variety of criteria are given below and they give some indication of the range of dimensions in which a bank must be able to perform. It should be noted that a similar exercise for subsidiary companies, for medium-sized companies and for small companies would undoubtedly produce different rankings and different criteria.

Table 6.1: Factors Affecting the Choice of Bank by Multinational Corporations

Criterion	US ranking	European ranking
Have global branch network	1	3
Officers knowledgeable in international services	2	n/a
Used as domestic lead bank	3	6
Efficient in international operating services	4	2
High quality forex services	5	1
Provide most foreign credit needs	6	7
Outstanding specialists in wide range of international services	7	n/a
Ability to meet multi-currency borrowing needs	8	n/a
Competitive pricing of international credit services	9	4
Efficient in international money transfer	10	5
Strong reputation among foreign governments and banks	11	n/a
Strong international cash management services	12	8

(Source: Adapted from Channon, D F (1986) Bank Strategic Management and Marketing)

Impact of product and organizational buying

The consumer's decision to purchase highly complex products and services which have high levels of consumer involvement (see Chapter 5 on consumer buying behaviour), e.g. the consumer's decision to buy a house, has more similarities with an organizational decision to buy equipment. Similarly, an organizational decision to buy pencils has more in common with a consumer, low-involvement, low-complexity product or service purchase decision, such as a consumer decision to buy toothpaste, than with an organizational equipment purchase decision. It is therefore important, when discussing organizational buying, to consider specifically the type of product or service being purchased.

Types of organizational buying

There are several approaches to classifying organizational buying behaviour. Two are presented: classification based on complexity and on whether the product has been purchased previously.

Classification of organizational buying based on complexity

One system of categorization is based on the complexity of the organizational buyer behaviour and the complexity of the buying process. Three types of buying situation can be identified:

simple re-ordering (say of a bank's stationery supplies) to complex purchasing decisions (a bank lending money to a third world government as part of a consortium).

1. *Routinized buyer behaviour.* This category deals with habitual buying where the buyer knows the offering and the item is frequently purchased. It is likely that the buyer has well-developed supplier preferences and any deviation from habitual behaviour is likely to be influenced by price and availability considerations.

2. *Limited problem solving.* This category deals with the purchase of a new or unfamiliar product/service but where the suppliers are known and the product is in a familiar class of products – for instance a new type of business bank account.

3. *Extensive problem solving.* This situation focuses on the purchase of unfamiliar products from unfamiliar suppliers. This process can take much time and effort and involve the need to develop criteria with which to judge the purchase – for instance a new type of finance arrangement to cover a new class of business.

Classification of organizational buying based on whether the product has been purchased previously

An alternative approach is to consider the degree to which the buying situation has changed. The three categories in this classification scheme are: new task purchase, modified re-buy purchase and straight re-buy purchase.

1. With a *new task purchase* the organization is facing a need or a problem for the first time. The organization will have to produce detailed specifications of both product and ordering routines for this and future purchases. Much information will generally be needed in order to make the purchase.

2. With a *modified re-buy* purchase something about the buying situation has changed, but a lot still remains the same. Such situations may include circumstances where a buyer requires faster delivery, different prices or a slightly different product specification.

3. A *straight re-buy* purchase occurs when the buyer routinely purchases the same products under the same terms of sale. In such situations the buying process is much truncated.

In marketing products or services to corporate clients, the role of the sales representative is vital to the supplier. As the human face of the producer company, the sales representative is a key figure in establishing the relationships between the supplier and the customer. In practice there are two types of dimensions to the relationship:

- *Formal dimensions.* These dimensions include objectively measurable supplier characteristics such as price, credit terms, delivery speed, documentation, product training;

- *Informal dimensions.* These dimensions include subjectively evaluated supplier characteristics such as technical product responsiveness, producer credibility, perceived sales representative quality, perceived ease of contact.

The reasons for making the distinction between formal and informal dimensions is to emphasize the role that marketing can play in the producer's attempt to influence this interface. In addition the distinction serves to emphasize the importance of customer service in the marketing mix of producers and, as will become clear, this is a key dimension of service quality in the banking sector.

Much of the research work on organizational buyer behaviour stresses the rationality with which buyers defend their purchasing decisions. It is much more difficult to identify and evaluate the importance of informal dimensions of the interface between supplier and customer than it is to deal with objectively measurable dimensions. Nevertheless, it is important that factors such as personal motivations are given some consideration and that the need to build up good personal relations with the individuals involved in the purchase decision is of considerable importance.

6.2 The Organization Decision-making Unit (DMU)

This is the person, or group of people, involved in the process of making a buying decision. It is a particularly useful concept in business-to-business marketing where the customer is a commercial business or a public-sector organization. The marketing manager needs to know who in each organization influences and makes buying decisions. This may not always be evident because the DMU is rarely a formal self-contained unit. Quite often it is an informal group with many sources of influence on the buying decision. Many large organizations employ buyers – but the autonomy of the buyers will vary not simply among organizations but according to the type of production services to be purchased.

Purchasing decisions may be influenced by several people in the consuming organization.

- Employees or managers in operational departments might make recommendations about what type of supplies should be purchased.

- A junior buying manager might decide what is required, but may have to submit a recommendation to a superior for approval.

- In large organizations, there will be several buying managers, who might work independently, but might also work closely together, either formally or informally.

- Technical specifications for component purchases might be provided by engineers or other technical staff.

- Accountants might set a limit on the price the organization will pay.

- Large items of purchase might require approval from the board of directors.

The marketing department of a supplier aiming at corporate clients therefore needs to be aware of:

- how buying decisions are made by the DMU;

- how the DMU is constructed; and

- the identities of the most influential figures in the DMU.

The relationships between members of the buying centre are also important. Webster and Wind (1972) provided a framework for understanding the operation of buying centres. Their framework included several roles, five of which are presented.

1. The '*Initiator*' is the person who starts the process towards making a purchase. The purchase may be motivated by a desire to improve productivity and performance by someone who will not use the product or service being considered.

2. The *user* may have influence on the technical characteristics of the equipment (and hence the cost) and on reliability and performance criteria.

3. The *influencer* is particularly useful where the purchase relies on technical knowledge. Unlike personal purchasing behaviour where opinions may be sought from colleagues, friends and family, competitive pressures and trade secret constraints may limit the sharing of information between companies. In this environment the salesperson can be a respected technical link with the buyer and so be able to influence the purchasing process. Trade journals and trade associations or professional bodies can often be a good source of influential information in addition to sales staff of the supplying company.

4. The *buyer* is the person who actually makes the purchase. Professional buyers buy on behalf of organizations. For large purchases, they may have to seek prior approaval from 'the decider' before undertaking their buying role.

5. The *decider* is the person who is the ultimate decision maker. For large project decisions this may be the board of the whole company. For smaller project decisions the decider may be the finance director etc.

6. The *gatekeeper* controls the flow of information about the purchase. This person may be senior or junior, but is important as he or she influences the communication flow within the organization.

As already noted, each role may be undertaken by individuals or groups of individuals. These people have personal idiosyncrasies, social pressures and organizational and environmental pressures. Thus each individual and group has a set of rational factors (task variables) and non-economic factors (non-task variables) which influence the final buying choice.

6.3   Stages in the Buying Process

The corporate decision-making process is shown diagrammatically in Figure 6.2. The process will vary according to the type of purchase being made. You should realize that the diagram is a somewhat idealistic portrayal of reality. Such a systematic and dispassionate approach might apply only where an organization:

- has yet to establish a relationship with an actual or potential supplier of a particular good;

● is under some particularly strong (possibly statutory) reason to achieve strict ethical standards in its search for suppliers (for example, the public sector).

Figure 6.2: A Decision Process Model of Business-to-Business Buyer Behaviour

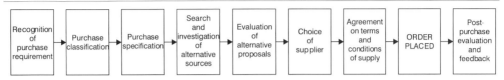

6.4   Influences on Behaviour

Organizational buyers share the influences of their personal characteristics (such as motivation and personality) and individual circumstances (e.g. age, education and training history) with consumer buyers. However, in addition they must operate within an organizational buying context in which the internal and external business environments may be relevant. They must adhere to the 'internal' organizational objectives and procedures and the external environment which may change the legislation governing their products or the technological environment which may alter the buying process and approach, for example through implementing automatic reordering for 'Just-In-Time' supply.

Consumer buyers, when buying relatively 'expensive' goods and services, such as cars, white goods, long-haul air tickets, season tickets to arts and sports venues etc., share in common with organizational buyers the concept of 'economic value'. Here the buyer assesses the benefits of the purchase against the costs which will result and compares these with a competitor's offer. For example, the purchase of a new computer system will attract a variety of costs and benefits (Table 6.2):

Table 6.2: Comparison of Product Attributes of a Computer System in Consumer Buying

COSTS	BENEFITS
● Purchase price ● Annual service fee	● Performance specification and productivity implications ● Speed of delivery ● Speed of repair/ maintenance ● Life expectancy ● Upgradability ● 'Comfort factor' of respected brand, i.e. a 'safe' purchase choice.

It will not be possible to convert some of the 'benefits' into cash terms. However the impact of, for example, the safety of buying a known brand, especially if the service or product fails, will result in the buyer being prepared to pay more for the 'reassurance' aspect of the purchase.

We shall now look more closely at the influences on buying behaviour in organizations by working though a descriptive (rather than 'process') framework published by the American Marketing Association: the AMA model.

The American Marketing Association Model

The AMA model suggests that influences come from within the buying department, from other departments within the organization, and from buying and other departments in other organizations. These ideas may be summarized on a positioning map and the location of individual organizations plotted (Figure 6.3).

Figure 6.3: Positioning Map for Influences on Organizational Buying Behaviour

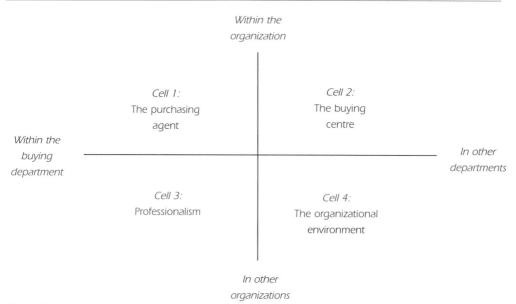

The Purchasing Agent

The purchasing agent is the buyer within the buying department within the organization. The intra-departmental, intra-organizational influences on the agent's decisions are:

Social factors, mainly the personal relationship of the purchase agent with the supplier or supplier's representative, which is believed to have considerable importance – despite inconsistency with the supposed rationality of organizational decisions. The influence of other members of the DMU is also relevant.

Price/cost factors. Price may be more or less important, depending on:

- the product, and the value/benefits it offers;
- pressure on profit margins in the buying organization;
- budgetary control on the purchasing function;
- competition on price in the market for the product;
- the background and price-consciousness of the purchasing agent.

Supply continuity. The desire to keep a consistent source of supply will be greater if the number of potential suppliers is small.

Risk-aversion. The purchase agent may perceive the risks of a decision to be high or low, depending on the price of the product, reputation of the supplier or manufacturer, reputation of the brand, and past experience. Agents may try to reduce or avoid risk by further information search, premium brand choice, product sampling etc. – just like individual customers.

The buying centre

The 'buying centre' is, like the DMU, the group of people within an organization, but in different departments, who participate in the buying decision. The inter-departmental, intra-organizational influences on the decision are as follows:

The organizational structure. This will determine the composition of the DMU, and the authority delegated to the purchasing function. Some decisions will be centralized (kept at a senior level or within a specialized function) while others will be decentralized (delegated downwards or outwards from the centre of authority): the purchasing department may make decisions, or implement the decisions of a planning department – or purchasing may be done by the user departments themselves. Inter-departmental decisions depend on the effectiveness of communication and coordination mechanisms.

Organizational politics. 'Politics' in organizations is the way in which individuals and groups compete for power and resources. The extent of perceived conflict of interest between departments, and the mechanisms for conflict resolution, will determine how effectively departments can work together in cooperative buying decisions, and who has the greatest influence or power to enforce their preferences.

The *gatekeeper.* An important role in the DMU belongs to the person who gathers, 'edits' and disseminates information about new brands, suppliers and terms of business to other members of the buying centre.

Professionalism

Professionalism links members of the same department, or function, in different organizations: all marketers, say – or in this case, all purchasing professionals. Intra-departmental, inter-organizational influences are:

- *Word-of-mouth communication* between fellow professionals in the purchasing field. This allows the exchange of information about products and suppliers, which can be used as one of the inputs to the buying decision. A professional body – or perceived professionalism – acts as a reference group;

- *Specialist journals and conferences*, trade shows etc. Specialist publications and meetings also allow the exchange of targeted, technical information, and reference-group effects. (They also offer opportunities for suppliers to advertise or be represented to the defined market segment.);

- *Supply-purchase reciprocity.* Two organizations may supply each other as part of the trading relationship.

The organizational environment

The environment of the organization includes those outside the purchasing function and outside the organization. Inter-departmental, inter-organizational influences on the purchaser include:

- technology and technological change;

- the legal, political and social environment: influencing trading practices, contracts, and purchaser 'values' – such as buying environmentally-friendly products, supporting trade sanctions etc.;

- economic, commercial and competitive factors – influencing price/cost sensitivity, purchasing power etc.;

- the nature of the supplier: large companies may offer less risk, but be less flexible and accommodating, and less willing to enter into price competition with other suppliers;

- cooperative buying: organizations may get together as purchasing consortia, in which case compromises on all the other factors may have to be reached.

This model is merely a framework within which the various influences on the buying decision can be categorized. In order to trace the effects of these factors on the decision-making process itself, we need to look at a process model of business-to-business buyer behaviour.

Figure 6.4: A Model of Industrial Source Loyalty

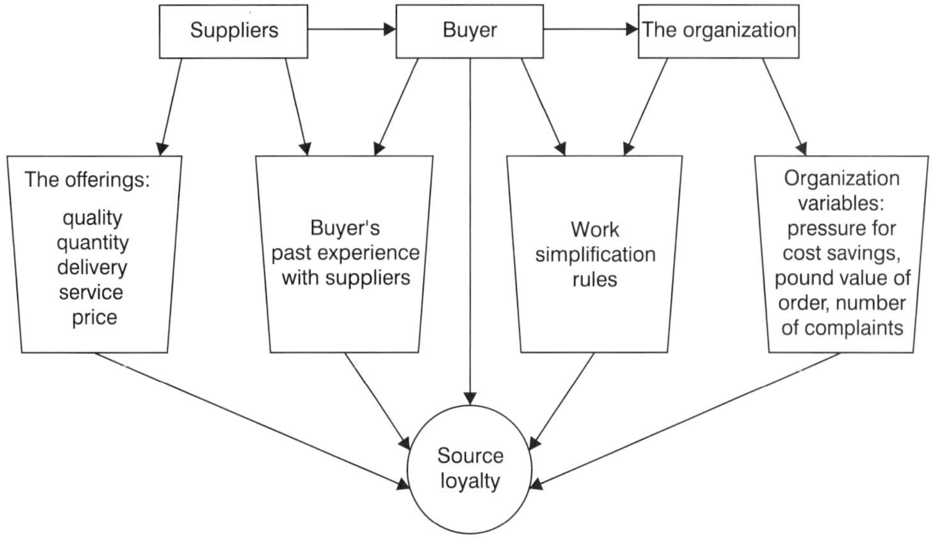

Source: Adapted from Webster & Wind (1972)

This model stresses loyalty to the supplier. *Source loyalty* is defined as the tendency for customers to continue to rely on the same supplier unless there are good reasons not to do so. This decision is based on the following factors:

● the offerings and dimension of the relationship with the customer;

● the past relationship with the supplier;

● organizational variables such as the degree of pressure for cost savings, the number of complaints;

● ways in which the organizational customer thinks the task can be simplified, such as convenience of access to the supplier, inertia and resistance to change.

Webster and Wind (1972) see organizational buyer behaviour and the decision-making unit (DMU) as influenced by a number of sets of variables, which may be grouped under one of four categories:

1. *Individual characteristics* of the members of the buying centre, such as personality and preference, must be considered. These factors are similar to personal buying processes;

2. The *buying team;*

3. The *organization*, including organizational structure, function and culture;

4. The *business environment.*

Webster and Wind present a model of organizational buyer behaviour which includes the influence of buying task (Figure 6.5).

Figure 6.5: Factors Influencing the DMU and Organizational Buyer Behaviour

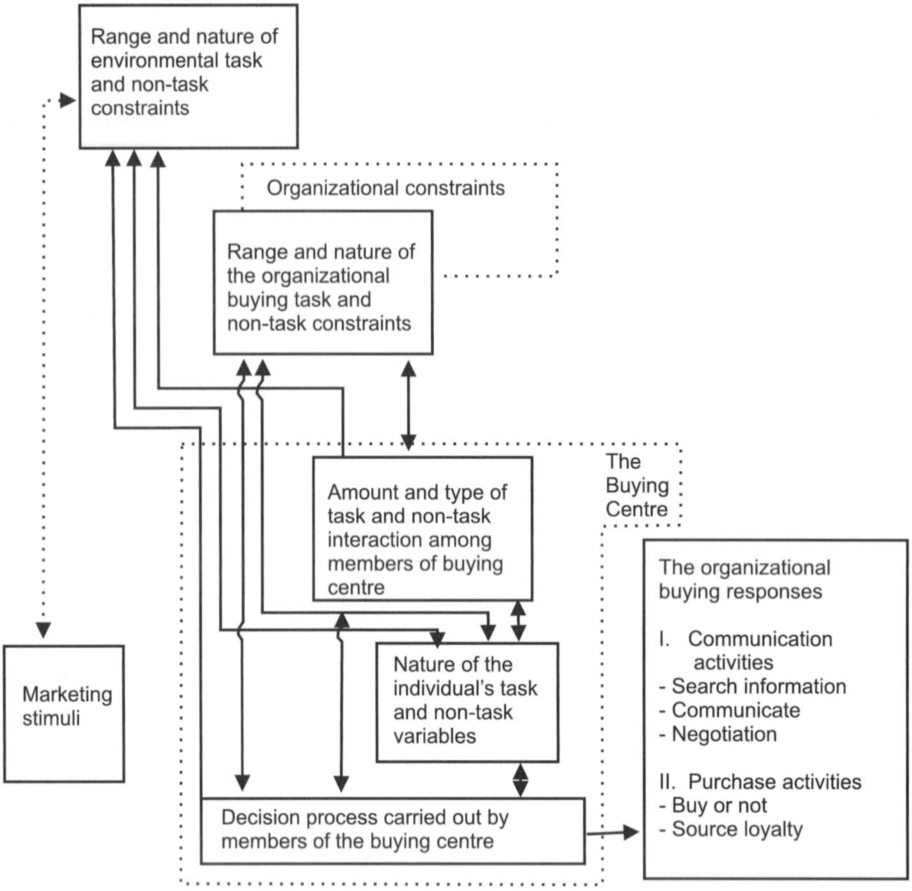

Source: Adapted from Webster, F and Wind, (1972) Organizational Buyer Behaviour

6.5 B2B, Technology and International Organizational Buying

The explosive growth in B2B e-commerce has received much less attention than its B2C equivalent. That is in spite of it being a much more significant marketplace, i.e. an estimated 9 out of every 10 transactions in the world take place between companies rather than between companies and consumers (World Trade Organization, 2000). E-commerce is facilitating the rapid expansion in transactions. Forrester Research, the e-commerce specialist agency, estimate that B2B online sales will grow from an estimated $40 billion in 1999 to $1.8 trillion by 2003.

Technology, in particular company intranets and the Internet, has resulted in developments in buying practices and behaviour. The form that this buying behaviour takes varies according to the market structure formed between sellers and buyers. Three broad structures exist:

Table 6.3: Market Structures for B2B Marketing

Structure	Number of sellers	Number of buyers
e-channel	One	One
e-market – type 1	One	Many
e-market – type 2 (also termed e-procurement)	Many	One
e-exchange	Many	Many

e-channels result in an integrated supply relationship between buyer and seller. The seller becomes an integral part of the buyer's manufacturing and supply structure. Prior to such a high degree of interdependency, the managers in both businesses must agree long-term buying/selling relationships in detail.

e-markets are where a supplier has several or many customers or a buyer has several or many suppliers. That is not to suggest that they are the only supplier or buyer in the marketplace, but to explain the broad situation in terms of the relationship between suppliers and buyers. Technology must facilitate a buyer obtaining competitive price quotations from selected suppliers, or for suppliers to auction off non-contracted production in the wider B2B marketplace. e-procurement can allow organizations to minimize costs by automating and speeding up the lengthy procurement function. It minimizes waste in the marketing channel and long term should result in lower costs.

The third category of market structure, e-exchange, implies there is not a contractual relationship between organizations. In this context, technology must provide a means for buyers to interact with sellers. Perhaps the best known examples of such markets are currency, share and commodity markets.

Digital markets are beginning to spread with the lure of cost savings and efficiency. One of the largest recent digital markets to be developed is in the car industry.

Creating a Global Marketplace

The automotive industry is already a global industry with a global supply chain and marketplace. Internet technology provides an unprecedented opportunity to speed the flow of material through the supply chain, increases response to consumer demand, and delivers new products to market faster than ever before. Covisint is a software-enabled environment which harnesses the power of Internet technology to create visibility within a company's supply chain – transforming the linear chain into a far more productive and efficient networked model. Furthermore, it delivers build-to-order capability and does so with proven secure technologies that will reinforce customers' individual competitiveness.

MARKETING IN PRACTICE

Covisint

Covisint is an independent e-business exchange, the global automotive business-to-business exchange, developed by DaimlerChrysler, Ford, General Motors, Nissan, Renault, Commerce One and Oracle to meet the needs of the automotive industry. Covisint provides original equipment manufacturers (OEMs) and suppliers with the ability to reduce costs and bring efficiencies to their business operations. Its temporary headquarters are located in Southfield, Michigan. Covisint Europe has temporary offices in Stuttgart, Germany, and the exchange also expects to establish offices in Asia.

The campaign debuts with a global advertisement in business and trade publications throughout the United States, Canada, the UK, France, Germany and Japan. In addition, Internet advertising will be posted on targeted automotive and financial web sites. It does this through a comprehensive and integrated product offering focusing on product development, procurement, and supply chain management

Today, Covisint has more than 250 customers on two continents engaged in activities on the exchange including catalogues, auctions, quote management and collaborative design. Its current product and service offering is focused on procurement, supply chain and product development solutions.

Covisint provides the software environment for clients to set up an auction, whether as a buyer or a seller, using easy-to-use, intuitive software. Clients may specify price bands, delivery times, quantities, who may bid, whether bids are sealed or open, who sees the bids, whether the bid history is open for all to view etc. The organization therefore facilitates the setting up of a whole new supply chain in minimal time, if this is required. Consequently the whole dynamics of traditional B2B is being changed dramatically.

Source: http://www.covisint.com/

Summary

Organization buying, or business-to-business (B2B) marketing, differs from consumer buying in several respects, most notably because fewer high-value purchases tend to be involved as do professional buyers and buying processes and structures (the organizational decision-making unit – DMU). As in consumer buying the organization buying unit is likely to move through a series of stages in the buying process. Understanding the members who play each role in the buying unit, and the stages through which they progress, gives a marketer a competitive edge over rivals in the B2B market.

Organization buyers share the influences of their personal characteristics and individual circumstances with consumer buyers, but in addition they must operate within an organizational buying context. This requires them to adhere to the constraints of the internal business environment, including organizational objectives and procedures. They must also

---

be responsive to the external environment adjusting and pre-empting changes in particular to legal, technological and economic factors.

Technology has had a profound effect in changing B2B marketing. This has ranged from automation of business-to-business transactions, thereby tying businesses together for the longer term, as they must integrate their systems. Digital markets and supply networks are being rolled out, increasing efficiency in the supply chain but at the same time increasing the level of competition, as products and services are sourced more widely, frequently globally.

References

Channon D F (1986) *Bank Strategic Management and Marketing*, Wiley

Webster F E & Wind Y (1972) *Organizational Buying Behaviour*, Prentice Hall, New York

World Trade Organization 2000

7

MARKETING SEGMENTATION, TARGETING AND POSITIONING

Learning Objectives

After reading this chapter students should:

- Be able to define segmentation;

- Know the four main approaches to consumer segmentation and three main approaches to the segmentation of business markets;

- Understand what makes a market segment valid;

- Understand the three target market strategies;

- Understand the meaning of positioning;

- Understand and be able to apply segmentation, targeting and positioning to a product or service.

Figure 7.1: Chapter Map

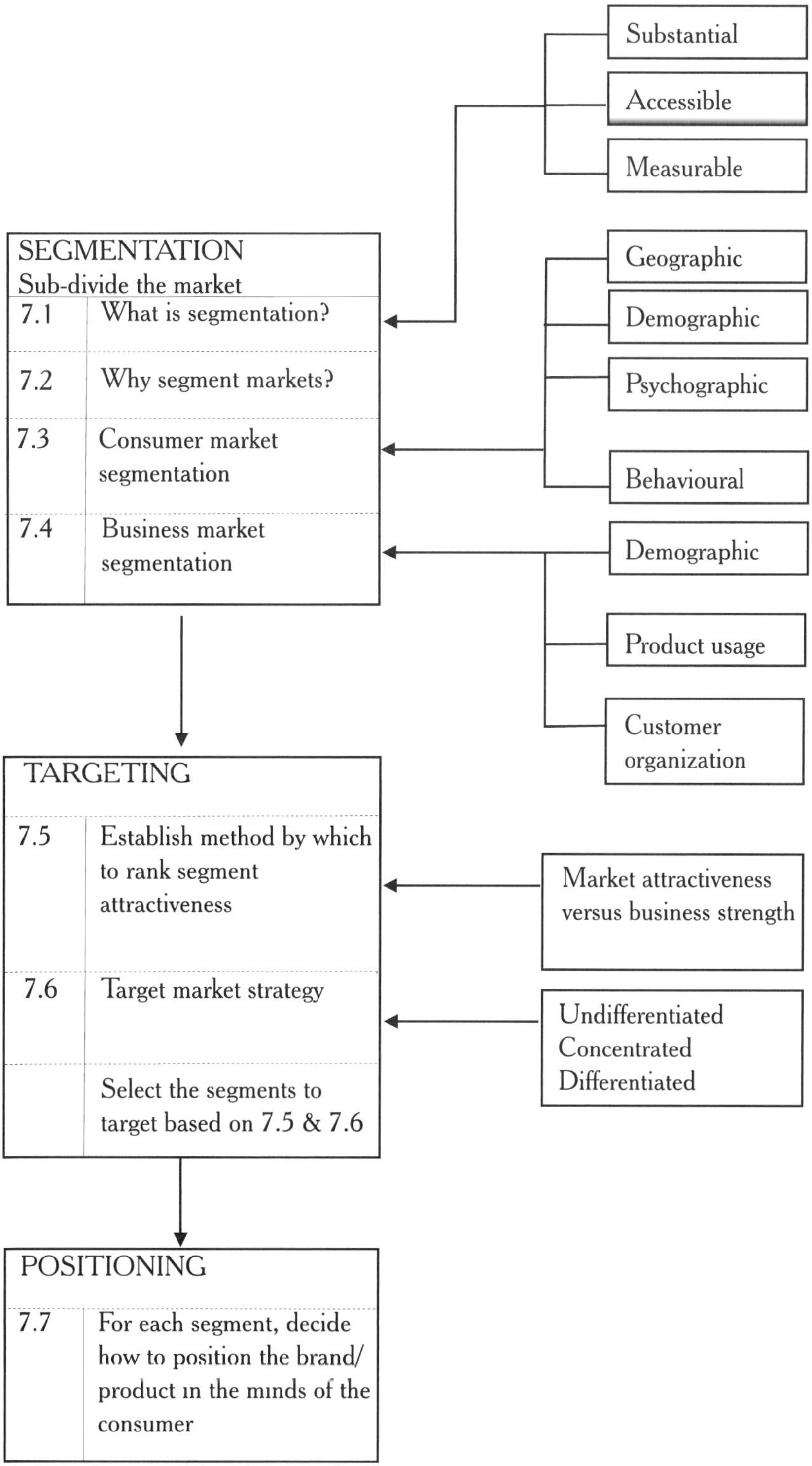

	Substantial
	Accessible
	Measurable

SEGMENTATION		
Sub-divide the market		
7.1	What is segmentation?	
7.2	Why segment markets?	
7.3	Consumer market segmentation	
7.4	Business market segmentation	

Geographic
Demographic
Psychographic
Behavioural

Demographic
Product usage
Customer organization

TARGETING		
7.5	Establish method by which to rank segment attractiveness	
7.6	Target market strategy	
	Select the segments to target based on 7.5 & 7.6	

Market attractiveness versus business strength

Undifferentiated
Concentrated
Differentiated

POSITIONING		
7.7	For each segment, decide how to position the brand/ product in the minds of the consumer	

Introduction

Segmentation, targeting and positioning are the very essence of marketing. These are the key concepts around which all marketing activity revolves. Marketers require ingenuity in devising new segments and such ingenuity can be highly rewarding for their businesses. Once an approach has been established for splitting up the market into homogeneous groups of consumers, the organization must decide on the most attractive groups of segments to target. It is unlikely that all potentially attractive segments may be targeted, because organizational resources are limited. Criteria must be established for selecting the most attractive target segments.

It is not sufficient to establish effective segmentation criteria and then to select optimal segments to target. The marketer must also achieve an effective and differentiated positioning stance for consumers in the target market segment(s). One of the most accessible tools for depicting alternative positioning stances is the positioning map. The map itself is a simplistic tool. The critical aspect of positioning maps is the selection of optimal positioning criteria for use as the map axis labels.

7.1   What is Segmentation?

It is not usually possible to develop a service or product that satisfies all customers in a market. Therefore it is necessary to identify groups of consumers who have similar requirements for the service, or product, offered by the organization.

Market segmentation may be defined as:

> *The subdividing of a market into distinct and increasingly homogeneous subgroups of customers, where any subgroup can conceivably be selected as a target market to be met with a distinct marketing mix.*

> *(Kotler et al. 1999)*

Market segmentation is the subdivision of a market according to *consumer buying behaviour*. It is not the subdivision of markets for the convenience of planning the deployment of the salesforce, or of any other aspect of the marketing mix.

To achieve successful segmentation it must be possible to identify the segments in practice rather than only as a concept, to measure the segment size and to be able to communicate directly with the segment using the marketing mix. For example, it would be very difficult and costly to identify and communicate with people who like to write with green ink. A useful checklist of criteria that a segment must pass is 'SAM':

- S ubstantiality
- A ccessibility
- M easurability

S ubstantiality

Is the segment large enough for the cost of marketing activity to be justified? All segments ultimately could be reached, given infinite resources. But would it make commercial sense? If the segment is too small, is it possible to use fewer factors to define homogeneous segment members so that the segment could increase in size?

A ccessibility

Can the segment be reached by the marketing mix? There are many segments with media devoted to them. For example, magazines for women under 35 years old or for gardeners. These segments are therefore accessible.

M easurability

Data has to be available on the size of the population. This is not a problem for people with credit cards, current accounts, car owners etc., but is a problem for identifying people with a preference for using green ink.

All three elements of the SAM checklist must be used when assessing a market segment. Sometimes the SAM checklist elements are linked. For example, a large customer base (for mass-marketed products and services) automatically makes this segment 'accessible' and 'substantial'.

If companies with big brands such as Kodak, Sony, Federal Express and HSBC want to communicate with their customers they cannot use highly-targeted media as these do not necessarily exist. However, these brands have sufficient numbers of customers, or potential customers, that it is cost-effective to use mass media, such as national commercial TV, to communicate directly.

Small segments tend to be 'inaccessible' unless they have special-interest media devoted to their interests. Stamp collectors would form an 'accessible' small segment because specialist media are devoted to this hobby. However, users of green ink would be 'inaccessible' even though they may be 'substantial'. Because this fails one of the three tests of 'SAM', this is not a marketing segment.

7.2   Why Segment Markets?

The marketing-orientated firm seeks to identify customer needs. It does this because not all customers have the same requirements of the products and services that they buy. Everyone drinks some water for its thirst-quenching benefits, however some people are prepared to pay more for this benefit for a drink that is more interesting to consume than water. The consumer is better off if a new product is provided and the company that provides that new product is likely to receive a financial reward for this innovation. Everyone therefore benefits.

Segmentation is a key aspect of marketing. It is where companies try to attune their product and service 'offers' more closely to the needs of the market. The first banks to provide 'automated teller machines', telephone banking and subsequently Internet banking, realized that some customers, with particular lifestyles, were fundamentally unhappy with a banking system that required them to visit branches in person to conduct transactions. Segmentation by 'access to accounts/financial transactions' became an important approach to aligning bank services and products to customer needs.

In theory, there are two opposing forces operating when an organization considers how to segment its market: consumer demand and attractiveness for the company to supply.

Customer demand	$\neq$	Company supply
Each customer requires a unique combination of product and service attributes		Organizations would like to supply all consumers with a single, uniform product or service. In this case each service encounter or product could be provided at minimum cost to the company.*

* Assumes that firms try to maximize their profits at lowest-cost supply.

The fundamental requirements of the consumer and the company have in the past been different. The compromise, which marketing specialists devised, was to suggest that consumers in a market may be allocated to sub-groups where their service or product requirements are very similar. In that way, groups of consumers with relatively homogeneous interests are created and at the same time the firm is not required to tailor products and services to each individual consumer.

In many fast-moving consumer goods (FMCG) markets there are relatively few market segments. For example, there are only a limited number of combinations of soap powder, or cola, which all consumers would like to purchase. In practice, therefore, for these markets only a few segments exist and most consumers may be allocated to one of these few segments.

It is perhaps over-simplistic to suggest that consumers have a unique set of requirements for any single product or service. The example of soap powder suggests that often only a limited number of segments exist. These ideas may be generalized to a principle of a 'continuum of consumer demand for product attributes'. Some services must be tailored to individual consumer needs, while there is a limited number of segments for other products and services. The attributes of salt, for example, are in universal demand, whereas an order for books purchased over the Internet must be tailored to individual requirements (Table 7.1).

Table 7.1: Continuum of Consumer Demand for Product Attributes

MASS PRODUCT				INDIVIDUALLY TAILORED PRODUCT
● Salt	● Cola drinks	● Non-designer clothing	● Designer clothing	● Internet book purchases
	● Cars	● Pension products	● Specialist cars	● Prescription spectacles
	● Specialist magazines			● Hair cut
	● Current accounts			● Made-to-measure clothing
	● Mortgages			
	● Deposit accounts			
	● Petrol (gas)			

7.3   Segmenting Consumer Markets

There are three main stages involved in target market selection:

● segmentation of the market into various groups;

● targeting of selected segments;

● positioning the product/service in the mind of the consumer using the marketing mix.

This section discusses methods that allow the first stage to be completed. There are many methods of segmenting consumer markets. All may however be categorized under one of four main approaches: geographical segmentation, demographic segmentation, psychographic segmentation and behavioural segmentation.

Geographic segmentation

Geographical approaches to segmentation include the subdivision of the market by country, region, state, county, topography (lowlands, uplands, mountain), climatology (arid, tropical, sub-tropical, temperate etc.), or any other meaningful criterion.

The basis of 'meaningful' geographic segmentation depends on the size of the company and the type of product it markets. It is a highly meaningful segmentation approach for products such as dehumidifiers and air conditioning units, for example. It may also be meaningful in the marketing of food, if for example people are mainly Moslem in the north of a country and of some other religion, e.g. Christian, in the south. Pork and pigmeat products would not be consumed in the north, possibly beef or lamb would be consumed in its place. Similarly for banking practice, Moslem banking practice must be adhered to without the payment of interest on the borrowing of funds, etc.

International consumer market segmentation

The principles of segmentation applied across national boundaries has aspects that are additional to those purely for a single country. Segmentation criteria may be used which may be categorized under the main environmental factors.

Political/legal

Marketing activity is constrained and influenced by political and legal (discussed in Chapter 4 on the Marketing Environment) factors. Countries may be categorized according to the degree of democracy or autocracy, or to the particular legal code that operates within the country.

Economic

The most commonly employed economic factor is wealth, measured on a per head basis (per capita GNP). Wealth is important in determining the consumption patterns within an economy and this is a readily accessible indicator of consumption.

Social/cultural

Because culture has a profound impact on how the marketing mix is used in a country, this is an appropriate approach to segmentation, especially with regard to marketing communications activity. One of several classification approaches that may be used is that of Hall (1987) who produced a classification continuum based on how literal communication is in the country. In Germanic and Scandinavian countries, the meaning of communication can be taken literally from what is stated (termed 'low context' cultures). In 'high context' cultures (examples including Japan and Arab countries) the social context of the message (i.e. who has said what to whom, and where) all add meaning to what is communicated. An understanding of the context is vital for a complete understanding of the message.

Technological

As a broad approximation to the technological state of development of a country, one of the economy classification systems may be used. A three-category system is, for example:

1. Advanced Industrial Country (AIC), i.e. members of the Organization for Economic Co-operation and Development (OECD);

2. Newly Industrialized Country (NIC);

3. Less Developed Country (LDC).

A useful objective means of categorizing economies is to use the percentage of national output generated by the service sector. A relatively simple scale could be applied in which AICs are over 45%, NICs between 15 and 44% and LDCs under 15%.

Demographic segmentation

This is where markets are subdivided on the basis of attributes of the human population. These can include 'physical' aspects, for example: age, gender, race, nationality, family size, 'family life cycle' stage as well as 'socioeconomic' population attributes such as religion, education and income.

Demographic segmentation is an approach in common use because of its widespread applicability across markets and products. Age, for example, is one of the most significant determinants of buyer behaviour from toys, e.g. pre-school, to financial products (personal insurance products).

Family life cycle

This approach has been one of the most widely applied demographic approaches. It has much immediate appeal. Consumers pass through a series of stages as they grow up, mature and ultimately retire. Individuals do not necessarily pass through every stage of the model. At each stage of the family life cycle, consumers exhibit different buying behaviour.

Supermarkets' customers are potentially everyone, so these businesses need a segmentation approach for the whole population. The family life cycle is very much in evidence when you select a shopping trolley at a large supermarket. There are trolleys:

- with no child seats;
- with a seat for a single young child;
- for two young children;
- extra large trolleys for large families;
- small shallow trolleys for the elderly so they do not have to bend down too low.

This segmentation model has also been used by the travel industry and as part of a combination of segmentation variables used by the financial services sector. Table 7.2 illustrates the various stages in the family life cycle. Lawson's (1988) classification system covers over 80% of the population. Particularly difficult households to track are excluded, e.g. households made up of young people living in joint households and households with more than one family.

Table 7.2: Updated Family Life Cycle Model (Lawson 1988)

STAGE	% OF UK HOUSEHOLDS
Bachelor	1.42
Newly married couples	3.11
Full nest 1 (with pre-school children)	11.91
Full nest 1 (lone parent)	1.26
Middle-aged (no children)	1.19

Table 7.2: Updated Family Life Cycle Model (Lawson 1988) (continued)

STAGE	% OF UK HOUSEHOLDS
Full nest 2 (school-age children)	16.97
Full nest 2 (lone parent)	1.92
Launching families (with no dependent children)	6.3
Launching families (lone parent)	1.45
Empty nest 1 (childless, aged 45-54)	9.45
Empty nest 2 (retired)	9.51
Solitary survivor under 65	2.66
Solitary survivor retired	14.17
TOTAL	81.31

Geo-demographic segmentation

This combines geographic segmentation with demographic segmentation. The popularity of this combined approach arises from the need to locate consumers (for marketing activity) who exhibit certain demographically-determined buying characteristics.

The central themes of geo-demographic segmentation are that:

1. Two people who live in the same neighbourhood are more likely to exhibit similar characteristics than are two people chosen at random;

2. Neighbourhoods can be categorized in terms of the characteristics of the population they contain. Two neighbourhoods may be placed in the same category, if they contain similar types of people, even though they are widely separated geographically.

Geo-demographics is thus able to target customers in particular areas who exhibit similar behaviour patterns. The implication for the financial industry is very significant, because this system allows them to profile the users or potential users of a product or service and then proceed to target customers who match these profiles. This of course should increase the profitability of take-up of the offered product/service.

There are several geo-demographic approaches in common use. Here we shall focus on two approaches: ACORN and FinPin.

ACORN

'A Classification of Neighbourhoods' (ACORN) divides the UK into 6 categories which are sub-divided into a total of 17 groups. Together these comprise a total of 54 different types of areas, which share common socio-economic characteristics.

The 17 ACORN groups for 1995 are as follows:

Table 7.3: The ACORN Targeting Classification: Abbreviated List

		% of population
A	**Thriving** (19.7%)	
A1	Wealthy achievers, suburban areas	15.0
A2	Affluent greys, rural communities	2.3
A3	Prosperous pensioners, retirement areas	2.4
B	Expanding **(11.6%)**	
B4	Affluent executives, family areas	7.8
B5	Well-off workers, family areas	7.8
C	**Rising** (7.8%)	
C6	Affluent urbanites, town and city areas	2.3
C7	Prosperous professionals, metropolitan areas	2.1
C8	Better-off executives, inner city areas	3.4
D	**Settling** (24.1%)	
D9	Comfortable middle-agers, mature home owning areas	13.4
D10	Skilled workers, home-owning areas	10.7
E	**Aspiring** (13.7%)	
E11	New home owners, mature communities	9.7
E12	White-collar workers, better-off multi-ethnic areas	4.0
F	**Striving** (22.7%)	
F13	Older people, less prosperous areas	3.6
F14	Council estate residents, better-off homes	11.5
F15	Council estate residents, high unemployment	2.7
F16	Council estate residents, greatest hardships	2.8
F17	People in multi-ethnic, low-income areas	2.1

As an example of a more detailed breakdown of the main six groups, group E ('Aspiring') is presented.

E   *Aspiring (13.7% of population)*

E11   *New homeowners, mature communities (9.7%)*

11.33 Council areas, some new home owners   3.8

Table 7.3: The ACORN Targeting Classification: Abbreviated List (cont.)	
11.34 Mature home-owning areas, skilled workers	3.1
11.35 Low-rise estates, older workers, new homeowners	2.8
E12 White-collar workers, better-off multi-ethnic areas (4.0%)	
12.36 Home owning multi-ethnic areas, young families	1.1
12.37 Multi-occupied town centres, mixed occupations	1.8
12.38 Multi-ethnic areas, white-collar workers	1.1

These various classifications share certain characteristics, including:

a)   car ownership;

b)   unemployment rates;

c)   purchase of financial service products;

d)   number of holidays;

e)   age profile.

Unlike geographical segmentation, which is fairly crude, geo-demographics enables similar groups of people to be targeted, even though they might exist in different areas of the country.

Psychographic Segmentation

Opinions, activities and interests of people are based on their psychological orientation and are therefore termed psychographic segmentation variables. The most common types of variables to use for psychographic segmentation are 'lifestyle', 'social class' and 'personality'.

Social class

'Social class' is a very widely used psychographic classification in the UK, based on socio-economic status (determined largely by occupation and assumptions about income). The JICNAR's social class system has been especially popular in usage. While it remains moderately useful as a classification for newspaper readership, for example, it is both outdated and too imprecise for most other applications. The UK 2001 census will instead use an updated version, which will include an additional classification group as outlined in Chapter 5.

Table 7.4: JICNARS' 'Old' Social Class System

Social class	Status/occupations	Examples
A	Upper middle class – higher managerial and professional	Professionals and directors
B	Middle class – intermediate managerial	Managers and teachers
C1	Lower middle class – junior managerial, supervisory and clerical	Office workers and shop assistants
C2	Skilled working class – skilled manual labour	Electricians and plumbers
D	Working class – semi-skilled and unskilled manual labour	Assembly workers
E	Subsistence – no occupation	Pensioners, students, unemployed.

From a practical marketing perspective, these classifications on their own are unlikely to be useful predictors of homogeneous consumer buying behaviour segments. This is because they are still heavily based on occupation, which can be indicative only of general purchasing behaviour. The main use of such a segmentation approach is in combination with other segmentation approaches such as other psychographic segmentation (e.g. lifestyle) and behavioural segmentation (e.g. benefits sought).

Lifestyle Segmentation Models

Lifestyle models are among the most popular methods of market segmentation analysis. Various models have been suggested by leading commercial research organizations. Four of these include: Young and Rubicam's 4Cs, Taylor Nelson's 'Lifestyle motivation groups', SRI International's VALS model and the Henley Centre of Forecasting.

Young and Rubicam's 4C's (a Cross-Cultural Consumer Characterization) was developed to help to target advertising and marketing activities. It identifies three groups and sub-groups.

- The constrained
  - the resigned poor
  - the struggling poor
- The middle majority
  - mainstreamers
  - aspirers
  - succeeders

- The innovators
  - transitionals
  - reformers.

Taylor Nelson's 'Lifestyle motivation groups' also identifies three main groups which in turn have sub-groups.

A. Sustenance-driven group

  - *Belongers.* What they seek is a quiet undisturbed family life. They are conservative, conventional, rule followers. Not all are sustenance driven.

  - *Survivors.* Strongly class-conscious, and community spirited, their motivation is to 'get by'.

  - *Aimless.* Comprises two groups,

  - the young unemployed, who are often anti-authority

  - the old, whose motivation is day-to-day existence.

B. *Outer-directed group*

  - The balance of the belongers.

  - Conspicuous consumers. They are materialistic and pushy, motivated by acquisition, competition, and getting ahead. Pro-authority, law and order.

C. *Inner-directed group*

  - *Self-explorers.* Motivated by self-expression and self-realization. Less materialistic than other groups, and showing high tolerance levels.

  - *Social resistors.* The caring group, concerned with fairness and social values, but often appearing intolerant and moralistic.

  - *Experimentalists.* Highly individualistic, motivated by fast-moving enjoyment. They are materialistic, pro-technology but anti-traditional authority.

SRI International's VALS model. This identifies nine segments:

1. *Integrated.* Such people are psychologically mature, with an inner sense of what is balanced, self-fulfilling. They have strong feelings on some issues, such as ecology;

2. *Socially conscious.* This group is acutely aware of social and environmental issues. Many choose a simple, non-consumerist lifestyle;

3. *Experiential.* These people are seekers of sensations, and into everything from astrology to Zen. Often intellectual, they welcome the new;

4. *I-am-me.* Such people are described as fiercely individualistic in purchasing patterns. They are show-offs and are impulsive, dramatic and narcissistic;

5. *Achievers* are self-confident, ambitious, materialistic. Their homes and offices are used as symbols of success. They see themselves, quite rightly, as running the show;

6. *Emulators'* chief characteristic is their wish to copy what they believe to be the buying patterns of the rich and successful. They are flamboyant;

7. *Belongers*. This group's motivation is to fit in with the crowd, not stand out. They are often conservative and intolerant of other lifestyles;

8. *Sustainers*. Under economic pressure, they seek to sustain and, if possible, improve their position over time. They are insecure and are nervous of experimenting or taking unnecessary risks;

9. *Survivors* are the most disadvantaged. Their struggle to survive is the dominant force in their lives. Haphazard buying patterns reflect the availability of cash and the impulse of the moment.

Variations on the lifestyle or psychographic approach have been developed, analysing more precisely people's attitudes towards certain goods or services. *The Henley Centre for Forecasting* (1995) has outlined four different kinds of consumers in the market for technological and media products.

Technophiles (24% of the population) 'are enthusiastic about technology in a general sense and also show a high level of interest in applications of new technology. They are concentrated among the under-35s, are more likely to be male than female, and are more likely to belong to social grade C1 than AB'.

Aspirational technophiles (22% of the population) 'are excited in a general sense about technology but are much less interested in its applications. They are more likely to be male than female, and are concentrated in the AB social grade'.

Functionals (25% of the population) 'claim to be uninterested in technology but are not hostile to its applications, especially those areas which offer an enhancement of existing services. These consumers are more likely to be family ... and are most numerous among the over 45s'.

Technophobes (28% of the population) 'are hostile to technology at all levels and are sceptical about whether technology can offer anything new. Technophobes are concentrated in the over-60 age group, are more likely to be female than male, and are distributed fairly evenly through the social grades'.

Personality

This is the behaviour pattern of an individual that is consistent and enduring. Psychologists have developed a variety of theories of personality. Many of these theories attempt to classify the population into personality types. Two different classification approaches from two different models are presented in Table 7.5.

Table 7.5: Examples of Two Personality Types Taken from Two Different Personality Classification Models.

	Personality type A	*Personality type B*
Extract from personality model 1.	*Inner-directed* Where an individual has a strong sense of what is correct (in terms of the behavioural rules of society).	*Other-directed* Where an individual takes a lead from others as to the correct forms of behaviour.
Extract from personality behaviour.	*Compliant* Conformists who seek approval from others and are highly sensitive to the views of others.	*Aggressive* Domineering people who want to 'achieve' and to be seen as 'achievers'.

Application of this work to marketing promotion could use the attributes of 'other-directed' or 'compliant' people who are likely to be followers of fashion or of the role models in the segment to which they belong. Advertising would then focus on role models who would be depicted endorsing the products a firm is marketing. This type of advertising would not appeal to 'aggressive' individuals who would be interested only in products and services that are perceived as being attainable only by the few.

In practice, many psychographic segmentation approaches combine lifestyle and personality segmentation elements, for example *Taylor Nelson's 'Lifestyle motivation groups'*.

Behavioural segmentation

This segmentation approach focuses on aspects of product usage rather than on attributes of the individual consumer. These include segmentation by: usage frequency (e.g. occassional/ regular), usage status (non-user, user, lapsed user), benefits sought, purchase occasion and attitude (towards the product). In addition, buyer readiness state, frequently employed in marketing communications, is also used for behavioural segmentation.

MARKETING IN PRACTICE

Internet shopping and customer segmentation

Shopping online is still a relatively new phenomenon. As consumers get into the swing of clicking, rather then queuing for their goods, they develop new shopping habits – habits that retailers are keen to cash in on.

According to a recent survey by market analysts Datamonitor, web consumers have quite different habits from those shopping on the High Street. Online customers fall into certain categories, exhibiting characteristics that identify them as a particular 'breed' of e-shopper.

One of the most telling results of the survey is that, despite the flurry of dot.com adverts filling the airwaves and billboards, many of us are still wary of making a purchase over the Internet. Although 80% of respondents had browsed the net for anything from CDs to cars, less than a third had actually taken the plunge and ordered online, and even fewer – just 15% – had paid over the Internet.

But, according to the report, all this is about to change. Falling prices mean that computer ownership 'is ceasing to be the preserve of the young and affluent'. And the increasing popularity of interactive TV, games consoles and WAP phones means you do not even need a computer to shop online. More than 70% of Europeans already own at least one interactive device and it is thought that by 2004, more than three-quarters of all households with PCs will be connected to the Internet, increasing the potential online shopping population from its current 19m brave speculators to a whopping 100m big spenders.

Overall, the proportion of Internet users who buy items online is expected to rise from 25% to 70% over the next four years.

Once consumers progress from starter to expert they will inevitably spend more time, and money, on the Internet. Datamonitor spoke to a total of 12,000 people, aged from 18 upwards, in the UK, Sweden, Germany, France and Spain. According to their findings, we are all shopping animals. Which one are you?

The rhino

Not always, but mostly elderly, with 61% of the group being over 65. Rhinos tend to belong to a relatively low-income household, often because of retirement. This consumer wants to see, feel – and if possible sniff – their groceries before they hand over the ready cash. In fact, cash is the preferred method of payment and the thought of putting credit card details onto a computer and clicking on a 'mouse' which sends them to someone they have never met or spoken to is enough to send even the toughest, most thick-skinned rhino charging into the bushes for cover. Only a third of all rhinos have gone online at least once.

The puma

At the opposite end of the shopping jungle lies the puma. Usually young, often single, with a high income and fearless disposition, these predators want their shopping delivered yesterday and are not afraid to try out new technology. If you can get it online, they will buy it, anything from the latest Nike (or possibly Puma?) trainers to a new car. They will even hunt for food online – provided it can be delivered within the hour – and can usually be relied on to try anything once. However, these big cats should remember what curiosity did and be a little more cautious when handing over their financial details, if they do not want to get their claws burned.

The gazelle

Generally 30-somethings, and usually computer literate, these are the lowest-spending group in the younger categories. Youthful and energetic, yes, but unlike the puma, the gazelle has a more timid approach to shopping on the Internet. Moving in herds, often with a young family in tow, they prefer to hang back, saving their hard-earned cash for the things they really need. They are not averse to the web, and will occasionally dip their toe in the water, but they would rather wait to see if it is safe before wading in. Their average online spend in the past six months was £170.

The gorilla

Still preferring to spend most of their substantial income in the High Street, this group is not as conservative as the rhinos and is open to new suggestions. They will eventually get into the swing of shopping on the net, but only after carefully weighing up the pros and cons. Classic gorilla behaviour involves starting slowly with low-risk, familiar items – something from Amazon perhaps and then moving on to bigger transactions as confidence builds. Despite being financially better off than rhinos only 18% of this group had logged on to the Internet.

The jackal

This pack animal has got the Internet sussed and spends most of its day persuading other, less adventurous types, to try out the latest technology. If they are not surfing for a new coat or digging up a bargain CD, they are ordering groceries at home and breathing a contented sigh at not having to fight their way through the crowds in the High Street. Around 10 years younger than gorillas or rhinos, jackals spend approximately 10 times more money on Internet shopping – an impressive average of £440 over six months.

Source: The Guardian *25 May 2000*

Segmentation by benefit sought

This is an almost infinite category and allows the marketer greatest scope for ingenuity. Companies have frequently gained an advantage over competitors by discovering through research or by creating new benefits sought. Benefits sought include anything that the consumer values in a product or service. For example, low price, speed, frequency, easy access to information (for tracking parcel movements), ease of purchase (telephone/ Internet). As for all segmentation variables, the company must deliver, and been seen to deliver, the benefit sought for a given price to a better level than competitors, if this is to be a successful segmentation approach.

'Time saved' continues to be an important benefit sought, which has wide appeal to consumers across markets and products. This ranges from fast-food outlets, ready meals, microwave chips (French fries), photographic developing services, ophthalmic services to Internet banking and stockbroking services.

To conclude this section on segmentation, an example is provided of segmentation of the consumer market for toothpaste, using a range of segmentation approaches.

Table 7.6: Demographic, Psychographic and Behavioural Segmentation of the Toothpaste Market

SEGMENTATION METHOD				
DEMOGRAPHIC Strengths	Children	Teens, young people	Large families	Men
PSYCHOGRAPHIC Personality	High self-involvement	High sociability	High hypochondriasis	High autonomy
PSYCHOGRAPHIC Lifestyle	Hedonistic	Active	Conservative	Value orientated
BEHAVIOURAL Principal benefit sought	Flavour, product appearance	Brightness of teeth	Decay prevention	Price
BEHAVIOURAL Special characteristics	Users of spearmint-flavoured toothpaste	Smokers	Heavy users	Medium users

---

MARKETING IN PRACTICE

FiNPiN

The financial services sector has been active in generating its own approaches to the segmentation of the customer base. PiNPOINT Analysis has developed FiNPiN, a 40 variable-classification system using data from Financial Research Services (FRS).

(See over page.)

Level FiNPiN Types	10 Level FiNPiN Types	40 Level FiNPiN Types
A Financially	i) Most active ii) Financially secure savers	1 'Wealthy' families with older children 2 'Wealthy' families 3 Families with young children and two working adults 4 'Wealthy' families with students and older children 5 Families with growing children and two working adults 6 'Wealthy' empty-nesters 7 'Wealthy' retired
B Financially informed	iii) Multiproduct savers and investors iv) Traditional multiproduct users v) Net savers	8 Established families with older children 9 'Wealthy' urban areas with few children 10 Agricultural families 11 'Wealthy' rural empty-nesters 12 Rural or suburban elderly 13 Suburban families 14 Established families with two working adults 15 Army families 16 'Wealthy' farmers and agricultural workers 17 'Wealthy' self-employed with older children 18 Young professional singles and families 19 Elderly empty-nesters 20 'Wealthy' in flats
C Financially conscious	vi) Average users vii) Uncommitted investors viii) Basic product users	21 Young professional adults, students and ethnic populations in rented accommodation 22 Families with young children in owner-occupied housing 23 Elderly rural empty-nesters 24 Young families in council flats in deprived areas 25 Smallholding and farming families 26 Young adults and ethnic populations in crowded rented property 27 Large families in council houses, mother working part-time 28 Small families in council accommodation with women in part-time work 29 Deprived areas with few children 30 Elderly in small council dwellings
D Financially passive	ix) Inactive borrowers (x) Least active	31 Young adults and ethnic populations in bedsits 32 Established families in council accommodation 33 Young families and ethnic populations in small inner-city dwellings 34 Empty-nesters in council accommodation 35 Large young families in council accommodation 36 Large families in crowded council accommodation, mainly in Scotland 37 Elderly in small council accommodation, in ethnic neighbourhoods 38 Elderly in crowded council neighbourhoods 39 Families with older children in deprived council neighbourhoods 40 Crowded council neighbourhoods with ethnic populations

7.4   Segmenting Business Markets

Segmentation of business markets uses different methods to consumer markets. A framework for segmenting business marketers has been provided by Webster and Wind (1972). Although the detail requires updating, the framework remains valid today. Three main approaches to the segmentation of business customers are on the basis of:

(1) demographic information, although this is a little different to consumer demographic information;

(2) The buyer's usage profile of the product and of the company's product range;

(3) How the firm buys products and services.

1.   Demographic information

● Company size (various measures are used, e.g.: turnover, number of employees, asset value)

● Geographic location

● Type of business most commonly identified by Standard Industrial Classification (SIC) code.

2.   Product usage

● Frequency of purchase

● Volume used (heavy, medium, light)

● Context of use (glass for car windscreens will require particular features). Similarly, a retailer with high asset turnover will have different financing needs to a manufacturer of industrial equipment with low asset turnover.

3.   Customer organization

● Centralized purchasing

● Buying decision-making unit (single person or groups of people)

● Short delivery lead times (e.g. supermarkets for replenishment orders or just-in-time manufacturing)

● Order size

● Loyalty status (sole supplier, preferred supplier, occasional supplier, not yet a customer of the firm).

Market segmentation tools

Tools for creating segments range from 'expert opinion' to statistical techniques. 'Expert opinion' is where someone with industry experience perceives a gap in the market, very probably based on a behavioural segmentation variable. Idea generation is discussed briefly in Chapter 9.

There are several statistical techniques used to create segments. The most common are cluster analysis, factor analysis and conjoint analysis. In principle, these techniques compare the attributes of a subject (e.g. an individual or a product/service) with all other subjects. Subjects are allocated to groups (or clusters) where the differences between subjects are smaller than the differences between groups.

7.5   Targeting

Once an organization has segmented a market, it must select particular market segments to target. Targeting is a two-stage process. The organization must decide:

- how to rank each of the identified segments so that the most favoured segments can be identified (discussed in this section);
- how many of the most favoured segments to target (section 7.6).

Ranking markets

There are two important dimensions that an organization must consider when ranking markets:

1. *Market attractiveness*. How attractive is a market intrinsically? For example, two commonly agreed 'attractive' attributes are market size (large) and growth rate (rapid);

2. *Business strength*. This is about the internal strengths of the business and whether they are appropriate to compete successfully in a chosen market, i.e. the competitive advantage of the business. For example, strong success in telephone banking may be regarded as a business strength when considering a large Internet presence.

Table 7.7: Factors to Consider When Ranking Markets

Market attractiveness	Business strength
● Profitability	● Relative market share
● Market growth rate	● Company image
● Entry costs	● Learning curve effects
● Economies of scale	● Relative product quality
● Price competition	● R&D
● Distribution costs	● Financial strength of the business
● Effect on working capital – what stock levels are needed	● Patents held

The tools and techniques of portfolio analysis (see Chapter 3) may then be used to produce a summary numerical assessment of (a) market attractiveness and (b) business strength. Each market may then be plotted on a market assessment matrix (Figure 7.2).

Figure 7.2: Market Attractiveness-Business Strength Assessment Matrix

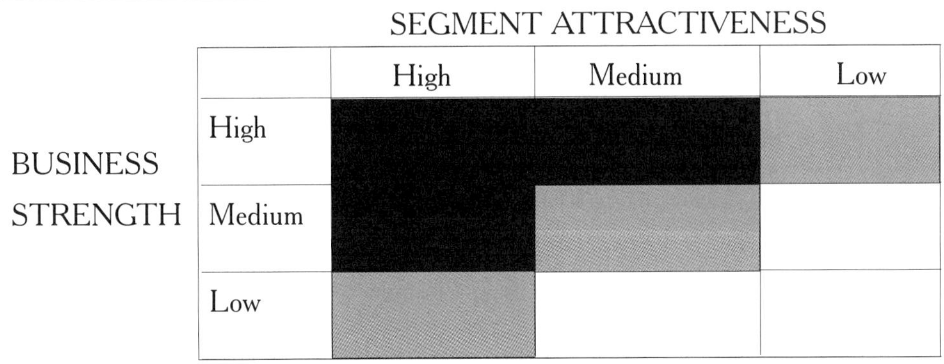

SEGMENT ATTRACTIVENESS

		High	Medium	Low
BUSINESS STRENGTH	High	██████	██████	▒▒▒▒▒
	Medium	██████	▒▒▒▒▒	
	Low	▒▒▒▒▒		

Assuming the risks and resources required are similar for each segment, the company will choose to concentrate its resources and efforts in the segments that offer the best combination of segment attractiveness and competitive advantage (i.e. high segment attractiveness and high business strength). In general, three major zones are identifiable in declining order of interest (more heavily shaded zones preferred). The zone without any shading should be avoided, unless there is an *exceptional* reason for the firm to compete.

Porter's five forces (see Chapter 1) may also be used to assess market attractiveness. For example, a segment that has high barriers to entry might cost more to enter but will be less vulnerable to *competitors*. Retail banking as an industry is difficult to enter because of the high costs of establishing and maintaining a branch network. Banks that only have an Internet presence have found that lack of physical presence constrains their activities so that they can compete individually only in part of the banking market.

Strategically attractive segments
Segments that are most attractive are those whose needs can be met by building on the company's strengths and where forecasts for demand, sales profitability and growth are favourable.

7.6   Target Market Strategy

A target market is a market segment selected for special attention by an organization (possibly served with a distinct marketing mix). Once the attractiveness of each segment has been analysed, and ranked, the organization must choose:

●   one

●   few

- many or
- all segments

to target for marketing activity.

Organizations are not usually able to sell with equal efficiency and success to the entire market, i.e. to every market segment. The marketing management of a company may choose *one of three* general targeting strategies depending on a combination of company resources and market requirements.

1. *Undifferentiated marketing*: this policy is to produce a single product and hope to get as many customers as possible to buy it. No attempt is made to segment the market.

2. *Concentrated marketing*: the company attempts to produce the ideal product for a single segment of the market (for example Rolls Royce cars, Mothercare mother and baby shops).

3. *Differentiated marketing*: the company attempts to introduce several product versions, each aimed at a different market segment, for example:

    - the manufacture of different types of washing powders and liquids (natural and gentle formulations, biological action, environmentally friendly formulations, concentrated liquids, tablets, etc.);

    - different levels of credit cards (standard, silver, gold, platinum).

Figure 7.3: Target Market Strategies

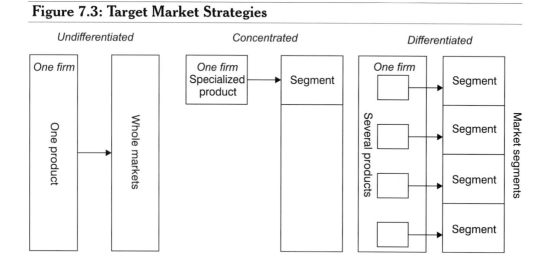

The benefits and problems of each targeting strategy are summarized below (Table 7.8).

Table 7.8: Advantages and Disadvantages of Each Targeting Strategy

	Advantages	Disadvantages
Undifferentiated targeting	Minimize the costs of marketing and production (e.g. product design and development, promotion and administrative costs etc.). Maximize economies of scale in production and storage.	The firm risks being only of general interest to many customers but of no particular interest to any. This means that it is not sufficiently attuned to any particular segment – customers may prefer products and services from companies that are targeting their particular segment.
Concentrated targeting	Specialization in a particular market segment can give a firm a profitable, although perhaps temporary, competitive edge over rival firms. The firm gains detailed market knowledge of the segment and experience of servicing consumer needs.	The major disadvantage of concentrated marketing is the business risk of relying on a single segment of a single market.
Differentiated targeting	The company is maximizing the alignment of the marketing mix to the segment requirements. Customer needs are therefore met. Some of the additional costs listed under 'disadvantages' may not be doubled but only marginally higher as a result of duplication. This will depend on individual products, markets and company circumstances.	Additional costs of marketing and production (e.g. product design and development, promotion and administrative costs etc.) as a result of supplying the needs of different segments. The company foregoes the opportunity of economies of scale in production and storage. When the costs of further differentiation of the market exceed the benefits from further segmentation and target marketing, a firm is said to have 'over-differentiated'. Some firms have tried to overcome this problem by selling the same product to two market segments (for example Johnson's baby powder is sold to many adults for

Table 7.8: Advantages and Disadvantages of Each Targeting Strategy (cont.)

	Advantages	Disadvantages
Differentiated targeting (cont.)		their own use; in the fairly recent past, many hairdressing salons switched from serving women only to serving both sexes). Company resources may be spread too thinly and the company can end up supplying services that are of general interest to all segments but preferred by none.

Organizations are constrained by internal company resource factors and external market factors when they select either an undifferentiated, differentiated or concentrated marketing strategy. Constraints include:

- Limited company resources. Small firms may succeed better by concentrating on one segment only;

- Competition (and the ability of some competitors to match consumer requirements more closely based on expertise, resources, experience etc.);

- Market homogeneity, i.e. the extent to which the product and/or the market may be considered homogeneous. Mass marketing may be 'sufficient' if the market is largely homogeneous (for example, for safety matches);

- Stage in product life cycle. The product must be sufficiently advanced in its life cycle to have attracted a substantial total market (see Chapter 9 on 'Product'); otherwise segmentation and target marketing is unlikely to be profitable, because each segment would be too small in size. An organization with substantial finacial resources may support a small segment if it believes that this segment will grow to become 'substantial';

- Large market size (which may be beyond the capacity of the firm to service).

These are the product, or service, attributes that the organization has control over. In combination, they provide tangible and intangible signals to the consumer, or potential consumer. A consumer purchasing ice cream will be sent very different signals in the following two situations:

1. Hand-made ice cream from an exclusive restaurant in the most fashionable district of the city;

2. Mass-produced ice cream, with skimmed milk powdered added during manufacture to reduce product costs, purchased from a street vendor.

At a basic level, one firm is providing readily available low-cost ice cream. The other firm is providing a luxurious memorable product.

7.7   Positioning

Positioning is where the marketer uses the marketing mix to affect the consumer's perception of the product. The reason why marketers are able to do this is because positioning is not intrinsic to the product or service. Consumers position products and services in their minds according to their perception and this depends on individual, social and cultural factors.

Consumer perception differs even for very basic products. For example, one consumer will perceive a grapefruit as sour and in need of sugar, whereas another will perceive the taste as refreshing and would not want to add sugar. Sensitivity of individual palates is one factor, however social and cultural factors will be influential in forming consumers' opinions as to how acidic a grapefruit must be before it is perceived as 'sour'. North Americans tend to have greater fondness for sweetness. The impact of this ranges from the production of sweeter grapefruits to the manufacture of sweeter burger buns by McDonalds, for the North American market.

Marketers can, instead of changing the product formulation, change the way the existing formulation is perceived. In the grapefruit example, grapefruit producers may decide to market to a segment that values the refreshing properties of grapefruit. A degree of sourness could be marketed as a 'refreshing', 'invigorating' start to the day. A targeted consumer segment would seek these attributes, including a proportion of consumers who previously dismissed the product as unpalatable.

In this grapefruit example, 'positioning' is demonstrated as more than simply intrinsic product attributes. There are no absolute intrinsic attributes. Even the five senses (taste, touch, sight, sound, smell) can be modified with regard to consumer perception. In addition, positioning involves many other attributes, which have no direct relationship with a particular product. For example, while the degree of sweetness/sourness may be linked to grapefruits, attributes such as 'invigorating' are not commonly ascribed to grapefruits, unless marketers choose to devote marketing resources to positioning on this.

Consumer perception of services works in a similar way. It may not be the case that bank A is any more 'receptive' and 'sympathetic' to customer needs than bank B. However if bank A believes, through research, that 'receptive to customer needs' is a segmentation dimension which consumers value, then it will focus its communications, and full service mix, on securing in the minds of consumers that it is the leading bank on this. In other words, it will 'position' on 'receptive to customer needs' and seek to be perceived as the leading bank on this one criterion.

Consumer perception can, for practical purposes, be reduced to product or service attributes, for example 'receptive to customer needs'. The marketer tries to:

1.   Find attributes which the consumer values *and* which are not offered by competitors (using marketing research);

2.   Achieve consumer perception that the firm, or its products and services, has/have the valued attributes to the greatest extent, at a given price level. (This is where another firm is trying to position on the same attribute).

The attributes on which the firm 'positions' must be highly valued by consumers in the target segment, otherwise the positioning will not work.

Influential marketers' views on positioning

'Competitive positioning requires the firm to develop a general idea of what kind of offer to make to the target market in relation to competitors' offers.' (Kotler *et al.* 1999).

Theodore Levitt, writing in the *Harvard Business Review* in 1965, gave a useful commentary on market positioning in the case of banks.

> '. . . no bank can be the best bank for all customers. A bank must choose. It must examine its opportunities and 'take a position' in a market. Positioning goes beyond image-making. The image-making bank seeks to cultivate an image in the customer's mind as a large, friendly or efficient bank . . . Yet the customer may see the competing banks as basically alike.
>
> . . . Positioning is an attempt to distinguish the bank from its competitors along real dimensions in order to be the preferred bank to certain segments of the market. Positioning aims to help customers know the real differences between competing banks so that they can match themselves to the bank that can be of most value to them.'

Positioning maps

Positioning maps are used to present positioning on two attributes. They can also be used to identify gaps in the market. One simple perceptual map that can be used is to plot brands, or competing products, in terms of two key characteristics such as price and quality is presented in Figure 7.4.

Figure 7.4: A Brand Perception Map on the Two Attributes of Price and Quality

This example might suggest that there could be potential in the market for a low-price high-quality 'bargain brand'. A company that carries out such an analysis might decide to conduct further research to find out whether there is scope in the market for a new product that would be targeted at a market position where there are few or no rivals.

Marketers are searching for distinctive positions. That is with clear space (on positioning maps) versus competitors. However there may be logical reasons why there are no competitors in a particular position. In the simple example presented in figure 7.5, the lack of any low-price + high-quality brand may be due to this being unprofitable.

In practice, marketing researchers will establish the most favourable positioning attributes using statistical approaches, such as cluster and regression analysis, which examine many attributes simultaneously. The most favoured attributes are then presented, in two dimensions, using positioning maps.

'Valued' positioning

The positioning stance selected must be valued by consumers. The focus of positioning may be on product and service attributes which are valued by consumers (1). Where the focus is on the consumer, rather than on the product or service, this may be on either the attributes of individual consumers (the user or purchaser of the product/service) or on how and where the individual uses the product or service (2). Regardless of whether the focus is (1) and/or (2), the organization must, in addition to considering the consumer, consider the positioning stance in relation to competitors (3).

1.   Positioning in relation to attributes

This essentially involves positioning the product on the basis of very specific attributes such as performance, durability etc., or positioning on the basis of benefits sought by consumers. For example, many life assurance policies cannot be successfully differentiated and so rely heavily on the issuing companies' reputation for high and stable performance.

2.   Positioning in relation to the user (psychographic)/usage (behavioural)

This can involve positioning on the basis of specific types of users/specific user lifestyles. Amex charge cards were once positioned (e.g. via endorsement by business people as a 'corporate' card. Now Amex emphasizes quality of service). Equally, it may be possible to position the product in relation to usage occasion – summer/winter, day/night, regular/emergency use etc.

These may be linked to one, or some, of the main segmentation categories. Two of the four segmentation categories tend to be favoured:

● Psychographic segmentation

● Behavioural segmentation.

An example of each is provided to illustrate this.

Example of **psychographic** positioning:

Individual/personal

'Travellers cheques are for people who are experienced travellers'

'I almost always keep some travellers cheques in my wallet'

'I think about my safety and security when planning a trip'

'I use a seat belt even when going to the local store for milk'

Product specific ————————————————————— **General**

'We wouldn't even go on an overnight trip without travellers cheques'

'We really appreciate the peace of mind that travellers cheques provide'

'When we go on holiday, our family is always shopping'

'We use the hotel safe to store our valuables when away on a family trip'

Family/household

Example of **behavioural** positioning:

Document movement and delivery may be considered on many dimensions. Two attributes (i.e. benefits sought) that are valued differently depending on market segment are:

- speed
- security.

Very high security

Very fast

Armoured vehicle courier

Motorbike courier

Regular mail/ post – recorded delivery

Regular mail/post

Regular /slow

Low security

3.   Positioning in relation to competitors

This entails presenting the product with features that are to some extent directly comparable with those of competitors. In this situation, there are three basic approaches that could be adopted.

1. *Positioning directly against competitors.* The aim is to present the product as having all the important features of the competitor and a lower price. Obviously this is dependent on whether, from the production/technology side, such a product is feasible. If it is, then there is potentially much to be gained from such a strategy.

2. *Positioning away from competitors.* The product is positioned as having quite distinct/ different features but fulfilling the same consumer requirements. This may be necessary if the competitor's product is patent protected or if it is not feasible to produce a comparable product.

3. *Positioning in relation to a different product class*, but a class that fulfils similar consumer requirements. The current accounts launched by building societies when compared with bank current accounts are strictly speaking different types of product, but they were positioned directly against bank current accounts because they could fulfil the same basic consumer needs.

Other important product decisions concern the precise form of the product and the features that it is to offer. Although we are treating these topics separately it is important to remember that they are clearly interlinked and that the length of the product range and the position selected for the product will obviously have considerable bearing on the features and attributes offered. Equally, the features and attributes which currently exist or which could be offered will themselves have an important bearing on the product's position and the length of the range.

Target marketing by a company involves:

1. The selection of its market (undifferentiated, concentrated or differentiated marketing);

2. Setting as an objective a target share of each market segment (or of the market as a whole, with a policy of undifferentiated marketing).

Competitive Positioning Approaches

There are two main positioning approaches. Focus on the:

- Unique selling proposition (USP), i.e. the functional attribute(s) which differentiates the product from the competition;

- Emotional selling proposition (EMS), i.e. non-functional attributes of the brand. Rolls Royce focuses on supreme luxury, Coca Cola on fun and vibrancy.

USP

Functional attributes, as a positioning stance, are relatively easy to copy and surpass and unless the firm continues to maintain the market position for a set of attributes, through continuous product and service development and innovation, exemplified by the Japanese electronics group Sony, then the product and service range will become dated.

Important functional attributes in positioning are product quality and price, and Kotler *et al.* (1999) identified a 3×3 matrix of nine different positioning strategies.

Table 7.9: Positioning Strategies (Kotler *et al.* 1999)

PRODUCT QUALITY	PRODUCT PRICE		
	High price	*Medium price*	*Low price*
High	Premium strategy	Penetration strategy	Super bargain strategy
Medium	Overpricing strategy	Average quality strategy	Bargain strategy
Low	Hit-and-run strategy	Shoddy goods strategy	Cheap goods strategy

ESP

Emotional selling propositions are less easy to copy. They tend to be used in the medium to long term to develop a personality for a product, service or brand. This is necessary in mature product markets where the differences between products and services are marginal. In addition, this approach is undertaken in markets where the product or service is relatively simple or for markets in which the consumer has very little interest (low-involvement purchases). In these markets, the consumer is unlikely to value minor differences in product and service attributes.

Car manufacturers, as a very large, mature industry, is one of the largest-spending industries on advertising. Close similarities among each of the leading brands results in manufacturers focusing mainly, in their European car advertising, on building an emotional selling proposition with the customer base.

Summary

Segmentation, targeting and positioning are fundamental to marketing. Segmentation involves dividing the market into homogeneous groups of customers. Only valid segmentation methods should be employed. Valid segments are those that possess all the following attributes: substantiality, accessibility and measurability.

Segmentation is a highly strategic decision as all other marketing activity is based on segmentation policy. The success of marketing activity is decided by whether the subdivision of consumers, through the particular segmentation method selected, is meaningful. A wide range of segmentation strategies may be pursued by the marketer. At one extreme each consumer is considered as an individual, i.e. one-to-one marketing. At the other extreme, the market may be considered as consisting of homogeneous individuals. The principles of segmentation strategy may be similar in consumer and business markets, but the segmentation criteria used differ. The main consumer segmentation dimensions are: psychographic, behavioural, geographic and demographic, although geo-demographic is also considered an additional category. Business segmentation has in common with consumer segmentation the demographic approach but in addition business marketers commonly employ two other segmentation approaches, namely segmentation by product usage and by customer organization.

Targeting is also highly strategic, as the organization must decide whether to concentrate resources on one or a few segments, or try to service many or all segments. Three main target market strategies may be followed: undifferentiated, concentrated or differentiated marketing. Such decisions have a profound impact on the resource requirements for the organization, which may constrain its activities in other markets. The fundamental impact of targeting strategy on the business requires strict adherence to predetermined methods for ranking the most attractive segments, once the optimal combination and number of segments to target have been decided.

Positioning is what marketers do to the minds of consumers, relative to the competition. The marketing mix is used to affect consumers' perception of products and services. This may be undertaken without altering product attributes and specifications.

References

Eames L (2000) Consumer shopping animals: so what kind of Internet consumer are you – a gazelle or a gorilla? *Guardian* 25 May

Green P A, Tull D S & Albaum G (1988) *Research for Marketing Decisions*, Upper Saddle River, NJ, Prentice-Hall

Hall E T & Hall M R (1987) *Hidden Differences: Doing Business in Japan*, Anchor Press

Kotler P, Armstrong G, Saunders J & Wong V (1999) *Principles of Marketing*, 2nd European Edition, Prentice Hall Europe

Lawson R W (1988) The family lifecycle: a demographic analysis, *Journal of Marketing Management*, Vol. 4, No 1.

Levitt T (1965) *Harvard Business Review* (September)

The Henley Centre for Forecasting (1995) *The Financial Times*, 30 March

Webster F E & Wind Y (1972) *Organizational Buying Behaviour*, Prentice Hall, New York

8

MARKETING INFORMATION AND RESEARCH

Learning Objectives

After reading this chapter students should:

- Understand the difference between market research and marketing research;

- Know the marketing research process and understand each stage;

- Know the main three research designs and understand the different types of research problems for which each is appropriate;

- Know the main sources of secondary research;

- Understand why primary research should be used rather than secondary research;

- Know the main elements of a marketing information system and understand how these may be used to support marketing decision making;

- Know the four stages in research sampling and understand how they may be applied.

Figure 8.1: Chapter Map

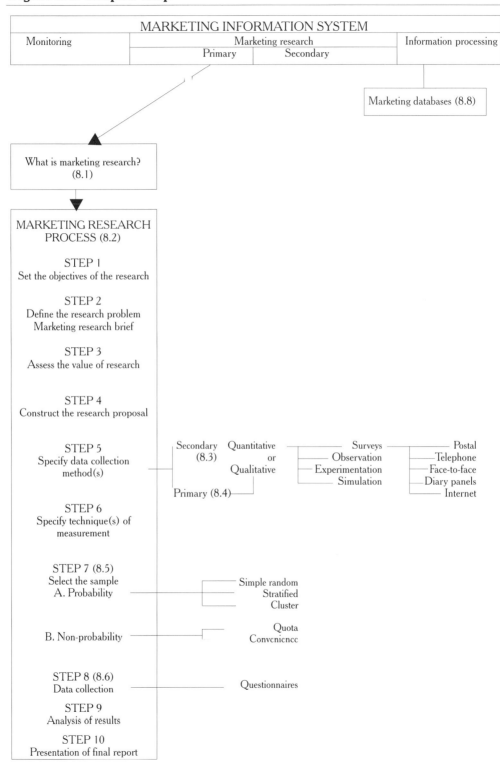

Introduction

Marketing decision making requires information in order for managers to make the best decisions. Where relevant information is not already available to the organization, marketing researchers must obtain the information directly through marketing research. This involves several stages, which begin with translating the marketing problem in to a research problem which may be solved using research techniques. The research process is one of the most important aspects of marketing research. However, within the context of the organization, marketing research is only one element in the marketing information system, which in its turn is a part of the organizational information system. To use marketing research effectively it is necessary to have an understanding of its context within the organization.

8.1   What is Marketing Research?

This chapter explores how marketing research methods and techniques can be used to gain information about the marketplace as an aid to marketing decision making.

Market research and marketing research are often used interchangeably although there is a difference of scope.

Market research refers to finding out information about the market for a particular product or service.

Marketing research (MR) was defined more broadly by the American Marketing Association as:

> '*the systematic gathering, recording and analysing of data about problems relating to the marketing of goods and services.*'

MR thus:

- includes 'problem' (or 'opportunity') identification;
- provides information as an aid to decision making.

Why are Marketing Research and Market Research Important?

Marketing and market research provide information, which can be used in making marketing decisions. The extra information should reduce the risk involved in the decision and thus increase the chances of making the right choice. The trade-off between cost and accuracy is important, particularly because risk cannot be eliminated – there is no such thing as perfect information when dealing with decision making in an uncertain world.

8.2   The Marketing Research Process

Webb suggested ten steps in the marketing research process. These are summarized in Figure 8.2 and each step is discussed separately.

Step 1   Set the Objectives of the Research

Webb suggests that 'marketing research should reduce the need for a company to have to *react*, by making the organization *proactive*, i.e. by sensitizing management to oncoming threats and opportunities in a timely way, such that steps can be taken to avoid those threats or to take maximum advantage of the opportunities'. This may be the general objective of marketing research but individual investigations will need to be concentrated on a specific event or situation.

Marketing research objectives are the result of marketing problems.

Marketing problems

The more accurate the information, the higher the cost. Examples of the types of marketing decision, or marketing problems, which *marketing research* can help with include the following:

a)   Market statistics

- What is the size of the market for a particular bank service?

- What are the trends in the market?

- What is our market share?

b)   Consumer buying behaviour

- What are customers' buying motives?

c)   Marketing communications

- Is our advertising being well received?

d)   Product research

- Are customers satisfied with our products?

- What are the most attractive/least attractive features of our products and of our competitors' products?

- Competitive product research is particularly important in banking in that it is relatively easy for rival banks to copy new products. Hence a new feature introduced by one financial serice provider could easily be copied by others. Market research to identify customer reaction to the new feature should be an essential prerequisite to this process. The response by competitors could aim to improve on any weak points of the new feature which are perceived by customers.

Another example is *cannibalization*. If a bank introduces a new service it is important to identify where the demand is coming from. Ideally, the new service will draw customers from rival banks or building societies. However, if the new service causes customers to drop another of the same bank's services in switching to the new product, then overall profitability could fall if the new service makes a lower contribution than does the one from which customers are switching. This process is known as cannibalization and is to be avoided unless:

- the new service is more profitable than the old service; or

- the new service is less profitable but the alternative would be to switch to a rival's service (obviously with a loss of overall profitability).

Figure 8.2: The Marketing Research Process

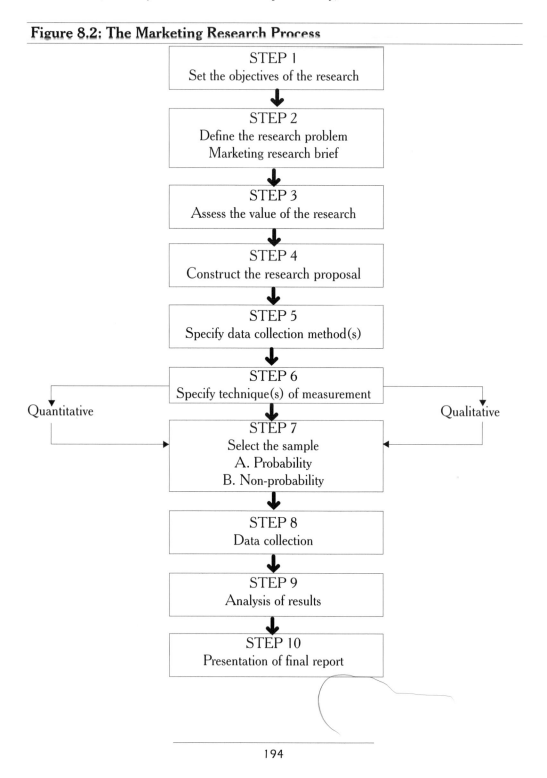

Step 2   Define the Research Problem

This step in the process is of vital importance. It establishes the area of research and the type(s) of data required. Exploratory research may need to be undertaken but at the end of this step it is imperative that there is valid understanding and definition of the problem/opportunity and that an accurate assessment of the environment in which the problem/opportunity exists has been made.

An assessment of the environment may necessitate building a model of the situation so as to allow researchers to put forward hypotheses (possible ways in which the research question may be answered).

Figure 8.3: Summary Stages of Step 2

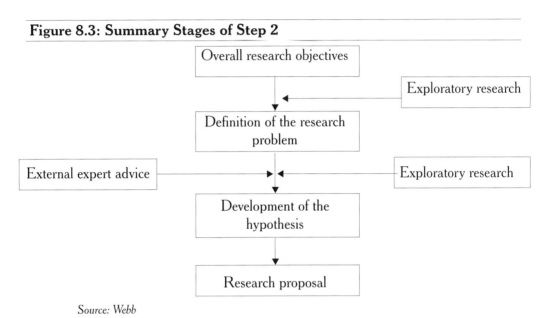

Source: Webb

The end result of Step 2 will lead to the construction of the research proposal (Step 4) but before this an assessment of the value of the research must be made.

Step 3   Assess the Value of the Research

This step involves carrying out a cost-benefit exercise on the desired information. The cost of a research project should always be less than the value of the information provided.

Step 4   Construct the Research Proposal

If the results of marketing research are to prove useful they must provide 'a true, life-like representation of the situation and not a distorted cartoon-like image' (Webb). They can do this only if 'at the problem definition stage of the project there has been an unambiguous request for data relevant to the situation under investigation, data which will be useful to those empowered to take decisions' (Webb). Both client and researcher must therefore agree on the exact constituents of the research proposal. The agreed proposal should therefore be written down and signed by both parties.

The category of research (exploratory, descriptive or causal) must be decided upon. Exploratory research is the least formal and most flexible; causal the most formal but least flexible. Exploratory research looks at the variables which impact on a situation, descriptive research describes them and causal research looks at the relationships between them.

Research approaches (research designs)

Exploratory research

Exploratory research is a blanket term covering whatever style of research is adopted *before* the main research effort is enacted. Any technique might be used: it is the purpose to which it is put that makes this research exploratory.

Initial investigation may help to clarify what is currently uncharted territory. Exploratory research arises, more specifically, in the following situations:

- Where the researcher does not know enough (about a country, a market or some aspect of consumer behaviour) to be able to design a formal research proposal or methodology until the parameters of the situation have been identified;
- Where the researcher wants to generate some meaningful hypotheses before embarking on the main study, and to diagnose the 'problem' in a meaningful way;
- Where the researcher needs to design questionnaires in which consumer perceptions need to be tested but are not known in advance, or where descriptive words and phrases relative to markets or products need to be checked;
- Where the researcher wishes to establish the priorities and objectives of the main research;
- Where the researcher needs information on practical problems (e.g. will certain organizations cooperate?).

Exploratory research is characterized by flexibility, informality and personal intervention.

Descriptive research

Descriptive research measures or estimates the frequencies with which things happen and the degree of correlation between different variables. It aims to discover or elucidate 'facts'. Descriptive research might offer conclusions on the following:

- The overall size of the market
- Market share
- Customer attitudes and behaviour
- Characteristics of various segments.

Descriptive research is often designed to secure specific information (e.g. 'what do you think of banks' approaches to customer care?'), and often rests on a *hypothesis* (e.g. 'customer care is important in the financial services sector').

Descriptive research (design) tries to find the answer to questions such as:

- How many people…?
- What is the favourite…?
- What type of people like…?
- What is the distribution of attitudes on a product or service? E.g. how many people 'strongly agree' that our new investment product is the best on the market?

Causal research

If descriptive research discovers facts, causal research, as its name suggests, aims to ensure the underlying causes for these facts (e.g. 'customer care is important in financial services because customers expect higher standards these days').

Such research is sometimes experimental, and its aim might be to assess which factors are more important than others (e.g. 'inertia, rather than customer satisfaction, explains why customers are often unwilling to switch bank accounts').

Types of research information – Quantitative and qualitative research

There are two types of marketing research information that may be collected, using one of the three research designs: quantitative and qualitative data.

1. *Quantitative research* involves the analysis of numerical information. The main question to be answered is 'How many?' Quantitative analysis ranges from the simple, counting, averages, ranges, to the complex where statistical and other numerical methods are used.

2. *Qualitative research* involves the collection of information on attitudes, beliefs and behaviour. It is mainly concerned with the question 'Why?' This does not aim to establish simple statistical relationships, but instead a group of people explore their feelings and responses to a product offer. This gives information of greater depth than quantitative information, but of less breadth.

Step 5   Specify Data Collection Methods

Data can be collected from either primary or secondary data sources. Secondary data, is 'data neither collected directly by the user nor specifically for the user, often under conditions that are not well known to the user' (American Marketing Association). Most research begins with secondary data collection because it is relatively cheaper and quicker to obtain. Primary data is information collected specifically for the study under consideration and is only undertaken if secondary data is regarded as insufficient (e.g. too old or without appropriate detail).

Step 6   Specify the Techniques of Measurement

This is an issue for quantitative research rather than qualitative, because qualitative research mainly focuses on summarizing attitudes and beliefs in a textual format. Measurement is the process of turning the factors under investigation into quantitative data and requires an appropriate scale of measurement on which the property's characteristics can be measured. In this context, scale means the levels of response that the interviewee is offered. For example:

- Five different salary ranges with a spread of £5,000 within each range;

- Scale for attitude towards a product: Strongly agree, agree, neither agree nor disagree, disagree, strongly disagree.

Step 7   Select the Sample

Time and money will, more often than not, preclude the researcher from conducting a census of each member of the population in which he/she has an interest, unless the population is very small. The researcher must therefore examine a sample. We shall be looking at sampling in detail shortly. Samples may be selected on a probability or non-probability basis.

Step 8   Data Collection Forms

This is when the researcher actually goes out and gets the data. The most common data collection form used for descriptive research is the questionnaire. Observation and experimentation research designs will use other data collection form types.

Step 9   Analysis of Results

The data collected in Step 8 will not itself answer the research problem defined in Step 2. The data will have to be processed into information, which can be communicated to interested parties. Note that certain types or levels of analysis are possible only if the data has been collected in a certain way and has been measured using certain instruments and scales of measurement. The researcher, prior to Steps 6, 7 and 8, should therefore have decided upon the way in which the data should be analysed.

Step 10   Reporting Research Findings

Once the research process has been completed, the researcher will usually present the findings to the client in a face-to-face session at the client's own premises, giving managers the opportunity to ask questions about the results. It takes time and skill to convert the findings into a well-structured oral presentation. The researcher should bear in mind the following factors:

a)   The original problems presented in the research brief;

b)   The extent to which those problems have been resolved;

c)   The people at the presentation (and the key people among those present);

d)   The available time;

e)   The use of visual aids;

f)   The formality (or otherwise) of the occasion;

g)   Avoiding the use of jargon and technical language if necessary;

h)   Making the presentation enjoyable and entertaining;

i)   Methods for involving the audience;

j)   Ways to focus on the results, conclusions and recommendations (the topics likely to be of major concern to senior executives).

It is very likely that the research must be organized in *report form* as well. It is always a mistake simply to prepare the oral presentation from the already written report, because the conventions of report writing are quite different from the criteria that govern effective presentations. A typical report will include the following:

a)   A title page;

b)   A contents page;

c)   An executive summary containing an abstract or synopsis of the whole report (not just the recommendations);

d)   An introduction, giving the background to the research;

e)   The terms of reference (that is, the objectives for the research);

f)   The methods and sampling used;

g)   The main findings;

(h)   The conclusions drawn from the findings;

i)   The recommendations;

(j)   Appendices containing tables, diagrams, copies of research instruments, and other supporting information too detailed to be placed in the main body of the report.

Specific parts of the marketing research process will be discussed in more detail in sections 8.4 to 8.8.

Note

The whole process is *iterative*. In other words, though the arrows (in Figure 8.2) show a logical and progressive sequence, it is possible that earlier phases in the process will have to be revisited, as a result of either information gathered or fresh thoughts or both, at later stages. Once the research proposal has been put together, for example, it may be necessary to rewrite the research objectives, because it has become apparent that some of the objectives are unattainable.

Figure 8.4: The Marketing Research Brief and Research Proposal (Steps 1, 2 & 4 – Figure 8.2)

The key to good research information, whether collected in-house (i.e. by company staff) or an external agency lies in the quality of the research brief. This is a crucial document which includes:

Background. This covers relevant information about the company product, marketplace and the factors that have led to the current need for market information.

The marketing problem. This specifies the marketing problem which the research is trying to support. Writing down the marketing problem helps to clarify the purpose of the research. It is important that vague general statements are not used. For example, the marketing problem is that we are not competiting successfully is too vague. It is better to specify this as the marketing problem is that sales of our new savings product are very low. Greater precision in specifying the marketing problem will help in the specification of the marketing research problem.

The marketing research problem. This may be undertaken in conjunction with the researcher, but defining the problem carefully and agreeing objectives for the research is an essential first step in the research process and is central to the brief.

Too broad a definition leaves the researcher looking for 'everything and anything' whereas too narrow a view can blinker the researcher and limit the potential value of any research. However, once agreed, the objectives should be written down clearly.

For example, the *objectives* of a research study into students' choices of textbooks are as follows:

- Identify the main factors students consider when selecting a textbook;
- Assess the importance of the tutor as influencer in a decision-making process;
- Assess the importance of availability in the final selection of a textbook.

The brief should also contain any constraining factors relevant to the process. These can involve timescale, budget or the degree of secrecy necessary.

8.3 Data Collection – Secondary Research (Step 5)

Market and marketing research data can either be primary or secondary:

- *Primary data is information collected specifically for the study under consideration;*

- *Secondary data*, sometimes called desk research, has been defined by the American Marketing Association as 'data neither collected directly by the user, nor specifically for the user, often under considerations that are not well known to the user'.

Sources of secondary data should always be assessed first. If it already exists, this information is usually relatively cheap and quickly available. That being said, secondary data should be used with caution, because:

- It can be out of date;

- It may be difficult to confirm who produced it, and why;

- Definitions and categories may not be consistent or relevant to the user.

External secondary data sources

1. Trade sources
   Trade associations. Many industries have an industry body, which provides useful marketing research data.

   - The Association of British Insurers (ABI) provides market share data on the life insurance industry.

   - The Society of Motor Manufacturers and Trades (SMMT) provides detailed data on the registration of new vehicles by brand on a regular basis.

   - Chartered Institute of Marketing (CIM), Cookham, England.

   - In addition, the trade press is often a valuable source of information about competitors (for example *Financial World*).

2. Chambers of commerce
   Operate in most countries. In the UK information can be obtained from the British Chamber of Commerce, London tel: 020 7823 2811; the International Chamber of Commerce, London tel: 020 7565 2000.

3. Government statistics
   National government. Government agencies publish a wealth of information, especially about customers. In the UK this includes Social Trends, Census of Population, Family Expenditure Survey and on market conditions, Economic Trends, which can be very valuable and which are easily accessible through libraries. The UK government publishes 'Government Statistics a Brief Guide to Sources' and 'Guide to Official Statistics'. The latter publication is comprehensive and there is a charge in excess of £20 for this.

Pan-regional government. The European Union produces a wide range of publications, details of which may be obtained from the European Union website. The statistical service of the EU usually publishes material through 'Eurostat'.

Pan-regional agencies. The Organization for Economic Co-operation and Development publishes economic analyses of member countries (OECD, Paris). The United Nations, New York, publishes a range of statistics on most countries of the world, which are on a comparable basis. These tend to focus on economic and social statistics.

4. Media
   In an attempt to get more people to advertise with them, TV stations, press and magazine publishers provide detailed analyses of their audiences, which can be useful in market research studies. These are usually available free.

5. 'Off-the-shelf' reports
   A number of research organizations carry out analyses of particular markets and publish and sell the results. Although these reports can be general and/or expensive they can provide a quick way to analyse a new market or competitor. Mintel, Euromonitor and the Economist Intelligence Unit are examples of publishers of this type of study. 'Which?' reports could also be classified into this category.

   One particular example of a research report, which can be purchased, is the National Opinion Poll's Financial Research Survey (FRS). The FRS provides market penetration data over time for a range of personal financial services. It details by sex, age and social class the holders of various financial services (e.g. bank account, credit card etc.).

6. Directories
   Examples of business directories include the following (although there are many others):

   a) *Kompass Register* (Kompass);

   b) *Kompass Financial Information* (Kompass) – Provides the last three years' accounts of listed companies;

   c) *Who Owns Whom* (Dunn and Bradstreet);

   d) *Key British Enterprises* (Dunn and Bradstreet);

   e) *The World's Major Companies Directory* (Euromonitor, London).

   As mentioned above, these directories can make a good starting point. The information provided is usually on industries and markets, manufacturers (size, location), products, sales and profits.

7. Computerized databases include the following:

   a) 'www.ft.com' gains free access to the *Financial Times* website. In addition, free access, at the time of writing, is provided to many thousands of archived articles published by many hundreds of sources, including the *Financial Times*

b) ACORN (consumption indices by class of neighbourhood)

c) PRESTEL (British Telecom)

d) TEXTLINE (abstracts and articles from approximately 80 newspapers)

e) Marketing Surveys Index (CIM)

f) MRS Yearbook (Market Research Agencies and their specialisms).

8. Syndicated services
   If the expense of conducting their own surveys is too great, companies and organizations can obtain general surveys that they can buy into on a shared basis, for example the *Nielsen Retail Audit*. A particular form of shared-cost research is the *omnibus survey*, which are conducted weekly or monthly with a specified target sample and sample profile. Companies can then buy space in the survey for one, or a few, of their own questions. Examples of omnibus surveys include:

   - NOP Financial Research Survey. 60,000 sample each year allows for in-depth interviews (computer-assisted in-home interviews);

   - Youth Omnibus – Carrick James Market Research, London. Surveys 1,200 people aged 11-24, every other month;

   - Omnicar Motoring Omnibus Survey. Motoring omnibus survey sample of 1,000 motorists conducted monthly, in-home at the weekend.

   The advantage is that for a few hundred, as opposed to a few thousand, pounds a company can ask some questions of a reasonably representative sample and have a report sent within two or three weeks. Companies can also link up with others in an industry through their federations so as to conduct shared-cost marketing research surveys.

9. Continuous tracking using panels
   The Nielsen Retail Index. The panel is a representative sample of grocery shops. Researchers audit sales since the last visit. Infrequently purchased items are analysed in greater detail by means of in-home interviews with consumers. Nielsen was the first market research organization to establish continuous retail tracking operations in the UK. The *Nielsen Index* is not an index in the statistical sense, but refers instead to a range of continuous sales and distribution measurements, embracing ten separate product fields, covering consumer goods rather than services. Data is collected from the major supermarket grocery multiples through their EPOS systems. For other types of shop, where EPOS data are not available, researchers undertake a monthly audit of stock, check computer records, invoices and delivery notes to get a precise measure of using data from deliveries, and the level of what sales must have been since the last audit is determined. It is essential to take account of non-EPOS retail units otherwise the survey would generate misleading data.

AGB's Superpanel consists of 8,500 households, covering the purchases of some 28,000 individuals aged between 5 and 79, who are resident in domestic households across

Great Britain which are equipped with telephones. Data collection is through personal data terminals equipped with a laser light pen. The terminal is designed to resemble a digital phone and is kept in a modem linked to the domestic power supply and the telephone socket. Data capture is via overnight polling (which means that AGB's central computer dials each panel number in turn and accesses the data stored in the modem). All that is required from informants is that when they unpack their shopping, they pass the laser light pen over the barcode for each item, and also enter standardized data about the date, shop(s) visited, prices paid and so on. The process incorporates procedures for entering details of products either without barcodes or that have a barcode that is difficult to read.

Taylor Nelson claims *Omnimas* to be one of the largest single random omnibus surveys in the world, with some 2,100 adults being interviewed face-to-face every week.

BMRB's Target Group Index (TGI). TGI's purpose is to increase the efficiency of marketing operations by identifying and describing target groups of consumers and their exposure to the media (newspapers, magazines, television and radio) and the extent to which they see or hear other media.

In design, the TGI is a regular interval survey and is also 'single source', in that it covers both product usage data and media exposure data. Respondents are questioned on a number of areas:

● Their use of 400 different products covering 3,500 brands;

● Their readership of over 170 magazines and newspapers;

● Cinema attendance;

● Independent (i.e. commercial) television viewing habits;

● Listening patterns for commercial radio stations;

● Their lifestyles, based on nearly 200 attitude questions.

The major product fields covered are foods, household goods, medicaments, toiletries and cosmetics, drink, confectionery, tobacco, motoring, clothing, leisure, holidays, financial services and consumer durables. It is worth noting that respondents are only asked about the use, ownership and consumption of the products identified, not about purchases made or prices paid.

Lifestyle questions are in the form of Likert-type attitude statements, with which people are asked to agree or disagree on a five-point scale from 'definitely agree' to 'definitely disagree'. These attitude statements cover the main areas of food, drink, shopping, diet/health, personal appearance, DIY, holidays, finance, travel, media, motivation/self-perception, plus questions on some specific products and attitudes to sponsorship.

TGI results supply enormous amounts of information, both within categories and cross-tabulated against other relevant categories.

a) Total numbers of product users for each demographic category

b) Percentages of product users in each demographic category

c) Information on heavy/medium/light and non-users for each product or product category

d) For brands and product fields with more than one million claimed users, consumption can be cross-tabulated against a range of demographic variables including sex, age, social class, area, number of children, and media usage.

e) Brand usage tables, listing the following:

    i) *Solus users* – users of the product group who use the brand exclusively;

    ii) *Most-often users* – those who prefer it, but use another brand as well;

    iii) *Minor users* – whose who do not discriminate between brands.

Company secondary data sources (Internal data)

Internal secondary data are records inside the organization, gathered by another department or section for the research task in hand. They therefore include the following:

a) Production data about quantities produced, materials and labour resources used and so on;

b) Data about inventory;

c) Data about sales volumes, analysed by sales area, sales person, quantity, price, profitability, distribution outlet, customer and the like;

d) Data about marketing itself, such as promotion and brand data;

d) All cost and management accounting data;

e) Financial management data relating to the capital structure of the firm, capital tied up in stocks and debtors, and so on.

Webb (1992) gives an alternative summary of internal sources of data:

a) *Accounts* contain information on:

    i) customer's name and location;

    ii) type and quantity of product purchased;

    iii) costs of sales, advertising and so on.

b) *Sales records* contain information on:

    i) markets;

    ii) products;

    iii) distribution systems.

c) *Other reports* contain information on:

i) trade associations and trade fairs;

ii) exhibitions;

iii) customers complaint letters;

iv) previous marketing research reports;

v) conferences.

You can see that some of the information collected by particular departments in an organization would be useful to other departments within the business. It is often the case, however, that there is little inter-departmental communication of such information. In an organization with good information channels between departments, such data would be reported to other interested departments. For example, bad debt and credit control analysis should be passed from accounts to the sales department. Similarly, the breakdown of customers by geographic location indicated by the return of guarantee cards could be sent to the sales department from the customer service department. A problem may be that information passed from one department to another is in a format that is unsuitable for that second department to use. The increasing use of management information systems has made data manipulation straightforward. This allows inter-departmental data to be adjusted as required.

Despite the problems associated with internal secondary data, it can be extremely useful for sales and marketing, as the following examples show. Not all of them, as you will see, relate to financial services as such.

a) *Order/sales statistics (by customer)*. An understanding of who the customers are allows marketing activity to be directed appropriately (promotions, invitation to sponsored events, and so on). Having a correct view of the types of existing customers and where they live allows consumer product companies to use geodemographic databases to target other like-minded people susceptible to buying the product.

i) Sales representatives need to understand who their most important customers are to be able to manager their time effectively. Very important customers may be categorized as needing contact once a month, medium-sized customers as needing to be seen every quarter, and so on.

ii) Trends need to be monitored as the 'league table' of customers will change and new important customers should be given the most appropriate treatment.

b) *Sales statistics (by product)*. These allow product managers to monitor the popularity of products to help to decide where to direct the marketing activity and which products to withdraw so that the most appropriate ones are available. Having an appropriate mix of products is required to maintain good customer relationships.

c) *Delivery details*. Where these are different from customer/order details, they help the representatives to identify new contacts and new sites/establishments.

d) *Profitability (by product/by customer).* It is important that the salesforce put their energy into spending time with their most profitable customers and building relations with them accordingly.

e) *Complaints.* Having an understanding of the nature of complaints can help sales and marketing people to communicate with the customers more effectively. It may be a question of explaining the functioning of the product differently or changing the customers' expectation and perceptions.

f) *Stock levels.* Knowing that there is stock that needs to be shifted quickly or that a particular item will need two weeks' notice can help the sales staff seem more professional and interested in their customers.

g) *Debtor information.* A representative could have spent a lot of time building up a good relationship only to have the time wasted by a letter going out from the accounts department threatening to withdraw credit facilities. It would be preferable to discuss such matters with the sales manager and in certain instances ask the manager or representative to discuss it directly with the customer (or at least know that it may not be a good time to call!).

The basis of good relationships with customers is having the right amount of information about one's own business and the customers' business. Much of that information is available in-house and it is important that sales and marketing staff are given such data and that they communicate back to other departments any intelligence acquired (impending bankruptcy or an imminent large order for example) so that the appropriate steps can be taken by other departments.

The use of secondary data will generally come early in the process of marketing research. In some cases, secondary data may be sufficient in itself, but not always.

Advantages and Disadvantages of Secondary Data

Advantages of secondary data

Secondary data may solve the problem without the need for any primary research; time and money is thereby saved.

Cost savings can be substantial because secondary data sources are a great deal cheaper than those for primary research.

Backdrop to primary research
In unfamiliar territory, it is natural that the marketer will carry out some basic research in the area, using journals, existing market reports, the press and any contacts with relevant knowledge. Such investigations will aid the marketer by providing guidance on a number of areas:

a)   Possible data sources

b)   Data collection

c)   Methods of collection (relevant populations, sampling methods and so on)

d)   The general state of the market (demand, competition and the like).

A *technique in itself*

Some types of information can be acquired only through secondary data, in particular trends over time. The historical data published on, say, trends in the behaviour of a market over time cannot realistically be replaced by a one-off study.

Secondary data, while not necessarily fulfilling all the needs of the business, can be of great use by:

a)   Setting the parameters, defining a hypothesis, highlighting variables – in other words, helping to focus on the central problem;

b)   Providing guidance, by showing past methods of research and so on, for primary data collection;

c)   Helping to assimilate the primary research with past research, highlighting trends and the like;

d)   Defining sampling parameters (target populations, variables etc.).

Acquisition studies

In the secretive and competitive world of take-overs (particularly contested take-overs), primary research is not always possible. Field research would show the aggressor's hand too soon and so secondary data sources would be exploited, mainly in two areas:

a)   *Company description:* history, structure, financial situation, production methods, employee resources etc.;

b)   *Products and markets:* products and product policy, promotional activity, competitors and markets.

In spite of all these uses of secondary data, it has been shown that many businesses do not use secondary data to full advantage. Many sources are left untapped.

Disadvantages of secondary data

1.   Relevance. The data may not be relevant to the research objectives in terms of the data content itself, classifications used or units of measurement.

2.   Cost. Although secondary data is usually cheaper than primary data, some specialist reports can cost large amounts of money. A cost-benefit analysis will determine whether such secondary data should be used or whether primary research would be more economical.

3.   Availability. Secondary data may not exist in the specific product or market area.

4.   Bias. The secondary data may be biased, depending on who originally carried it out and for what purpose. Attempts should be made to obtain the most original source of the data, to assess it for such bias.

5. Accuracy. The accuracy of the data should be questioned. Weiers (1988) suggests the following checklist:

    i)   Was the sample representative?

    ii) Was the questionnaire or other measurement instrument(s) properly constructed?

    iii) Were possible biases in response or in non-response corrected and accounted for?

    iv) Was the data properly analysed using appropriate statistical techniques?

    v)   Was a sufficiently large sample used?

    vi) Does the report include the raw data?

    vii) To what degree were the field-workers supervised?

    In addition, was any raw data omitted from the final report, and why?

6. Sufficiency. Even after fulfilling all the above criteria, the secondary data may be insufficient and primary research would therefore still be necessary.

The golden rule when using secondary data is use *only* meaningful data. It is obviously sensible to begin with internal sources and a firm with a good management information system should be able to provide a great deal of data. External information should be consulted in order of ease and speed of access: directories, catalogues and indexes before books, abstracts and periodicals. A good librarian can be a great help.

It is worth remembering Peter Jackson's comment (on Desk Research):

> *All that is published is not necessarily accurate. It may even be quite untrue. However, print conveys authority and there is a common tendency to take published data, uncritically, at face value. Computer databases possibly legitimize dubious data to an even greater degree. The thorough researcher should therefore attempt, wherever possible, to evaluate the accuracy and reliability of secondary data.*

8.4   Data Collection – Primary Research

Primary research is required if secondary research does not provide enough information to support marketing decision making, perhaps because it is:

- out of date
- too general
- from an unreliable source
- provides highly unexpected results which need to be corroborated.

The type of primary research required depends on the marketing problem that needs to be solved and whether a descriptive, exploratory or causal research design (section 8.2) has been selected. Primary research may be placed into two categories: quantitative research or qualitative research. In general, where little is known about the attitudes and beliefs of the target segment, or their views on a product area, then exploratory research will be undertaken – an approach that emphasizes qualitative research. Where much is known but the relative number of people holding different views is uncertain, then descriptive research is undertaken and this tends to rely on quantitative research. Experimental research tends to be used less frequently and commonly to support decision making in specific areas such as test marketing.

Quantitative research techniques

There are four main approaches to quantitative research:

- Surveys
- Observation research
- Experimentation
- Simulation.

Surveys

This is the most commonly used quantitative research method. Individuals may be selected using probability sampling or non-probability sampling, information may be collected anonymously or not, individuals will always be aware that they are providing information, but in some cases the research sponsor may be anonymous. Information may be collected by survey in one of five ways, by:

1. Postal research questionnaires
2. Telephone research
3. Face-to-face interviews
4. Diary panels
5. Internet research.

Postal research questionnaires

Questionnaires are sent to respondents for self-completion using postal services, or other appropriate means of distribution. The major limitation of postal research is the low response rate. Anything higher than 10% is considered a reasonably good rate of return. Response rates may be increased by follow-up reminders, telephone reminders, freepost return envelopes and a carefully selected target audience who may have more interest in the topics under investigation than would a random sample. Response rate ranges, however, could vary from 1% to over 90%.

Pre-coding the questionnaire makes analysis of the data more straightforward. Tick box questionnaires are easy for respondents and stand more chance of providing the researcher with a higher response. Good clear layout with space and not too many words on the page are more attractive and stand a better chance of completion. A covering letter explaining the purpose of the survey and the benefits to the respondent are more successful in achieving reasonable response rates.

Telephone research

Telephone research is a relatively fast and low-cost means of gathering data compared to personal interviews. It is most useful when only a small amount of information is required. It also has benefits to the respondent in terms of the short amount of their time taken up by interview. It has been particularly useful in industrial research, although the technique has been widely used for consumer research with the growth in home telecommunications. There are a number of other benefits to telephone research: a wide geographical area can be covered cheaply from a central location, the researcher having no need to travel between respondents; it may be easier to ask sensitive or embarrassing questions.

Disadvantages of telephone research

1) A biased sample may result from the fact that a proportion of people do not have telephones and many of those who do are ex-directory.

2) It is not possible to use 'showcards' or pictures.

3) The refusal rate is much higher than with face-to-face interviews.

4) It is not possible to see the interviewee's expression or to develop the rapport that is possible with personal interviews.

5) The interview must be short.

6) Respondents may be unwilling to participate for fear of being sold something.

CATI (computer assisted telephone interviewing) has been used successfully by insurance services and banks as well as consumer research organizations. The telephone interviewer calls up a questionnaire on screen and reads questions to the respondent. Answers are then recorded instantly on computer. Complex questions with questionnaire routing may be handled in this way. For example, if the answer to question 4 is yes, proceed to question 10 and so on.

Face-to-face interviews

Most survey work in the UK is conducted through face-to-face interviews, usually by employees of a market research company. Their prevalence as a data collection method and the quality of the data collected are probably due to their obvious advantages.

Advantages of face-to-face interviews

1) The interviewer can check the respondent is suitable before beginning the interview.

2) The use of an interviewer ensures that all questions are answered in the correct order.

3) The interviewer can check that the respondent has understood the questions and can encourage respondents to answer as fully as possible.

4) Response rates are generally higher than with other forms of questionnaire administration.

5) Where quotas are applied (such as 20 women under 30), the interviewer can ensure that the target number of interviews is achieved.

6) Interviewers can attempt to persuade respondents to take part in the survey.

Interview surveys can be classified according to where they are carried out.

Store/mall intercept surveys are carried out in busy town centres, especially shopping centres/ malls. The interviewer tends to stand in one position and approaches potential respondents as soon as the previous interview is completed, thereby eliminating time between interviews. The interviews need to be brief, however, because respondents are unlikely to want to stop for more than ten minutes.

In-house (or more accurately door-step) interviews are part of those surveys where respondent recruitment is door-to-door. Interviewers may be given a list of names and addressees, or they may be limited to certain areas. Moreover, they may be given additional information such as call at every fourth house. In contrast to mall intercept interviews, in-house interviews may be prearranged by telephone. Such interview methods can be time consuming but longer interviews than in mall intercept surveys are possible (although likely to be interrupted).

Hall tests refer to interviews carried out in a pre-booked location. Recruitment is usually from a nearby street and respondents are often given refreshments. Materials, videos and displays can be used.

In-store surveys may take place in a shop or just outside. Permission will of course be needed from the shop. Recruitment could be on the basis of people leaving or entering the store. A study of shopping intentions would require recruitment from the latter.

Business interviews will normally take place at the interviewee's place of business but will need to be arranged in advance.

Diary panels

A diary panel may be an important source of continuous data. These are usually run by an independent market research agency that will sell the results to interested companies. It is a useful method of research when a decision-maker wants to discover the effects of various decisions on a target audience. For example, the effects of promotional messages or price change. Panel data is most effective in consumer research.

A representative sample of respondents is selected and respondents are asked to keep a diary. The diary is provided by the researcher and respondents are asked to record specific data of interest to the recorder. The diary builds up continuous data from the panel who are (should be) representative of a larger population. Inferences can be drawn from diary data.

Internet research

The Internet can be a valuable research tool and can be used to conduct both secondary and primary research. There are in excess of one billion web pages containing information on the Internet and therefore it is often difficult to find the required information. However, the wealth of information available at the touch of a button makes this sometimes-difficult task worthwhile. Search engines such as Yahoo and Alta Vista, and multiple search engine software, such as Copernic and Ask Jeeves, are invaluable methods of using key words to identify relevant websites. Information that is in the public domain, such as company reports, government reports and newspaper articles, are often available free of charge. Commercial information, such as Mintel reports, is also available via the Internet but often only if purchased. Many different forms of information can be gathered via the Internet such as:

- Information about the macro-environment, such as economic trends, government legislation, technological developments;

- Competitor and other company information, such as annual reports, takeovers and partnerships;

- Customer information such as buying trends and customer characteristics.

Increasingly primary research is being carried out over the Internet. This is restricted to some extent by the number of people who have Internet access. However, with the higher penetration of Internet access in businesses, this is an approach that many B2B companies are now adopting.

Observation

Observation is frequently used when managers want to evaluate the impact of a new store layout or the response to a proposed new package design. In these situations, asking questions may produce responses of limited value. It is better to simply observe, and possibly video, customer behaviour. Customer browsing habits in a store may be observed to assess the impact of new floor layouts of merchandise. In a bank, customer movement and queuing may be observed and assessed, before altering branch layouts to improve customer service.

Experimentation

In a controlled *experiment*, a controlled research environment is established and selected stimuli are then introduced. For example, in assessing magazine advertising, consumers may be shown a 'made up' magazine (i.e. which looks like a real magazine) with adverts. Their response to the adverts will be assessed. They will then be shown other copies of the magazine with different adverts or with the adverts in different locations. Each magazine is a different experiment and consumer reaction to each experiment will be assessed in this relatively controlled environment.

An environment may be described as 'controlled' to the extent that 'outside' factors can be eliminated from the environment (e.g. other marketing stimuli and competitive products).

Depending on the degree to which a controlled environment is established, the observed effects can be measured and related to each stimulus. Controlled experiments have been used to find the best advertising campaign, the best price level, the best incentive scheme, the best sales training method etc.

When experiments are conducted in more realistic market settings, results are less reliable because of the researcher's inability to control outside factors. Nevertheless, the local market reaction to a new product, for example, is often a prerequisite to a national launch. This is known as a test market. It is expensive and time consuming because it is necessary to establish the repeat purchase rate. Nonetheless it provides valuable information to the marketing team prior to a national launch.

Simulation

This is a mathematical representation of the world. Simulations are often combined with a visual representation of the situation that is being simulated. For example, in simulating shoppers in a supermarket, to help in deciding how to arrange store layout, the simulation model could visually represent the store layout and the movement of people in the store and at the checkout tills. In constructing even the most basic simulation, the modeller would require information on:

a)   The number of shoppers arriving at the store and the time of arrival throughout the day;

b)   The amount of time people spent in the store;

c)   The amount of time it takes to process a customer at the checkout tills.

In addition, to introduce some realism in to the simulation it would be necessary not simply to use a single average figure for (b) and (c), but to make assumptions about whether all shoppers could be allocated to one of several groups which exhibit similar shopping behaviour. For example, a retired couple would have a very different behaviour profile to someone shopping on behalf of a family with children. The family life cycle (see Chapter 7) may be an appropriate way to segment the population for this type of simulation.

Qualitative Research

Qualitative research in marketing is characterized by these features:

a)   It is based on open-ended interview methods;

a)   It collects data that is largely qualitative and in the form of narrative rather than isolated statements;

c)   It is not susceptible to statistical analysis.

There are other features which are common to qualitative research, but which are not defining characteristics.

●   The use of small samples of respondents who are not necessarily representative of a larger population.

- The direct involvement of the research executive in a number of stages of the research, including the planning and design phases, conduct of the interviews, results analysis, and presentation of the data to the client(s).

- A concern for understanding consumer perceptions and consumer behaviour, rather than measuring the extent of their occurrence.

Until the 1970s, qualitative research was often dismissed as not serious, lacking in scientific rigour, non-replicable, non-generalizable and subjective. In the past few years, however, qualitative techniques have enjoyed a rapid growth in popularity for a number of reasons:

- Greater understanding and appreciation of the roles that qualitative research can perform;

- Its relative cheapness and speed;

- Its proven effectiveness in a growing range of applications.

With techniques like group discussions, depth interviews and projective tests, the results are reached not by a scientific and objective process, but by subjective, interpretative approach. This is not to dismiss this approach because it has produced many useful insights for the marketers. Researchers must be dispassionate. In fact it is no different from acting on the advice of an 'expert' whom one expects to provide conclusions that weigh all sides of an argument.

Qualitative research techniques

1. Depth interviews

2. Group discussions/focus groups

Depth interviews

Motivational research often uses the psychoanalytic method of *depth interviews*. The pattern of questioning should assist the respondent to explore deeper levels of thought. Motives and explanations of behaviour often lie well below the surface, which is only scraped by structured and semi-structured techniques of interviewing. It is a time-consuming and expensive method of data collection. Taped interviews and analysis of transcripts is often the way in which the depth interview and subsequent data analysis are conducted. A single individual or a small team may conduct depth interviewing. Depth interviews may have fewer than ten separate respondents.

Advantages of depth interviews:

1) Detailed information, such as information on decision-making processes, can be gathered from one respondent at a time, thereby aiding clarity of interpretation and analysis;

2) Intimate and personal material can be more easily accessed and discussed;

3) Respondents are less likely to confine themselves simply to reiterating socially acceptable attitudes.

Disadvantages of depth interviews:

1) They are time consuming to conduct and to analyse. If each interview lasts between one and two hours, a maximum of three or four per day is often all that is possible;

2) They are more costly than group discussions;

3) There is a temptation to begin treating depth interviews as if they were simply another form of questionnaire survey (see below), thinking in terms of quantitative questions like 'how many' rather than qualitative issues like 'how', 'why' or 'what'. A skilled interview 'moderator' will ensure that this problem does not arise.

Projective techniques

People may find difficulty in articulating their motives which lie buried deep within the sub-conscious mind or may tell people what they think others want to hear. So as to overcome problems associated with articulating complex or subconscious motives, researchers have borrowed techniques developed by psychologists in their studies of mentally disturbed people who have difficulty explaining why they do things. These techniques are referred to as *projective techniques*. Attitudes, opinions and motives are drawn out from the individual in response to given stimuli. A number of techniques might be employed. Here are some examples.

Word association

This method is based on an assumption that if a question is answered quickly, it is spontaneous and subconscious thoughts are therefore revealed. The person's conscious mind does not have time to think up an alternative response.

Sentence completion is a useful way to get people to respond quickly so that underlying attitudes and opinions are revealed. Interviewees may be asked to complete the following types of sentences

> Banks are places where ...?
> People who use Internet banking are ...?
> Someone who has not taken out a life insurance policy is...?

In *thematic apperception tests* (TAT tests), people are shown a picture and asked to describe what is happening in the picture. They may be asked what happened just before or just after the picture. It is hoped that the descriptions reveal information about deeply-held attitudes, beliefs, motives and opinions stored in the subconscious mind.

Potential problems with projective techniques
1) Hard evidence of their validity is lacking. Highly exotic motives can be imputed to quite ordinary buying decisions.

2) Analysis of projective test findings is highly subjective and prone to bias.

3) Many of the tests were not developed for the study of marketing or consumer behaviour, and may not therefore be considered scientifically valid as methods of enquiry in those areas.

4) There are ethical problems with 'invasion' of an individual's subconscious mind.

5) The major drawback with projective techniques is that answers given by respondents require considerable and skilled analysis and interpretation. The techniques are most valuable in providing insights rather than answers to specific research questions.

Marketing decisions where projective techniques are most suitable
Since motivational research often reveals hidden motives for product/brand purchase and usage, its main value lies in the following:

1) Developing new promotional messages which will appeal to deep, often unrecognized, needs and associations;

2) Allowing the testing of brand names, symbols and advertising copy, to check for positive, negative and/or irrelevant associations and interpretations;

3) Providing hypotheses that can be tested on larger, more representative samples of the population, using more structured quantitative techniques (questionnaires, surveys etc.).

Group discussions/focus groups
Group discussions are useful in providing the researcher with qualitative data. Qualitative data can often provide greater insight than quantitative data and does not lend itself to the simple application of standard statistical methods. A focus group is retained for several discussions.

Group discussions usually consist of eight to ten respondents and an interviewer taking the role of group moderator. The group moderator introduces topics for discussion and intervenes as necessary to encourage respondents or to direct discussions if they threaten to wander too far off the point. The moderator will also need to control any powerful personalities and prevent them from dominating the group. Group discussions may be audio or videotape recorded for later analysis and interpretation. The researcher must be careful not to generalize too much from such small-scale qualitative research.

Group discussions are often used at the early stage of research to get a feel for the subject matter under discussion and to create possibilities for more structured research. Four to eight groups may be assembled and each group interviewed for one, two or three hours.

Advantages of group discussions:
1) The group environment with 'everybody in the same boat' can be less intimidating than other techniques of research, which rely on one-to-one contact (such as depth interviews);

2) What respondents say in a group often sparks off experiences or ideas on the part of others;

3) Differences between consumers are highlighted, making it possible to understand a range of attitudes in a short space of time;

4) It is easier to observe groups and there is more to observe simply because of the intricate behaviour patterns within a collection of people;

5) Social and cultural influences are highlighted;

6) Groups provide a social context that is a 'hot-house' reflection of the real world;

7) Groups are cheaper and faster than depth interviews.

Disadvantages of group discussions

1) Group processes may inhibit some people from making a full contribution and may encourage others to become exhibitionistic.

2) Group processes may stall to the point where they cannot be retrieved by the moderator.

3) Some groups may take a life of their own, so that what is said has validity only in the short-lived context of the group.

4) It is not usually possible to identify which group members said what, unless the proceedings have been video recorded. This can be very time consuming and costly to analyse.

8.5   Sampling

Most primary research is based on a survey rather than on a full population census.

Advantages of sampling

- Saves money
- Saves labour
- Saves time
- More elaborate and detailed information can be collected

There are four sampling questions that the researcher must answer:

1. Who or what is the target population?

2. Which population list will be used as the basis for selecting a sample? [Sampling frame]

3. Which sampling approach will be used? [Sampling procedure]

4. How large a sample to select? [Sample size]

1.   *Who or what is the target population?*
Define the population of interest, which is all those people likely to be interested in buying a particular bank service in a defined region. 'Population' in statistical terms does not

necessarily refer to people; it means the entire body of items about which we require information. It may be people who play golf, or it may be all golf clubs manufactured by a company (when sampling for quality control purposes).

Before any statistical work is attempted the population must be properly defined. This is not always easy. For example, attempt to define 'housewife'. Is a housewife a woman with no other occupation or is she a working woman who also looks after a house? Is she a woman who lives in a house, a flat or a caravan? Does she have to do the housework or can she employ someone to do it for her? Is she single or married? And finally is the 'housewife' actually a woman in the first place? Changing employment patterns mean that men frequently share in jobs with the home and family, as well as having sole responsibility for these tasks.

In marketing research for consumer goods, it will be impossible to obtain data from every consumer in the market, because not only would this take too much time and cost too much money, but it would also be impracticable. (In a small market, however, such as an industrial market or government market, a census might be practicable and preferable to a sample survey.) To obtain data, it is therefore usually necessary to obtain a sample to provide an estimate of the characteristics of the entire 'population'. A survey approach is used which involves asking questions of the target market or population. The larger the sample, the greater the likelihood that the sample will provide an accurate reflection of the population as a whole. Questions can be limited and highly structured, in the form of questionnaires delivered by post, telephone, e-mail or in person. This generates quantitative data providing factual responses such as how much, how many, when and where purchases were made.

Another problem associated with defining the population is that its full extent may not be known, e.g. the number of people with a suspected disease.

2. *Which population list will be used as the basis for selecting a sample? [Sampling frame]*

Specify the sampling frame. A sampling frame is a list of all those in the population of interest. If the population of interest is solicitors, for example, *Yellow Pages* or a list of local members of the Law Society may be suitable as a sampling frame.

Every factor of the survey design is influenced by the sampling frame – the population coverage, the stratification that is used, the method of sample selection. Questions to ask about a sampling frame are offered below:

● Does it adequately cover the population to be surveyed?

● Is it complete?

● Are all members of the population on it?

● Is it accurate and as up-to-date as possible?

● Do any items appear more than once?

● Is it arranged in a convenient way for sampling? Is it readily accessible?

No frame is likely to completely satisfy all the above criteria. It is important, however, in view of the influence of the frame on the following stages of the survey they should all be considered.

Sampling frames can be broadly classified as follows:

1) *Lists of individuals*, either of the whole population or of the groups within it. Examples include the electoral register, the lists of members of professional bodies and lists of company employees;

2) *Complete census returns.* Unfortunately the manner in which the data is collected and processed tends to prevent its use as a frame;

3) *Returns from an earlier census.* How useful previous surveys are depends on the questions asked in the original survey and if the data is up to date;

4) *Lists of dwellings as a frame.* Council tax lists are useful as a frame for obtaining samples of dwellings;

5) *Large-scale maps.* Ordnance survey maps have a grid system which enables areas to be broken down into suitably sized blocks. Sometimes a problem is the availability of up-to-date large-scale maps – there has been much town and city redevelopment in recent years.

The two frames most generally available are:

● Local government lists of people living in every house in the area, used mainly to collect local government (council) taxes;

● Electoral register.

3. *Which sampling approach will be used? [Sampling procedure]*
Sampling requires clearly defined sampling procedures. The first procedural decision is which one of the main two approaches to sampling to select?

● probability sampling or

● non-probability sampling

For each approach there are several sampling methods. These are:

Probability sampling

● Simple random sampling

● Stratified random sampling

● Cluster sampling

Non-probability sampling

● Quota sampling

● Convenience sampling

The best method for any particular enquiry depends on:

- the nature of the population to be sampled;
- the resources, e.g. time and money available;
- the degree of accuracy required.

In general, probability sampling tends to be more expensive and time consuming, but produces a greater degree of accuracy. This is only a general principle because technology has reduced the cost of probability sampling, which is incurred mainly in the selection and interviewing of the sample. For example, telephone surveys where computer-controlled random dialling is used adds very little additional cost to any single survey.

Probability sampling
To obtain a representative sample is far from easy.

All probability sampling approaches include an element of random sampling. The strengths of random sampling as an approach are that it allows:

- the accuracy of the target variables to be measured (e.g. number of people who prefer a product, the annual fee for a credit card which a particular segment is prepared to pay, etc.);
- probability estimates to be made of the degree of confidence which the researcher has in the survey results (e.g. 95% confident that consumers prefer our branch design to those of our two main competitors).

A *random sample* is a sample selected in such a way that every item of the population has an *equal chance of being selected*.

Random samples are not perfect samples. There are potential problems with random sampling:

- A random sample of all the people living in England could result, simply by chance, in all of the people selected living in one county, e.g. Cornwall. Random selection does not guarantee that the sample will be free from bias – only that the *method of selection* is free from bias;
- Random sampling is likely to result in a large geographical spread of the sample to be surveyed and this will be expensive to research;
- There may be no suitable sampling frame (e.g. bald men). Multistage, quota and cluster sampling are used to overcome these difficulties.

There are various probability sampling approaches which include random sampling:

1. Simple random sampling
2. Stratified random sampling
3. Cluster sampling (including multi-stage sampling).

Simple random sampling

This is where a sample to be interviewed or assessed is selected *at random* from a population list. The population list may be:

- people in a telephone directory;
- customers who have returned product registration forms;
- customers/potential customers who have logged onto the company Internet site;
- people visiting a branch outlet;
- every 10,000th credit card transaction;
- every 100th component coming off a production line.

Stratified random sampling

In stratified sampling the researcher does not want to risk a pure random sample producing, by chance, a sample with limited application. For example, if a conclusion on customer behaviour is required comparing male and female customers, then a sample with only male customers will not be of much use. It is possible that a simple random sample will produce a list with only male customers. In this example, the researcher may specify two strata to include 50 males and 50 females.

In stratified random sampling the population must be capable of being divided into strata, which may conform to a consumer characteristic or a market segment. For example, a bank analyst may regard age and average account balance as the two main factors influencing customer up-take of a new financial service product. In this situation, it will be important to ensure that customers selected for interview are spread across age and account balance levels. Stratification by age (five levels) and by average account balance (4 levels) will result in 20 segments. In this simple example the analyst will expect results in each of these segments to be different. This will test the hypothesis that uptake of the new product will vary according to age and average account balance.

Table 8.1: Sample Stratification by Age and Average Monthly Account Balance

Age	Average monthly balance (£)				
	1-10,000	10,001-20,000	20,001-30,000	Over 30,000	Total
Under 18	16	3	1	0	20
18-25	5	10	4	1	20
26-40	2	3	7	8	20
41-60	1	4	10	5	20
Over 60	1	5	3	11	20
Total	25	25	25	25	100

Note: Percentages refer to allocation of total sample, e.g. of 1,000 consumers.

Cluster sampling

This method is normally used to cut down the number of investigators and the costs of travelling etc. This approach is usually used on a geographical area. It uses a two-stage sampling approach, like stratified random sampling, which requires that a geographical area is divided into smaller areas. For example, in the UK:

● the country is divided into counties or regions;

● each county/region is subdivided into parts – the parishes.

In the stylized example (Figure 8.5) of a country cluster sampling process, seven UK counties have been selected, two at random. The second stage of sampling requires selection within each of the two areas selected at the first stage, in order to minimize travelling distances to interview people. In this example, three parishes (UK) have been selected at random in each of the two counties (UK).

Figure 8.5: Stylized Country Illustrating Two-Stage Cluster Sampling

Sub-region PARISHES	COUNTIES (UK)						
	1	2	3	4	5	6	7
1					X		
2		X					
3					X		
4							
5		X					
6		X			X		
7							
8							

Note: In the USA, for example, the country is divided into states which could equate with the UK counties. Each USA state may be subdivided into counties, which are the American subdivisions of a state.

Non-probability sampling

In practice non-random methods are used frequently, but these are more prone to bias. There are various non-probability sampling approach. Discussing the two main methods, convenience sampling and quota sampling, provides an understanding of this approach.

Convenience sampling

This is based on the convenience of the researcher. If a researcher is asked to undertake a street interview with a large number of people, then for convenience a location will be selected where large numbers of people pass. For example, train stations, football grounds, shopping centres etc. In some cases this will obviously create a very biased sample. If a survey is on the attitude of people to shopping centres rather than to traditional main street shopping, then interviewing people in shopping centres, for convenience, will bias the results of this research towards a positive response. Traditional shoppers will largely be excluded from this convenience sample.

Quota sampling
Investigators are instructed to interview all the people they meet up to a certain quota. A large degree of bias can be introduced. For example, an interviewer may fill his or her quota by only meeting housewives out shopping. In practice, this problem is partially overcome by subdividing the quota into different types of people, e.g. on the basis of age, sex and social class.

Sample bias

In dealing with the unknown, we need to be sure that our sample is not unrepresentative or biased. If the characteristics of the sample are different from those of the population, then the inferences we draw from studying the sample will be unreliable. Bias can occur for any number of reasons:

1) The conscious or unconscious preconceptions of the researcher about the nature of the population can cause bias. It is not possible to obtain an unbiased sample by selecting *deliberately* the items to be included;

2) Another type of bias arises if members of the population are allowed to select themselves. Mail surveys show this form of bias;

3) Substitution of an item selected by a random process by another (chosen at whim);

4) Bias is introduced if part of the sample is missed. This is particularly common in mail surveys. Ideally *everyone* should reply;

5) Other causes of bias are:

   i. badly phrased questions, e.g. 'You do have a car'?

   ii. the tendency of the person being interviewed to give answers he or she thinks will be acceptable to the interviewer.

4 How large a sample to select? [Sample size]
The general principles of sample size selection are based on a compromise between 'survey precision' and 'survey confidence'. We can be 100% confident that everyone in the country earns between £0 and £100 million per month. The level of precision of this estimate is however very low. It is so low that it is meaningless.

In contrast we could talk to a few people and calculate an average of £1017.12 per month. This is a very precise estimate. It is so precise that we would have very little confidence that it was a meaningful, useful result.

Figure 8.6: Trade-off Between Precision, Confidence and Sample Size

High precision	Medium sample size	Large sample size
Low precision	Small sample size	Medium sample size
	Low confidence	High confidence

The trade-off between accuracy and cost is an important consideration in the determination of sample size. It is possible to use statistical theory to specify how large a sample is required. In practice, the sample needs to be big enough to get a representative view of the total market. Opinion poll research on voting intentions of 22 million voters are based on about a thousand interviews, for example.

8.6 Data Collection Forms

Data may be collected and summarized in various ways which range from structured approaches, using observation forms and questionnaires, to unstructured approaches. In the latter approach, the recorder simply notes down points of interest, perhaps when conducting part of a focus group or in noting shopping behaviour. The larger the volume of data collected the more important it is to structure information as it is collected. This makes the task of processing and analysing the data much quicker and easier.

By far the most common approach to the collection of data is the 'questionnaire'.

Questionnaire Design

The first step in any type of survey is the outlining of the information to be obtained. The researcher has then to develop a set of questions, which can be answered correctly by the respondents.

a. All the factors which seem to have some bearing on the problem must be set out.

b. These factors must be discussed with people likely to have some special knowledge of the problem.

Once the list of factors is verified, questions can be drawn up and the questionnaire designed. Each question should be tested against the following criteria.

a) What is the interviewer trying to find out by asking this question?

b) Will all the target respondents understand the question?

c) Will all the target respondents know how to answer?

d) Have clear unequivocal instructions been given on the format of the answer?

e) Having got answers to the question, can they be analysed meaningfully?

The initial draft of the questionnaire should be discussed with colleagues prior to being tested in a pilot survey.

Table 8.2: Checklist for Questionnaire Design

1	Be clear about the purpose of the research.	9	Try to find out why people did not respond and take actions by re-designing future questionnaires as appropriate.
2	Select your target group or sample very carefully.	10	Analyse non-responses.
3	Construct questions carefully to avoid bias.	11	Make sure your responses are representative of the whole sample.
4	Do not make the questions too difficult or too long.	12	Use open as well as closed questions when appropriate.
5	Keep questions unambiguous.	13	Give considerable thought as to how the data will be processed and analysed.
6	Do not provide too many choices.	14	Never lose sight of the purpose.
7	Keep the questionnaire relatively short (this should give a higher response rate).	15	Balance cost and benefit.
8	Be prepared to send a second questionnaire to a respondent as appropriate.	16	Always pilot the questionnaire by trying it out on a few respondents before sending it to your sample. This gives you the opportunity to refine it.

8.7   The Marketing Information System

A marketing information system is more than just data collection. Data by itself is often of little use. It is simply a set of facts and figures. To be of use, data must be transformed into information; that is to say, it must be organized into a systematic and meaningful framework. This is the function of a marketing information system. It will typically comprise a structure of individuals, procedures and equipment which are organized to collect, sort, analyse, evaluate and distribute up-to-date information required by marketers in the planning management and control of marketing activities. Traditional market research, which is often thought to be concerned primarily with consumers and their buying behaviour, is only one component of this information system.

Figure 8.7: Question Types

Name	Description	Example

CLOSED-END QUESTIONS

Dichotomous — A question with two possible answers.

In arranging this trip, did you personally phone British Airways?

Yes ☐ No ☐

Multiple choice — A question with three or more answers.

With whom are you travelling on this flight?

No one	☐	Children only	☐
Spouse	☐	Business associates/	
Spouse and		friends/relatives	☐
children	☐	An organized tour group	☐

Likert scale — A statement with which the respondent shows the amount of agreement/disagreement.

Small airlines generally give a better service.

Strongly disagree	Disagree	Neither agree nor disagree	Agree	Strongly agree
1	2	3	4	5

Semantic differential — A scale connecting two bipolar words, where the respondent selects the point.

British Airways
Large .... Small ....
Experienced .... Inexperienced ....

Importance scale — A scale that rates the importance of some attribute.

Extremely important	Very important	Somewhat important	Not very important	Not at all important
1	2	3	4	5

Rating scale — A scale that rates some attribute from 'poor' to 'excellent'.

Excellent   Very Good   Good   Fair   Poor

Intention-to-buy scale — A scale that describes the respondent's intention to buy.

If an inflight telephone was available on a long flight, I would

Definitely buy	Probably buy	Not sure	Probably not buy	Definitely not buy
1	2	3	4	5

OPEN-END QUESTIONS

Completely unstructured — A question that respondents can answer in an almost unlimited number of ways.

What is your opinion of British Airways?

Word association — Words are presented, one at a time, and respondents mention the first word that comes into their mind.

What is the first word that comes to mind when you hear the following:
Airline _____
British _____
Travel _____

Sentence completion — An incomplete sentence is presented and respondents complete the statement.

When I choose an airline, the most important consideration in my decision is _____
_____

Story completion — An incomplete story is presented, and respondents are asked to complete the sentence.

I flew BA a few days ago, I noticed that the exterior and interior of the plane had bright colours. This aroused in me the following feelings

Picture completion — A picture of two characters is presented with one making a statement. Respondents are asked to identify with the other and to fill in the empty balloon.

The inflight entertainment's good

Thematic Apperception Test (TAT) — A picture is presented and respondents are asked to make up a story about what they think is happening or may happen in the picture.

Figure 8.8: A Marketing Information System

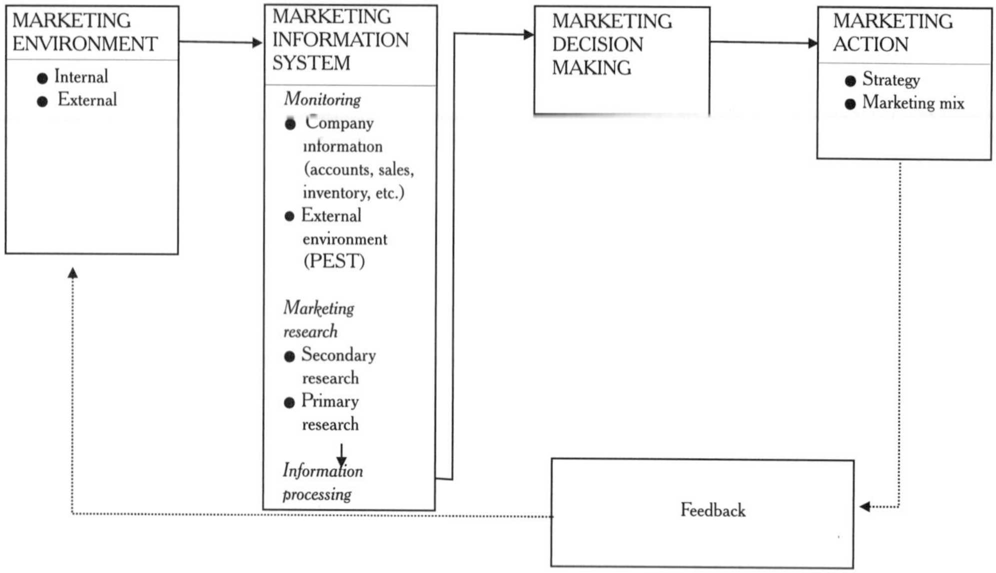

Typically, a marketing information system will have three main inter-linked components.

Monitoring

This comprises two main elements: company data monitoring (internal data) and external environment monitoring (Figure 8.8).

Company information monitoring. Essentially this refers to all data generated internally and often originates from accounting databases. In a manufacturing company, it covers information on costs, production schedules, orders, sales and may also include some types of financial information relating to customers. Where available it would also include product profitability information. For a financial services company, accounting databases would also be a major source of information with fixed costs and information technology costs of major interest as well as financial information which allows the calculation of product profitability.

External database. This covers all types of information (PEST) collected from external sources. It may simply take the form of press cuttings, trade journals or discussions and information from competing organizations. However, it may also include subscriptions to external databases such as those supplied by Prestel, Dun and Bradstreet etc. Some organizations may also subscribe to databases supplying information on consumers and their personal profiles, credit ratings such as those supplied by CCN or by other systems such as Pinpoint and Finpin.

The marketing research system

While the internal and external databases generally focus on information that flows into an organization on a regular basis, marketing research is normally a process of information collection and analysis that is undertaken on an 'as needed' basis, although this 'as needed' basis may often be sufficiently frequent to support a specialist department for this function. Such research can provide a variety of information from consumer views of the product or the supplier through to evaluations of the efficiency of distribution systems and the effectiveness of advertising.

Information processing

Information processing consists of a series of analytical techniques that enable marketing managers to make full use of the information provided by the monitoring and marketing research systems.

- Some of the information available may be used in the form in which it is presented but much requires further processing and analysis – increasingly, the simple retrieval of information from databases is insufficient to aid decision making. Basic processing and analysis may involve only the selection of appropriate people for the distribution of information or the reformatting and summarizing of information, e.g. sales patterns. Other tasks may include simple financial ratios to more complex statistical models.

- The information may be utilized in various decision-making models/tools. For example, with a simple econometric model of sales/advertising responsiveness linked to marketing accounts, the manager can analyse the impact of changes in advertising expenditure on sales, revenues and profitability.

- Developments in expert systems can be used to guide more complex marketing decisions. Increasingly, decision-support tools are available directly to managers rather than requiring specific programming expertise. However, it is typically the task of marketing information systems to develop and operationalize the appropriate tools and provide the necessary access to the data.

The *information system* is linked to the various sources of data and will process and analyse information for management use. The information may be available from existing databases or may require more specific analysis of the marketing environment. The marketing information system receives internal and external information. This information, once collected and analysed, is transmitted back to management to enable planning decisions to be taken and strategies developed.

Strategies in turn will have some impact on the business environment and monitoring this impact is a key component of the marketing management function. Therefore, further analysis is required from the information system during the course of plan implementation to enable monitoring and control.

In response to management requirements the information system will collect and analyse data relevant to the marketing plan; any significant deviations from targets can then be identified and management is in a position to develop tactical responses.

The ability to develop and use marketing information systems has been greatly enhanced by the rapid pace of developments in information technology, which now allow large volumes of information to be stored, organized and analysed. The development, internally, of sophisticated customer databases is one key aspect of a marketing information system, which could have considerable implications for the development of effective targeted marketing campaigns. The banking sector has, in the past, played an important role in the computerization of business activities and all the banks have large and sophisticated electronic data processing and communication systems. The development of information systems has not been neglected as such, but rather it has developed in different directions. Historically, many of the developments in banking information systems have been orientated towards the internal needs of management rather than the external needs of marketing. Thus, although all banks held detailed databases concerning customers and their accounts, these were organized around:

- the need to manage and monitor the accounts; rather than
- the need to build up profiles of and relationships with their customers.

Databases in the banking sector have traditionally been account (not customer) based. The pressures of increasing competition have encouraged the banks to move towards a system centred on customers, but even so the sector still lags behind consumer goods organizations in terms of the development and use of marketing information systems.

The typical problem with computerized databases that have been developed by banks is that they were constructed for accounting purposes and to facilitate the handling of transactions in the most efficient manner. It was noted above that this kind of system might not be particularly suitable for marketing purposes. If a marketing campaign is planned with the intention of targeting a certain segment of the customer base with a direct mail shot promoting a new product, accounts-based information may make it impossible to select customers with the characteristics of those identified as most likely to purchase the product. This issue is of particular significance given the growing importance of direct mail, a trend that is expected to continue.

More generally, the kind of marketing information system referred to above may be developed in an IT context. Routine contact with customers, for example, provides a crucial source of data. Detailed information may be obtained, for instance, from mortgage applications or new account application forms. Together with other marketing information on general trends in the financial services sector, it is possible to construct a computerized database to aid various marketing functions. The marketing information system so developed is shown to be a sub-system of the firm's overall management information system and is required to be consistent with and able to coordinate with the firm's overall corporate strategy.

In the development and use of such as system there is a need to ensure quality control of the information which is input. Where the intention is to enable branch managers, for example, to use it to undertake decentralized marketing campaigns, it is essential that they know how to use the system effectively (and actually do so). A general issue in the development of databases using significant amounts of personal details for marketing purposes concerns the need for accuracy and other security issues.

MARKETING IN PRACTICE

Predicting the future

Forget forecasting. When it comes to predicting consumer behaviour, the tools and techniques available today to financial services firms are much more sophisticated. By analysing real data, they can make scientific and reliable projections.

Given large amounts of data on customer behaviour, there are many techniques that can be used to predict future behaviour. It is an extremely complex area and there are only a handful of experts in Europe able to build models using the best techniques for different cases. Some models are based on the following:

- Algorithms
- Decision trees
- Case-based learning
- Knowledge-based induction rules
- Supervised neural nets
- Unsupervised neural nets.

The main choice is between the expert system and the neural network. These are techniques used commonly in the high-volume, low-amount credit arena, the main example being in credit cards. It is, perhaps, easiest to explain the difference between the rules-based expert systems and the artificial intelligence technique of neural nets by looking at credit cards.

Man versus machine

Both types of system aim to use knowledge of the pattern of payments to determine the probability that a payment may be fraudulent for that card and that extra security precautions should be taken.

For example, if the system recognises that a three-year-old card has only been used to buy groceries in a supermarket in South London, when it suddenly appears in Geneva and is being used to buy a £5,000 watch, the system will alert this as a potentially fraudulent transaction. Expert systems and neural networks have different approaches to achieving the same conclusion.

With expert systems the programs take a set of rules and apply these rules to all the transactions passing through the central system. As with all such systems, the rules are created and applied in a hierarchical fashion. Each transaction must therefore pass a hierarchical set of tests. When a test is failed, the system increases the probability that the transaction is fraudulent. The rules themselves are set by experts who write their knowledge into the system usually based on a statistical analysis of an expert's experience of fraud.

The alternative, the neural network, is being increasingly used. In this case the system is allowed to work out its own set of rules. A neural network is a self-training computer program that can take its experiences and derive new rules to apply to future events. If these events do not have the expected outcome then the results are fed back into the system so that the rule set is adapted and reapplied over time.

Neural networks require vast amounts of information from which to extrapolate rule sets. It will be fed large amounts of transaction information and, by looking for correlations, flag what it defines as fraudulent transactions.

The main problem with such systems, especially neural nets, is that they require vast amounts of data. These correlations form the basis for the set of rules by which the neural network operates. It all used to be seen as a very grandiose technology requiring vast amounts of computer power and data facilities. Now, however, with most large retail finance organizations developing data warehousing technologies to support their marketing and customer service operations, the information needed by the network is more readily available.

In comparison, a neural network can learn over time and can react to change automatically, while the process of updating an expert system can be complex due to the impact a change in one rule may have on others. The availability of data warehouses and very powerful on-line processors also makes neural network technology more accessible.

Expert applications

These two artificial intelligence technologies can be used at many levels. Card issuers can look at customer behaviour while merchant acquirers can apply it to the other major area of fraud, that of merchant or retailer fraud. In turn, card schemes can look at international transactions to spot cross-border activity. The card schemes are not universally adopting one technology, and indeed most neural networks are a combination of a network and some expert rules. Some companies, such as American Express, use only expert systems because of the fear that neural networks do not always catch all possible fraud types.

The same techniques can be used for predicting behaviour change that may lead to the opportunity to deepen a relationship, prevent the potential loss of a customer or help gain a new one. The main problem in the use of such systems, especially neural nets, is that they require vast amounts of data. In the UK, as is explained overleaf, institutions may be able to do this for internal customers, but for marketing to potential customers, there are some information limitations.

Source: Financial World, February 1999, pp34-35

8.8   Database Marketing

Databases are introduced here in the context of marketing within the marketing information system. Application of databases to marketing communications is discussed in Chapter 10 on 'promotion'.

Database marketing is an approach to marketing adopted by a number of firms to get more information about their customers. Many manufacturers realized that retailers knew more about their customers than they did. Database marketing, according to the *Economist*

(1 April 1995) 'hold out a vision of marketing nirvana: instead of advertising their products indiscriminately to fuzzy sections of the population, marketers can speak directly to individuals!'

Banks and financial service companies should, with the right technology, be in a good position to exploit this development. American Express is quoted as using its customer database to 'tailor offers to small groups of cardholders according to their spending patterns... In Britain ... a database that ranks business outlets which might be persuaded to accept its card ... has allowed it to recruit thousands of new outlets without expanding its sale force.'

Customer Databases

Customer databases can often be used by organizations that actually hold detailed data on customers, such as banks, building societies and insurance companies. The systems are based on the array of data held about each customer in a relational database. In other words, a sub-sample of customers could be formed by the use of any one specifying variable (or combination of variables). Thus all customers aged 18-24 could be identified for the development of long-term relations, as discussed above, as could all customers aged 25-34 with incomes over £20,000 p.a. and who live in ACORN type B6 housing. This data has become more important as POS (point-of-sale) information is routinely gathered, and personal computer systems have become cheaper, more widely available and more 'user-friendly'.

Such customer database systems allow highly specific target marketing. The most obvious marketing use is by direct mail methods, the particular advantage of which is the capability for exact monitoring of results using a computer system. The costs of each mailshot can be related to the increase in business that results and the types of customers who do buy can be used to refine the target marketing further.

Figure 8.9: Application of Customer Databases to the Customer Communications Planning Cycle

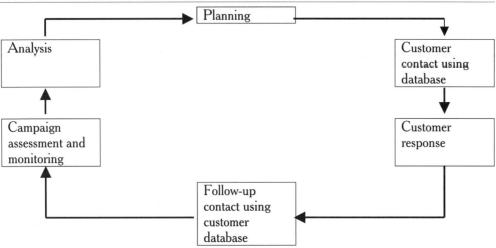

The benefits of using databases to support marketing activity have led to the construction of very large databases. There are two main types of databases used by organizations: data warehouses and data marts.

Data warehouses are much larger and broader in scope, usually built for whole organizations. These take many months and even years to build because of their size and complexity, a result of the wide range of user requirements.

Some organizations have preferred to follow the *data mart* route, where a database is constructed for use by a single functional area within an organization, such as marketing. These are smaller databases with narrower, more specific functions, which can be constructed much more quickly than a data warehouse. Data marts may include a facility whereby the database is integrated with other organizational databases. For example, in financial services marketing it is important to have access to customer account information. Customer transaction history may be used in conjunction with predictive tools from the marketing information system for improved targeting of customers (see 'Marketing in Practice').

MARKETING IN PRACTICE

Making information work in the front line – Canadian Imperial Bank of Commerce

Data warehousing projects sometimes come in for criticism for their complexity and lack of end results. The problem of achieving a return on the large investment made is often due to the fact that such projects are led with a technological goal to create an integrated data environment. Too often the projects have been led by the need to create the central warehouse; how it is then used is a secondary issue.

The Canadian bank, CIBC, is an organization that is using data warehousing technology and local sales assets to create an integrated marketing and sales environment. It is trying to improve long-term relationships and reduce attrition while targeting profitable, or potentially profitable, customer groups.

The bank has a network of 1,400 branches with 24 million accounts held. According to an interview in *American Banker* with James Allen, senior vice president of relational sales and markets, CIBC has spent $10m to $15m on database marketing capabilities in the last three years.

Two of the initiatives are a customer profitability modelling and targeting capability and a branch-level sales support programme.

The bank has implemented a package called the Customer Profitability Management System from the Profit Management Group. The goal for the bank was to produce targeted marketing plans based on potential customer profit, rather than the traditional regional and product-based campaigns.

The bank was aware that up to 50% of its customers were unprofitable, but how could they identify them and how could they then take appropriate action? The PMG software measures a customer's use of bank resources, compares this to the value of the products they own and the potential profit which that customer could contribute given what is known about that customer's economic situation and interaction with other institutions. In cases where the customer is unprofitable, but has the potential to improve, individual marketing strategies can be tailored for expanding the relationship. For other customers, the bank could encourage them to move to lower-cost channels and reduce their use of bank resources.

The goal was to reduce customer profitability reporting from 30 days to 48 hours so that marketing strategies were always acted upon with the freshest information on the customer's behaviour.

The system uses an Oracle customer information warehouse running on three Compaq Alpha Servers in a cluster format. The whole system was tested at Compaq's CRM Centre of Excellence for performance, scalability and the other essential features necessary to make best use of the warehouse.

However, once customers are identified and is assessed on the basis of their behaviour and potential profitability, how best to access them? One method is to use the PMG system to drive central campaigns. However, the bank has also implemented a method of driving knowledge-based sales in the branches.

After a pilot covering 24 branches, the bank has made the decision to invest $6m-$7m in a rollout of a branch-level customer relationship and sales management environment called ENACT from Dallas-based ActionSystems. The ENACT system enables the local branch to execute local, highly-targeted campaigns. In the past, the basic strategy was to get local branch staff to contact customers if there was a specific product offering which the customer did not have. Even this was rare as most marketing was centrally driven. Now that the bank has a better model of the variances in contribution by each relationship and a view of how this value could be increased, local branch staff have been given the tools to act independently.

Each month the branch is sent a CD-ROM with 200 fields of customer data on it taken from the central database. This enables the branch to view in detail the total relationship the bank has with a customer and household, to do their own targeting and manage direct contacts with the most profitable customers. This benefits the customers with more timely advice, but, as importantly, it gives the branch staff confidence to act in their increasingly sales-orientated role. Says Allen: 'They feel they have a more compelling reason to call. They feel they are making the right call and the right offer. There are higher hit rates and better coordination between what we're doing centrally from a direct mail perspective, and locally.'

The CIBC application is the stand-alone version of the ENACT software. Currently, ActionSystems is working with a major UK bank to create an even greater tie-in between the local representative and the central marketing system by enabling an intranet version of the package which eventually will also tie in the call centres to the central customer management tool kit.

Source: Financial World *February 1999, p27*

Summary

Market research refers to a narrow range of activity, principally finding out information about the market for a particular product. Marketing research, which includes market research, is all embracing, relating to all research activity in support of marketing decision making. There are several stages in the marketing research process. Separation into ten discrete stages is presented in the text, starting with setting the objectives of the research and ending with the presentation of the final report.

There are three main types of research design: exploratory, descriptive or causal research. The research design (approach) selected depends on the research problem. Exploratory research is defined not by technique but by the purpose of the research, i.e. to generate hypotheses, or to establish the priorities and objectives of the main research. Descriptive research measures the frequencies with which things happen, or attitudes are held, while causal research tries to establish a connection between variables, e.g. what factors cause an increase in expenditure on a service?

An enormous number of secondary data sources exist, ranging from national and pan-national government statistics, chambers of commerce to commercial databases and directories. Organizations may even buy into a wide range of continuous, specialist research data. Company secondary data, i.e. internal company records gathered by another department within the organization, is often an underused source of information.

Where secondary data is out of date, does not cover the topic of interest, does not provide sufficient detail or do so with sufficient accuracy, then primary research must be undertaken.

A key aspect of successful primary research is sample selection. This can be considered as a four-stage process, which requires answering four questions:

1. Who or what is the target population?

2. Which population to use as the basis for selecting a sample?

3. Which sampling approach to use?

4. How large a sample to select?

A marketing information system has several components that combine to support marketing decision making. These include a **monitoring** element, where internal and external data are monitored and important information collected on a daily, weekly or monthly basis, a **marketing research** function which gathers secondary data and commissions primary data to fill gaps in the secondary data and a **processing** function, which analyses and then disseminates key findings and results.

References

Churchill G A (1996) *Basic Marketing Research*, International Edition, The Dryden Press Harcourt Brace College Publishers, Fort Worth

Crouch S & Housden M (1999) *Marketing Research for Managers*, Butterworth Heinemann, Oxford

Dillon W R, Madden T J & Firtle (1994) *Marketing Research in a Marketing Environment*, Irwin, Burr Ridge Illinois

(1999) *Financial World* February pp34-35

Levitt T (1965) *Harvard Business Review* (September)

(1999) Making information work in the front line, Canadian Imperial Bank of Commerce *Financial World* February, p27

Proctor T (2000) *Essentials of Marketing Research*, Financial Times – Prentice Hall, Harlow

Part 2

CASE STUDIES

NOP 'FRuitS – Behavioural Segmentation

NOP Financial, in conjunction with Berry Consulting, has developed a behavioural segmentation approach which groups the adult population of Great Britain into eight segments. FRuitS is based on a three-dimensional description of each adult aged 18 and over. The three dimensions include: 'lifestage', 'financial strength' and 'product portfolio'.

Lifestage comprises ten rule-based lifestage groups based on (a) age/sex (b) marital status (c) presence of children under 15. **Financial strength** is formed by interlacing two measures of wealth; 'household income' and 'total value of savings and investments'. **Product portfolio** is the basket of financial products held and used by the individual, principally current/savings accounts, investments, borrowings and credit cards.

The survey, which is used to generate the FRuitS segments, examines the financial behaviour of consumers through 60,000 interviews each year. Examples of six of the segments are:

Plums (10% of the adult population of Great Britain). Plums tend to be college-educated married men aged 44-65 living in the South with an income of at least £17,000 and high savings. They are likely to own their home and two or more cars, and are three-and-a-half times more likely than other groups to own shares.

Pears (9% of the adult population of Great Britain). Likely to be older than plums and more likely to be retired. With an income of £7,500 to £17,499, they are at least twice as likley as other groups to own stocks and shares. They may be interested in National Savings but not mortgages.

Cherries (15% of the adult population of Great Britain). Aged 35 to 54 and married with a family, earn above £17,500, usually own their own home and possess two cars. They usually live in the South, have moderate savings and are regarded as prime candidates for mortgages, loans and credit cards.

Apples (12% of the adult population of Great Britain). Tend to be similar in age to cherries, have a lower income (£7,500 to £17,499) and are likely to live in the North, the Midlands or Wales. Usually married they have one car and tend to be self-employed. Good bet for loans and mortgages.

Dates (15% of the adult population of Great Britain). Dates tend to be women over 55, widowed or retired and living alone, often as owner-occupiers. Income usually below £7,499. They tend not to have a car and are likely to have life insurance and a building society account.

Oranges (13% of the adult population of Great Britain). Probably single and aged 16 to 34, with an income of up to £7,499, or students. Likely to be living in private, rented accommodation, they are seen as an interesting segment by financial institutions because of their potential in later life.

Research organizations, such as NOP Financial, employ a variety of segmentation approaches depending on the objectives of the research. For example, attitudinal segmentation is employed when there is a need to understand customer motivations, especially when there is a requirement to develop communications activity. However, the advantage of behavioural segmentation in general, and of the FRuitS segmentation approach in particular, include:

- based on the characteristics of the individual rather than a profile of the postcode or neighbourhood;

- it provides an indication of an individual's market-wide financial behaviour and so can identify customers with most potential for buying certain products; and

- segments are defined relatively simply in terms of lifestage and financial strength, and these can therefore be understood relatively easily within an organization;

- such a segmentation approach is relatively easy to overlay onto databases held by financial service organizations.

The ability to overlay FRuitS data is a key benefit of this particular segmentation method. This allows clients to use of this segmentation approach in direct marketing campaigns. More detailed marketing application includes:

- Developing marketing plans by segment;

- Targeted communications with each individual customer using segment attributes;

- Evaluation of customer performance by FRuitS segment, including recruitment, cross-sale and retention;

- Providing actual data for the development of models to predict customer membership of specific groups (e.g. large savers in the Plum segment).

Compliance

Compliance issues are raised by the use of individual customer records for attribution and in the context of potential use for targeted marketing activity. The use and application of this methodology has resulted in achieving full compliance.

Compliance Issue	Compliance in relation to the use of FruitS
The Data Protection Act (and subsequent EU data protection legislation)	The assistant Data Protection Registrar has approved procedures.
Good Banking Voluntary Code of Practice	Complies. For example the data is not used for direct marketing to individuals but to create statistical relationships.
Market Research Society Code of Conduct.	Approval for compliance obtained.

Source: The authors are grateful to 'NOP Financial' for their support and permission to use the above material.

- Consider how the FRuitS segmentation approach could be applied to regional targeting (e.g. pan-European) and the potential problems of using this FRuitS segmentation outside of the UK.

- Select a market sector, other than financial services, and consider how behavioural segmentation may be used effectively.

- Powerful segmentation methods allow companies to target profitable segments. By definition, unprofitable segments can be excluded. Consider whether this raises any ethical issues, with regard to compliance and ethics, especially for key industry sectors. (Ethics are discussed in Chapter 1.)

Abbey National – defying convention

Abbey National's committed e-strategy is proving to be a resounding success.

Following multi-million pound investment, Abbey National's new ebanking service is the fruition of its 'bricks & clicks' strategy. ebanking is the first example of Abbey's 'Flexible Finance' concept, designed to put the customer in complete control of his or her day-to-day finances through the click of a button.

Abbey National has been providing WAP-based mobile financial services since July 2000. Early services provide useful customer tools as well as special offers. All options carry a speed-dial approach which allows the customer to ring directly into Abbey National avoiding the need to write numbers down and key them into the phone manually.

John Reynolds, head of e-commerce strategy for the bank, says: 'We have rolled out these basic services rapidly and have had thousands of WAP visits to both the cahoot and Abbey National sites. The feedback we have received from customers is that they are delighted with these services and are looking for more. We have clear plans to be an innovator in this space and are currently developing a range of value-added services.'

Providing new services

Abbey has recently launched some innovative services via mobile phones, such as a mortgage and personal loan quotation service and an ATM locator service. The first such service of its kind in the UK, the ATM locator service, works by simply dialling into wap.abbeynational.co.uk and typing in the name of a town, city or postcode. Abbey customers can then get details of their nearest Abbeylink machines.

Ambrose McGinn, Abbey's director of e-commerce, says:

> The Abbeylink locator is a new and unique WAP service that will be very popular with our customers who use this technology. Wherever you are in the UK you'll now be able to get cash quickly and easily.

> This service is part of Abbey National's new portfolio of interactive WAP functions, which include instant mortgage quotes and a personal loan repayment calculator. We have been careful to make sure that the services we provide are appropriate for WAP mobile phones.

Peace of mind

Abbey is bolstering customer confidence in electronic banking channels by offering a 'peace of mind guarantee', a promise that its customers' money will be safe. Abbey will also guarantee to cover any losses in the event of Internet fraud. Abbey intends to roll out a number of appropriate mobile financial services – share dealing, for example, was available by the end of 2000.

Reynolds says: 'We want our services to be available to everyone. It is critical that our services are network agnostic. In addition, we intend to offer our e-banking on the portal of every network provider.'

Abbey has also been busy developing e-banking via interactive TV. The banking services are already available via Open, and are currently being rolled out by NTL and TeleWest. Abbey intends to be a dominant player using this medium, and has become one of the first banks in the world to offer interactive services on the Internet, digital TV and WAP.

Old habits die hard

Abbey knows that despite its innovative range of services, customers do not easily switch their banking arrangements. Research carried out in the US by Dove Associates shows that people are more likely to get divorced than change banks.

To counteract this, Abbey has launched a new 'switcher' service, designed to shake up the industry and win new bank account customers. Abbey National expects that one million customers will be registered to use the service within 12 months, and predicts that at least five million will be using its online services within four years.

Abbey National expects e-banking to have dramatic results on the business: its own research from North America indicates that it increases cross-holdings per customer by up to 150%, and improves customer retention by up to 50%. In addition, with the cost of simple transactions online being only a fraction (and in some cases as little as 1%) of the cost in traditional channels, the service will achieve significant cost efficiency benefits for the company in the medium term.

McGinn comments: 'We have invested millions in providing what we believe to be the best e-banking service yet launched. We have taken time to research the market in the finest detail, listened to our customers' views and developed the most straightforward, comprehensive and easy-to-use service available.'

Unconventional to the last

Cahoot, Abbey National's new, stand-alone interactive bank which launched in 2000, is heralding a new era in customized banking.

The entire venture was set up with brand new processing systems. This gives Cahoot the opportunity to provide customers bespoke banking services. The flexibility offered in the new systems gives Cahoot the ability to exploit not only new services but also new partnerships.

Cahoot offers an unprecedented level of pricing to its customers, including 0% APR on credit cards and overdrafts until the end of June 2001 for at least the first 25,000 accounts. Rates for customers after the initial offer of 0% will remain among the most competitive in the marketplace.

Value for money

The rates are part of Cahoot's long-term commitment to offer outstanding value for money to all of its customers. Cahoot's marketing director Tim Sawyer says: 'Cahoot is all about doing things differently. We intend to put customers in complete control of their finances. We will provide all of our customers with outstanding value for money and levels of service.

> *We are the lowest cost provider and our excellent rates are sustainable because we will pass on these cost savings directly to our customers.'*

Cahoot is not a 'one-size-fits-all' bank account – instead it works with its customers to shape the products and services that meet their banking needs. Customers can receive any advice they need via the state-of-the-art, purpose-built contact centre recently opened in Coventry.

It has joined forces with BT Cellnet to make 150,000 mobile phones available to customers, who will be able to conduct a full range of banking services via their mobile devices.

Using Genie, BT's mobile Internet service provider, customers will be able to access banking and non-banking services such as news, sport and travel information.

Source: Financial World, *January 2001, pp46-47*

- Outline the main influences on buyer behaviour in this market.

- Identify the bases that Cahoot could use to segment their market and select the most appropriate method(s).

- Think about what criteria Cahoot could use to evaluate the various segments.

- Recommend an appropriate segmentation and targeting positioning strategy for Cahoot.

Part Three

THE MARKETING MIX

9

Product Management

Learning Objectives

After reading this chapter students should understand:

- The marketing definition of a product;

- The importance of product management and how it is affected by the stage of industry maturity and type of industry sector;

- Portfolio planning models and how they may be applied to product management;

- The impact of stage in the product life cycle on marketing decision making and the linkage of the product life cycle to the BCG matrix;

- A classification system of product innovation according to (a) newness to the firm and (b) newness to the consumer;

- The diffusion of innovation model;

- The meaning of product line decisions.

Figure 9.1: Chapter Map

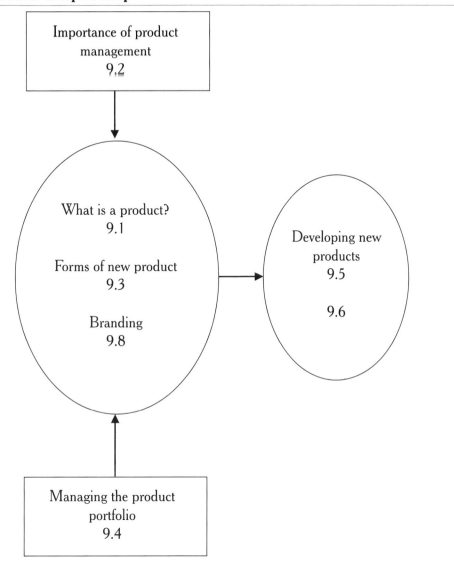

Introduction

In order to understand fully the marketing of products it is first necessary to have a concept of what a product is, i.e. What are the essential elements that make up a product? Such a concept may be used to analyse the suitability of a particular product for target market segments.

Product management decisions are not static or made in isolation. As a product is rolled out into the marketplace, the rate of uptake (diffusion) in each market will differ depending on the attributes of the product and of the market. At each stage in its life cycle within any specified market, product management needs to change. In addition, the organization must consider product fit within the product range. This is because consumer perception is affected not simply by individual products but by their relationship with other products offered by the same company, as well as by competitors.

9.1   What is a Product?

Consumers do not buy a product for its own sake, only for the benefits that the product offers them. Focusing too much attention on the product itself can lead to the 'marketing myopia' trap. The consumer who buys a drill does not generally do so for the pleasures of owning a drill but in order to have a facility to make holes in things. In the same way, the consumer who purchases a pension plan does so not because he or she wants to own a pension plan, but rather because of a need for financial security in the future. Therefore, in thinking about products it is necessary to think in terms of the needs that the product fulfils, and not the product's features.

However, the concept of a product is a little more complex. We can analyse a product on three levels (Figure 9.2).

1.   For any particular type of product, there are certain basic or essential features and these are likely to be identical across all products. All drills must offer the capability for making holes and all current accounts must offer basic money transmission facilities. These basic features can be thought of as the ***core or generic product***. At this level, all products are effectively the same. For example, all unit trusts offer basic investment facilities to the buyer through the purchase and management of a portfolio of shares. All cars offer basic transport.

2.   Differentiation begins to appear at the next layer – often described as the ***tangible or expected product***. At this stage various features, which might be regarded as desirable from the point of view of the consumer, are added to the product. These features will incorporate brand names, certain types of packaging, different quality levels and other additional, non-essential features. In the case of the unit trust, this might include particular options regarding the realization of the initial investment, the degree of liquidity and the degree of risk.

3.   There is also a third layer in the product concept, that of the ***augmented product***. The augmented product covers the additional aspects of the product offering which go beyond what consumers might generally expect, and hence provides a basis for the organization to gain a competitive edge. Features of the augmented product are often in the form of customer service facilities. Certain features may be added to a product such as interest on current accounts, insurance company help lines etc., which initially appear to be part of the augmented product – the 'added extras'; but soon they will become features which are expected as an integral part of the normal product offering, i.e. the 'tangible product'. It is typically at the level of the tangible product that the greatest competition between different suppliers will emerge.

Figure 9.2: The Product Concept

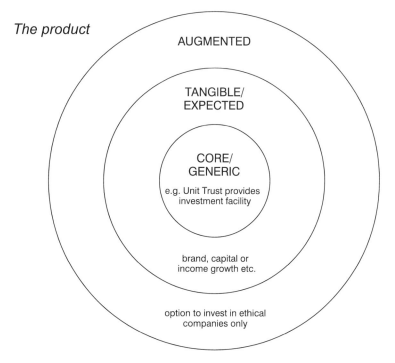

In developing the product, the key considerations are features that must be present to ensure that consumer needs are being fulfilled. Other features need to be present to differentiate the product from its competitors and match consumer expectations for that type of product. By exploiting the potential and opportunities to augment a product and provide something that is noticeably different, the organization has the basis on which a distinct competitive advantage can be built.

Services

There are particular problems in differentiating the service offer at the augmented level compared with differentiating products. In mature product markets most competition takes place in the augmented product, which is substantially concerned with service issues around the product. However, for services, there is seemingly comparatively less scope to differentiate the augmented offer. To achieve successful differentiation the service marketer must focus on excellence in the extended marketing mix. The extended marketing mix is discussed in Chapter 13.

Potential marketing problems

These may arise from the degree of complexity that characterizes services, especially financial services.

A further difference, which stems from the characteristic of *inseparability,* is the difficulty for consumers to distinguish between the financial product itself and its delivery system. Distribution issues are examined in Chapter 12 but it is worth recognizing that the delivery system will be inextricably linked with the product itself and will often be considered as a component of that product. In this sense, there will be some aspects of the delivery system which must be seen as components of the core or tangible product while others may usefully be characterized as part of the augmented product.

9.2   Importance of Product Management

Product management is highly influenced by industry sector and this in turn is influenced by the stage an industry has reached, in terms of its evolution or maturity. A useful guiding principle to use is the product life cycle. Consider the consumer electronics sector and the stage of maturity of the television sector within consumer electronics. Successive product innovations of televisions resulted in a blurring of this major sector with other industry sectors. Beginning from stage 3, televisions have been used and integrated with other devices. They may therefore be considered as a part of other sectors, e.g. electronic games, home entertainment, communications etc.

Table 9.1: Successive Product Innovation in the Television Industry

Stage	Product
1.	Black-and-white television
2.	Colour television
3.	Colour television with 'Dolby' high-quality sound
4.	Flat-screen televisions
5.	Wide-screen televisions
6	Home cinema surround-sound televisions
7.	Digital television
8.	Televisions that may be used to send e-mails and to connect to the Internet

Product management of televisions was relatively simple when market penetration levels in excess of 90% existed for black-and-white sets and colour televisions had been introduced. In the decline stage of the product life cycle, black-and-white sets, which had been made in factories that had written off their capital costs, were sold at heavily discounted rates in developed economy markets. At the same time this allowed these products to be rolled out in large volumes to less developed economy markets.

The television as a product class has endured mainly because it has become an essential element in the delivery of high-growth services such as electronic games, home shopping and communications. Product management has become more complicated with many more products within the product line and branding supporting products that are more varied and complex than a 'simple television'. No longer does the television have a single function, i.e. to watch shows broadcast on a narrow selection of terrestrial channels. Now many product forms exist within the product class. In turn, there is a multiplicity of new and improved models within each product form. Many 'television' products are at the growth stage of the product life cycle, while only basic models, such as small portables and non-digital sets, are being managed at the decline stage.

Product management within services requires responding more quickly to developments. Technology has resulted in the development of new product classes, for example Internet bank accounts, Internet grocery shopping, execution-only stockbroking etc. Within each product class new product innovation proliferates. Managers must respond to these market developments within days and weeks, especially as technology facilitates rapid implementation of product management decisions. Most recent technological developments require product managers to consider in advance the criteria that they apply. These may then be programmed into automated systems. For example, investors and users of financial services now have access to information services that alert customers to the financial products that offer 'best' returns. In such a marketplace, waiting several days for the launch of a new service, or the adjustment of features offered for existing products, is inadequate.

9.3   Forms of New Product

Any organization must constantly monitor and review its product range to ensure that it provides the desired extent of market coverage; where the aim is to provide a varied range of products to a number of market segments it is necessary to ensure that the range of products on offer meets the needs of those segments.

Furthermore, since customer needs will change over time, product ranges should be monitored and modifications made as and when necessary. Indeed, such modifications are often implemented when products have reached the maturity stage of their life cycle in order to stimulate a renewed interest from consumers and encourage an expansion in sales. How different must a product be before consumer interest is encouraged? There are two aspects of this for a commercial firm.

1. *The consumer perspective.* If we consider an 'innovation' to refer to any good, service or idea that is perceived by someone to be new, it is important to ask, How new is the product? The answer to this question is subjective, because a new product idea may have a long history but be an innovation to the person concerned. However, the newer the innovation, the more probable it is that the firm will be able to use the innovation for competitive advantage, although it is likely to present a more complex marketing communications task explaining to consumers how they may use substantial innovations.

2. ***The perspective of the firm***. The newer the innovation to the firm, the more probable it is that:

    ● a substantial investment in development was involved;

    ● that the risk of failure in the marketplace will be higher;

    ● the financial risk of the project (including a combination of the size of the investment and the probability of success) will be greater.

In order to support the analysis of product innovation, various classifications of 'newness of innovation' have been developed, both from the perspective of the firm (Table 9.2) and from the perspective of the consumer (Table 9.3).

'Continuous innovation' is probably the most common form of innovation from the perspective of the consumer. This refers to products which, although new to the organization, are not new to the market, at least not in their basic form. The development of a new service line will typically involve developing an organization's own variant of a particular product which is already available, but possibly adding additional features to differentiate it from existing versions of the product. The development of new service or product lines is arguably the most common form of NPD in any business area, but particularly so in financial services.

Table 9.2: Types of Newness to the Firm (Increasing Level of Product Innovation)

TYPE OF CORPORATE STRATEGY	TYPE OF NEW PRODUCT	TYPICAL EXTENT OF NEWNESS
Market penetration	● Product modification (to meet or beat competition)	● No change in market ● Small change in technology
Market development	● Technical extension ● Change in form	● New use ● User-related technology
Product development	● Line extension	● New segment ● New technology possibly
Diversification	● Completely new ● Brand franchise extension	● New market ● New technology probably

Table 9.3: Types of Newness to Market

TYPE OF INNOVATION	TYPE OF NEWNESS	CHANGE REQUIRED OF BUYER
Discontinuous (Rare – e.g. result of technical breakthrough)	New product class	Creates a new consumption pattern e.g. TV, mobile phone
Dynamically continuous (Major evolutionary improvement in a product class)	New product form	Not significantly altering existing patterns of consumer buying or product use. Buyers aware of product class. What share will be won of product class? (E.g. personal computer, portable radio)
Continuous (Modest enhancement within a product form)	New or improved model	This causes the least disruption to established patterns of consumer behaviour. Possible impact on buyer perception of brand. (E.g. IBM PS/2, Celeron processor, Sony Walkman)
Non-innovative (Imitations that offer a repackaged version of a competing brand)	New brand	Minimal impact on consumer behaviour (E.g. IBM computer clones, own-label breakfast cereals)

9.4   Managing the Product Portfolio

Product management decisions are supported by several marketing theories, in particular: the diffusion of innovation, the theory of the product life cycle and porfolio planning methods.

The use of portfolio models in product management is discussed in Chapter 2. First we must consider what 'product' is being managed.

Products and product lines

The term 'product' is used frequently when in fact 'product lines' are being discussed. Companies seldom market single products. More commonly groups of products are marketed that are related in terms of the benefits they offer, or in terms of their functions. Car manufacturers, for example, offer a selection of family cars with different engine sizes and features. Companies must decide how many products to offer within a product line. This depends on how homogeneous the target market segment is (see Chapter 7) and on the product line marketed by the competition. Each additional product marketed, within a product line, creates costs for the business (production, marketing, inventory management, customer support). These costs must be balanced against the size of the target market segment and the 'value' ascribed to an additional product which is more attuned to the demands of the segment.

Diffusion of innovation

Much marketing activity is related to the launching of new products. Of particular interest to marketers, in this context, is the propensity of consumers to respond to communication about new products. One of the major writers in this area was Rogers who, in 1962, defined 'diffusion' as the process by which an innovation is communicated over time among the individuals within society who comprise the target market.

Any innovation will take time to permeate (or diffuse) through the social system and Rogers defines the diffusion process as 'the spread of a new idea from its source of invention or creation to its ultimate users or adopters'. Research in this area identifies four key elements as being significant to the process of diffusion:

- The innovation itself;
- The communication processes and channels used (including how well the innovation is communicated);
- The time at which individuals decide to adopt the product;
- The social systems involved.

Marketing communication can be a crucial factor in determining the rate of diffusion. Consider the consumer world before Sony invented the 'Walkman'. At this time, the concept of music on the move, on foot, did not exist. People could legitimately ask, Why would anyone want, and be willing to buy, a highly portable music system? The success of this product relied on the diffusion of the idea that there was a distinct benefit to 'music on the move'. Marketing communications was vital in demonstrating the practical applications of this technology and therefore the relevance to many consumer segments.

Adoption

At the heart of the diffusion process is the decision by an individual to adopt the innovative product or service. This process of adoption focuses on 'the mental processes through which an individual passes from first hearing about the innovation to final adoption' (Rogers 1962).

Adoption is the decision of an individual to become a regular user of a product.

Kotler *et al.* (1999) states that adopters of new products have been observed to move through the following five stages:

Awareness. The consumer becomes aware of the innovation but lacks information about it.

Interest. The consumer is stimulated to seek information about the innovation.

Evaluation. The consumer considers whether to try the innovation.

Trial. The consumer tries the innovation to improve his or her estimate of its value.

Adoption. The consumer decides to make full and regular use of the innovation.

The progression suggests that the marketer of the innovative product should aim to facilitate consumer movement through these stages. The process of adoption of innovation described here bears a remarkable similarity to the 'core' process of consumer buying behaviour described earlier. Indeed, when considering the adoption process, all we are considering is the consumer buying behaviour process for a new rather than an existing product – the differences between the two processes being ones of emphasis rather than content.

Categories of Adopters

It is a fact, however, that people differ markedly in their readiness to try new products. Rogers defines a person's innovativeness as 'the degree to which an individual is relatively earlier in adopting new ideas than other members of his social system', and identifies five categories of adopters, which are often described diagrammatically in terms of a normal distribution curve, showing their relative numerical importance (Figure 9.3).

Figure 9.3: Adoptors of Innovations as a % of Total Potential Adoptors (Rogers 1962)

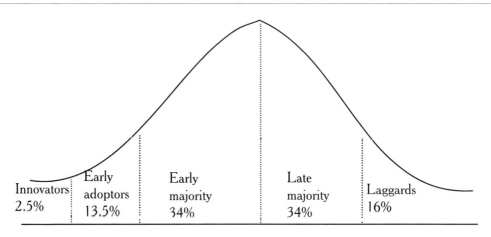

Time of adoption of an innovation

Rogers (1962) describes the characteristics of the various groups.

Innovators represent on average the first 2.5% of all those who adopt. They are eager to try new ideas and products almost as an obsession. They have higher incomes, are better educated, and are more active outside their community than non-innovators. They are less reliant on group norms, more self-confident, and more likely to obtain their information from scientific sources and experts.

Early adopters represent on average the next 13.5% to adopt the product, adopting early in the product's life cycle. They are much more reliant on group norms and values than innovators, and are much more oriented to the local community than the innovators who have a more cosmopolitan outlook. Early adopters are more likely to be opinion leaders because of their closer affiliation to groups. This group is probably the most important one in determining whether a new product will be successful because they are more likely to transmit word-of-mouth influence.

The *early majority* represent the next 34% to adopt. They will deliberate more carefully before adopting a new product, collecting more information and evaluating more brands than will the early adopters. Therefore, the process of adoption takes longer. They are an important link in the diffusion process because they are positioned between the earlier and later adopters.

The *late majority* represent the next 34% to adopt, and are described by Rogers as sceptical: they adopt because most of their friends have already done so. Since they rely on group norms, adoption is the result of the pressure to conform. They tend to be older, with below average income and education, relying primarily on word-of-mouth communication rather than the mass media.

Laggards represent the final 16% to adopt. They are similar to innovators in not relying on the norms of the group. They are independent because they are tradition-bound, with decisions made in terms of the past. By the time they adopt an innovation, it has probably been superseded by something else. Laggards have the lowest socioeconomic status.

Encouraging Adoption

It is a common assertion that 90% of new products fail. How, therefore, can a marketer ensure that his or her new product stands the best chance of success in the market? Rogers and Shoemaker (1971) identify five characteristics that increase the acceptance of a new product:

1. *Relative advantage*: the extent to which the consumer perceives the product to have an advantage over the product it supersedes, implying that, the greater the perceived advantage, the greater the probability of adoption;

2. *Compatibility*: the degree to which the product is consistent with existing values and past experiences of the potential customers, the assumption being that the less a product is compatible with consumer values, the longer it will take to be adopted;

3. *Simplicity*: the degree to which a new product is perceived to be simple and easy to use. The more difficult it is perceived to be, the harder it will be for the product to be accepted;

4. *Trialability*. It is believed that new products are more likely to be adopted when customers can try them out on an experimental basis. This can often prove to be a difficulty for financial services because people cannot 'try before they buy';

5. *Observability*: a measure of the degree to which adoption of the product, or the results of using the product, is visible to friends, neighbours and colleagues. This seems to affect the diffusion process by allowing potential customers to see the benefits of the product, and thus increase (or even create) a 'want' for themselves. This process can be given added impetus if the product is seen to be used by celebrities or other role models. This factor obviously lends itself more to some products than others.

In operational terms the organization has a number of strategies at its disposal to influence customers to adopt innovations and, within this, marketing communication is obviously very important. For example, in markets where continuous innovation is the norm, organizations can encourage trial through free samples and price promotion.

Encouraging adoption for a discontinuation is more problematic because the product cannot be purchased on a trial basis and therefore advertising may have to be used to promote awareness and communicate product features. One advertising strategy used by organizations to promote innovative behaviour is to show astute buyers purchasing the most advanced products.

The rate of diffusion will influence the marketing strategy of the organization. There are two main strategic options, depending on the rate of diffusion: skimming, where the marketer predicts a slow rate of diffusion, and penetration, where the marketer anticipates, or wishes to achieve, a faster rate of diffusion.

With a *skimming* policy a slower rate of diffusion is anticipated and therefore prices are initially set at a high level to sustain the costs of introduction. The target market is the smaller, price-insensitive segment, which will probably be quite well defined. Advertising will probably be orientated towards the supply of information in order to create awareness. Distribution will be selective. This policy is most likely for discontinuous innovations as there may be barriers to widespread acceptance because the product is not likely to be simple and may not be compatible with existing products or systems.

With a *penetration* strategy the marketer encourages as rapid and as widespread a diffusion as possible by introducing the product at a low price. The intention is to try to sell to a general market through an intensive communication campaign that uses imagery and symbolism. Distribution is widespread. This strategy is most appropriate for continuous innovations, because closely competitive product substitutes exist.

The Product Life Cycle

The concept of the product or service life cycle is a tool that is widely used for market planning. It can be employed both to guide an organization in the determination of the appropriate balance of products in its portfolio and in the development of a suitable strategy for the marketing of those products. The concept is one that is familiar to most students of marketing and the basic idea is that a product will follow a life cycle from development and introduction, through to growth, maturity and finally decline. If products are thought to follow such a life cycle, then in principle there is no reason why services should not follow a similar life cycle. A typical product life cycle is shown below.

Figure 9.4: The Product Life Cycle

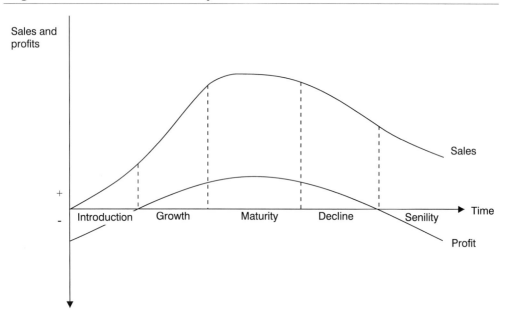

By considering the characteristics of each of the product life cycle positions we can obtain some indication of the use of this approach both in balancing the product portfolio and guiding the development of the marketing mix.

Development refers to the period during which an idea is developed into a specific form which can be launched to consumers (see sections 9.6 and 9.7). At this stage the product will be absorbing resources for development and testing and in many industries this can be a time-consuming business. In the banking sector, given the ease of copying products, the pressure is for the development phase to be kept as short as possible to ensure that innovative products are moved into the market to ensure that the bank can benefit as much as possible from its first mover advantage. If the product is likely to be successful, competitors will soon follow with their own versions.

Introduction is a period of slow growth, with sales being primarily to customers who are most receptive to new ideas. At this stage, because considerable marketing resources are being devoted to obtaining widespread acceptance for the new service, cash flows and profits will typically be negative. From a marketing perspective, the priority is to raise awareness and appreciation of the product. Marketing communications is therefore a particularly important marketing mix element at this stage. In the financial services sector it is of considerable importance that new products are introduced quickly and that this phase of the life cycle is shortened, because of the ease with which new products can be copied. Operating a current account from a WAP phone is currently at the introduction stage.

Growth is the stage when sales volumes increase steadily, the service is accepted across a much broader range of consumers and the product begins to make a significant contribution to profitability. Increases in sales can be maintained by improvements in features, targeting more segments or increased price competitiveness. However, it is at this stage that the new service product will begin to attract significant competition. Growth services include do-it-yourself investment in the stock market with finacial institutions providing 'execution only' services.

Maturity sets in when the rate of change in sales begins to stabilize and the product is known to the majority of consumers in the market. At this stage of the life cycle of many consumer and industrial goods, replacement purchases tend to be more common than new purchases. The market itself is mature and the product is well established. Competition is probably at its most intense at this stage. It may be necessary to consider modification and rejuvenation of the service to arrest future decline. Building society ordinary share accounts and bank current accounts are products which can be seen as having reached maturity and in many cases are being modified in attempts to prolong their life cycles.

Decline occurs when sales begin to drop away noticeably, leaving management with the option of withdrawing the product. This may be implemented in one of two ways:

a)   Immediate withdrawal of the product and of all marketing resources.

b)   Retain the product but to maximize cash flow all marketing support may be withdrawn. Often with long-term investment products this may be the only option The main danger of this is that there may be a knock-on impact on the rest of the company's products if consumers see an organization owning a dying product.

In the financial services sector it should be noted that barriers to product withdrawal are often high; some products such as life insurance cannot simply be withdrawn from the market because some customers will still be paying premiums.

Alternatively, if the product is seen as one with a potential long-term future then the appropriate strategy may be one of *rejuvenation*. It is more efficient for this strategy to be planned and implemented during the 'maturity' phase before the additional burden of decline is encountered.

A difficulty in the banking sector is the possibility of some confusion between the cash flow into a product and the product itself. For example, in the launch of a loan product cash resources will be absorbed, as would be the case with any new product. However, a basic feature of such a product is of course that it involves making money available to finance purchases by the borrower; thus the product itself will be a net user of financial resources.

The reverse will be true of a savings product. Thus, consideration of the resource use characteristics of financial services at different stages of their life cycle must distinguish between:

a)   the resource use for the development and marketing of the service; and

b)   the resource use which is an integral feature of the service itself.

Hence, it may be unwise to take the analogy too literally and assume that every product follows this sort of stylized life cycle. Life cycles may take many different forms; some very short, others very long and the time period associated with each possible phase can vary considerably. The idea that the product life cycle attempts to convey is that the position of a product in a particular market will change with time and that the understanding and analysis of those changes can be of use in guiding marketing decisions and maintaining some balance within the product portfolio.

Furthermore, the role of marketing is generally considered to be one of prolonging the growth and maturity phases, often using strategies of product modification or product improvement which are frequently regarded as less risky than new product development.

What is often unclear in discussions of the product life cycle is the actual meaning attached to the word product (or service). The life cycle could refer to a product class (loans), or a product form (car loans) or to a specific brand (NatWest Car Loans). It may be equally useful in each case, but the distinction is of some importance since the life cycle is typically longer for the product class than it is for the product form and longer for the product form than it is for the specific brand. The pattern of development of a product class or product form is also likely to be much smoother than that of a brand simply because of the influence of changing competitive strategies and changes in the marketing mix which will affect consumer take up.

Portfolio planning methods

Portfolio planning methods may be used in strategic planning or for planning the management of the product portfolio. These are discussed, in Chapter 2, in the context of strategic analysis.

9.5   New Product Development (NPD)

Product development and product modification are key elements in the maintenance and development of a product range which meets the constantly changing needs of consumers. However, for every new product that actually reaches the stage of being launched there will be perhaps hundreds that have failed to get through the development phase. NPD is therefore one of the most costly, and risky, aspects of marketing.

We have discussed the different types of new products that may be considered. The costs, risks and potential returns of NPD are correlated with the degree of 'newness' of the product which has been developed and the financial resources committed to its development.

Invention versus innovation

These two terms are frequently confused. Invention may be totally unrelated to consumer demand. It is solely about the creation of new products. In contrast, innovation is intimately concerned with consumer demand. It includes invention but in addition it is about the satisfaction of identified consumer wants. This requires the new product to be tailored to particular consumer needs, in identified consumers. Innovation is not always about new products. It could also include new processes, new distribution methods, etc.

Issues surrounding NPD

Before discussing the NPD process, it is important to realize that this must be supported by:

1. An organizational structure and a corporate culture which encourages NPD. Suggestions should be actively solicited from within the organization and all ideas should be allowed to go forward without criticism to a screening phase. This has been described as 'creating a climate of trying';

2. The maintenance of regular contacts with the external environment to identify changes in market characteristics and customer requirements;

3. A need to develop a flexible management structure which stimulates and encourages the NPD process;

4. Identifying key individuals with specific responsibility for the NPD process.

Research into the characteristics of successful new consumer financial products indicates that the most important are:

- overall quality (the product, the delivery system, after sales service, the organization's reputation for quality);

- having a differentiated product (being first, being innovative), product fit and internal marketing (the new product complements existing products and receives the support of staff);

- the application of technology.

Given the costs and risks involved, and the importance of NPD in marketing strategies, it is important to apply an organized and systematic approach to the process. Such an approach cannot in itself guarantee that new products will be successful but it can at least attempt to reduce the possibility of failure.

9.6   New Product Development Process

The NPD Process: Overview

Because NPD is a costly and risky activity and is also one that is important to the long-term competitive success of a business, a systematic and structured approach to new product development is important. Adopting such an approach will ensure that new product ideas which are consistent with an organization's strategies can be fully tested and evaluated, so that only those with a real chance of success will actually reach the marketplace. There are a number of different approaches that can be used for NPD but all will involve broadly similar sets of activities and stages. A simple framework is outlined in Figure 9.5. In brief, the NPD process is as follows:

- *Rationale* As a starting point an organization requires a strategy for new product development which sets the general approach to be followed and which itself is consistent with the firm's overall strategy.

- The second stage is to *generate ideas* or concepts, which may be entirely new ones or derivatives from existing products.

- The range of new ideas generated needs to be *screened* to identify those which appear to have at least some potential for success and, as part of this process, the viability of the idea ought to be tested.

Figure 9.5: New Product Development Process

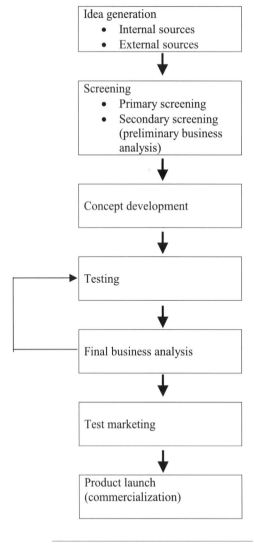

- Assuming the idea has some support from the initial test, the next stage is to *develop it into a recognizable product* and to test again for acceptability.

- Following refinement, the next stage is to undertake a *pilot launch*, to a segment of the intended market, perhaps in a sample of geographical locations.

- After further refinements, a product which successfully passes through this stage will be *launched fully* into the intended market.

The rationale for NPD

For the effective organization and management of NPD it is important that the rationale for the process is made clear. This requires some identification of why the organization is involved in NPD and what it expects to achieve. In essence, this can almost be thought of as a statement of the organization's new product development strategy. By clearly identifying the motivations for NPD it is possible to provide some guidance to those involved in the process of formulating ideas.

- If the process of NPD is to be orientated towards taking advantage of new market segments, then those involved need some clear indication of the needs and expectations of customers in the particular segments.

- By contrast, if NPD is to be concerned with reducing excess capacity or evening out fluctuating levels of demand, the focus of attention, particularly in generating ideas, will be different.

Idea generation: internal sources

Ideas are the basic raw material for any NPD process; because only a very small proportion of ideas ever become products, the importance of generating many and varied ideas should not be overstated. The possible sources of new product ideas can be classified according to whether they are internal or external. Internal sources include any ideas which are generated by employees within the organization, the most obvious being the following.

New product development groups. It is possible to establish groups within the organization who meet on a regular basis to 'brainstorm' ideas for new products. Although this is an important management function in many organizations, it appears to have developed rather more slowly in the banking sector. Approaches adopted include:

- The formation of small, inter-departmental teams to handle some of the aspects of new product development;

- The formation of new product development groups on an ad hoc basis, with individuals brought into the group on a special assignment basis, either from within the organization or from specialist agencies.

The danger in using internal staff without adequate staff development for the role is that they will bring with them their functional department perspectives which may not be appropriate. One product, launched by a financial services firm, was targeted at people who did not operate a current account. Although it was produced with the best systems available, little emphasis had been placed on researching what this target population required, with the end result of failure and repositioning of the product.

A strong research finding is that the conservative culture and systems of organizations frequently conflict with and constrain new product development and reinforce copying of other firms' products. As such the process of new product development may be a political issue, with emphasis being placed on which functional specialisms dominate the institution.

Market research department. Through regular monitoring and analysis of the marketplace, management within the marketing research function are potentially well placed to come forward with new ideas. These ideas may stem from the analysis of changes in consumer requirements but may equally well arise from an appreciation of changes in technology or changes in legislation. The development of many new financial service products is the result of legislation or other forms of government action, for example PEPs, ISAs and stakeholder pensions.

Increasingly, financial service firms are using their substantial customer databases to support the development of new services.

Informal management suggestions. Management, both within the marketing department and elsewhere in the organization, can also be a useful source of ideas and many financial service organizations make considerable use of informal suggestions from this source.

Employee suggestions. Staff involved in day-to-day dealing with customers are often encouraged to submit their own suggestions for new products. This is a potentially useful source of ideas, because such staff, by virtue of their regular contact with customers, may have a clearer understanding of customer attitudes and problems with the existing product. Many companies are recognizing the wealth of ideas employees can generate and are introducing schemes to reward good ideas.

Ideas generation: external sources

A significant number of new product ideas are developed either formally or informally from external sources. There are numerous possible external sources, but the major ones include customers, agencies and competitors.

Customers. Ideas may be generated by an organization's customers either through informal suggestion or as a result of formal market research. This produces the most obvious expression of the nature of customer wants and needs and is seen as an important source of ideas by many banks and building societies.

Outside agencies (outsourcing). These include suggestions from market research agencies, advertising agencies and specialist new product development agencies. An outside agency is able to distance itself from the organization, and is not constrained by internal traditions and cultures. This will tend to encourage the generation of new ideas from a different perspective.

Competitors. Copying and modifying products developed by competitors is a common source of ideas for new product development in many organizations. It is perhaps particularly common in the financial service sector where oligopolistic market behaviour practice is evident.

Since very few ideas will ever reach the stage of product launch, it is important to ensure that ideas are generated regularly and in significant numbers to increase the probability of finding a successful idea. At this stage ideas should be encouraged, however unusual or eccentric they may seem; their suitability will be evaluated at a later stage.

Screening

The next stage of the NPD process is to screen the available ideas in order to establish which should proceed to the development stage. Essentially, screening will seek to establish whether the ideas will be of benefit to the organization in attempting to achieve its objectives. In order to do this each idea must be judged according to a variety of criteria. Typically the screening process will fall into two stages, primary and secondary screening.

Primary screening
Primary screening will seek to eliminate those product ideas which are clearly outside the company's capabilities, which do not fit the current strategies, which duplicate existing products or those which are technologically, politically or legally impractical. The precise criteria used for a primary screening will vary according to the nature of the organization's NPD strategy, but it is important that a clear set of criteria are determined and clearly laid down in advance: a simple example is given in Figure 9.6.

Figure 9.6: Sample Criteria for Primary Screening

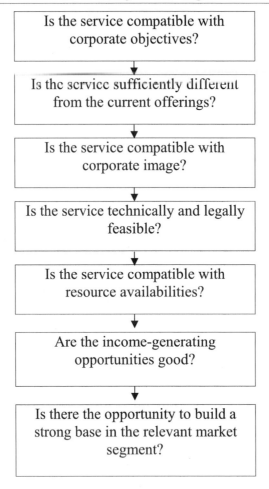

The primary screen may well eliminate as many as 80-90% of new product ideas. While this may seem to be a particularly high failure rate it is nevertheless necessary because once beyond the primary screen into secondary screening and product development the costs of ideas begin to increase substantially. Thus it is important to eliminate ideas that are clearly not practical. At the same time, it is important not to be too ruthless and eliminate potentially successful ideas. At the primary screening phase, it is possible to err on the optimistic side, because the secondary screen should identify any obviously weak ideas that have escaped the primary screen.

Secondary screening

The secondary screen is a much more detailed evaluation of the potential of an idea and is often referred to as the preliminary business analysis stage of NPD. Again, it involves comparing and ideally ranking products according to their performance over a set of evaluative criteria. These criteria may include the following:

1) Measurement of the size and growth potential of target markets;

2) Evaluation of the nature and extent of competition;

3) The costs of producing and marketing the product;

4) Projected sales volumes under a variety of assumptions;

5) Projected profits;

6) How long it will take for profits to be realized;

7) How easily the product can be copied;

8) The likely length of the product life cycle.

Obviously there is a variety of criteria that can be used and their precise nature will again differ according to the requirements of the organization. At the end of the secondary screening process there may be as few as 5% of the original ideas that proceed to the stage of development and testing.

Concept development

The ideas that have passed through the screening phase must now be transformed into product concepts and a clear statement of the product positioning.

● The product concept involves translating the basic idea into a specific set of features and attributes which the product will offer to potential consumers.

Product positioning is concerned with determining the way the product should be perceived by the customer, and included in this is some notion of how the product will be marketed to those consumers. Positioning maps, discussed in Chapter 7, can be a useful tool in supporting this work.

Concept development may include, in declining level of investment, the construction of a prototype, the building of a model or simply concept sketches on a drawing board. The larger the investment in product development, and consequently the greater the risk, the more likely the it is that a prototype will be constructed. Prototype construction is common in products as far removed as shampoos in bottles to new car designs. In service marketing, full-scale prototypes may be constructed for new bank layouts, chain restaurant designs. Where process issues (see Chapter 13) are especially important for successful service delivery, concept development may focus on the building of computer models to simulate activity. For example, a queuing computer model may be constructed of a call centre that allows managers to investigate the robustness of any particular system and staffing level. The model could allow managers to explore the implications on service levels of different call volumes, call lengths, the distribution of calls during the day and the construction of call diversion systems for non-standard queries.

Testing

Once a clear product concept has been developed, it would be normal to progress by testing (sometimes referred to as test marketing) either the concept or a sample product, or both, in the market. This is the clearest source of real evidence on the suitability of the product and will provide the development team with information on consumer and market reactions. The feedback from the testing process will identify:

- any modifications which may be necessary; and
- perhaps more importantly, will provide some indication of whether the product is likely to be successful.

The *product concept* is often tested by the use of focus groups, consumer panels or consumer experiments. The test marketing exercise involves the actual marketing of the product to a small group of consumers who should ideally be representative of the targeted market as a whole.

Research has shown that financial services firms can avoid full-scale product testing by using previous studies of the type of consumer reactions generated by certain factors. The problem with this approach may be that question marks exist over whether the information is accurate or up-to-date (because consumer tastes are continually redefined as a result of many interrelated extraneous factors).

To test (market) or not?
An important factor influencing financial services suppliers not to engage in full test marketing is the possibility that it will give competitors advance warning of an organization's latest ideas. Since copying financial services products is comparatively easy, the test marketing exercise offers competitors the ideal opportunity to imitate.

By missing out the test marketing stage, the probability of a product failing to achieve market success will be increased. However, many suppliers of financial services feel that this is not such a great problem as it may seem. Compared with many other industries, the costs of NPD for financial services are low, but the losses from giving advance warning to competitors may be quite high, so there is a preference in many organizations to accept the risk of a higher failure rate and to avoid test marketing. This view is by no means universal; some would argue that the test marketing exercise provides invaluable information, not only about the prospects for success, but also about the most appropriate methods of marketing the product. Furthermore, it is often said that it is better to be second in the market with a good service rather than first with a faulty one.

Comprehensive business analysis

At this stage only one or two products are left, the remainder having been discarded, or placed in abeyance. Now that a precise product concept has been produced, with clearly defined market segments identified, a full business analysis may be undertaken. The criteria applied during secondary screening may be examined in greater detail as refined product specifications enable market size, growth rate and competitors to be defined, and predicted, with greater precision.

Product launch

The product launch provides the true test of the viability of a newly developed product. At this point the organization makes a full-scale business commitment to the product and the product moves from the development phase of its life cycle into the introductory phases. As far as the actual launch is concerned, the key decisions are essentially of an operational nature – decisions regarding the timing of the launch, the geographical location of the launch and the specific marketing tactics to be used in support of that launch.

9.7 Brands and Branding

Marketing managers make the following distinctions:

Product class. This is a broad category of product, such as cars, washing machines etc. This corresponds to the core or generic product identified in Section 9.1.

Product form. This is a sub-division of the product class. The product class 'cars' may have several product forms including: five-door hatchbacks, four-wheel drive vehicles, hearses etc.

Brand or make. This is the means by which companies distinguish different products within a product form to consumers. Thus in the five-door hatch product form individual brands competing in this market include: Ford, Vauxhall/GM, Mercedes Benz, Toyota, VW etc.

Branding removes anonymity and gives identification to a company and its goods and services. 'Branding' is actually a very general term for attributes that may be used to distinguish one organization's goods and services from another's. This includes: brand names, designs, trademarks, symbols, a distinctive letterhead, even an identifiable shop front etc. ('Trademark' is a legal term covering words and symbols that can be registered and protected.)

According to Kotler *et al.* (1999) a *brand* is 'a name, term, sign, symbol or design or combination of them, intended to identify the goods or services of one seller, or group of sellers (as in the case of a franchise for example), and to differentiate them from those of competitors'. Branding and a firm's reputation are heavily linked. It is taking VW many years to replace the highly negative brand image which the brand 'Skoda' represents in the minds of consumers. This is in spite of highly positive consumer perception of the product in blind tests (i.e. when consumers are not aware of the brand of the car they are assessing).

Reasons for branding

1) It is a form of product differentiation.

2) Advertising needs a brand name to sell to customers.

3) It facilitates self-selection of goods in self-service stores.

4) It reduces the importance of price differentials between goods and services.

5) Brand loyalty in customers gives a manufacturer more control over marketing strategy and the choice of channels of distribution.

6) Other products can be introduced into a brand range to 'piggy back' on the articles already known to the customer (brand extension strategy).

7) It eases the task of personal selling.

8) Branding makes market segmentation easier.

Branding creates value for the company. In addition to a return factor, there is a financial cost, or investment, which the firm must undertake if it is to develop a brand. Although brands have an obvious marketing appeal, some products are inherently more difficult to brand than others. These are low-value, low-involvement products, i.e. products where the consumer has very little interest (see Chapter 5 on consumer buying behaviour). Consequently, the consumer is unlikely to remember brand names. For example, while brand names are important in buying coffee, snacks and confectionery, they have very little significance when buying light bulbs or milk. A higher level of investment is therefore required to build brands for low-involvement products, consequently a favourable return on investment is less likely. This accounts for the low numbers of brands in these markets.

Branding strategies

There are three main branding strategies:

● Individual branding

● Overall family branding

● Brand extension branding.

Table 9.4: Branding Strategies

Branding strategy	Description	Examples
Individual branding	Providing a different name for each product. The consumer is not aware of the brand owner.	Procter and Gamble with washing machine powers/ soaps – Tide, Bold, Daz, Dreft.
Overall family branding	All products branded with the same name or at least part of the name. The company name is nearly always mentioned when the individual product is mentioned.	Heinz, Microsoft, Ford. ● Heinz beans ● Ford Focus
Brand extension branding	Use successful existing brand to launch a new related product	Timotei shampoo then Timotei hair conditioner. Disney's latest film from the makers of, for example, 'Beauty and the Beast'.

The decision as to whether a brand name should be given to a range of products or whether products should be branded individually depends on several factors.

- If the brand name is associated with quality, all goods in the range must be of that standard. An example of a successful promotion of a brand name to a wide product range is the Marks & Spencer brand, formally presented to the consumer, partially through the 'St Michael' brand. This brand name applies to clothes and food, and more recently to household goods and financial services.

- If a company produces different quality (and price) goods for different market segments, it would be unwise to give the same brand name to the higher- and the lower-quality goods because this would deter buyers in the high-quality/price market segment.

Branding and Services

Service firms have found it possible to succeed mainly through family branding. Differentiation at the level of the product is very difficult, for example all current accounts are much the same. Consequently, firms are forced to fall back on their corporate image. One of the most memorable attempts at individual product branding, in the UK financial services sector, was Midland Bank's attempt to brand its current accounts (e.g. Vector, Orchard and Meridian), but this was generally regarded as unsuccessful.

Family branding continues to be the favoured branding approach for service firms. Service staff deliver a wide range of corporate products. The service is the product and this makes it difficult for the service firm to brand individual products. This has resulted in as diverse firms as fast food outlets to banks operating a family branding startegy. For example, McDonalds introduced a new chicken burger and called it 'McChicken', while banks introducing their new Internet service closely link the name of the Internet service to the name of the bank. This trend is set to continue as numerous consumer surveys have stressed the importance of organizational image, in the financial services sector, and as a consequence many financial products are identified primarily by the supplier's name.

Brand stretching

The summary of branding strategy presented in Table 9.4 assumes that the firm is using its brand within a specified product form (see Section 9.3). Where a firm uses its brand in another product form, or even within another product class, then the firm is 'stretching' the brand (also referred to as brand extension).

Table 9.5: Examples of Successful 'Stretched' Brands

Brand	Initial product/ service markets	'Stretched' markets
Virgin	Music	Trains Planes Travel Financial services Cola
Marks & Spencer	Food and clothing	Financial services
Tesco	Food retailing	Petrol retailing Financial services

Several firms have attempted to 'stretch' their brands. The stretchability of a brand depends on how narrowly defined the consumer perception of the brand is and on the brand personality. 'Virgin' is one of the most highly stretchable brands and this has enabled the company to use the brand to enter a variety of different product classes. In keeping with its original personality, the firm tends to 'stretch' into markets that are consistent with its existing personality. Words such as fashionable, trendy, style consciousness, may be used to describe this particular brand. These are all suitable attributes for its new product markets. Most brands have much more limited stretchability, some none at all. Financial service providers have not attempted to stretch their brands beyond their original markets in spite of a variety of non-financial service providers 'stretching' directly into financial services.

Brand Equity

Brand equity is the asset value of the brand which is based on positive brand attributes. Awareness and preference are perhaps the two most important factors. It is possible for a brand to have a relatively high awareness, e.g. Skoda cars before VW took over, but to have a low brand preference.

Issues of brand valuation surfaced in the 1980s, but they got tangled up in the controversy over financial reporting: if brands were treated as assets, companies could borrow more. They were considered a kind of goodwill. The main criticism of brand values in balance sheets is that they are so subjective. The counter argument to this is that they are no more subjective than other assets, and possibly less subjective than some, where brands (or at least the companies that own the brands) may be bought and sold.

Brands, perhaps unlike most other assets except property, can lose their values overnight (e.g. Perrier water, which was found to contain benzene).

The inclusion of *brand values* in the budgeting process can be justified on the following grounds (according to Guilding and Moorehouse):

1. *Authorization.* A brand evaluation exercise can help to justify discretionary marketing expenditure (e.g. advertising). Advertising can be seen as supporting the brand 'assets', like upgrading machinery.

2. *Forecasting/planning*
   - Brand values can be used to determine, over the long term, the optimum price/quantity equation. Selling at a low price increases volume in the short term but might devalue the brand in the long term.
   - Brand value itself can encourage planning, by becoming an objective in its own right. (In other words: 'what do we have to do to develop a brand that will generate £1m sales per year?')
3. *Communication and coordination.* The brand valuation exercise can effect enhanced communications between marketing staff and accountants.
4. *Motivation.* The inclusion of brand value motivates marketing management to participate in the budgeting process.
5. *Performance evaluation.* Conventional ways of measuring the performance of marketing management have relied too much on market share, without considering the law of diminishing returns (e.g. the extra percentage point may not be justified by the huge amount of money necessary). At the same time, short-term profit considerations may act to the detriment of brand value, and its ability to deliver profits in the long term. If brand values and expenditures are brought into performance evaluation, it can help both marketers and accountants to take better decisions.

Brand valuation exercise
This includes the following process:
- A brand audit discovers the strength of the brand;
- The current earnings of the brand are assessed together with the brand's ability to deliver future profits;
- The brand is then given a 'capital' value.

According to Guilding and Moorehouse, seven factors underlie the strength of a brand, and these can be given weights.

Table 9.6: Brand Strength Weightings

Item	Max. weighting %
Leadership	25
Market characteristics	10
Stability	15
Internationality	25
Trend	10
Support	10
Protection	5
	100

1. *Leadership.* How dominant is the brand in its sector? High scores are earned for dominance.

2. *Market.* What are the growth characteristics of the market?

3. *Stability.* 'Well-established brands that enjoy consumer loyalty will receive higher strength scores'.

4. *Internationality.* International brands are generally worth more than national ones, because they are not vulnerable to one market. In addition, a brand might be in another stage of its life cycle in an overseas market.

5. *Trend.* A trend indicates a brand's ability to sustain itself. Reductions in sales volume lower profit, but also make price increases harder to justify.

6. *Support.* Marketing expenditure can support a brand, but it must be of the right quality (e.g. a successful repositioning).

7. *Protection* (e.g. patent protection, copyright, imitation etc.)

Guilding and Moorehouse suggest that brand strength can be plotted against a multiple of earnings per share.

Figure 9.7: Brand Strength versus a Multiple of Earnings per Share

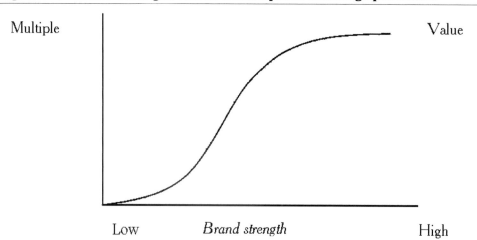

The multiple to be applied to brand strength will be:

●   higher than the average P/E ratio for the company's sector if the brand is strong;

●   lower than the average P/E ratio for this sector if the brand is weak.

The fastest growth in brand value occurs when the brand moves from the second of these to the first.

Summary

A product or service may be perceived as having three elements:

(1) the core product which provides the basic/essential features shared by similar products;

(2) the tangible (expected) product, i.e. the range of product features, included services, expected to exist in such products by most consumers; and

(3) the augmented product which includes features and services which exceed those commonly provided by similar products.

The importance of product management changes as the level of industry maturity develops. As industries mature, the focus of competition in product management moves from the core product to the tangible product and eventually to the augmented product.

Product analysis can take place at the level of the individual product or of the product line. The results of such analysis may be very different at these two levels.

Portfolio models may be used to manage an individual product in its life cycle in combination with other products in the company's portfolio (discussed in detail in Chapter 2). The dual function of such models is best demonstrated by the BCG matrix, where products move through four stages which equate broadly to the PLC stages of 'introduction', 'growth', 'maturity', and 'decline'. As products move through the marketing mix the level of competition that they face changes drastically and so does the approach to product management.

Product innovation is a key aspect of product management. New products differ greatly, both in terms of how new they are to the firm and to consumers. There are gradations of innovation for both groups. The most innovative on either or both scales are most infrequent and risky but potentially yield the highest financial returns. How innovative a product is, from the perspective of the consumer, can have a large impact on the rate of diffusion of the innovation. This concept concerns the speed at which products are purchased by the target population, not the whole population. A stylized model of diffusion considers the population as comprising five main groups, each group with a different propensity to purchase new products.

References

Kotler P, Armstrong G, Saunders J & Wong V (1999) *Principles of Marketing*, 2nd European Edition, Prentice Hall Europe

Rogers E M (1962) *Diffusion of Innovations*, Free Press, New York

Rogers E M & Shoemaker F F (1971) *Communications of Innovations*, 2nd edition, Free Press, New York.

10

MARKETING COMMUNICATIONS

Learning Objectives

After reading this chapter students should:

- Understand the application of branding to the building and support of corporate identity;

- Understand how to develop a communications plan;

- Know the difference between above- and below-the-line communications;

- Know the different types of agency and understand key issues in ensuring an effective partnership between agency and client;

- Understand the key issues in sales management and direct marketing;

- Be aware of the impact of technology on marketing communications;

- Understand the factors affecting the selection of communications media.

Figure 10.1: Chapter Map

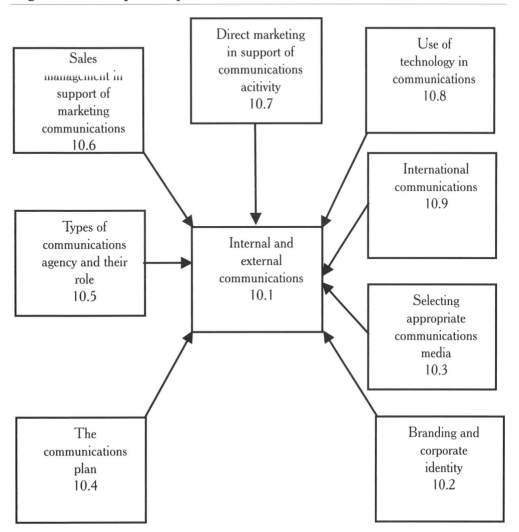

Introduction

In studying the communications mix, it is helpful to first consider general models that describe communications. These are helpful in that they allow for a common conceptualization of the communications process. This allows practitioners to analyse communications with a view to understanding problems and to suggest improvements.

Objective setting, targeting and positioning, and understanding how these marketing tasks should be implemented, is crucial when communicating to consumers, intermediaries or all stakeholders, including those who are internal as well as those external to the organization.

A common mistake made by students when considering the communications mix is to overemphasize the importance of TV advertising, even within advertising as a medium. In terms of the advertising budget, newspaper advertising exceeds TV advertising in many countries. A further oversight is the importance of regional newspapers which in many countries are as important as national papers, in terms of the value of spending within the communications mix.

Table 10.1: Marketing Communications Mix

Advertising [TV- press- radio- cinema- outdoor media such as in football stadia and on the outside of bus shelters, taxis etc.]	● Paid for non-personal communications targeted through mass media with the purpose of achieving set objectives, e.g. one element in the AIDA model.
	● Publicity surrounding AXA's sponsorship of the FA cup, following Manchester United's withdrawal in 1999, is not advertising, because it is not paid for. One-to-one communications, as in a direct mailing from a bank to recruit new credit card holders from a comprehensive database, is not advertising, because it *is* personal.
Public relations	● The development and maintenance of good relationships with different publics, e.g. press relations, lobbying.
Direct marketing	● Marketing through various advertising media that interact directly with consumers, generally calling for the consumer to make a direct response, e.g. direct mail, telemarketing.
Sales promotion	● Incentives to consumers, trade or the salesforce designed to increase sales in the short term.
Sponsorship	● This is where the cost of an event, broadcast or publication is paid for in part or in whole by another individual or organization with a view to promoting its commercial interests.
Packaging and merchandizing	● Packaging has three basic roles:
	1. Protect and contain – especially important where the contents are delicate, toxic or potentially harmful, e.g. tamper-proof pill bottles, child protection lids on bleach, food preserved in controlled atmosphere packs.
	2. Offer convenience – e.g. microwaveable food containers, stand up toothpaste tube dispensers, Heinz squeezable plastic bottles.
	3. Communication – of the brand and of functional activity, e.g. how to cook, frequency to take pills etc.

Table 10.1: Marketing Communications Mix (cont.)

	● Merchandising includes techniques that encourage consumers to purchase when browsing product and service displays. Examples of tools include shelf displays, posters, stickers, store sampling, leaflets and window displays.
Personal selling	● In addition to selling the role can include customer care, key account management and relationship marketing. Telephone sales is the most common consumer channel.
Internal communications	● Internal customers, i.e. employees, are a key target for much marketing communications. Internal communications can include activities such as newsletters, e-mails/memos, presentations, briefings, workshops etc.
New communications technologies	● Use of digital communications including the Internet, WAP phones, interactive digital television.
ABOVE THE LINE	● Any paid-for communications (e.g. TV, press) on which commission is paid by the media to the agency.
BELOW THE LINE	● Marketing communications activities that are not subject to commission being paid to the advertising agency.

10.1   Internal and External Communications

Communications

In developing a communications strategy, the particular problem facing suppliers of services is that they have no physical product to present to consumers. The task of promotion is therefore to develop a message, and a form of presentation, that allows the organization to present an intangible product in a tangible form. The elements of a simple model based on this framework are presented below. There are basically *nine* components.

1. *Source*: the party sending the message which will typically be the organization itself, although for some aspects of publicity or public relations, the source could be classed as a quasi-independent body.

2. *Encoding*: finding some verbal or symbolic representation for the concepts and ideas that are to be conveyed in the communications process.

3. *Message*: the set of words and symbols created by the encoding process which the sender then transmits.

4. *Medium*: the particular channel through which the message is transmitted, either personal (sales staff) or non-personal (advertising, publicity or sales promotion).

5. *Decoding*: the process whereby the receiver interprets and assigns some meanings to the message.

6. *Receiver*: the party receiving the message.

7. *Response*: the way in which the receiver reacts to the message, based on its interpretation of it.

8. *Feedback*: information on the receiver's response that is transmitted back to the sender.

9. *Noise*: any unplanned interference with the communications process that distorts the message.

Effective Communication

The simple model described above highlights the important components of effective communication. An audience must be identified to receive the message.

●   The message itself must be presented (encoded) in a way that makes clear what the source wants to convey to the audience and in a way that will attract attention.

●   The communications process itself must then be managed to minimize the effects of noise. The presence of noise in any communications process is unavoidable. There will be few messages that are not distorted in some way; the target audience may receive only part of the message being communicated, they may interpret it in accordance with their own preconceptions and they may recall only parts of the message.

Figure 10.2: General Communications Model

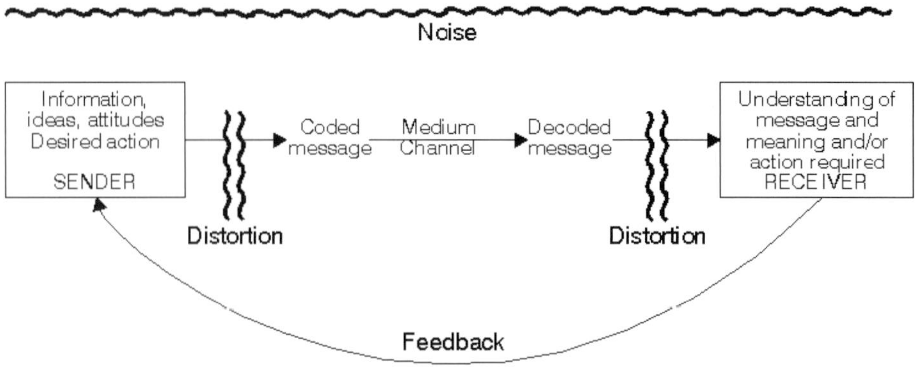

Marketing Communications Models

In Chapter 5, we identified various categories of buyer behaviour. Similar models have been developed for the communications process. All of these models concentrate on the behaviour of the target audience and what the communications exercise should do to alter this behaviour.

In practice, all buyer behaviour models propose a sequence of behaviour as follows:

1. *Cognitive*: learning about a product;

2. *Affective*: developing feelings about a product;

3. *Conative*: doing something about the product (e.g. purchase).

Two of the more popular models used to support communications planning, namely AIDA and DAGMAR, are presented.

AIDA

The AIDA model (Strong 1925) was originally designed to represent the sequential stages a salesperson must go through during personal selling, although it has been applied to marketing communications in general. The AIDA model suggests that marketers should use the marketing mix in general, and the communications mix in particular, to:

- Gain consumer **A**WARENESS;

- Generate customer **I**NTEREST;

- Stimulate customer **D**ESIRE;

- Instigate customer **A**CTION to buy.

The AIDA model is relevant, and the following situations exemplify this:

- A promotional message that is concerned with creating awareness of, or interest in, a product is likely to differ from one that is trying to create a desire to purchase or stimulate an actual purchase;

- It is often useful to distinguish between those groups who actually make decisions regarding purchases and those who influence decisions;

- In the small business sector of the corporate market, although the business owner may decide which bank to use, an accountant or a solicitor may exert an important influence on that choice and as such may need to be considered as part of the target audience;

- In the personal sector, the consumers of the increasing number of specialist children's savings products are the children themselves, but the decision maker is typically a parent or relative. In this instance, promotion would be directed not to the consumer but to the decision-maker, i.e. the person who actually makes the purchase.

The DAGMAR Model

Colley devised the DAGMAR model ('Defining Advertising Goals for Measure Advertising Response') in 1961. This showed that before purchase, customers move through five *stages* – unawareness, awareness, comprehension, conviction, action – and that progress through each stage was measurable. From this it was a short step to designing promotional work to influence each step, and to the devising of more detailed promotions, each specific to a particular target market.

Table 10.2: Amplification of DAGMAR Model of Consumer Communications

Awareness		This is obviously necessary before purchase behaviour can be expected.
	Build	A new product must be brought to people's attention.
	Associate	People may not know *how* the product will satisfy their needs.
	Sustain	Awareness must be maintained.
	Define	The firm may wish to *change* people's awareness in some way.
Comprehension		People need to understand the product; mere awareness is not enough.
Conviction		Having established that a product has particular attributes which lead to benefits perceived by the target audience as being important, people need to be convinced that the product is the right one.
Action		Advertising can guide people to purchase. The use of personal selling may be appropriate here.

Model criticisisms

A number of criticisms have been directed at these models, and models which are similar to them. The main two are that:

- The 'learn-feel-do' sequence implies 'rationality' and this cannot be validated consistently by all research data;

- The links between 'attitudes towards' a product and the 'intention to buy it' are sometimes tenuous. Market researchers are readily able to measure attitude and changes in attitude and this in part has been the reason for focusing on attitude as a precurser of purchase behaviour.

10.2   Branding and Corporate Identity

Branding is often discussed in the context of corporate identity and image. Branding is discussed in Chapter 9 on 'product' and the discussion here will focus on corporate identity.

Corporate identity

Corporate image is the consumer/potential consumer's perception of the organization which the organization projects from one of three corporate identity sources:

1. Symbolism, i.e. the visual cues that the organization projects, especially in terms of design in the servicescape (e.g. from logos to buildings);

2. Behaviour of staff and they way they interact, with each other and with the public, which is determined by corporate culture;

---

3.   Communications from the organization received by stakeholders.

These three identity cues, according to the corporate identity design consultancy Wolf Olins, project for the organization:

● Who it is

● What it does

● How it does it.

Why is corporate image important?

In mature product and service markets where competition is intense, it is very difficult to sustain a competitive advantage. Consumers become increasingly confused by the array of services and products in the marketplace. Increasingly they simplify their buying decision process by reducing the list of potential purchases to a few, most of which are provided by companies that project an image in tune with customers in the target segment. Faced with a degree of uncertainty, consumers will select brands that tend to be well known and most trusted: HSBC in financial services, McDonalds in fast food catering, Starbucks in cafes, Sony in electronics etc.

Poor corporate image can develop rapidly. In the UK services market Barclays was a high-profile casualty of poor corporate image, largely based on consumer perception of two elements of corporate identity; behaviour and communications. In 2000, corporate communications of branch closures in sparsely populated areas was perceived as uncaring. In addition, management action to try to introduce charges in a previously free cooperative financial services network, which the bank had only recently joined, was perceived as evidence of corporate greed. Consumers were not interested in any debate over the strategic reasons for such action.

Building a new corporate identity

Developing a new corporate identity is a complex process which involves repositioning the identity. This is assessed and depicted in the same way that products and services are positioned and repositioned (see Chapter 7 on positioning maps). How is this achieved? Corporate identities are also repositioned on attributes. While many models and systems of this process have been proposed, a fundamental understanding of this is perhaps best achieved by considering the work of Spector (1961). Here it was suggested that corporate image is perceived on six dimensions. Each dimension does not have a single meaning but a range of possible meanings within a central attribute. Sometimes these meanings can be mutually exclusive (Table 10.3).

Table 10.3: Attributes on which Corporate Image is Perceived

ATTRIBUTE	Characteristic
Dynamic	pioneering and active
Cooperative	friendly and well liked
Character	ethical, reputable, respectable
Business	wise, shrewd and well organized
Successful	financial performance
Withdrawn	cautious, aloof

Source: adapted from Spector (1961)

Organizations must therefore use the three identity cues (symbolism, behaviour and communications) to reposition corporate image on each of the six attributes that are relevant, if one employs Spector's six attributes of image.

10.3 Selecting Appropriate Communications Media

There are two main decisions to be made when selecting the most suitable communications media.

1.   Which media to use (inter-media decision)?

2.   Once a particular medium has been selected, e.g. television or magazines, which programme slots or titles to use (intra-media decision)?

Before discussing this topic it is necessary to be clear about three concepts:

1.   REACH – percentage of target market who are exposed to the communication in a given time period;

2.   FREQUENCY – how many times the average person in the target market is exposed to the communication;

3.   IMPACT – qualitative value of a message, What effect did it have on the target audience?

The objective of media planning is to ensure that a reasonably large target audience (high percentage reach) see/receive the communications a sufficient number of times (high frequency percentage) with a high level of impact.

There are many influences that guide the selection of optimal media combination (Table 10.4).

Table 10.4: Influences on the Inter-media Decision

Money available	Budget size places a substantial constraint on media options. To obtain large audience reach on a small/medium budget eliminates the effective use of TV advertising. Some companies opt for inappropriate low-cost alternatives such as stills with voice overs, especially in regional TV and cinema advertising. This may achieve high reach but with a substantial reduction in 'impact'. Many companies have opted to use PR as a relatively low-cost approach to high percentage reach, at the risk of reduced control, the delivery of the message and how it may be received by the target audience.
Client's preference	Companies often favour a particular medium over periods of 1 to 3 years, for example the back page of glossy magazines, or magazine supplements in weekend newspapers. It may be difficult to change a client from a particular communications mix.
Target audience	This partly makes the decision of media on its own. Middle-aged women have several magazine titles devoted to their interests, specialist interest magazines are available for homogeneous groups, e.g. golf, astrology etc.
Type of product	Communications to support a product retailed in a supermarket, for example, must deliver its message prior to peak supermarket sales activity at the weekend. This communication has short lead times, therefore glossy magazines could not be used. Instead, local and national press may be used, as supported by local radio. Female products are likely to reach a large target audience if women's magazines are used.
Competitive activity	There are two possible strategies; avoid where competitors advertise or out-advertise in the same media.
Retail trade reaction	Selection of media is not always used purely to reach the final consumer. National press and TV advertising may be used to encourage the distribution channel to stock the product, or in the service context, to support agents and franchisees in their marketing.
Relative effectiveness	Each medium has different relative strengths. Cinema and TV have a high impact on audiences, TV generates high awareness/coverage (although a profusion of channels may require multi-TV channel communication). Press is favoured when issues, or rationale, have to be explained, e.g. Häagan Dazs when entering the UK market explained the rationale for the product in the quality press, supported by complementary pictures.

Intra-medium decision

The intra-media decision concerns media selection within a particular category. For example, choosing the most appropriate magazines, once the decision has been made to proceed with magazine advertising.

- Choice of publication or radio/TV station.
  The main consideration is how cost-effective is the choice against the target audience? This is measured in cost per thousand people in the target audience. In many countries, independently audited audience viewing and readership data is available. This allows detailed estimates to be made of the cost of communications. For example, if an advert costs £50,000 in a magazine with a readership of 100,000 people, 20% of whom are in a target audience of women 25-40 years old, then the advert costs per thousand people seeing it may be calculated:

  Number of people in the target audience who will see the advert:

  $$100,000 \times 0.2 = 20,000$$

  Advert cost per *thousand* readers $£50,000/20 = £2,500$

- Size/length of spot.
  How long a TV slot to buy? Whether to include short ads which are less than 30 seconds in length? How large a print ad to use? How frequently to repeat ads? Insufficiently detailed research is available to answer these questions. Advertisers have to rely on experience in assessing where diminishing returns set in and more repetitions, longer or larger ads do not justify their costs.

- Choice of position in the medium.
  The advertiser wants to reach the target audience in sufficient numbers. Published information and research studies support decision making in this area.

- Poster sites are graded in terms of the volume of traffic passing them.

- In the press, agencies rely on research (their own) to judge the best locations, e.g. bottom right better than bottom left on the right hand page.

- TV rating systems lets advertisers know how many people are watching and fees are structured accordingly.

10.4   The Communications Plan

Where are we now?	Situation analysis	This is much more detailed and specific than the more general marketing situation analysis. Communications analysis must include potential segments and decision-making units.
Where do we want to be?	Objectives – Marketing	Generally to increase market share or to reduce the rate of decline in market share.
	Objectives – Communications	To change the viewpoint of the target audience. The objective is specified as moving consumers in the target segment from one stage of a buyer behaviour model to another stage (see AIDA and DAGMAR in section 10.1). E.g. move the consumer from being unaware of the brand to being aware of the brand.
How do we get there?	Communications strategy	Communications strategies are not defined precisely. Essential elements include:
		● Specifying a positioning stance that is to be communicated.
		● Specifying the relative emphasis on each communications medium [*inter*-media decision].
		● Identify the relative weighting of a push versus a pull strategy.
	Tactics = implementation	Here the weekly, or monthly, plan of activity for each communications medium is specified [*intra*-media decision].
	Budgets Internal people Other resources	These are vitally important elements of the plan and should not be overlooked.
How can we be sure we got there?	Control/ measurement	How is success measured? ● Number of people who remember (prompted or unprompted) seeing the advert.
		● Percentage of target segment who consider, for example, a particular perfume as the brand most likely to be purchased.
		● Measure changes in attitude.

Advertising plan stages

1.   Advertising plan for … (e.g. pensions for ABC1 women, 25 – 40 years of age).

2.   Advertising objectives.

3.   Target segment.

4.   Message.

5.   Inter-media selection: allocate 100 percentage points across all possible media to show relative emphasis on each.

6.   Media selected (a) For broadcast media state the times of broadcast and the type of programmes around which the adverts will appear. (b) For print media provide examples of print titles in which adverts will appear.

7.   Timing (most usefully presented in Gannt chart format).

8.   Estimated cost (include in Gannt chart).

9.   How will success be measured?

Setting the budget

A budget must be established for the promotional exercise as a whole, and, at a later stage, for the individual components of the promotional mix. There are no hard-and-fast rules for determining the size of the promotional budget and organizations even within the same broad market vary enormously in terms of promotional expenditure. A number of methods are available to provide guidelines on expenditure.

The affordable method

This simply suggests that the organization's expenditure on promotion is determined according to what the overall corporate budget indicates is available. A target level of expenditure is thus determined without reference to the needs of the campaign and the marketing department must tailor its activities to that budget. This approach is common among smaller organizations with limited resources.

Sales revenue method

The promotional budget is set as some percentage of sales revenue. By implication this means that sales 'lead' promotion rather promotion leading sales, which is what might be expected. Although this approach does at least establish a link between the success of the product and the level of promotional expenditure, it may present difficulties when budgeting promotional campaigns for new products and it also tends to limit the opportunity for increased promotional expenditure in periods when demand seems weak.

The incremental method

The budget is set as an increment on the previous year's expenditure. Although this method is often used by smaller firms it offers no real link between the market and promotional expenditure and does not allow promotional or marketing objectives to guide the level of expenditure.

The competitive parity approach

This approach focuses on the importance of promotion as a competitive tool and entails setting budgets to match those of competitors. It is a rather more market-orientated approach but one which ties the firm to following its competitors and ignores possible fundamental differences between different organizations in the same broad markets.

The objective/task method

This is probably the most rational approach to the establishment of promotional budgets, but perhaps also the most difficult to implement. It requires specific objectives for promotion in terms of the numbers of customers to be reached (exposed to a message), means of reaching them (advertising, direct mail etc.), the frequency of the message (number of adverts, mail shots, leaflets) and, of course, the precise costs associated with each stage. On this basis, a budget can be established which should enable the organization to achieve its specified promotional objectives and, furthermore, it gives the marketing department a systematic basis on which to evaluate the merits of alternative promotional strategies.

10.5   Types of Communications Agencies and their Role

Before considering types of agency, organizations should consider whether they have the resources and/or staff with suitable qualifications and experience to undertake a campaign. If not then several types of agency are available.

Types of agency

Full service agency

The typical full service advertising agency would cover much of a firm's communications activity, including media advertising (e.g. TV), media buying (i.e. purchasing TV advertising time and newspaper space), and creative work, including copyrighting. Examples of full service agencies include Saatchi & Saatchi, J. Walter Thompson and Leo Burnett.

À la carte

It is possible to use a wide variety of specialist agencies. These agencies have grown in importance, particularly in the last ten years. The main types of specialist agencies undertake each one of the main functions undertaken by the full service agencies, such as media buying and creative work. In addition, there has been a growth in the number specialist agencies that have evolved as a result of new technology, for example, direct marketing agencies and those specializing in the use of the Internet as a communications medium. Examples of two types of agencies include:

Creative boutiques

Sometimes also known as creative workshops or creative independents. The sole function of these agencies is to provide assistance in creative planning and execution. They are able to assemble a group of highly creative people to work on big-budget campaigns such as those involving television commercials.

Media buying agencies

These specialize in buying media. They have grown in importance because of the increasing complexity of media and the need for computer-based analysis facilities. They also operate on large volumes and low margins. A fee of 5% of the media spend is frequently charged but depending on the particular relationship with the agency, some or all of the media commission can be reimbursed to the client company.

Agency remuneration

Three approaches to payment for agency work are:

- Commission
- Fees
- Payment by results.

Commission

The long-established method of remunerating agencies is that of commission paid by the media owners. Agencies started life as media space sellers and have traditionally received 15% commission. To a large degree this is an arbitrary amount which has to cover the cost of planning, designing, preparing and placing advertisements. The client, of course, pays for the media space bought and it is this on which the 15% commission is calculated. These activities are described as 'above-the-line' because they incur commission paid by the media owners. 'Below-the-line' activities include public relations, direct marketing, sales promotion, exhibitions and literature. These services are billed as a direct cost.

Because the 15% is an arbitrary figure variations are made to allow for differing scales of work. For example, for a relatively simple but large-budget account the 15% may be too generous and clients have sought to claw back a percentage based on a sliding scale. Likewise in a relatively low-budget account with lots of activity the 15% may not be sufficient and the agency will either seek to enhance the 15% or will seek to get the client to agree to pay an additional fee.

Fees

A retainer is paid regularly, e.g. quarterly/monthly, and the client in addition pays for each project with the agency. Agencies are able to estimate costs accurately and use this as a basis for a mark-up.

Payment by results
Agency payment is linked directly to results. It can sometimes be difficult to agree on the particular results that should be used as an indicator of success. Two options include recorded sales or research on target segment attitudes and behaviour, pre- and post-communications activity. The main problem with payment by results is that factors outside of the control of the agency can affect the results. These include factors that are internal to the client company (poorly trained staff on a new service product which is being marketed) and external factors (such as the launch of a new service product by a competitor).

There has been a shift away from commission payments towards payment by fees, due to inflation in media prices and the growth of specialist agencies, which are comfortable with working on a fee basis. The method of payment selected is fundamental to the client-agency relationship, both working and contractual.

Major roles within agencies

Account management
Responsible for:

● Day-to-day contact with the client;

● Project manager for the client work within the agency.

Account managers are the main point of contact between the client and the agency. Their function is to channel the client's brief to the agency and to act as a link between the client and the agency. Through this role they develop close, long-term relationships with the client. They are ultimately responsible for coordinating activity within the agency to ensure that client deadlines are met.

Account planning
Main role to commission, understand and interpret research. Responsible for:

● Advertising strategy

● Creative brief

● Consumer research

● Measurement of advertising effectiveness.

Account planning is mainly a feature of the large consumer agencies. The planner must have an ability to know the detailed intricacies of research. Requires a highly numerate individual who is very skilled in phrasing problems, commissioning relevant research and in interpreting its findings. The planner's role also includes identifying gaps in the picture of the market provided by the client, and to suggest research to fill important gaps.

Creative team
● Art director (visual aspects of campaign)

● Copywriter (textual aspects of the campaign)

Media planners and buyers
Responsible for placing communications in the most appropriate media to reach the campaign target audience.

10.6 Sales Management in Support of Marketing Communications

Personal selling

This may be viewed as the traditional 'direct marketing' or 'relationship marketing' approach. Overall, the emphasis placed on the sales force has declined as other marketing channels have risen in importance. However the sales force continues to be an important tool in the marketing of financial services with most employees now charged with supporting sales, although for many this will be in delivering efficient and effective processes. Personal selling continues to consume a large proportion of the marketing communication budget for many B2B companies.

Important sales force issues include: objectives; organization and structure; motivation, recruitment; training; evaluation and assessment; and the stages of the selling process.

10.7 Direct marketing in support of communications activity

Direct marketing and database marketing are often used interchangeably. There is no single term in common usage. Direct marketing emphasises the whole process of communicating directly with consumers, based on a database of customer records, with the objective of obtaining a direct response. This implies a short-term tactical objective. Direct marketing may also be used to support strategic marketing activity. If new markets (i.e. customers) are sought for a product (i.e. one of the four quadrants in Ansoff's matrix (see Chapter 2)), then analysis of the database may be undertaken to identify these customers.

The term database marketing emphasises the exploitation of the database. The main functions include storing customer information in a structured manner and tracking customer purchase behaviour. Additional customer demographics may be updated, including life and lifestyle changes. Various techniques are employed in analysing the customer database and in integrating purchased data with the database (see the example at the end of Part 2 on financial behavioural segmentation provided by 'NOP Financial').

There are now many potential vehicles for direct marketing including direct mail, telephone sales, newspaper advertising, direct response television advertising, promotional competitions and the new possibilities provided by digital media, especially via the Internet, cable services and satellite broadcasting.

Direct marketing and new media

What is direct marketing (DM)?

> '*An interactive system of marketing which uses one or more advertising media to effect a measurable response and/or transaction at any location*'

Direct Marketing Association of the USA.

The tenet of direct marketing is that the organization needs to build a one-to-one relationship with the customer. It is not the single sale that is important but the lifetime relationship with the customer. Directing marketing is regarded as an important tool in moving consumers up 'the ladder of loyalty', as part of this process of building a lifelong relationship. Branded consumer goods manufacturers have used direct marketing strategically to counteract the power which retailers have in the marketing chain through the knowledge they have of their customer base. In the mid-1990s Heinz focused marketing communications on direct marketing, supported by television advertising, exploiting their extensive customer database. Their company consumer magazine *At Home with Heinz* was a major vehicle for this strategy, which included targeted coupon offers.

DM terminology

- *Proposition* – the benefit which you claim to provide, e.g. 'A Mars a day helps you work rest and play'; 'Persil washes whiter'; Ford 'Everything we do is driven by you'.
- *Offer* – the trigger that makes you buy the product, frequently a sales promotion.
- *Fulfilment* – this involves getting the right goods to the customer (i.e. without expensive errors to resolve). The fulfilment process controls cash flow, e.g. cheque/card clearance before dispatch.

DM activity split

Table 10.5: General Allocation of Costs for a Direct Marketing Campaign

	%
Account handling, planning, consultancy	25
Production	25
Creative	20
Media buying	20
Database operations	5
Fulfilment	5
TOTAL	100

MARKETING IN PRACTICE

Legal & General attract last-minute PEP business through Direct Marketing activity

Legal and General was identified by the journal *Campaign* as one of the biggest spenders on PEP advertising. In the first quarter of 1999 this activity cost £3 million. Direct marketing activity was concentrated in three areas; direct response; press advertising and inserts; and direct mail. The company tried to market three PEP product offers: a UK Index Tracker, a European Index Tracker and a corporate bond. Direct mail activity included a pack with information leaflets, testimonial press coverage and a simple application form – all presented in corporate livery. There were two objectives, to attract customers of competitors as well as for new business. Direct mail was supplemented by national press advertising, including press inserts.

Databases

The established view of database marketing is relatively simplistic. This is where the company stores information, including customer details, quantities, values and frequencies of transactions (i.e. customer behaviour) and uses this information for informing customers of new products, special offers and to cross-sell to existing customers. Techniques evolved with list brokers selling lists of new potential customers. Specific attributes of the potential customers' list (i.e. one or a few data fields) could be matched with the existing customer lists thereby allowing the two lists to be merged, e.g. on income or credit card payment history.

Data warehouses represented a development that was more quantitative than qualitative. They allow for the storage of very large data sets in a highly structured way that allows organizations to:

● access data, according to need, on a company-wide basis; and

● update records relatively easily.

Data warehouses may be used to analyse customer information in order to undertake integrated marketing communications activity. It is a facility that has two main functions in addition to simply storing data:

1. Presenting clearly structured summary information, often in table and graph form;

2. It allows data mining to take place which allows for patterns in data to be identified in order to predict behaviour of existing customers. In addition, it allows cross-linking of behaviour of existing customers, with given characteristics, with a dataset of potential, non-existing customers who have similar characteristics.

New media (principally the Internet and digital television) is another vehicle for direct marketing. It warrants particular emphasis, due to the profound influence that this will have on marketing competitiveness (i.e. e-business). The distinction between place (i.e. distribution), product and promotion becomes blurred in the case of new media and it is no

---

longer possible to make complete distinctions between these tools. The marketing tool classification allocated to an Internet bank account, for example, only has meaning depending on the perspective taken. It may be regarded as a product (service), a marketing communications vehicle, a distribution channel or as a product line providing a 'value' price offer.

Intelligent agents

This represents a major change in the application of technology to database marketing and is especially effective when used with new media. In the past databases could only be exploited by undertaking sorts on selected data fields. More sophisticated sorts would be on artificial fields which had been generated using complex analytical software.

Intelligent agents or 'agents' are self-contained programs which analyse data and 'learn' from this analysis. They automatically change rules of data classification as different connections in the data are discerned. They are especially useful where textual information has to be classified, e.g. reports on key customers or client calls/visits. The more an 'agent' is used, the more it learns about the data it is analysing and consequently the more effective it will become. 'Agents' can for example be used to monitor consumer visits to company websites, to monitor who are customers and where and what is read, and perhaps the entry and exit websites. They are then able to generate a profile of users. Within the context of a company intranet, 'agents' may be used to inform one user of previous users with the same interest. For example, if someone interrogates the corporate knowledge base on high-income customers who have moved their credit card business, then information on other users who have undertaken this research will be provided.

'Agents' are also used in online banner advertising where information browsed by visitors to a site will be used as the basis for targeting the product or service advertised in the banner.

MARKETING IN PRACTICE

Technology and direct marketing

Technology has turned banking competition on its head. In the past it was necessary to have an extensive branch network in prime-site locations to run a bank. Now, First Direct runs a bank in the UK from a call centre. At the centre of this shift is technology, the web as well as database technology. The latter in particular has facilitated a rapid growth in the use of direct marketing by financial sector organizations. Maintaining and updating databases is essential to the continuing success of direct marketing. For example, in 1998 when the Bradford and Bingly wanted to test the strength of opinion about its mutual status, it targeted 2 million customers in a direct mailing and additionally used the questions asked to enhance and expand their database. The motivation for this activity, like all similar activities, is to create accurate data that can lead to improved targeting and therefore allow effective cross-selling.

Direct marketing is increasingly the vehicle employed to keep customers loyal to the company. On a cautionary note, however, one commentator suggested that too many financial service organizations were concentrating on customer recruitment, leaving existing customers to become disillusioned and open to approach by the competition.

See further reading cited in *The Banker* (June and Nov 1998) and in *Precision Marketing*.

The process of facilitating interaction is important in developing corporate brand image, in addition to the more usual communication vehicles. Up until 1998, new media represented less than 10% of direct marketing spend. It is therefore a tool for the future, however due to its explosive growth, this will be the near future. Some financial services firms are in the vanguard of the development of this tool. The Nationwide Building Society has for some time offered Internet banking to its customers, while the Prudential restricted access to Internet customers for its 'Egg' accounts. Abbey National and Standard Life Bank are examples of just two banks which followed the lead of these innovators, in the autumn of 1999, although in the case of Abbey it will be an 'innovator' if their 'Aquarius' accounts actually succeed in exploiting digital TV, in offering totally interactive banking. In spite of these developments by some, there are still many laggard companies. A straw poll, by the authors, in the summer of 1999, found some leading High Street banks still without any internet accounts/products in their portfolios.

10.8   Use of Technology in Communications

The principal technological development has been the Internet, which has permitted communications to become interactive.

General, basic use of the technology

Electronic (digital) communications using each element of the communications mix	This is the digital (electronic) equivalent of non-digital advertising. The most important difference is that it can become one-to-one advertising.
Direct marketing	Electronic equivalent of direct mail.
Building databases	Electronic equivalent of paper-based technology.
Internal marketing	Shared company information databases and the use of company intranets to broadcast information.

Advanced exploitation of the technology

'Push' technology	This is where communications are delivered to the consumer without the consumer directly requesting the information. For example, receiving notification from a book website of the latest publications in the topic area of interest, or the latest news stories on a particular

industry sector. All the consumer has to do is to request to be informed and provide some details.

Internet service providers are offering attractive gateway services that the subscriber can personalize to obtain information as efficiently as possible, from finding a plumber, a new distance learning course to buying a house. Users must enter the site via a gateway and this provides a valuable location for advertising space.

Technology enables new businesses to gain access to consumers relatively inexpensively. An important element of communications using new media technology is the creation of a company website. There are different levels of sophistication the organization may achieve in the use of a website.

1. Electronic publisher At the most basic level the organization will simply use the website to produce an electronic, rather than paper, version of its communications.

2. Customer interactive The organization has a dialogue with its customers or potential customers. This can include requests for product information, the location of showrooms or hotels. The website may also provide information on linked products in an attempt to cross-sell.

3. Process/people substitution Train companies in the UK, for example, allow customers to book tickets online, while the success of amazon.com has been based on the automation of functions. Intelligent agent and virtual assistant technology will take the 'people' out of services. Intelligent agents will provide 'intelligently' sifted information, while virtual assistants will be able to undertake low-level dialogue with customers on a narrow topic area linked to products and services offered by the organization.

The 'three levels of sophistication' model in Internet usage is a useful starting point in assessing the need for company development of websites. Organizations operating at level one are not really exploiting the technology.

IBM considered that organizations needed to appraise their use of the whole of their e-marketing activity. This would allow them to integrate their communications activity with the rest of the marketing mix. They tentatively suggested six e-marketing characteristics for success.

e-marketing success characteristics

IBM suggests that there are six e-marketing success characteristics against which the success potential of products or services, marketed on the Internet, can be rated. The characteristics are (1) target market, (2) marketing environment, (3) product/service and branding, (4) promotion, (5) price and (6) distribution. This information can be used to identify issues that may impact the potential of the organization to conduct electronic commerce. A range of criteria is used to derive a single measure for a product/service for each characteristic.

This produces a profile against which other products/services may be assessed or benchmarked. The six criteria presented by IBM may be used in a portfolio-matrix style of analysis (see Chapter 2).

Table 10.6: Portfolio Analysis to Appraise the Potential Success of a Product or Service Marketed through the Internet, Using Six e-marketing Success Characteristics

	Score	Weight	Total
1. Target Market **Advantage(s)** ● Offering is targeted at people who have resources to sustain volume purchases of your proposed offering. ● Sustained volume sales of the offering may be possible because Internet usage is common at the education level of the target audience. ● Sustained volume sales of the offering may be possible because Internet usage is currently high among males and growing among females. ● Internet users are a significant part of the target audience. **Disadvantage(s)** ● Target market is difficult to identify and reach. **2. Marketing Environment** **Advantages** ● The potential to save money by using the Internet appears to exist. ● Regional or national economic factors appear positive and may help in increasing sales. ● Targeted geographical areas appear to have strong Internet infrastructure and/or usage to warrant the offering. **Disadvantages** ● Offering is currently available on the Internet from competitors. ● Demand appears low.			

Table 10.6: Portfolio Analysis to Appraise the Potential Success of a Product or Service Marketed through the Internet, Using Six e-marketing Success Characteristics (continued)

	Score	Weight	Total
3. Product/Service and Branding			
Advantages			
● Offering is easy to order via the Internet.			
● Offering provides new capabilities and features that could provide customers with a competitive advantage.			
● Offering has multinational market potential.			
● Customers recognize the brand and/or the company.			
Disadvantages			
● The offering is not significantly computer-related.			
● The offering is low-tech and therefore may not appeal to a large portion of Internet users.			
● Offering may be too unique to be successful on the Internet and customers may not know what to expect if they make a purchase.			
4. Promotion			
Advantages			
● Traditional advertising media can be leveraged.			
5. Pricing			
Advantages			
● Pricing appears adequate for Internet marketing.			
6. Distribution			
Advantages			
● International distribution should allow the offering to attain its full marketing potential.			
Disadvantages			
● Competition from traditional channels may be damaging to the offering's sales potential.			
TOTAL		1.00	

If the product or service scores highly, according to the above criteria, then it should potentially be a successful Internet service or product. Examples of products/services that would achieve a high score are books, music, software and flowers.

Internal Communications

The importance of internal customers cannot be overstated, as discussed in Chapters 3 and 14. Employees are a key stakeholder group with which an organization will wish to communicate. Communication is an important element of the internal marketing mix and many companies continually strive to develop better and more effective means with which to communicate with employees. This is particularly important for financial service companies because they are to a large extent reliant on the staff to deliver the service and therefore they must be kept informed about latest developments.

MARKETING IN PRACTICE

BUPA

BUPA is an international private health care provider employing approximately 25,000 people. The task of communicating effectively with these employees is a complex yet essential task. BUPA adopts a multi-channel strategy approach utilizing e-mail, team meetings, a quarterly staff magazine and video. These are all controlled by the PR department to ensure they are integrated and that the various messages are consistent with each other. Internal communication is also integrated with external communication – the strapline 'You're Amazing' used in the recent advertising campaign has also been used internally. BUPA has recognized that one of its greatest assets is its staff and that effective internal communications is a means of retaining their loyalty and commitment.

Technology has had a major impact on internal communications in the form of e-mail and intranets. Intranets are proving to be valuable tools for companies to communicate with their staff locally, nationally or internationally. Intranets can provide information of all types from telephone numbers to details about a new advertising campaign. They can be updated continuously, facilitate interaction and provide the opportunity for two-way communication. Extranets are also being utilized to provide specific groups with access to particular areas of the intranet while preventing open access to all Internet users. This is a particularly effective way to communicate with suppliers, distributors, customers and other stakeholder groups. The relationship between intranets, extranets and the Internet is illustrated in Figure 10.3.

Figure 10.3: The Relationship Between Intranets, Extranets and the Internet

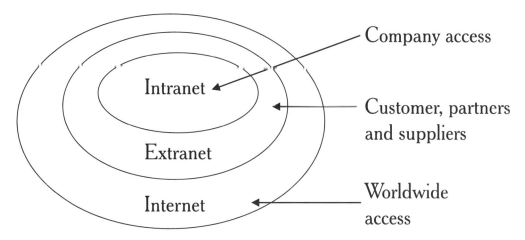

Many companies are recognizing the power of the intranet in communicating with their staff; BP is one such company. It is developing the 'Virtual Village', an online shopping mall accessed through the company portal where employees can purchase anything from holidays to computers. The objective is to get employees logging on and then BP can start to talk to them. The intranet plays an important role in updating staff about new developments. For example, BP broadcasts live events such as the launch of its new brand and logo to its employees via the 'In Motion' section of its intranet. The advantage of this method of communication over the traditional newsletter is that it encourages staff to respond and provide feedback. It also ensures staff can find out about new developments as they take place.

The development of a company intranet does not guarantee effective communications because staff can feel overburdened by e-mail and the intranet can simply add to their workload. The development and implementation of the intranet must be well thought out and its objectives clearly identified. Once the intranet is established it is important that sufficient resources are devoted to it to ensure that it is maintained.

10.9　International Communications

Key international communications issues are:

1. Overcoming communications barriers in the business environment;
2. Whether to standardize or adapt marketing communications activity;
3. Whether to adopt a 'push' or a 'pull' strategy.

Overcoming communications barriers

Communications barriers, or lack of acceptance of marketing communications, may result from numerous sources. Some of these, which cover all marketing communications methods, are summarized in the following table.

Table 10.7: Potential Communications Barriers

Potential barrier	Example
Language	This can also be a problem when another country seemingly speaks the same language – Germany and Austria, France and Belgium, UK and USA. In the latter case English words often have a different meaning in the USA: trousers = pants, bumper = fender, boot = trunk etc.
Buying criteria	The decider in the decision-making unit may be different. For example in the purchase of white goods (i.e. household electrical items) in Latin America the male member of the household tends to be the decider, whereas in the USA and UK a joint decision is usually made between the male and female.
Business etiquette	In conducting business the use of informal first names at first meeting is common in the USA and increasingly the UK, but would not be acceptable in Germany.
Use of the brand	In the USA there is heavy emphasis on pack shots to promote products in TV advertising. This is highly unusual in UK TV advertising where the use of humour, satire etc. tends to predominate.
Aesthetics	This ranges from pack size (also influenced by economic wealth), shape and colour. Femininity is denoted by pink in the USA but by yellow in many other cultures. The colour of death is black in many cultures, but white in others. Incorrect use of colour can potentially ruin an advertising campaign.
Culture	Sarah Lee, owners of the Wonderbra brand, ran a worldwide campaign using a standard image of a woman wearing one of its products, with strong emphasis on the fit of the product. In Mexico, posters with this image were regarded as offensive and the model was changed to wearing a suit.

Standardization or adaptation?

Key drivers of whether to standardize or adapt include similarities in the marketing environment, in media cost and availability, and in product usage. For example, in France and Finland, top-loading washing machines are favoured – therefore these models have to feature in advertising.

Pan-regional and global marketing communications require both the supply side and demand side to facilitate this development. Increasingly there has been an international shift towards cross-media mergers and vertical integration of content and service providers. The largest merger of this type, so far, is that between America Online and Time Warner. Global media provision is therefore becoming more of a reality.

On the demand side, very few worldwide brands exist. Of these even fewer have a common global message. Apart from the already well-known global brands, most supra-national branding is at a pan-regional level.

In general, attempts by retailers to eliminate a physical presence from their retailing operations, and to focus on Internet distribution and communication, has resulted in poor levels of brand development. A study by Harris Interactive showed that recognition levels of online brands by Internet users is 'poor if not non-existent', with 40% of shoppers failing to identify one online retailer in 12 of 13 categories.

'Push' or 'pull' strategy?

As markets differ, so must strategies. A fundamental strategic communications consideration is whether to adopt a 'push' or a 'pull' strategy. The suitability of each strategy is highly influenced by the level of economic development and by culture (Table 10.8).

Table 10.8: Factors that Influence the Selection of a 'Push' or 'Pull' Strategy According to the Level of Economic Development and Culture 'Type'

Non-Western 'type' culture – less developed economy	Western 'type' culture – advanced industrial economy.
A **Push Strategy** is favoured when:	A **Pull Strategy** is favoured when:
1. The consumer culture is less Westernized.	1. Advertising has great leverage in the consumer culture.
2. Wages are low and it is cheaper to employ salespeople than advertise.	2. Wide media choice, together with wide availability of other marketing communications tools.
3. A variety of languages, ethnic and racial groupings are present.	3. Marketing communications budgets are high.
4. Limited media availability exists.	4. Self-service predominates, i.e. supermarket culture.
5. Channels are short and direct.	5. The trade is influenced by advertising.
6. The culture dictates its use (e.g. business etiquette).	

Culture is a universally significant factor that must be considered in every aspect of international marketing communications. De Beers, the international diamond business, must pay particular attention to culture in the marketing of its products. This required adverts to feature different products and cultural contexts in different countries (see Marketing in Practice).

MARKETING IN PRACTICE

De Beers – diamonds are for love

De Beers wanted to promote the buying of diamonds. The theme they selected was to emphasise the connection between the giving of diamonds and eternal love and to keep this theme common to all advertising.

Consider three contrasting environments: the UK, the Arab region and Spain. The company decided to use a common themed communication in all three areas. In particular, shadows of people were shown in the context of gift giving to denote very special occasions in the life of people and of families, with a key theme of love. Special occasions included: birth, confirmation, betrothal, coming of age, engagement, marriage, reconfirmation of devotion (e.g. eternity ring), etc.

In each environment the most prominent of occasions was featured for the local context. For example, advertising in the Arab region featured ankle bracelets with diamonds, but this was not featured in the other two regions. An additional advantage of the campaign was that with the use of shadows, there was less risk of offending the cultural sensitivities of people in the Arab region, when portraying the theme of love and gift giving.

Summary

Corporate identity is formed from one of three sources: symbolism, behaviour of the organization and its staff, and organizational communications. These combine to form an image of the corporation in the minds of consumers. In mature product and service markets in which competition is intense, positive corporate image can provide organizations with a competitive edge.

Whether above-the-line (where media is paid for) or below-the-line (non-paid for media or sales promotion) is favoured, the marketer must decide on which communications media to use. There is never a single solution to this question. Several factors must be considered in making this decision including: money available, media preference (perhaps based on previous usage), suitability for the target audience, type of product and consequently employing the medium which is relatively most cost-effective, and the reaction of the retail trade.

Communications planning is similar in structure to marketing planning and includes a situation analysis, objective setting (which must be preceded by marketing objective setting), communication strategy, budget setting, tactical implementation, monitoring and control.

There are four main types of agency: full service, à la carte, creative boutiques and media buying specialists. One of the keys to a successful agency partnership is to agree a suitable means of payment that both parties can support. This ranges from payment by results to flat fees or commission percentages, and all combinations in between. The favoured approach depends on the type of communication, the budget size and the form of relationship between the client and the agency, especially if the client is a frequent, long-standing customer.

Technology has changed the emphasis of marketing communications and facilitated the growth in one-to-one communication, by delivering the systems and processes and at lower cost. The Internet has been the main driver of change and this has resulted in new forms of communications being developed, especially communications via organizational websites and banner advertising. Internet-only organizations have quickly realized the need to achieve a physical presence and have invested heavily in traditional media. Technology has also supported the growth in direct marketing; prior to the Internet direct marketing via the post was the fastest growing communications medium.

The emphasis placed on the sales force has declined with the growth in direct marketing activity and the costs associated with maintaining a sales force. The major areas for sales forces are in specific B2B markets, i.e. marketing to channels where independent, large or specialist retailers dominate or are significant. Where sales forces are employed, database technology is used to maximize their efficiency in targeting customers and in managing the sales team.

References

Colley R H (1961) cited in Smith P (1998) *Marketing Communications an Integrated Approach*, Koogan Page

Spector A J (1961) Basic dimensions of the corporate image, *Journal of Marketing*, 25 October, pp47-51

Strong E K (1925) *The Psychology of Selling*, McGraw-Hill, New York

11

PRICE

Learning Objectives

After reading this chapter students should understand:

- The factors influencing pricing levels;
- The general approaches to pricing;
- Strategies for pricing new products;
- How prices change throughout the product life cycle;
- Key issues affecting price adjustment strategies.

Figure 11.1: Chapter Map

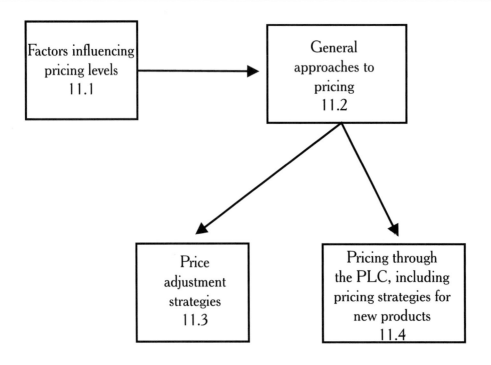

Introduction

Price is the mix element that can be changed most rapidly, but this should not mislead us from the highly strategic role which it can play. Price has a profound influence on all aspects of the business; setting it too high can be as damaging as setting it too low, impacting greatly on volume and margin. Price intrinsically communicates 'worth' and over time will impact on the perception of the organizational brand. Increasingly, high prices in the financial sector run the risk not only of low sales and margins, but also of public opprobrium and charges of profiteering and exploitation. The impact of price on the brand is therefore rising in importance as price transparency increases in the financial sector.

Factors influencing the determination of price are discussed, as are specific tools that assist in setting price (e.g. price elasticity, average costs).

11.1   Factors Influencing Pricing Levels

There are many factors that affect price determination. These may be considered as comprising factors that are internal or external to the organization (Kotler *et al.* 1999). An alternative approach to classifying factors is to consider them as comprising those which directly influence (1) consumer demand or (2) organizational supply, mediated by (3) organizational pricing objectives.

The underlying principles which influence pricing strategy are:

Demand factors

Elasticity of demand

Price elasticity of demand is the responsiveness of demand to changes in price.

It is very important to have an idea of how elastic or inelastic the demand for each of your products is because this determines whether revenues rise or decline as prices are raised. This depends on a range of factors which include:

● Price of complementary products;

● Price of substitute products;

● The degree of product/service differentiation. The more differentiated the service, e.g. through branding, the lower the elasticity of demand;

● How fashionable the product or service is. Relatively inelastic price segments exist for highly fashionable goods and services;

● Information availability and ease of comparison for the consumer – affects price transparency. If it is difficult to compare prices this makes the product/service more price inelastic. Financial services, new cars and many services offered to domestic consumers (e.g. plumbers, electricians, professions, 'alternative' medical therapies etc.)

are difficult to compare, especially for the occasional user. Many new entrants to some of these markets have made a marketing virtue over their low prices and facilitated consumer price comparison when presenting their combined product plus service offer;

● The number of competitors in the marketplace.

For example, where there are many competitors in the marketplace, and the company's products are not highly differentiated or branded, then a rise in price is likely to result in a more than proportionally larger decline in quantity demanded. The total revenue earned by the firm will decline. Figure 11.2 illustrates this point with initial price and quantity supplied Q1-P1. After the price rise this moved to Q2-P2. The decline in revenue (price times quantity) as a result of lower numbers of people buying at the higher price totals the area of the grey box, which is not compensated by the rise in revenue (generated by selling each unit at a higher price), i.e. the black shaded area.

Figure 11.2: Elastic Demand Line and the Impact of a Price Rise on Revenue

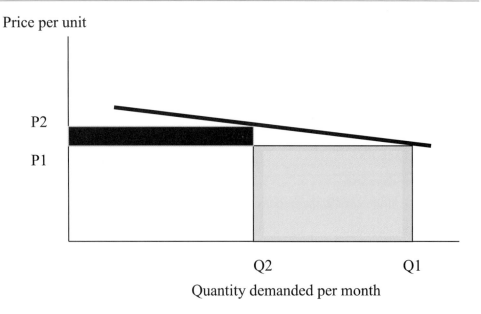

Price per unit

P2

P1

Q2   Q1

Quantity demanded per month

Supply factors

Total and average costs

The determination of total costs (i.e. fixed plus variable) and average costs (total cost / volume sold) is straightforward; however the point of interest here is how do these costs behave as sales volumes rise? This matter of cost structure is critical when setting price.

To understand this it is necessary to understand the relative importance of fixed and variable costs. Where fixed costs are a large proportion of total costs, average costs tend to diminish with higher volumes. Clear understanding of cost structures (in particular economies of scale) in setting prices was one of the principles behind the success of Japanese products in European and North American markets several decades ago. This principle is employed in the competitive pricing of investment funds (i.e. in terms of entry/exit charges, annual management fees and bid offer spreads).

Average costs tend to rise in the *non*-service sector because factory efficiency eventually diminishes as output rises. However this is much less the case in the service sector, where constraints tend to be in terms of available, experienced staff. Cost structures are obviously important in making decisions about undertaking activity in-house or not, e.g. call centres to support marketing activity. However the main problem for the service sector is in the calculation of costs and their allocation to specific products.

Competition and market type

Market type/structure has a strong influence on pricing. The more competitors in an industry, and the less differentiated the product or service offering, the lower the price which the consumer will be able to achieve. Most organizations compete in either monopolistic or oligopolistic markets (Table 11.1).

There is an additional, geographical dimension to service markets as services are 'inseparable' (see Chapter 4). Consider product markets. Goods may be stored and shipped to anywhere in the world. Potentially all consumers in the world may compare the retail price with those of competitors. However as services are 'inseparable' and 'perishable' the potential market is restricted to a much narrower geographical range for many services, e.g. hotels, gyms, cinemas, haircuts, professional services. In these markets businesses must be price competitive with local businesses that are marketing to similar segments.

As services increasingly use technology to reach customer segments, the geographical size of the market increases, and consequently the number of competitors who consumers use to compare prices increases. Branding, to reduce price comparison, becomes increasingly more important in these types of markets, unless the firm is to go for a penetration pricing strategy.

Table 11.1: Main Types of Market Structure

Market structure	Key price related features
Perfect competition	Many buyers and many sellers. Extreme, rarely achieved market structure which requires goods and services to be virtually identical and for full price transparency to exist. Little scope for branding. Some markets are beginning to operate more like this as a result of Internet sales.
Monopolistic competition	Many buyers and many sellers. Products and services are differentiated. Branding exists to increase differentiation for customer segments. Relatively inelastic customer segments exist for small price rises – see discussion above on factors that affect price elasticity.
Oligopoly	Many buyers and few sellers. Product/service differentiation a key element of market success, usually achieved through branding. Non-price competition a key feature of this type of market structure. Duopoly is a cross between a monopoly and oligopoly. The features of this market structure are similar to an oligopoly, except where collusion exists, then it operates more like a monopoly.
Monopoly	One or a few sellers. Under UK legislation a monopolist is defined as a firm with a market share in excess of 25%. Monopolists are able to segment markets in order to charge higher prices to segments that are unable to select alternative products or services – travelling on commuter trains charged at a high price, while leisure travellers are charged a lower tariff because they can make alternative, non-train arrangements.

Service organizations compete mainly in two types of retail market – monopolistic competition and oligopoly. Financial service organizations, for example, compete mainly in monopolistically competitive markets where there are many buyers and sellers, e.g. car loans, and in oligopolistic markets where a few sellers (i.e. a few large-volume sellers have most of the market share) and many buyers, e.g. mortgages in the UK. It is important to understand which type of structure your organization competes in because this allows for a greater understanding of the market behaviour of competitors.

Government regulation

This directly affects the behaviour of the firm, i.e. what is and is not legally acceptable, as well as encouraging different types of market structure to develop. For example, deregulation of the utilities, and of financial services, is at different stages in various European countries. Prior to deregulation, a few domestic organizations, often single organizations in the utilities, 'competed', with varying degrees of state ownership, or detailed national regulation. Post deregulation, foreign service businesses began to compete and this resulted in mergers and acquisitions of the smaller domestic companies. Behaviour of firms then began to resemble that of an oligopolistic market structure in some national markets and monopolistic competition in others.

Organization pricing objectives

Rate of return required on projects

A requirement for a high rate of return implies charging a high price, but this depends on the elasticity of demand. For example, where demand is elastic, then large increases in price will be self-defeating, resulting in a decline in total revenue. This is because the additional revenue earned from the price rise will be more than offset by the decline in the number of people purchasing the service at the higher price.

MARKETING IN PRACTICE

ASDA to market discount insurance

ASDA applied its price discounting approach to the financial services sector for the first time in the summer of 1999. It did this through an own brand label 'ASDA for Travel', which offers policies that undercut traditional High Street products. This marks a departure from previous policy where the company was tied to Lloyds TSB, to the extent of having some of the bank's branches in-store. It is perhaps unsurprising when one considers that ASDA's competitors (e.g. M&S, Tesco and Sainsbury's) have offered own-brand financial services for some time.

This move has been linked to the purchase of ASDA by Wal-Mart, which has recently purchased a small bank in Oklahoma, the Federal BankCentre. Analysts have suggested that Wal-Mart may be developing a financial services format to roll out in the USA and in Europe. However, according to ASDA, it is not going to develop a banking operation form this base.

Market share

Several studies have shown a correlation between high market share and profit. Consequently, organizations have frequently pursued a high market share agenda and have used price as a key element in this approach. It does not always follow that a penetration pricing strategy is followed to gain market share. Whether this is appropriate will depend not simply on price, but in general on the product/service's elasticity of demand, especially on the ability of the firm to differentiate its products and services.

Key ways in which service pricing is different

The discussion has indicated differences between the pricing of goods and of services. Zeithaml & Bitner (1996) suggest three key differences between customer evaluation of pricing for services and goods:

1. Customers often have inaccurate or limited reference prices for services;

2. Price is a key signal to quality in services (especially where information on the service and the brand is limited);

3. Monetary price is not the only price to service customers. Non-monetary costs include time costs, search costs and psychic costs (e.g. fear of uncertainty or of not understanding the service provided – sometimes a problem with financial services).

11.2   General Approaches to Pricing

The main approaches to pricing are:

1. Cost-based pricing

2. Buyer-perception pricing

3. Competition-based pricing.

Some authors include bidding and tendering as an approach. They are in fact more a process by which the main approaches are manifested, therefore they will not be considered as an additional approach.

Cost-based pricing

Price is set with reference to the cost of producing the product/service. Once costs have been calculated the producer will add a margin to provide a profit, e.g. cost plus 30%.

Break-even analysis
A variation of cost-based pricing is break-even analysis. This is a calculation of the level of sales which covers cost. Normally this is undertaken for new projects to establish whether they are feasible. For example, if break-even sales are at a level equal to a market share of 90% (for comparable markets or in an existing market), then the project is unlikely to be viable because this level of sales is unsustainable.

Break-even analysis requires information on variable and fixed costs.

Various formulae may be used to answer questions on break-even analysis. The assumptions which are used for the question presented are:

Expected sales:	10,000 units at £8/unit = £80,000
Variable Costs:	£5 per unit
Fixed costs:	£21,000

Contribution: Total revenue – variable costs

⇒   £8 - £5 = £3

QUESTION : How many units must be sold in order for the firm to break-even?

Formula :

Total fixed costs

Contribution per unit   = Number of units which must be sold to break even.

$$\frac{£21,000}{£3} = 7,000 \text{ units}$$

At 7,000 units total revenue will equal £56,000 (i.e. £8 × 7,000).

At 7,000 units or sales revenue of £56,000 the firm will break even. Above this point profits will be earned.

Buyer-perception pricing

Rather than using internal cost structures as the reference point for price estimation, the firm uses consumer perception of value. Internal cost structures and consumer perception of value may be unrelated, e.g. perfume. Consumer perception of value is related to many factors, one of the most important of which is the level of consumer involvement. Consumers are more willing to invest in high-involvement goods and services because these can affect self-image. Consumers will be less resistant to spending an extra 30% on a haircut, or on special occasion clothing, due to their potential impact on self-image and on social standing.

Competition-based pricing

In this pricing approach competitors are considered to be an important reference point. Consumers are assumed to compare prices offered by competitors, and if prices offered by a single firm are substantially out of line, then demand will fall rapidly. Consumers normally work on 'tolerated differences' where small disparities are accepted (e.g. + or – 5%) but demand drops rapidly for greater disparities.

11.3   Price Adjustment Strategies

The strategic dimension of price setting includes the general approach to setting price in support of marketing objectives. This includes, in particular, market share; and price setting strategies that optimize not simply on a single product but on the whole product range offered by the organization.

Price setting and adjustment to optimize return on all products

The continuing relationship involving several services in turn gives rise to the potential for suppliers of financial services to price on the basis of cross-subsidies... Bank pricing frequently involves a network of complex cross-subsidies between sectors, customers and products.

Howcroft and Lavis (1995) p140

The ideas summarized in the above quotation are explored in the case example below.

MARKETING IN PRACTICE

Sustainable competitive disadvantage in financial services

Information technology enables new entrants to 'cream skim' a market and to target a company's most profitable customers. According to Eric Clemons, this has undermined the role of scale as a source of competitive advantage in financial services. Thanks to skill-based advantage, it is not necessary to be the low-cost producer, as long as you can be the low-price provider to the most profitable accounts.

In a wide range of financial service industries, recent changes in regulation, in the competitive environment and in technology have combined to erode the competitive advantage enjoyed by large, previously successful and apparently dominant institutions. New entrants are successfully challenging defenders that had considered themselves secure because of their scale, captive customers or other resources.

Markets that are attractive to attack

Consumers vary greatly in the costs associated with providing service to them and in the revenues that they produce for their service providers. This is equally true among customers for credit card services or for demand deposit banking products, among customers for health insurance or life insurance, or among customers for retail brokerage services. For example, some credit card customers maintain large outstanding balances and do not pay them off rapidly; rather they incur finance charges, which makes them profitable to serve. In addition, the best accounts have demonstrably low risk of default.

Very few banks impose charges for teller usage and most banks do not carefully differentiate the prices they charge retail customers for services; indeed, almost all British and French consumers enjoy free cheque-writing privileges, even those who are consistently unprofitable for their banks. Once again, profitable accounts are subsidizing the provision of services to unprofitable accounts, increasing the number of consumers who have access to banking services.

These simplistic pricing strategies have led to a significant gap between the costs that banks or financial service companies incur by providing services to most of their customers and the prices that these customers are actually charged. In the case of the most profitable customers, this gap represents the degree to which the customer is being overcharged for services, producing a surplus to subsidize less profitable accounts. Industries with extreme differences exhibit what is called a strong 'customer profitability gradient'.

> Simplistic pricing in the presence of a strong profitability gradient represents a money transfer between customers, and the stronger the gradient the greater the transfer. Significantly, the greater the transfer the more attractive it is for a new entrant to attack. By refusing to serve unprofitable accounts, and by focusing on the most profitable segments, new entrants can free themselves of the need to transfer money from good accounts to bad accounts; instead, they can feed some of the surplus back to the good accounts to 'buy' their business as low-price service providers, while transferring the rest of the money to themselves and their shareholders. New entrants without fully efficient scale can still find these industries attractive to attack via such 'cream-skimming' strategies.
>
> *Source: Sustainable competitive disadvantage in financial services* Financial Times; 29-Mar-1999

Pricing must not be undertaken in isolation for individual products. Account must be taken not simply of the product range, for example the gradations of charges for platinum, gold and standard credit cards should reflect their relative positioning in the marketplace. However in addition to consideration of pricing within the product range offered by the organization, consideration should be made of the pricing policies of competitors in the same marketplace. Only if another aspect of the marketing mix is also changed can an organization sustain a different, and profitable, pricing policy in the face of competitive pressures. For example, Direct Line was able to offer lower prices through low-cost distribution and the effective use of new technology.

Once standard prices have been set, a range of adjustment strategies is deployed to maximize return from each segment. For example, a retail mortgage rate will be specified based on prevailing wholesale money market rates. However mortgage customers taking out large loans may be given a discount compared to customers with small loans. Underpinning this approach are issues concerning volume, season, location within the marketing chain, level of competition, linkage with sales promotion activity and the psychological use of price to communicate value (Kotler *et al.* 1999, pp725-31).

International pricing

There are aspects of international pricing that are additional to those encountered in the domestic environment. This includes the potential for currency fluctuation (assuming foreign currency pricing), price escalation (i.e. the compounding of prices due to a longer marketing chain) and pricing strategy based on geographical distance, in addition to accommodating differences in currency (Kotler *et al.* 1999, pp731-4).

Doole and Lowe (1999) categorize factors affecting international pricing decisions into three main categories: company and product factors (e.g. cost structures), market factors (e.g. need for product adaptation) and environmental factors (e.g. business cycle stage).

11.4 Pricing through the Product Life Cycle, Including Pricing Strategies for New Products

Introductory stage

One of two strategic approaches may be taken to price setting for a new product or service; penetration pricing or price skimming.

Penetration pricing

This involves pricing at a comparatively low level at first:

● to gain maximum market share;

● to benefit from any cost reductions which may be realized as a result of high quantities;

● to discourage competitors.

An alternative to this is *price skimming*.

Price skimming

The product is deliberately priced at a high level to gain the maximum benefit in terms of margins.

● This approach is often used for new products in the early stages of their life cycle because it allows some of the development costs to be recovered before competitors are able to present their version of the product to the markets.

● The off-putting nature of the high price will be softened by relatively intense advertising and promotional activities.

● The objective of this approach is to sell initially to the consumers who are not particularly price sensitive while recognizing that the existing high level of price will need to be reduced in the longer term as competition increases.

Growth stage

In this stage prices tend to decline. The speed at which this happens depends on how easy it is for competitors to copy and market a rival product or service. This depends on:

● How innovative the product or service is. Changes in product form (see Chapter 9) are more difficult to imitate (e.g. Sony 'Walkman');

● The extent to which the product or service may be protected by copyright or patent;

● The nature of the product or service. The first firms to launch telephone insurance quotes while the caller waited were difficult to copy. These firms had invested time and resources in systems to process information and provide reliable, instant risk-based assessment. This is in contrast to most services which tend to be relatively easy for competitors to copy;

● The extent to which the firm wishes to use a high price as a means of supporting a premium product image within the marketing mix.

Mature stage

Competition is intense. Nearly all consumers who wish to have the product or service have purchased it. It is likely that at this stage at least one firm will have launched a successor product/service. Existing firms in the market have three possible approaches:

Options	Marketing/cost implications
1. Discount at increasingly higher levels to maintain demand prior to withdrawing the offer.	Expenditure on marketing communications to ensure consumers are aware of the discounts offered.
2. Maintain price, with limited discounts, to skim as much margin as possible	No expenditure
3. Withdraw the product/service immediately.	Cost savings. Expenditure more effectively used on other products/ services.

Summary

There are many factors that influence pricing levels. These may be grouped into one of three categories: consumer demand factors, organizational supply factors and pricing objectives of the organization, which may modify prices implied by the relative forces of supply and demand in the marketplace. Organizational approaches to pricing fall into one of three categories: cost-based pricing, buyer-perception pricing and competition-based pricing. The pricing approach selected by an organization must fit in with general marketing, and specifically pricing, strategy. For example, penetration pricing implies a cost-based approach to setting prices.

As products move through their life cycle, pricing strategies must be changed. This is to accommodate the fundamental change in the level of competition, which grows as the product moves towards the mature phase of the product life cycle. In addition to this feature of the marketplace, managers must decide on company strategy at each phase, i.e. is the firm operating a penetration or skimming strategy? Whatever strategy is pursued, it must be aligned with the rest of the marketing mix.

Launching new products is simply the introduction phase of the life cycle. It is a particularly important stage as it is highly influential in the almost irreversible positioning of the service or product. It is an expensive, or even impossible, task to market a product or service at a higher price point when it has been launched at an excessively low price.

When adjusting prices, marketers must consider the price point relative to other products or services in the range. Incremental prices must reflect differences in value perceived by target customers and this in turn will be influenced by the level of competition in the marketplace. The marketer must try to maximize returns for the product range in its entirety, rather than simply considering each product within the range in isolation.

References

Anon (1999) Substantial competitive disadvantage in financial services, *Financial Times*, 29 March

Doole I & Lowe R (1999) *International Marketing Strategy*, 2nd edition, Thomson Business Press

Howcroft & Lavir (1995) cited in Ennew C, Watkins T & Wright M (eds) *Marketing Financial Services*, Butterworth Heinemenn, Oxford

Kotler P, Armstrong G, Saunders J & Wong V (1999) *Principles of Marketing*, 2nd European edition, Prentice Hall Europe

Zeithaml V and Bitner M J (1996) *Services Marketing* McGraw-Hill International New York, Chapter 11

12

CHANNEL MANAGEMENT

Learning Objectives

After reading this chapter students should understand:

●   The factors and issues involved in channel selection;

●   The role and uses of technology in channel management;

●   Key issues in wholesale and retail channel management;

●   The role of physical outlets within marketing channel management.

Figure 12.1: Chapter Map

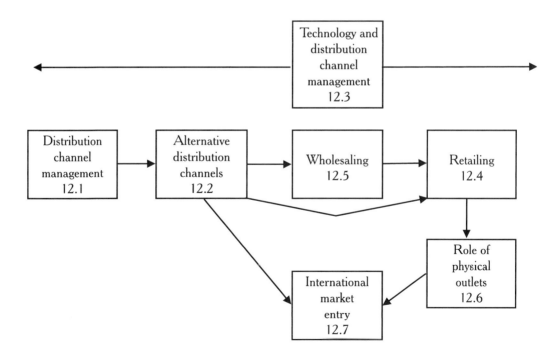

Introduction

Technology has revolutionized marketing channel management, especially though information and communication technologies. This has become a highly dynamic aspect of marketing since the Internet was widely taken up by businesses and consumers. However prior to that, change was a feature of channel management, especially with the growth in call centres and in services accessed by voice, via the telephone network. Technology has enabled channel lengths to be reduced and for producers to communicate directly with consumers. In spite of the impact of technology, for remote access of services, there is a need for service brands to maintain a physical presence. This requirement is met by physical outlets which provide tangibility for service firms. The importance of this function cannot be overstated, especially in defending existing players in an industry sector from low-cost, highly intangible, 'virtual' service providers.

12.1   Distribution Channel Management

This is an exciting and dynamic aspect of marketing with many companies using distribution as a key element of competitive strategy or for market entry. This has included, for example, the Korean company Daewoo entering the UK and European markets, Häagan Dazs using a selective distribution strategy to enter the UK market from the USA and Direct Line the first insurer to deal directly with consumers.

Distribution is relatively easily defined for products. It is the activity which results in the transfer of the product from the place of manufacturer, through the marketing chain, to a place, in a quantity and at the time which achieves consumer satisfaction.

A distribution channel is a set of interdependent organizations involved in the process of making a product or service available for use or consumption.

Logistics is often used with distribution. There is no precise definition from a marketing viewpoint. Logistics has been used by some to mean the physical aspects of distribution, including:

- Order processing
- Transportation
- Stock management
- Warehousing.

Logistics therefore includes the planning, implementation and control of the physical movement of goods and services. For this to be undertaken efficiently and effectively requires detailed information on customer needs and wants. Such needs and wants go beyond simply the delivery of goods and services. Companies now offer customers the facility to track the movement of goods and services, through the supply chain, or through their systems, as a means of gaining a competitive advantage. This additionally reduces business costs, requiring fewer customer support staff. For example, Federal Express provide world-wide tracking of the goods which they handle while, in the service sector, banks and building societies have for several years allowed customers to process transactions remotely.

Distribution management is the task of ensuring that this process takes place as efficiently and effectively as possible.

Product availability is a key area of competitive activity. Kotler identifies eight areas which should be considered. These are the:

● speed of filling and delivering an order;

● supplier's willingness to meet emergency product needs of the customer;

● care with which the product is delivered, so that it arrives in good condition;

● supplier's readiness to take back defects and to re-supply;

● availability of installation, repair services and parts from the supplier;

● number of options on shipment loads and carriers;

● supplier's willingness to carry inventory for the customer;

● service charges – are services 'free' or separately priced?

It is helpful to use Porter's (1985) model of the supply chain (see Chapter 1) when considering the strategic management of distribution channels, especially the first three, of the key four, distribution decisions faced by managers.

● **Channel Length** – How many intermediaries should be involved in connecting the company, its product and services and the end user or buyer?

● **Channel Integration** – The extent to which the business should be vertically integrated. What form of relationship to have within each stage of the marketing chain – ownership, short/long-term contracts, supply integration, e.g. through just-in-time production. How can relationships with the various intermediaries in the distribution chain be managed effectively?

● **Distribution Logistics** – How can physical flows of materials, goods and services be delivered to the customer, most efficiently and effectively?

● **Distribution Density** – What is the ideal number of sales outlets required to service the customer? More outlets imply better coverage but the trade-off is lower volume per outlet and therefore higher cost overheads. Does the volume of business justify the level of distribution density?

12.2   Alternative Distribution Channels

The term *channels of distribution* refers to the marketing institutions through which goods or services are transferred from the original producers to the ultimate customers. Channels of distribution include the following:

- *Retailers*, who may be classified by:
    - type of goods sold (e.g. hardware, furniture);
    - type of service (self-service, counter service);
    - size;
    - location (rural, city-centre, out-of-town shopping centre).
- *Wholesalers*, many of them specializing in particular products. Most wholesalers deal in consumer goods, but some specialize in industrial goods.
- *Dealers*. Organizations which contract to buy a manufacturer's goods and sell them to customers, e.g. car dealers.
- *Agents*. Agents do not purchase the manufacturer's goods, but earn a commission on whatever sales they make.
- *Franchisees*. In a franchise arrangement, the franchiser provides the franchisee with support, advice, an established brand name etc.; while the franchisee contributes capital and labour to open and run the franchise.
- *Multiple stores* (e.g. supermarkets) which buy goods for retailing direct from the producer, many of them under their 'own label' brand name.
- *Direct selling*, also an aspect of promotion.
- *Brokers*. Many financial services, such as insurance and/or pensions, have traditionally been sold through High Street brokers. In theory, the broker sells services from a number of different suppliers, on a commission basis, according to client needs. For example, in the 1980s, mortgage brokers would shop around for their clients, contacting a number of suppliers to find the best deals.

There are many potential routes for products between the manufacturer and the final consumer, including various combinations of channel intermediaries (Figure 12.2).

Figure 12.2: Examples of Different Channel Structures

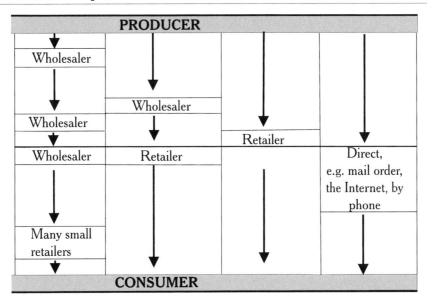

Business to consumer (B2C) and business to business (B2B) channels are essentially different. The major difference is that in the consumer market there are many small-value transactions, whereas in the business-to-business market, by contrast, there tends to be relatively fewer, larger transactions. Organizations continuously seek lower-cost channels to serve all markets. This is particularly pressing in the consumer market, and to a lesser extent in the small business market which shares the fundamental features of the consumer market. In the business market, the role of the sales force and the management of 'key accounts' remains influenced, but to a lesser degree, by cost pressures.

At any one time the financial institution has to select optimal combinations of distribution channels. However the factors that exert an underlying influence on the nature and structure of distribution systems in financial services are competition and technology (Ennew *at al.*, 1995, pp176-8).

In managing different members of the distribution channel, managers should be clear that channel members might have different objectives.

Table 12.1: Comparison between Producer and Channel Intermediary Objectives/Requirements

PRODUCER OBJECTIVES/ REQUIRMENTS	INTERMEDIARY, E.G. WHOLESALER OBJECTIVES/ REQUIREMENTS
Volume growth	Product price stability
Product promotion	Gross returns and gross margins
Market share	Good return on selling space
Profitability	Regular inventory turnover
High service level	Promotional allowance
Wide product range	Continuity of supply
Good market coverage	Managerial or technical assistance
High penetration level	Finance for consumer/business credit
Channel member loyalty	
Product extension	
Market feedback	
Customer loyalty	

Channel integration may prove to be difficult, especially where channel members emphasize objectives that directly compete with other members. For example, high market share, market coverage and service level provided by the wholesaler to satisfy the producer might only be possible through reducing price and consequently the wholesaler's margin. Unless sales volume rises sufficiently to compensate for the decline in unit margin, the wholesaler's gross margin will decline.

Functions of intermediaries

Cost-conscious firms are all too ready to eliminate channel members from parts of the distribution chain. This may be a good policy as long as the marketing functions of channel intermediaries are replaced by the firm. Some firms forget these functions and simply regard channel intermediaries as a cost. Table 12.1, in addition to listing channel member objectives and requirements, is also a list of the functions of channel members.

Figure 12.3: Contrasting Channel Lengths for Fresh Fruit

Fruit farm	→	Pick your own	→			Final customer

ONE INTERMEDIARY

Fruit farm	→	Supermarket	→			Final customer

TWO INTERMEDIARIES

Fruit farm	→	Wholesale market	→	Greengrocer	→	Final customer

What are the advantages and disadvantages of each channel for the farmer?

There are several issues to consider:

● Control

● Cost

● Feedback

● Customer service

● Ability of supplier (farmer) to meet objectives

● Predictability of sales.

Direct sales potentially offer the greatest control, margin and customer feedback. The farmer, as a supplier, is not under the domination of a large retail business. This is not necessarily ideal for the farmer because customers may:

● not come to pick the fruit

● damage or steal an unacceptably high proportion of the crop

● may not wish to pick their own fruit during extended periods of bad weather.

There are some benefits for the farmer in selling to the powerful supermarket. The supermarket buyer takes some of the risk from the farmer by guaranteeing payment (even though with a reduced margin). The downside of this is:

● the dependency on the supermarket, especially where a long-term relationship has not been established between the producer and the supermarket. There are many examples of buyers switching suppliers at short notice;

● the management burden placed on the producer to meet strict quality and quantity criteria, with severe financial penalties if they are not met. In bad weather, for example, producers may need to find, and pay for, more labour to gather, clean and sort the crop.

Channel members in all distribution channels have similar risk/reward trade-offs, which they must consider in arriving at the optimum combination to work with.

Reducing the number of distribution channel members

Channel members are declining in number. Cost pressures and strategic factors are resulting in a decline in the number of competing firms due to horizontal and vertical integration.

Horizontal integration
This is 'development into activities which are competitive with or directly complementary to a company's present activities'. For example, a milk-producer might acquire a bakery. A bookshop might start to sell compact discs and DVDs. A music publisher of CDs and tapes might finance the production of a film (as another, related, aspect of the entertainment industry).

Vertical integration (Vertical marketing system)
This is where a company becomes either one of the following:

- Its own supplier of raw materials, components or services (i.e. *backward vertical integration*). For example, backward integration would occur where a milk producer acquires its own dairy farms rather than buying raw milk from independent farmers.

- Its own distributor or sales agent (i.e. *forward vertical integration*). This would occur, for example:

  - where a manufacturer of synthetic yarn begins to produce shirts from the yarn instead of selling it to other shirt manufacturers;

  - where a manufacturer sells direct to customers by acquiring a retail network (e.g. Laura Ashley), or by establishing a direct-selling operation through mail order (e.g. Dell Computer Corporation).

The purpose of vertical integration may be to:

- provide a secure supply of components or raw materials with more control over quality, quantity and price. Supplier bargaining power is reduced;

- strengthen relationships and contacts of the manufacturer with the 'final consumer' of the product;

- win a share of the higher profits which might be obtainable in the raw materials market or end-user market;

- pursue a differentiation strategy more effectively;

- raise barriers to entry.

The disadvantages of vertical integration are that:

● the company, rather than spreading its risk, is in fact concentrating its risk exposure into the same end-market. Such a policy is fairly inflexible, more sensitive to instabilities and increases the firm's dependence on a particular aspect of economic demand;

● the firm fails to benefit from any economies of scale in the industry into which it has diversified. This is why, in the publishing industry, most printing is subcontracted to specialist printing firms, which can work machinery to capacity by doing work for many firms, or in the banking industry check clearance processing is subcontracted to one of a few firms.

Figure 12.4: Related Diversification Options

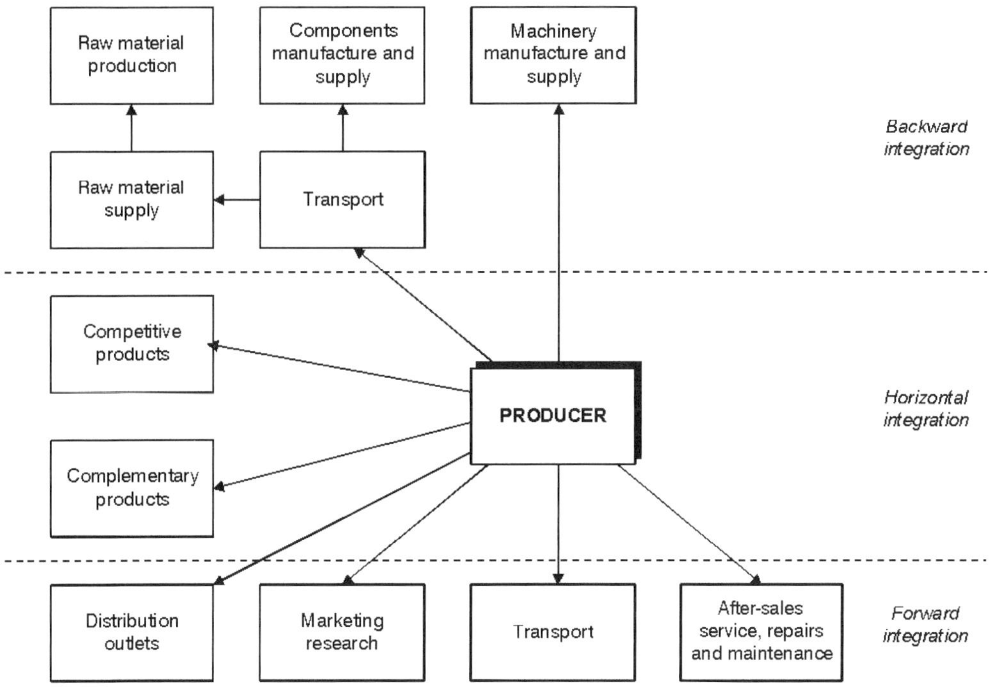

Source: Johnson and Scholes (1999)

In practice, vertical, as opposed to horizontal, integration need not involve the purchase and management of the entire distribution channel and its incorporation into the ownership structure. We can classify three types of *vertical marketing system (VMS)*.

● *Corporate* – as above, with all distribution functions under single ownership.

● *Administered* – although channel members are independent, they coordinate their activities. They might cooperate in joint promotional activities. Often, a single member exercises a predominant influence.

- *Contractual* – inter-organizational relationships are formalized through contracts, such as through franchise arrangements.

12.3 Technology and Distribution Channel Management

New distribution channels

Much is written on the rapid growth of the Internet as a distribution channel. Statistics, which provide an indicator of the rate of growth in the financial services sector, include:

- an annualized median growth rate in online banking customers in the leading 16 US internet banks of 118% (113,000 – March 1999);

- in the UK the Prudential's new direct banking arm 'Egg' accumulated £5 billion in deposits in eight months following its launch in October 1998; and

- doubling of Visa International Internet sales worldwide, in 1998, to $15 billion.

Source: The Banker (1999, June)

Interest in 'new media' has been heightened by the successful development of competitive advantage through new distribution channels. However interest comes from another direction, namely the growth of interest, facilitated by technology, in 'one-to-one' communication with the customer. At one level, technology has not in fact altered the principles of good distribution, i.e. to get the product to the customer at the desired location and to receive information back through the distribution channel on the customer. However, at another level, the new technology has facilitated a direct dialogue between customer and service provider and this has therefore allowed 'relationships' to develop between the two.

MARKETING IN PRACTICE

Internet Distribution – Publishing 'Best Seller' Novels

www.stephenking.com

Steven King, the novelist, decided to create his own channel of distribution for his novel *The Plant*, rather than using conventional publishers. On his website he provided information on the new novel and informed the reader that it will be realized in parts of 5000 to 7000 words. Each part was charged at $1 to download. The author suggested to readers that they might join him in 'becoming Big Publishing's worst nightmare'. Readers were provided with the option of paying before or after down-loading via the Internet. Steven King warned readers that for his new venture to succeed, everyone must adhere to the principle of 'plain honesty'. He suggested that if readers like the story enough they would want to pay to read more. However he provided potential 'thieves' with the warning that if after two parts have been released, and people do not pay for their downloads, then he will not continue with the venture. If you 'pay and the story rolls. Steal and the story folds'. This is a particularly

---

cleverly designed use of Internet distribution. Ultimately the author has little to lose because he can resort to conventional publishing if people do not pay for the novel via the Internet. He will have in effect run a promotional activity. However, if the strategy succeeds, then a whole tier of distribution costs is removed and the potential for greater concentration of financial reward exists for the author.

No service organization can ignore new media. The main issues are:

- the extent to which the organization should embrace it?

- how to integrate it with the rest of the marketing mix?

- to which segments to target new media?

MARKETING IN PRACTICE

Barclays b2 transactional web site

Barclays launched their b2 transactional web site in 1999. This was to encourage a take-up of unit trusts processed through the Internet. Unit trust ownership in Britain lags a long way behind the USA. This new approach to marketing unit trusts in Britain aimed to encourage uptake, facilitated by allowing investors to compare the performance of their own investments with comparable unit trust investments offered by competitors.

Integrating distribution channels
Integrating distribution channels is a strategy which the USA-based manufacturer and brand owner 'Levi's' pursues. The company seeks to service all potential customer segments using all possible distribution channels. In addition to the use of traditional distribution channels, Levis's allows customers to specify their measurements and to order online.

Technology and the implications for marketing management strategy
Technology has facilitated the rapid growth in:

- one-to-one relationship marketing;

- rapid order fulfilment;

- cost-effective, small-order fulfilment for order sizes that were previously non-viable – e.g. supermarket home delivery service;

- An alternative, electronic channel which may result in lower volumes through traditional physical channels. Growth in electronic distribution has been an important contributor to the bank branch closure strategy. As electronic transactions and customer communications grows the cost per transaction of direct customer contact starts to grow at untenable levels with unaltered, traditional bank networks;

- Efficiency of supply chains, allowing highly efficient management of stock levels and maximum use of in-store shelf space.

12.4   Retailing

Consumer retailing is the sale of products and services to the final consumer. There are several types of retail organizational structures:

1.   Multiple retailers: a single business that has many geographically dispersed outlets;

2.   Independents: a single (or a few) retail outlets with a single owner;

3.   Franchises: where the brand owner of a successful retail format sells the rights to another business to operate the format. This usually requires the franchisee to agree to maintain the format, including the purchase of consumables from the brand owner;

4.   Cooperatives: where individuals become members of the cooperative and they comprise the owners of the business. Any 'profits' made are distributed to members. This form of organization may include producers as well as retailers within the cooperative. Examples of this format, purely at the retail level, include: the UK Co-operative Wholesale Society, which has a substantial presence in the UK grocery and fast-moving consumer goods (fmcg) retailing marketplace, and the German, French and Dutch cooperative banks (e.g. Rabo Bank, Credit Agricole). In Denmark this format is more successful at the farm/processing level of the supply chain, rather than at the retail level.

Retailing has developed to allow consumers to purchase products and services in a variety of environments:

●   In person, for example in the company's outlet/store;

●   In person, for example from another company's outlet/store (e.g. perfume, designer goods, banking services);

●   by phone or post from a catalogue;

●   via the Internet (several possibilities exist, e.g. home PC, WAP phone, etc.);

●   via digital TV.

Value added by retailers
What is it that the retailer provides to the consumer, regardless of how the consumer makes the purchase?

●   a product/service range (product assortment).

●   a service function (ranging from support in product selection to after-sales product support).

●   time enjoyed – a pleasurable experience for consumers (e.g. the retail experience exemplified by Disney). The retailer may either try to get the consumer to stay longer at each visit (and hopefully therefore spend more money (e.g. shopping centres/malls)) or make the experience so enjoyable that a repeat purchases will result (especially important for service sector retailers such as hotel and catering outlets).

- Time saved. (There are degrees of 'time saved' which ranges from facilitating rapid transaction – fast food outlet, internet banking, telephone insurance, telephone/Internet flowers or stationery supplies. 'Time enjoyed' is the opposite of time saved.)

- Security (provided through an established retail brand).

- Familiar purchase experience (again provided by an established retail brand).

- Market information on consumers, which can be transmitted back through the marketing chain to increase marketing efficiency and effectiveness.

Positioning the retail format

The attributes, on which retailers position, are rarely unique. How therefore do they achieve a unique positioning stance? They do this by occupying a particular point on a range of attributes. Price, quality and service are regarded as the most common attributes employed by retailers. However some authors suggest that in reality the retailing situation is more complex. Retailers attempt to attract the consumer by the offer of 'more' attributes for the product or service. In addition, this provides the consumer with further benefits associated with the transactional exchange, benefits which the consumer would like less of (e.g. less effort searching for the product they require, perhaps facilitated by ICT). This is the basis of the 'more' for less in the retail 'value equation' (Figure 12.5).

Figure 12.5: Retail Value Equation

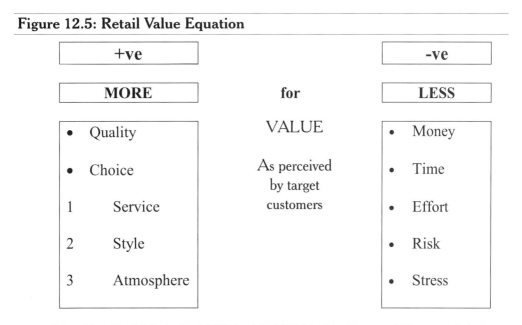

+ve		-ve
MORE	for	**LESS**

		VALUE	
•	Quality		• Money
•	Choice	As perceived by target customers	• Time
1	Service		• Effort
2	Style		• Risk
3	Atmosphere		• Stress

Adapted from The Marketing Book *M Baker (ed.) 2000 4th edition Butterworth Heinemann Oxford*

Product assortment

The range of products offered to the customer (product assortment) is a critical element in the retail marketing mix. Optimum product assortment will maximize:

- Profit per unit of shelf space and profit for the store;

- Interest in the shopping experience for the consumer (thereby maximizing the potential for repeat business);

- Reinforce the brand image for the retail format.

Retail marketing emphasis

Over the years retailers have emphasized different aspects of the marketing mix in an attempt to gain a competitive advantage. In the 1980s the focus of marketing activity was on obtaining optimal locations, before competitors, and ensuring efficient store design to maximize customer volumes. These concerns have now been replaced by an emphasis given to loyalty schemes and branding, in combination with a 'good value' price proposition. Marketing of retail formats has therefore become much more complicated.

Figure 12.6: Retail Mix Emphasis over the Last Three Decades

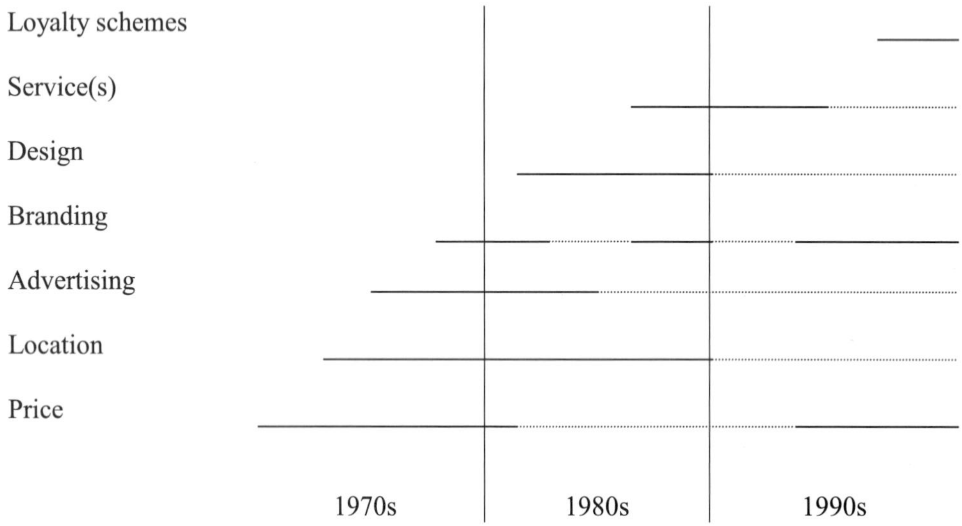

Loyalty schemes

Service(s)

Design

Branding

Advertising

Location

Price

1970s   1980s   1990s

Note: Solid lines refer to period when a particular retail mix was emphasized.

Source: McGoldrick PJ and Andre E (1997)

Changes and trends in retailing

There are several major trends affecting distribution. These include for example:

1.   *Growth in the number of international retailers*
Large retailers have found their domestic market maturing. This includes a large number of

firms; for example, McDonalds; Kentucky Fried Chicken; M&S; Laura Ashley; IKEA; Kmart etc.

The increasing international presence has been facilitated by enhanced data communications and lower barriers to entry. Customs unions such as the EU have encouraged retailers to expand within trade blocks and to grow through mergers and acquisitions.

M&S expanded overseas throughout Asia and was able to use its close working relationship with Coats Viyella, based on Coats' long experience of the Asian market, to gain customer knowledge into the fabrics and cut of clothing which Asian consumers required and demanded.

2. *Formal and informal horizontal integration*

This has included merger and acquisition activity in all sectors. In the grocery sector an alternative approach has been followed, with retailer groups engaged in cooperative buying in order to extract discounts from multinational manufacturing corporations. This has taken place in an international context with the formation of three major USA/EU buying groups. Increasingly, competition will take place, not simply between companies, but between whole supply chains.

3. *Proliferation of direct marketing channels*

This has increased the level of competition in markets and provided a means of entering new markets. For example, many overseas firms have entered the Japanese market through mail-order activity without having to enter the complex multi-layered Japanese distribution system. This has enabled price discounters to enter the market, a significant achievement on its own. Foreign firms required to enter into joint ventures with local Japanese partners and have been driven by demographic and technical factors, such as the rapid growth in the number of working Japanese women to over three-quarters of the female population. In addition, free phone numbers, cable TV and smart cards have facilitated the growth in this expansion. The success of this approach is indicated by Amway, the Japanese subsidiary of the US direct sales firm, achieving the accolade of becoming one of the most profitable foreign firms in Japan.

4. *The spread of discounting*

Pricing is an enduring element of the retail marketing mix (see Figure 12.6) and some firms have differentiated on this mix element. This has occurred internationally in a wide range of sectors. The US office supplies discounter (Staples) has taken their low-price proposition to several EU countries, French and German grocery discounters have entered several non-domestic markets including the UK, and in Japan the most rapid growth in retail sales is in the discount stores sector.

Table 12.2: Examples of Discount Retailers by Sector

Sector	Companies
Fast-food service	McDonalds, Burger King
Food retailing	Wal Mart, Aldi, Netto
Non-food retailing	Wal Mart
Office stationery	Staples
Banking	First e-banking
Toy retailing	Toys R Us

1. *Increasing overlap in the product assortment offered by retailers who were traditionally in different industries.*

This has made the task of the strategic marketing planner more complicated, when it is difficult to know who is in fact a competitor, or potential competitor.

Table 12.3: Product Assortment Overlap

Sector	New competitors
Banking and finance	Banks/building societies versus grocery retailing Government-owned Post Office, in UK
Grocery retailing	Petrol retailers
Travel/holidays	Motoring organizations (breakdown and general motorist support)
Restaurants (fast food on travel networks)	Hotel groups – through hotel chains offering customers to choose the rest facilities of the hotel complex and/or the restaurant facility, which supports the hotel facility and is located next to it.
Branded clothes retailing	Grocery retailing

In addition to assortment overlap through ownership, companies have also entered into strategic alliances with favoured partners, for example a car hire company with an airline.

2.   *The dominant role of information and communication technology to support a distribution strategy.*

This allows stores to keep detailed information on inventory and on purchase behaviour. Retailers are increasingly sharing data with manufacturers to increase profits. Because firms operate internationally information networks allow the coordination of complex businesses and the sharing of best practice across markets. Computer systems allow lower inventory and quicker stock turnover to be maintained. EPOS systems allow the linking of promotional activity to specific, targeted customers. In Japan, 7-eleven Japan coordinates sales through its 4000 franchised convenience stores via a computerized POS network. Small retail outlets with hundreds of products are tracked by the network which replenishes supplies automatically with three deliveries per day.

ICT has facilitated the rapid growth in demand for JIT delivery. The impact of this has been to:

- Increase order frequency with more smaller orders;

- Forge closer links between businesses (as dependency of such a system increases). This has increasingly led to 'favoured supplier' status and often to the industry becoming vertically integrated as suppliers are taken over. Companies follow this strategy, not simply to ensure and develop supply linkages, but to prevent a competitor from purchasing a key supplier;

- More frequent orders result in a reduction in order processing time, thus a need to further increase investment in information technology in particular and in systems in general.

The retailing of books has, in particular, been affected by the Internet as a new distribution channel. This has enabled Amazon books to become one of the largest suppliers of books in the world.

12.5   Wholesaling

Wholesalers buy goods and services from other businesses which they resell. To be defined as a wholesaler the business must not sell to the consumers of the product. The definition of wholesalers excludes businesses that manufacture products, or are involved in the primary sector of the economy, e.g. farming, forestry and mining.

The main reason for the existence of wholesalers is the need to provide a service to link manufacturers with consumers. Manufacturers want to produce long production runs of commodities, in one location, to obtain economies of scale in production. In complete contrast, consumers wish to buy small quantities of goods with no restriction on the geographic location of purchase. Retailers attempt to service the needs of consumers and, in some markets, retailers will also be relatively geographically dispersed and handle relatively small quantities of products, e.g. newsagents, independently-owned grocers, tobacconists and confectioners.

The greater the difference between the needs of the manufacturer and retailer, the greater the need for an intermediary, namely a wholesaler.

Wholesalers are also referred to as distributors. As they take ownership of the goods that they wholesale, they are involved in the use of the full marketing mix for their goods.

The main *additional* functions provided by a wholesaler are to:

Break bulk – where large quantities are purchased from a manufacturer (seeking large production runs) and broken down into smaller quantities for relatively low-volume retailing. Necessary services associated with this:

- Warehousing;
- Financing;
- Logistics (i.e. physical distribution). This includes order processing, transportation, stock management, warehousing and customer services;
- Marketing information receiver and transmitter. Information obtained from retailers is transmitted to manufacturers and information from manufacturers is communicated to retailers. This is a vital function for all businesses involved in the marketing chain. The success of this function will be influenced substantially by the form of relationship between businesses in the marketing chain. Where one member of the chain tries to dominate, then information flow is usually severely restricted.

Threats to wholesaling
- Large-scale multiple retailers that provide their own wholesaling function.
- Technology which:
  (a) makes it cost-effective to miss out channel intermediaries (e.g. wholesalers).
  (b) allows transactions to take place directly between the producer and the retailer. This demand comes from the producer, driven by cost pressures, and also from the consumer who in part expects to pay less (unless the producer can charge for the 'time saved' benefit) and who as part of a self-service culture likes to take greater control.

The number of wholesalers in the food sector, for example, has declined rapidly in the last two decades, as the above pressures have forced many to close.

12.6   Role of Physical Outlets

Physical outlets have been the main manifestation of a retailer. This topic is also discussed in Chapter 13 under 'physical evidence'. The development of dot com businesses has resulted in an enthusiastic debate about the role of physical outlets with extreme positions being taken. These range from,

- 'In the future all business will be conducted virtually' to

- 'Internet retailing will only ever be a peripheral activity'.

There are obviously many possible intermediate positions. Industries differ in the extent to which they tend towards either extreme. This depends on the extent to which the service must be consumed at the point of service delivery (see Table 12.4).

Table 12.4: Tactile Service Experience (Average Consumer)

(Requirement for the service to be consumed at the point of service delivery).

Highly tactile	Moderately tactile	Neutral	Moderately non-tactile	Non-tactile
- Haircut - Restaurant meal - Theme park - Overnight stay in a hotel - Transport by bus or train - Having a dental health check	- Getting a new exhaust fitted to the car - Sorting out legal problems with a lawyer	- Sourcing groceries and fast-moving consumer goods. - Sourcing electrical goods	- Purchasing car insurance	- Withdrawing money from a current account

The degree to which a service is highly tactile, i.e. must be consumed at the point of service delivery, depends on:

- the inherent nature of the service;

- consumer demand.

For example, a haircut must be consumed at the point of service delivery regardless of variations in consumer demand. In contrast, sourcing groceries need not inherently be consumed at the point of service delivery, i.e. in a retail store. Separation of the two was not uncommon over 50 years ago, when customers telephoned their orders to grocers. Delivery boys then provided the order, by bicycle, to the customer's doorstep. However some consumers enjoy the retail experience and prefer to consume the service at the point of delivery. Other consumers prefer the approach of the doorstep delivery and now use the technological version, via the Internet.

At the other extreme of the tactile service experience scale is the purely mundane and functional service activity of withdrawing money from a current account. This service has little or no inherent 'tactile' requirement for most consumers because it is regarded as a utilitarian, functional activity. Only consumers who are unable to use automated facilities would object to the withdrawal of a physical outlet for this service.

This discussion raises the question of what is meant by physical outlet. Where this discussion is least clear-cut is in the provision of banking services. Banking services are currently delivered by a range of physical outlets. These now include:

- traditional bricks-and-mortar bank buildings;

- ATMs;

- Supermarkets that provide 'cash back' services which allow consumers to obtain cash when they pay for their goods.

These different services increasingly educate the consumer in terms of their perception of what a bank is and how it should tangibly manifest itself. In spite of these other tangible, physical manifestations, retail bank outlets remain for the consumer a highly significant element of their perception of a bank.

Retail bank outlets

There is much discussion of new distribution channels. However their branch network continues to play a highly significant role for financial service providers.

The branch network is perpetually under attack to reduce the cost burden it imposes on the bank or building society. These cost pressures, and the virtues of direct banking, have led some to question whether there is a future for the branch network. An interesting article in defence of the network published in *Financial World* (June 1999, pp38-9) argues that the network is a key element in 'anchoring the brand and underpinning customer retention'. Currently it is argued that a narrow financial measure of branch profitability is used as a significant criterion for deciding on the retention of a branch, rather than its role within the mix.

Channel selection and evaluation

The broad evaluation criteria may be summarized under the headings of: *economic/financial control* that can be exerted over the channel and how *adaptive* the channel is to future trading conditions. The relative importance of each of these assessment criteria differs depending on individual circumstances (Kotler *et al.* (1999, pp921-5)).

12.7   International Market Entry

One of the decisions which is very different in international marketing concerns market entry. This is something that is usually kept constant in the domestic environment. Entry choices range from indirect exporting, where the firm markets to an overseas buyer operating in the domestic country, to full scale investment and manufacturing in the overseas market.

There is no single, ideal method of entry – many international organizations use a mixture of entry strategies, e.g. McDonalds have both wholly-owned and franchised outlets.

Table 12.5: Market Entry Choices

Indirect exporting	This is no different to selling to the domestic market. Many multinational procurement offices are located throughout the world, for example the Japanese trading companies (Soga Sosha).
Direct exporting	Direct exporting, also includes piggy backing. Here the manufacturer performs the export task rather than delegating it to others. This includes, for example, market contact, market research, physical distribution, export documentation, pricing etc.

Overseas
manufacture

without direct investment	● Licensing (of patents, trademarks, copyright). ● Contract manufacture.
with direct investment	● For example as JV or wholly owned subsidiary. ● The main benefit of this approach is shared risk. The firm is able to gain skills of, or linkage with, an important market player. This may be an important route of entry in to difficult markets. This was the preferred market entry strategy into China.

The main consideration for companies moving from indirect exporting towards overseas manufacture are:

● Increasing risk – due to rising levels of investment abroad;

● Increasing information on the market;

● Greater control over the channel of distribution;

● Greater opportunity to gain expertise.

Joint ventures can actually reduce risk, through working with established players in the marketplace who have complementary expertise (see Marketing in Practice).

MARKETING IN PRACTICE

Direct Line Insurance in Joint Venture in Japan

In October 1999, Direct Line, the UK's largest private motor insurer, entered into a joint venture with Japanese life insurer Yasuda Mutual Life Insurance to establish a new direct motor insurance company in Japan.

Direct Line contributed to the deal its operational expertise and strength in branding, while Yasuda Life provided a very large customer base, as well as specialist expertise in this

---

marketplace. The joint venture initially focused on insuring Japan's private motorists, a market valued at over £20 billion in annual insurance premiums. Impending deregulation in Japan precipitated this move.

Summary

The key channel selection decisions faced by marketers are:

(1) the length of the marketing channel

(2) the extent to which the business integrates with other channel members

(3) maximizing the efficiency of distribution logistics, i.e. the physical flow of goods from the producer to the end consumer

(4) selection of optimal distribution density.

Technology has improved the efficiency of channel management, allowing shorter lead times, from order to delivery, and more detailed inventory management. In addition to making, essentially traditional, systems work more efficiently, technology has allowed channel members to receive substantial volumes of information on the final consumer and even to market directly to the consumer.

Key issues in retailing involve positioning the retail format, deciding on the emphasis to give to individual marketing mix tools and competing successfully in the dynamically changing environment. Environmental change has constrained the scope for retailers to alter their positioning stance. The growth in the number of competitors, the widespread adoption of the 'value' proposition and the proliferation of direct marketing channels have contributed to this.

The wholesaling function is coming under increasing pressure from other members of the marketing chain, who have grown large enough to undertake their own wholesaling function. In addition, technology has facilitated this development and encouraged consumers of the 'self-service' culture to 'deal direct' with producers. Wholesalers must perform their key functions (of breaking bulk, warehousing, financing, logistics and as a marketing information transmitter and receiver) to a high level, and in market segments where retailers and producers can not compete effectively, in order to survive.

Physical outlets play an important role in support of brand perception, in particular providing tangibility to the brand. Their role has been underestimated by many dot com businesses. A key criterion in assessing the importance of the physical outlet is the requirement for the service to be consumed at the point of service delivery. Where this is important, e.g. for hotels and restaurants, then the role of the physical outlet is crucial.

References

(1999) How the Internet redefines banking, *The Banker*, June, pp27-30

(1999) *Financial World*, June, pp38-9

Baker M (ed) (2000) *The Marketing Book*, 4th edition, Butterworth Heinemenn Oxford

Johnson G & Scholes K (1999) *Exploring Corporate Strategy*, 5th edition, Prentice Hall Europe

McGoldrick P J & Andre E (1997) Consumer Misbehaviour: promiscuity or loyalty in grocery shopping, *Journal of Retail and Consumer Services*, 4 (2) pp73-81

Porter M E (1985) *Competitive Advantage*, New York, Free Press

13

EXTENDED MARKETING MIX

Learning Objectives

After reading this chapter students should:

- Understand the impact of customer contact level on service design;
- Understand the elements of 'people', 'process' and of 'physical evidence' (servicescape) and how these may be used to improve service marketing performance.

Figure 13.1: Chapter Map

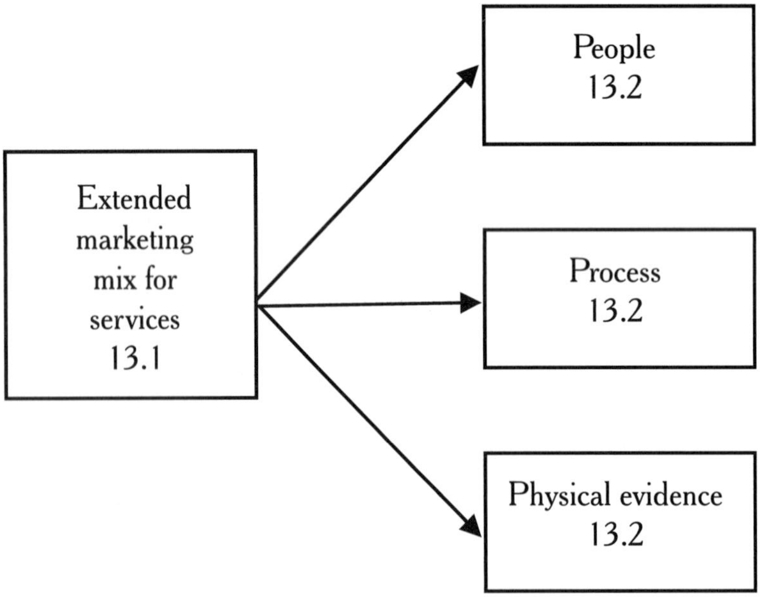

Introduction

In service marketing, unlike product marketing, the customer is often present and/or involved in the service delivery. Effective and efficient staff, processes and the physical environment surrounding service delivery are therefore even more critical in the context of marketing a service. In order to improve the performance of service delivery, it is necessary to understand the attributes of each of the service mix elements. Several models exist to support this; perhaps the best known of these is Zeithaml and Bitner's (1996) SERVQUAL model.

13.1   Extended Marketing Mix for Services

Due to the unique characteristics of services it has been suggested that the traditional marketing mix, i.e. the 4 Ps, is insufficient when dealing with services. Booms & Bitner (1981) suggested that the mix should be extended to include an additional 3 Ps. The services marketing mix (7Ps) consists of:

Product

Place

Promotion

Price

People

Process

Physical evidence.

People

Inseparability (see Chapter 4) in the marketing of services results in people having a much more important role. People can be identified with, or even as, the product (e.g. financial advisor or a dentist) unlike many products where product features and the manufacture's brand may be the dominant factors when consumers evaluate a product.

The role of people is particularly important in services because, due to its intangibility, the service is an act rather than an object and therefore the quality of the service can be influenced greatly by the service provider and its interaction with the customer.

Process

Process includes the systems and equipment required to deliver the service to the desired quality level. Perishability, inseparability and heterogeneity are the main reasons for the elevated importance of 'process' in service marketing. When a consumer orders a service, it is either required immediately (a meal or a quotation for car insurance), or at some time in the future (an airline ticket or cinema seat). In either case, systems must be in place to ensure that the service will be available at the time it has been ordered by the consumer.

Physical evidence

Physical evidence of the service offer or of the company are the only tangible attributes the service consumer may use to assess a service. This may include the physical state of repair, decoration and design of the building, company promotional information (brochures, letters, and business cards) and even the physical appearance of staff.

Often customers have difficulty in understanding the service offering due to its intangibility. For example, some years after the launch of individual savings accounts (ISAs) in the UK many consumers were still ignorant of their benefits.

A further challenge that faces the financial services industry is the nature of the service they are selling. Customers are not generally interested in financial services, unlike holidays, cars and other consumer goods. According to Roger Flynn, Managing Director of Prudential Retail, cited in Simms (1999) pp20-5:

> *They'd rather be down the pub or watching TV, so people who come in and try to turn it into a pull product with a fancy name will find it very difficult. You'll never turn financial services into a hot-to-trot purchase up there with holidays and cameras. But that doesn't mean you can't make it better than it is. The future will end up being a balance of better marketing along with sets of products that customers need to be sold.*

High-contact and low-contact services

Customer contact level refers to the extent to which customers interact with service staff and visit the physical organization. The distinction with regard to visiting, or interacting with, the physical organization originally meant visiting the building, as in a store, bank, office etc. and also interacting with the physical manifestation of the service, i.e. the staff. While these remain the most significant in terms of impact during interaction, for some services the customer may never experience the physical organization directly, but only indirectly via remote communications devices. Physical aspects of the organization may now also include remote communication interfaces such as computer screens, via the Internet, or any other remote devices, such as WAP phones and digital television. Interaction via such devices is considered as a low-contact service. Technological developments are likely to result in high levels of customer interaction with technology to such an extent that 'virtual interaction' will be experineced. At that stage remote technology-mediated communication could be considered as 'high virtual contact'.

The level of customer contact with a service is of great importance in the service design, including the relative emphases placed on people, process and physical evidence. In general, process is a very important aspect for all services (discussed in 13.3). Customer contact level has a direct association with the relative importance of 'physical evidence' and of 'people' (Figure 13.2).

Figure 13.2: Association between Level of Customer Contact and the Relative Importance of 'Physical Evidence' and 'People'

	CUSTOMER CONTACT LEVEL	
	Low	**High**
Relative importance of physical evidence	Low	High
Relative importance of people	Low	High
Examples	Electronic banking Phone insurance Use of a postal service	Hairdresser Doctor Dentist

13.2   People

The direct importance of the 'people' element of service delivery depends on the level of contact with the customer and on the skill level required. For example, medical services are high skill-high contact, building security is low skill-medium/low contact, while a car wash is low contact. In addition to the requirement to recruit, reward and train staff appropriately, organizations must also devote resources to the training of their customers. This is because customers perform ever-increasing proportions of services offered by organizations (e.g. transactions processing in banks and building societies, self-service in restaurants and supermarkets, check-in registration either by paper or touch screens at corporate offices and in hotels). Customers may need some basic training in how they can complete their part of the service and this may only require simple, clearly written and unambiguous instructions which are suitably located.

It is not sufficient that staff are able merely to do their work and achieve service level targets. They must understand what the brand and the company represents, and undertake their work in a way that is aligned with the brand. This requires the selection and recruitment of appropriate staff, and investment in their training and support systems to allow them to undertake their work to their maximum potential. Companies must therefore train and reward staff appropriately and provide systems and working environments (as part of the servicescape) which enable them to undertake their work effortlessly and efficiently.

The higher the customer contact level the greater the importance of 'people' in directly influencing customer perception of the service.

Research by Lovelock (1996) on employee-customer interaction concluded that there can be situations where the customer is not always right. A few 'problem' customers were the source of a disproportionately large proportion (22%) of unsatisfactory encounters. This may be even higher for industries in which the customer has a greater input into the service delivery process (e.g. health care, education and legal services). The implications for management are that:

- employees need to be provided with training in suitable coping and problem-solving skills;

- the organization must also clarify to its staff how they are to deal with such customers.

Such customers, in addition to the disproportionate amount of time which such customers account for, may also incur the company in additional expense, for example damaged rental cars and vans, damaged general physical environment (carpets, furniture, seating in planes).

Customers may require training

Further conclusions from Lovelock (1996) were that unsatisfactory customer interaction may result from customer ignorance of appropriate behaviour. This is an extension of research which concluded that where customers and staff share similar conclusions of the service encounter both parties have a clear understanding of their respective 'roles'. Customers who are ignorant of the detailed service offer may require training otherwise they may feel foolish and not revisit. For example, consider a restaurant that asks customers to cook their own meat, yet this must be served by staff. The potential for chaos, and for confused and uncomfortable customers, is great. Customer training, in such a context, is essential.

In the context of an up-market holiday resort, which offered large discounts in the off-peak season, customer training was essential. Customers who were unfamiliar with the dress code and general code of conduct expected, received education on expected behaviour. This minimized the potential for tension between traditional clients and off-peak clients.

Training of employees

As the expectations of the customers from the service businesses increase, companies have started to value investments in people as much as investments in machines (Schlesinger and Heskett, 1991). The largest portion of service employees includes receptionists, waiters, telephone operators, insurance company claims processors, flight attendants, sales clerks, and others with low pay and little input in their companies. Companies need to make recruitment and training as important for service employees as for managers. Service employees who are well trained and fairly compensated provide better service, need less supervision, and are much more likely to stay in the job. Consequently, customers who are in contact with well-trained service employees are likely to be more satisfied, return more often, and perhaps even purchase more than they otherwise would (Schlesinger and Heskett, 1991). Training provides service employees with the ability to identify and resolve problems and operational weaknesses hindering organizational effectiveness and efficiency. Training service employees to perform a variety of service activities will also provide an organization with a great deal of flexibility.

Proper training and empowerment will allow these workers to resolve any perceived conflicts before they become a negative service encounter for the customer. Hotel desk clerks or airline counter employees, for example, should have the training and authority to make a decision whether a customer should be given some form of restitution to ensure a positive service interaction.

Emotional labour

People operate at a physical and mental level, and in addition at an emotional level. Emotional labour refers to employee interaction with customers where staff, in addition to carrying out their tasks, give a little bit extra which makes customers feel good about the service (Hochschild 1983). This is where staff smile, are naturally interested in talking with customers, are friendly, courteous and strike an empathy with customers. It is the difference between 'having a service done to you' and 'feeling at home'. Many services are consumed when people are in their leisure time (e.g. hotels, sports centres and gyms, restaurants etc.) or when people are potentially stressed by the situation (doctors, dentists, lawyers, financial services). Customers really do 'need' to feel that they are not simply being processed by the organization. Staff may need to suppress their true feelings about their private situation in order to achieve high standards of emotional labour when dealing with customers. Effective recruitment and retention policies are required if organizations are to seek competitive advantage from the deployment of staff which are rated highly on 'emotional labour'.

Closing SERVQUAL 'Gap 3'

Zeithaml and Bitner (1996) identify employees as the cause for 'gap 3' (i.e. the difference between service quality specifications and actual service delivery) in the SERVQUAL disconfirmation model. Research which demonstrates the correlation between high customer satisfaction and 'surrogate' measures of employee satisfaction, such as staff turnover, is unsurprising. We have all experienced restaurant staff with 'bad attitude' whose service is very slow, rude, an ineffective. This situation should never arise if organizations pay close attention to the following critical human resource management issues:

- Accurate description of employee roles and reporting structures;
- Effective selection and recruitment;
- Effective training needs analysis and implementation;
- Suitable and motivating remuneration packages;
- Empowerment;
- Organizational socialization;
- Provision of support systems to enable staff to function effectively and thereby to enjoy their work.

13.3   Process

Processes include both the systems and the physical equipment which are involved in service delivery. Process elements are frequently unseen, or unrecognized, by customers. The main time they become aware of a process is when it fails. For example, an incorrect bank statement, the wrong order delivered by the flat pack company, a bouquet sent for a loved one's birthday which arrives late or a holiday taken in India where your baggage ends up in Singapore. Process failures can lead to substantial customer complaints and a loss of repeat business. The discussion of 'process' is linked to the topic of channel management (Chapter 12).

Process issues are becoming more complicated. Globalization and pressure to reduce costs has resulted in geographically dispersed supply chains. Companies are increasingly more dependent on other members of the supply chain. To understand where dependency and co-operation may exist, the concept of the value chain (Porter, 1980) is helpful. This includes the elements of the value chain which companies are likely to consider outsourcing, where these do not fit in with the core competencies of the business.

Increasingly, therefore, competition is taking place between supply chains, rather than between individual businesses. Grocery retailing is at an embryonic stage in this process where large European and North American companies work together (in terms of their buying activity) to form three major buying groups. The potential for greater cooperation in the future is evident. In the short term, these companies must enable inter-company buying processes and add these to processes already developed for their existing upstream supply chain. The essential elements of these processes include:

- marketing – efficient consumer response (ECR);
- production operations management and logistics; and
- information systems, especially electronic data interchange (EDI).

Inseparability of services means that the process by which the service is delivered may be visible to the customer, while the intangible aspect of services may result in the 'process' being a critical element when customers appraise service delivery. Flows of information to the customer, time queuing (Chapter 4) and ease of payment are frequent and substantial elements of most service offers.

Technological developments

Services are increasingly automated to:

- reduce costs;
- increase customer access (in terms of time and location, e.g. ATMs); and
- ensure consistency of service delivery.

These have resulted in:

- An improvement in supply chain linkages;
- Greater speed of business processes;
- Ability for companies to respond to the marketplace in less time;
- Ability to develop long-term customer relationships in a way that was previously not possible.

MARKETING IN PRACTICE

IBM and Long-term Customer Relationships

IBM offers complete, end-to-end business intelligence solutions to ensure long-term success in managing customer relationships based on an environment conducive to ongoing learning and improved results from every marketing effort.

Key elements include:

- *Marketing analysis*: The ability to classify customers into different groups to be managed differently, either tactically or strategically.

- *Predictive marketing*: Using data mining capabilities to discover new customers for specific marketing programmes and evaluate the responses to offers.

- *Campaign planning*: Cataloguing and organizing high-level campaign data so that multiple users can access what is happening across all campaigns.

- *Campaign management*: Target customer selections are made and contact lists are created – all based on the analytical work done and the intelligence generated in the preceding steps of the marketing process.

- *Campaign review*: The final step includes collecting, posting, summarizing, reporting, tracking and trending the results of each campaign and campaign segment.

Source: www.ibm.com

Service blueprints

It is essential that service firms develop efficient and well-considered processes if they are to achieve sustainable competitive advantage. Service blueprints, which are simply maps or diagrams of the service process, support the construction and development of an efficient service process. They are similar to flow diagrams which computer programmers construct, or which are constructed in various approaches to project planning. In addition, the blueprint may be used subsequently to analyse the performance of the service process in order to overcome problems and to increase process performance.

The service process includes elements which are invisible systems, from the customers' perspective, and systems which directly support customer-facing activity, e.g. airline check-in, bank transactions etc. Systems that directly support customer service may also include tangibility in terms of the machinery and equipment which are used by staff or customers to complete the process element of the service. Examples include touch screens, used by bank customers and increasingly by retailers ranging from cars to food. Consequently, consideration of process may often be connected directly with the physical environment (Zeithaml & Bitner 1996).

Customer satisfaction

Several elements contribute to the level of customer satisfaction with a service encounter. Zeithaml & Bitner (1996) suggest these include service quality, product quality, price, situational and personal factors. Customers contribute to their own service delivery (e.g. a student who reads course references versus one who does not) and because of this their role in service delivery is an important element of customer satisfaction.

The idea that customer satisfaction is strongly based on perceptions and expectations of service, rather than purely on actual service delivery, is well established in the literature, founded largely on the work of Parasuraman *et al.* (1985) which used service quality as the basis for determining satisfaction or dissatisfaction with a service.

Sources of customer satisfaction and dissatisfaction in memorable service encounters

Zeithaml & Bitner (1996) discuss the sources of potential customer pleasure or displeasure with the service offer under one of four main headings:

1. Recovery = employee response to service delivery system failures;

2. Adaptability = employee response to customer needs and requests;

3. Spontaneity = unprompted and unsolicited employee actions;

4. Coping = employee response to problem customers.

13.4   Physical Evidence

The tangibility provided by the physical service environment is important in the assessment of the service offered, especially where the customer is unfamiliar with the service, and/or with the brand. The term servicescape is used as a shorthand reference to aspects of the physical environment. This environment is highly influential in terms of the:

● behaviour of customers;

● behaviour and efficiency of employees; and

● extent to which the servicescape facilitates the socialization of employees and customers, in terms of their respective roles. This is important, especially where customers are new to the service and/or to the brand. In the worst servicescapes the customer is confused and perhaps concerned that he or she might look foolish. In this situation the customer is unlikely to repeat the experience, with obvious implications for long-term business profitability.

What is the servicescape?
Servicescape is the 'actual physical facility where the service is performed, delivered and consumed' (Zeithaml & Bitner (1996) p518).

Communications technology increasingly limits the coverage of this definition as the proportion of remote customer transactions and interactions rises. The only 'physical evidence' which many customers now see of an organization is its website.

As services are intangible, customers rely on tangible cues to evaluate a service, especially where they are either unfamiliar with the service or with the brand. Where customers visit the service provider in person, the most commonly employed tangible evidence cue which they use is the physical evidence.

Servicescape may be subdivided into:

1. The built environment – exterior;

2. The built environment – interior;

3. The virtual environment (e.g. interaction via websites, WAP phones, digital TV);

4. Tangible physical evidence (e.g. business cards, stationery, billing statements, uniforms etc.)

Servicescapes are classified according to their complexity and this will affect servicescape management.

The servicescape also affects:

● the behaviour of customers and customer perception;

● the performance of employees (i.e. some servicescapes impede performance compared to others which enhance performance);

● the socialization of employees and customers in terms of their expected roles and behaviour (Zeithaml & Bitner, 1996, pp524-6).

Impact of organization objectives on servicescape

Changes in retail formats have reflected organizational objectives to increase profits through a reduction in staff costs and an increase in throughput of customers. The self-service format has been the widely used servicescape 'formula' used to achieve these goals. More recently, the most dramatic example of change in retail servicescape has been in the banking sector (see 'Marketing in Practice').

MARKETING IN PRACTICE

Changes in banking servicescapes

In the past, the main function of the bank servicescape was as a transaction processing environment and one that could store the valuable commodity transacted (i.e. money) in complete safety. Hence the emphasis on staff protection with safety screens and bars.

Banks now have a more marketing-focused purpose. Much of the transaction processing function has been replaced by ATMs and direct funds transfers, as well as remote access banking. The main purpose of the banking servicescape now is to serve and to sell (and cross-sell) to customers. Major changes have resulted:

From

- a low customer-to-staff area ratio.

- extensive use of bandit screens, bars and small windows.

- a low adoption rate of retail merchandizing techniques in the banking hall area.

- personal interviewing conducted at the counter windows or in the branch manager's private offices.

To

- Standard branch design formats used to ensure that consistent colour schemes, formats and image are portrayed across the network.

- Exteriors consisting of high profile, glass, shop window-type frontages, with automatic doors, eye-catching signs and effective displays.

- Up to 80% of the branch interior is devoted to the customer and the sales area.

- Open planning and limited use of bandit screens.

- Prominent merchandizing techniques/activities and staff help desks.

- Traffic flow concepts, such as 'hard' and 'soft' zones and walkways, have been adopted to control the speed and direction of customer movement around the branch.

- Automated services grouped into lobby areas at the front of the branch, frequently with out-of-hours access to encourage the use of less expensive automated services.

- Ergonomically improved environments to ensure, for both staff and customers, efficient functioning and operation.

- Refurbishment accompanied by staff training/reorientation programmes to ease the pressures of change and to help to turn staff from bankers into retailers.

- A reduction in the average size of premises required to one-third, (e.g. from 6,000 sq. ft to 2,000 sq. ft), and this helps to reduce overheads.

- The fitting/refurbishment process itself has been reduced from about six months to about six or seven weeks.

The new branch formats are now much better aligned to current bank marketing objectives. The servicescape has played an essential role in this realignment process.

Sources: Information on new branch design taken from Greenland SJ (1994)

Summary

The marketing of services can often prove challenging as a result of their unique characteristics of intangibility, inseparability, variability, perishability and lack of ownership. Due to these features the traditional marketing mix, i.e. the 4 Ps, is often regarded as insufficient for dealing with services. Booms and Bitner developed the 7 Ps framework that consists of the original 4 Ps of product, place, promotion and price but with the additional 3 Ps of people, processes and physical evidence.

The extent to which the customer is involved in the production of the service can vary greatly. On the one hand the customer may not be involved in the service production at all, such as a visit to the dry cleaners. Alternatively there may be situations where customers are the co-producers of the service, for example a university tutorial, and this will greatly influence the quality of the service consumed. The extent to which customers participate in the service production and delivery is an important consideration for service companies. The greater the level of involvement and the higher the level of actual customer contact, the more important the 'people' and 'physical evidence' aspects of the mix. This can provide companies with the opportunity to tailor services to meet individual needs but it can also result in greater variability of services.

Due to the inseparability of services people play a key role in service delivery. This has major implications for staff recruitment and training. It also involves providing staff with the necessary skills and systems in order for them to undertake their work effectively. The people aspect of the mix can also be extended to include the customer. Increasingly customers are playing an important part in service production and may require some degree of basic training in order to complete their part of the service.

Services are often highly intangible and therefore customers find it difficult to judge their quality. Physical evidence, such as the physical service environment, is often used as a surrogate indicator of quality and is therefore an important element of the mix. The physical environment has been referred to as the servicescape and includes the interior and exterior of the built environment, the virtual environment and tangible physical evidence such as company literature.

Service delivery is often reliant on effective and efficient processes. Process failure can lead to customer complaints and therefore companies must ensure that they have systems in place to minimize failure. However, if processes do fail and this leads to customer complaints, companies must have processes in place to minimize the damage created.

References

Booms B H & Bitner M J (1981) *Marketing Strategies and Organizational Structures for Service Firms* in Donnelly J H & George W R (eds) *Marketing of Services* American Marketing Association pp 47-51

Canel C, Rosen D & Anderson EA (2000) Just-in-time is not just for manufacturing: a service perspective *Industrial Management & Data Systems*, Vol. 100 Issue 2

Greenland S J (1994) Rationalization and Restructuring in the Financial Services Sector *International Journal of Retail & Distribution Management*, Vol. 22 Issue 6

Hochschild A (1983) *The Managed Heart, Commercialization of Human Feeling* Berkely: University of California Press

Lovelock C (1996) *Services Marketing*, 3rd ed., Prentice Hall International, Englewood Cliffs, NJ

Porter M (1980) *Competitive Strategy* Free Press, New York

Schlesinger L A and Heskett J L (1991) *The Service-driven Company* Harvard Business Review Sept-Oct pp71-81

Sims J (1999) *Marketing Business* pp20-25 March

Zeithaml & Bitner (1996) *Services Marketing* McGraw-Hill International New York, Chapter 11

Part 3

Case Studies

The marketing mix

Credit card marketing has never been more active despite increasing competition but success rates depend upon the right blend of data

At first sight, this is not a good time to be a credit card marketer. Trends in the macro economy combined with a fiercely competitive environment as new entrants seek to carve out market share have led to increased levels of churn and pressure on margins. The most high-profile manifestation of these problems was the announcement made by Barclaycard that it was shedding over 1,000 jobs, having seen its market share fall from 32 per cent to 28 per cent in the last five years. Against this background, though, there are clear signs that credit card marketing can be successful both in terms of new customer recruitment and in respect of 'warm' customer management strategies. After all, several new credit card entrants have in recent years successfully marketed their products and built substantial portfolios. Bank One launched a card-based operation this year (1999) and it is very likely that other US-based issuers will establish operations in the UK next year (2000) as a springboard into Europe.

Their optimism is in no small part based on the European application of a data-driven card marketing strategy that has already been proven in the USA. This article seeks to argue that the key to successful card marketing lies in the better use of data and the integration of credit policy with marketing strategy to achieve optimal results. This needs to occur at the solicitation, application and behavioural parts of the customer life cycle, but this article will focus on the recruitment stage.

Most cards are marketed using a mix of broadcast media to build brand awareness (classic examples being Goldfish, Barclaycard and AMEX) supported by direct mail. Many of these mailings have been sourced from a variety of vertical lists selected on the basis of a profile match with the intended target audience. Extensive use is also made of lifestyle data, and mailings are deduplicated to provide a net file which is then commonly subdivided into different cells to test the most responsive pack/offer. This approach, much favoured by the creative agencies that also handle the above-the-line advertising, can lack sophistication if selections are made solely on the basis of response rather than according to the risk-response matrix shown below.

Optimizing response, usually the holy grail of the direct marketer, will not necessarily maximize the effectiveness of credit card mailing because of the adverse selection phenomenon. Put crudely, those most likely to respond to a credit offer will be those least likely to be accepted at point of application, while those most likely to be accepted are least likely to respond. The ideal segment – high response and low risk – unfortunately contains relatively few people and large-scale recruitment campaigns must focus therefore on the cells where adverse selection comes into play.

It is vital therefore that credit card marketers take proper account of credit policy if they are to avoid having a successful campaign in terms of response become a highly damaging and wasteful campaign when large numbers of solicited prospects are refused the card at point of application.

Unfortunately, many card issuers are divisionalised in such a way as to split the credit and marketing functions. This leads to each division being set contradictory goals (maximizing response v. minimizing risk) and can create tension between two departments whose close working relationship is essential if the benefits of a data-driven approach are to be fully realized. The more advanced card issuers, especially the new entrants, have sought to integrate these functions much more closely together, recognizing that both 'sides' have a common goal and are often using similar data and identical statistical techniques.

Integrating credit and marketing data

To address this issue, most but by no means all credit marketers pre-screen mailings against credit bureau information to remove the high-risk population but retain those likely to be responsive. This process may involve using a generic bureau risk score, and/or deselecting against county court judgements and high numbers of recent credit searches.

Mailing A

Volume mailed: 500,000 @ £0.60 per piece = £300,000 total mailing cost

Response rate: 0.6 per cent – 3,000 respondents

Accept rate: 50 per cent – 1,500 accounts opened

Overall mailing effectiveness: 0.3 per cent

Mailing cost per accept: £200 – almost certainly uneconomic

Mailing B

Volume mailed: 500,000 @ £0.60 per piece = £300,000 total mailing cost

Response rate: 1 per cent – 5,000 respondents

Accept rate: 70 per cent – 3,500 accounts opened

Overall mailing effectiveness: 0.7 per cent

Mailing cost per accept: £85.71 – probably economic

A simple rule, but one by no means universally adopted, is to confirm the person to be mailed as present on the electoral roll, since electoral roll confirmation is often a policy rule or a heavily weighted scorecard variable at point of application. It makes little sense to mail unconfirmed names if they are going to be instantly rejected when they apply.

More sophisticated marketers will recognize that the same names are going to be mailed over and over again as credit cards are targeted into broadly the same segment of the population. Although lightly mailed by US standards, nevertheless the amount of UK mail is increasing and response rates are falling. It is not unusual for a cold mailing to generate a response rate of half of one per cent with perhaps half of those responding rejected at point of application.

This implies the need to widen the mailing universe and make better use of comprehensive databases such as the electoral roll enhanced with actual data (years at address, household composition) or inferred estimates (geodemographics, financial wallet size and composition, age and income, for example).

A second strategy would be to differentiate the product offer to allow riskier groups falling just below the cut-off to be accepted for a card albeit on different terms. There is a large market in this C2/D/E group who are poorly served by traditional card providers who tend to have similar risk policies. However, if risk is properly managed and priced there is no reason why facilities should not be extended to this group – after all, the mail order catalogue business has been operating profitably in this market for many years.

The ability to use data in this way to overcome the adverse selection phenomenon varies widely across Europe. A general trend is for less data to be available as the privacy and data protection laws tighten, but there are large differences on a country-by-country basis. Some European states such as Sweden have relatively liberal laws concerning the use of personal data that is in the public domain, such as name and address and migration information, that can be used for targeting.

By contrast, Germany, for example, does not allow public record data to be used for marketing and the national credit referencing agency, Bundes-Schufa, does not offer pre-screening services due to legal constraints. In France the position is similar to Germany, whereas in Spain pre-screening can be undertaken for credit mailings.

As an aside, these enormous country-by-country variations contrast sharply with the universal availability of full data for pre-screening enjoyed by credit card marketers in the USA, a consequence of which is that American new entrants are often forced to re-examine their business models before launching on a pan-European scale. Whether such variations are desirable or even sustainable as we enter an aspatial world of ecu-denominated cards delivered by e-commerce is a point that will be returned to at the end of this article.

Small but significant

The importance of making the most intelligent use of data is clear when the economics of direct mail are considered. Even small percentage points of difference in response and acceptance rates have a profound effect on the profitability of recruitment, as shown in the above tables.

Implementing data-driven segmentation and targeting models for both risk and response will substantially improve the economics of card marketing using a direct channel. Similar metrics also apply to telemarketing of course. It is little wonder then that card marketers will celebrate when accepted response rates reach 1 per cent. However, it is hard to think of any other industry that would congratulate itself on being 99 per cent wrong, and this issue will be returned to later.

Note that there are many other cost and revenue dynamics to consider over and above mailing costs. These will include customer service costs, application processing and card issuing costs and the proportion of responses that are manually reviewed. On the revenue side, a monoline will add insurance-related revenues (card protection, sickness/unemployment protection etc.). A multi-product bank may take a different, customer-focused view across all other banking relationships to assess current customer worth and future profitability (see illustration below), whereas a retailer will also consider the effectiveness of the card in generating merchandise sales.

In all cases, the key driver of card profitability is utilization, downweighted by credit risk and attrition/dormancy. Again a data-driven approach can be used to model these factors not just at behavioural stage (i.e. after the account is a few months old) but also at point of solicitation. These powerful estimators enable the card to be targeted into the most profitable long-term prospects who are most likely to use the card, not repay each month, and who remain as loyal and responsible customers.

A view of the future

Reaching this holy grail, even with the most sophisticated data-driven models and strategies, is as we have seen extremely wasteful using traditional targeting media. The main reason for such low response rates, even when using modelling to best effect with traditional data sources, is that the credit card marketer is missing one vital piece of consumer information fundamental to response. Time is the key element that credit card marketers know too little about. Profiling and modelling will help to identify the target audience on the basis of static database characteristics and will point to the right segment and the best locations.

But the right time to make the offer will not be known. Collecting such data is massively expensive, and although lifestyle companies have tried to address this in their questionnaires, there is a wide gulf between declared intention and actual buying behaviour. And to complicate matters further, the use of personal data for marketing is becoming increasingly restricted as data protection regulations tighten. Where then does this leave the credit card marketer?

One view of the future comes from the USA where electronic commerce over the Internet is enabling not just new delivery channel options for financial services marketers, but is also providing the means for a radical reappraisal of the traditional relationship between buyer and seller.

Conventionally, credit cards have been taken to market by a 'push' model with service providers selling a packaged product at fixed terms to consumer segments. What if instead consumers empowered themselves with their own personal data (creditworthiness, wallet size and lifetime value) and promoted themselves in a new electronic marketplace where individual-level best offers would be selected by the consumer (note the reversal of the traditional power relationship) on the basis of validated personal information volunteered by the individual?

This is now beginning to happen, facilitated by a new type of company known as an 'infomediary' which acts as the virtual marketplace owner, hosting a site that brings consumers and service providers together, along with a validation certificate provided by a third party such as a credit bureau. Such a new world immediately addresses the fundamental dimension of time, raises response rates dramatically, and gives consumers direct and demonstrable benefits for their volunteering personal data.

We are just beginning to witness a new era in credit marketing as we move to the electronic marketplace. The winners and losers here will still be those companies making the best use of data, but the data sources and the response dynamics associated with them will be radically different from the '99 per cent wrong' world that credit marketers currently inhabit. And of course, with the best products made available to the best customers at the right time, the biggest winner of all in this brave new world, is the consumer.

Dr David Grafton is director of Equifax Consulting

Source: Financial World, May 1999, pp15-17

Imagine that you are the marketing manager for a European bank that is launching a pan-European credit card specifically targeting females aged 25 - 40. One of the features to be marketed for this product will be security in its use in Internet purchases. You have been asked to prepare a report for the marketing director outlining the following:

- Issues to be taken into consideration when developing a pan-European product.

- Select two contrasting countries and compare the promotional issues involved with launching this credit card. For one of these countries outline your initial ideas for a promotional strategy. Consider to what extent this strategy is appropriate for the other country. Identify the ways in which this strategy may have to be amended to accommodate the country differences.

● Think about how the extended marketing mix (people, physical evidence and processes) could be used in the launch of this new credit card.

New unified global brand for BP

In the summer of 2000, BP Amoco unveiled a new, unified global brand and announced plans for a radical update of its retail sites around the world. The re-vamp – which comes 12 years after BP's sites were last modernized and 20 years after the refurbishment of Amoco's network – is part of a major drive by the group to increase its worldwide retail business by over 10 per cent a year.

The move to a single brand follows a $120 billion series of mergers and acquisitions which, over the past two years, have brought together the former British Petroleum, Amoco Corporation, Atlantic Richfield (ARCO) and most recently Burmah Castrol, to create a combined group with a market value of more than $200 billion.

The enlarged group will in future be known simply as BP, with the familiar BP shield and Amoco torch replaced by a fresh new symbol depicting a vibrant sunburst of green, white and yellow. Named the Helios mark after the sun god of ancient Greece, the new logo is intended to exemplify dynamic energy – in all its forms, from oil and gas to solar – that the company delivers to its ten million daily customers around the world. It also echoes an original marble motif in the London headquarters of BP which was designed by the celebrated architect Sir Edwin Lutyens in the 1920s.

BP Amoco chief executive Sir John Browne said:

> *Put simply, we have adopted a single brand to show our customers around the world that, wherever they see the BP sign, they can consistently expect the highest quality of products and services.*

> *We also believe it will greatly strengthen the sense of identity and common purpose of our 100,000 staff in more than 100 countries on whom we depend to produce and distribute those products and services in a way that meets our aspiration to be a progressive, responsible company.*

The new logo will be rapidly introduced at company offices, manufacturing plants and on correspondence. But its appearance on retail pole-signs will be phased to coincide with the up-dating of the company's retail network, currently 28,000 sites around the world, which will take four years to complete.

The first new retail sites will open late in 2000 in London and in Cleveland and Indianapolis in the USA, based on a radical prototype service station perfected at a secret warehouse location in Atlanta, Georgia.

The new sites, liveried in green, white and yellow, will offer customers a radical new concept in refuelling and shopping. As well as proprietary cleaner-burning fuels and premier Castrol lubricants, the novel BP Connect service will feature in-store e-kiosks where customers can check weather and traffic conditions, pay without cash or credit cards and call up directions to local destinations. While filling their tanks, customers can use a touch-screen monitor to order sandwiches, pastries and snacks which will be waiting for them inside the store. The screens will also offer sports scores and the latest news headlines.

In line with its commitment to environmental improvement, and its major investment in solar, BP's new sites will be partly powered by energy from the sun, through solar panels forming the transparent canopy above the pumps.

The company said it had spent some $7 million on researching and preparing the new brand, principally on legal and copyright verification and protection in the countries where it operates or might wish to do business in the future. It plans to spend a further $25 million a quarter in support of the brand change, mainly non-retail signage and additional advertising. It said the cost of re-vamping its retail network was expected to be broadly in line with investment already earmarked by the pre-merged companies to upgrade their sites.

The company said that although BP will be the single global brand, it intended to retain the value of its strong product brands, with Castrol becoming its premier lubricants brand worldwide. All the company's US sites east of the Rockies would continue to sell Amoco fuel products and feature Amoco Ultimate, which is recognized as a leading quality fuel. It also intended to retain the ARCO brand and marketing strategy at its 1,800 retail outlets on the US West Coast.

Sir John Browne said: 'We expect the move to a global brand and the introduction of state-of-the-art retail sites to bring a significant increase in sales and to make a major contribution to our recently-announced target of growing underlying earnings for the group as a whole by at least ten per cent a year over the next three years.'

Source: http://www.bp.com/24 July 2000 BP Amoco Unveils New Global Brand to Drive Growth

- Think about the global branding strategy BP has adopted and why it has chosen this branding strategy.

- Present the case for and against BPs selected brand attributes in the markets in which BP *currently* operates.

- Consider the extent you think the BP brand could be stretched. Try to think of examples where the BP brand could be stretched

   (a)   successfully and

   (b)   where brand stretching would be problematic.

Part Four

MARKETING APPLICATIONS

14

RELATIONSHIP MARKETING

Learning Objectives

After studying this chapter students should:

- Understand the meaning of the term relationship marketing;

- Understand the contexts in which relationship marketing needs to be varied and how it should be varied;

- Be able to monitor retention levels;

- Understand the issues involved in working with the marketing chain to achieve improved relationships for future, mutual, long-term benefit;

- Understand the need to define clear objectives for agencies, the process which they are employed to undertake and how the work of agencies may be assessed;

- Understand the importance of internal marketing relationships in the marketing operations process;

- Be able to define internal marketing;

- Be able to appreciate the various organizational structures and their impact on organizational cultures and internal relationships.

Figure 14.1: Chapter Map

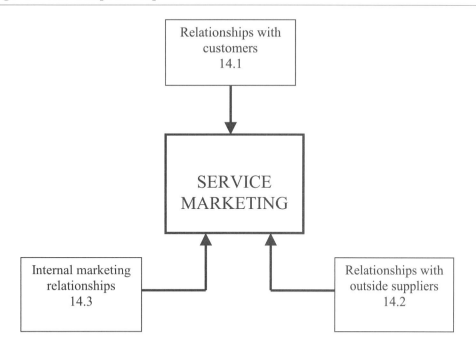

Introduction

Businesses must nurture wider relationships if they are to succeed. 'Relationships with customers' is concerned primarily with the competitive advantage that can be gained from customer retention and developing relationship marketing strategies. 'Relationships with suppliers' examines the management of external resources such as agencies, distributors, franchises and agents. In achieving lasting relationships with customers, organizations must depend on others in the supply chain. Porter's framework of the supply chain is a helpful concept to employ in understanding how suppliers must cooperate to achieve long-term customer relationships. One additional 'supplier' is included in the discussion, which is not described in Porter's supply chain, namely agencies. Effective use of agencies (most commonly advertising agencies, but also marketing research, public relations, design agencies etc.) requires clear specification of objectives, an understanding of the process which the agency is hired to undertake and clearly agreed approaches to the measurement of agency effectiveness.

Internal relationships play an important role in the marketing operations process. In order for a company to serve the needs of its external customer successfully, it is imperative that the needs of internal customers, i.e. employees, are also met. The concept of internal marketing was originally seen as applicable only to high-contact service organizations, such as financial service companies. However, it is now being acknowledged that all employees, regardless of the level of contact they have with customers, contribute both directly and indirectly to customer satisfaction. For example, counter staff in a bank contribute directly to the perceived level of customer service. However, the person working in the accounts department may have an indirect impact as he or she will contribute to the quality of the overall service provided. Many financial service organizations are recognizing the importance of ensuring that employees buy into the company's ideas. As a result some companies are implementing internal marketing schemes to ensure that staff are well informed and customer focused.

14.1   Relationships with Customers

Defining the 'relationship' concept, types of relationships and degree of importance

To understand the importance of relationship management one must first understand the idea of customer delivered value. This is defined as:

> *The difference between total customer value and total customer cost of a marketing offer*
>
> Kotler et al. (1999, p472)

What is meant by customer value (or more correctly, customer delivered value)? It is the value ascribed to the product and service provided by the staff of the financial service organization, including the image or brand value which customers perceive from buying financial services from a particular organization. Cost is not simply monetary cost, but the cost represented by time and 'hassle' involved in purchasing the financial product. This is the full meaning of the term 'economic value' which was discussed in Chapter 6 on organizational behaviour. Thus if the current account customer's bank, or building society, guarantees that they will not be undersold on household and car insurance *and* they facilitate simple purchase and post-purchase support (if a claim arises), there is no logical reason why the customer should buy from another provider. That of course assumes that the current insurance provider has included all product attributes that the consumer values in putting together a particular product, i.e. that superior customer delivered value is being offered.

A second important concept in relationship marketing is that of customer satisfaction. This is simply the difference between the product's performance and the buyer's expectation. Customer satisfaction is crucial in determining repeat purchases and in encouraging new business, through word of mouth communication. Thus the type of relationship which an organization develops with its customers will determine the degree of satisfaction they have and hence their level of loyalty to the organization.

According to Grönroos (1991)

> 'The purpose of relationship marketing is to establish, maintain and enhance long-term relationships with customers and other parties so that the objectives of both parties are met.'

Relationship marketing focuses on long-term relationships with profitable customers rather than on one-off transactions. Table 14.1 illustrates the major differences between relationship marketing and transaction marketing.

Table 14.1 Transaction Marketing versus Relationship Marketing

Transaction Marketing	Relationship Marketing
A focus on single sales	A focus on customer retention and building customer loyalty
An emphasis upon product features	An emphasis upon product benefits that are meaningful to the customer
Short timescales	Long timescales, recognizing that short-term costs may be higher, but so will long-term profits.
Little emphasis on customer retention	An emphasis upon high levels of service which are possible tailored to the individual customer
Limited customer commitment	High customer commitment
Moderate customer contact	High customer contact, with each contact being used to gain information and build the relationship
Quality is essentially the concern of production and no-one else	Quality is the concern of all, and it is the failure to recognize this that creates minor mistakes which lead to major problems

Source: Adapted from Christopher, Payne & Ballantyne (1994) cited in Wilson & Gilligan (1997)

Customer retention planning and monitoring, and the relationship marketing mix

Financial Services Institutions have to a large extent relied on customer inertia to retain customers. However, now with increased competition and the presence of new entrants into the marketplace offering attractive services, customers are becoming more discerning.

Research has shown that it takes significantly more investment to acquire a new customer that it does to retain an existing one. In fact studies have shown that it costs 5-10 times more to acquire a new customer than to retain an existing one (Murphy 1996). Analysts at Bain and Company Management Consultants have found that a 5% increase in customer retention can significantly increase profitably for example by 25% in a bank (Murphy 1996).

Of course all customers are not equally profitable and financial service companies may want to deselect those that are unprofitable. In financial services the Pareto effect is evident with 20% of customers accounting for 80% of profits (Murphy 1996).

The importance of relationships has led to the development of scales of customer relationships which organizations employ to monitor trends in their customer relationships. One such scale (of five levels) is presented in Figure 14.2.

Figure 14.2: Levels of Customer Relationship

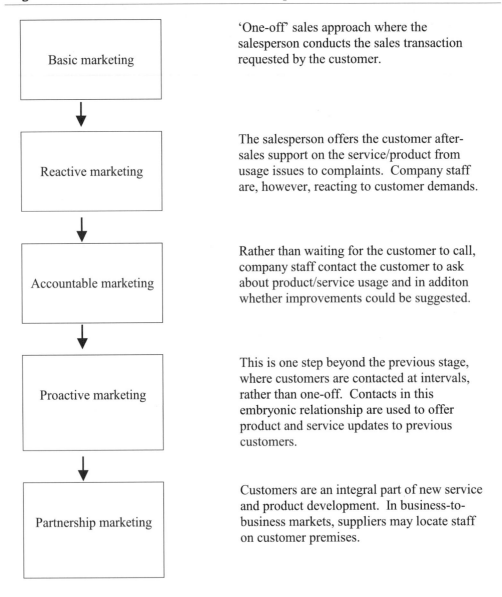

Basic marketing	'One-off' sales approach where the salesperson conducts the sales transaction requested by the customer.
Reactive marketing	The salesperson offers the customer after-sales support on the service/product from usage issues to complaints. Company staff are, however, reacting to customer demands.
Accountable marketing	Rather than waiting for the customer to call, company staff contact the customer to ask about product/service usage and in additon whether improvements could be suggested.
Proactive marketing	This is one step beyond the previous stage, where customers are contacted at intervals, rather than one-off. Contacts in this embryonic relationship are used to offer product and service updates to previous customers.
Partnership marketing	Customers are an integral part of new service and product development. In business-to-business markets, suppliers may locate staff on customer premises.

Adapted from Kotler P (2000) *Marketing Management* International edition Prentice Hall International

There is not simply one ultimate level of relationship that all companies should strive to achieve with all their customers, i.e. 'partnership' in Figure 14.2. Two important variables, which influence the type of relationship a company should develop with its customers, are profit margins and the number of customers that it serves. At one extreme, where the organization has many customers who yield high profit margins, the company should develop a partnership with each customer. However where there are many customers and each yields a low profit margin, it is appropriate to provide only basic customer support, e.g. a consumer helpline. Resources are scarce in organizations and they must be allocated to serving customer groups so as to maximize long-term profit margins.

Two additionally important variables, which are influential in determining the level of relationship the company develops with its customer base, are consumer time horizon and switching costs, from the consumer perspective. The highest level of relationship may not be appropriate, where consumers have short time horizons (e.g. travellers cheques/foreign exchange and holiday insurance), and similarly where switching costs are low.

Customer retention has a powerful more direct effect on profits that market share, scale economies and other variables commonly associated with competitive advantage. (De Souza 1992.) As customer retention increases associated marketing costs are reduced. In addition 'loyal' satisfied customers also bring in new business through word of mouth.

Relationships with dissatisfied customers

One of the surest signs of a bad or declining relationship is the absence of complaints from the customer. Nobody is ever that satisfied, especially not over an extended period. The customer is either not being candid or not being contacted, or both.

Payne et al. 1999, p27 thought provoking comment, in a paper by Theodore Levitt

Customers dissatisfied with their relationship, e.g. because of bad service, have one of three possible options:

1. Stop buying from the company;

2. Complain and demand satisfaction;

3. Continue to buy from the company without complaining – usually because alternatives do not exist or because the effort of change is outweighed by the problem encountered. The problem with this situation is that as soon as an alternative supplier is available the company will lose its customer base very rapidly.

Developing customer relationships
Marketers can develop stronger customer relationships through: (1) adding financial benefits (e.g. lower interest rates for platinum card holders), (2) adding social benefits (donating X% of profits from the sale of a product to a charity) and (3) adding structural ties (where the bank provides the Internet service link and customized accounts software when you set up an Internet account).

Two strategies which have been used by companies that are more advanced in relationship management are to (a) move towards 'zero defect' service management and (b) develop complaint management approaches and systems in which staff are fully trained. A well-handled complaint can convert a dissatisfied customer in to a loyal advocate of the organization. Studies have shown that converted dissatisfied customers can become an important element of the organization's hard-core loyals.

Relationship strategies available to service companies when developing a relationship-marketing plan include:

- core service marketing
- relationship customization
- service augmentation
- relationship pricing and
- internal marketing – where staff are fully briefed, trained and managed to deliver the required level of relationship.

MARKETING IN PRACTICE

Customer relationships and outside suppliers

Banks continue to seek ways to gain new customers. The very high costs of acquiring new customers through traditional communications methods resulted in banks going down the acquisition route. However as the costs of this have escalated, so banks have considered other approaches.

Banks are increasingly attempting to exploit the added value which may be obtained from pooling data with non-banking partners. The UK Data Protection Act provides guidelines which allows for the sharing of customer data. The Royal Bank of Canada and British Airways is one example of this. However cooperation and data pooling has been taken much further by HFC (the credit card firm) and General Motors. This has resulted in much more effective targeting of customers, with timely offerings of appropriate products, for the funding of major purchases, such as cars.

14.2   Relationships with Outside Suppliers

Briefing, working, control and review of agencies and consultancies (specifying needs/time/span/budgets)

The value chain requires that organizations work with and are dependent on outside suppliers. The key components of successful inter-organizational relations have been defined as:

- Common purpose
- Team work
- Long-term commitment
- Integrity
- On-going evaluation.

Worsam M (1998, p206)

Work by Buchanan and Gillies (presented in Payne *et al.* 1999, pp247-53) describes a 'collaborative and communicative partnership' which they suggest works by reducing systems costs and enhancing profitability and competitiveness. The four areas where it is suggested that typically most benefits arise are in: integrated design, manufacturing, quality control, and inventory systems. While this is a much-discussed topic in the manufacturing sector, parallel lessons may be learned in the service sector.

The recognition of distributors, intermediaries, agents and franchisees as customers

It is unremarkable to conclude that an important aspect of the final delivered value of a product to the consumer is the cost of the marketing chain that supplied the product.

Porter (1980) took the concept of the marketing chain one stage further when he proposed the 'value chain model' as a means of analysing each firm in the marketing chain. This provides managers of firms with an approach to reduce costs and to create more customer value. By ensuring cooperation with each chain member, in addition to maximizing the efficiency of each link in the chain, the total 'value delivery system' maximizes customer delivered value.

Briefing, working with, control and review of agencies and consultancies

This must be undertaken in the context of objective setting for the work which the agency must undertake. Once the agency planning and implementation process has been completed, effective evaluation of effectiveness must be undertaken. This should be agreed with the agency prior to undertaking the work. Clarity between the agency and the client company in each of these planning stages is essential for an effective, beneficial, long-term relationship. This is especially important with regard agency remuneration, where this is linked to some mutually agreed performance objective.

14.3   Internal Marketing Relationships

The concept, organizational structures and cultures

There is no one universal definition of internal marketing. The phrase has been used in many different contexts by various authors. However, it is generally accepted that the concept is concerned with treating staff as internal customers, defining internal marketing as:

> *coordinating internal exchanges between a firm and its employees to achieve successful external exchanges between the company and its customers.*

> Source: Dibb et al. (1997) p717

Internal marketing is seen by many as a prerequisite to external marketing. Without satisfied and motivated employees, in service industries it is hard to see how they could satisfy external customers.

Three important issues to be considered for successful internal marketing are (1) successful implementation, (2) senior management support and (3) appropriate organizational structure.

1. The implementation stage of any plan is often more difficult than the planning stage. It is therefore imperative that managers plan for implementation to ensure the barriers to planning are overcome. Internal marketing is seen as the vehicle for ensuring that staff 'buy into' any form of change, whether it is the implementation of a marketing orientation or the introduction of a new organizational structure.

2. Despite companies recognizing the growing importance of internal marketing it is still rare to find UK companies that have implemented formal internal marketing campaigns. Instead, internal marketing programmes have been part of quality initiatives or attempts to help to improve communication within the organization. A key driver to ensure success is formal support from senior management.

3. The type of organizational structure can impact on the level of marketing orientation that exists in an organization and also the culture of the company.

Internal marketing techniques include ensuring that appropriate people are recruited in the first place and that suitable training programmes are developed to ensure that people continually update their skills. Some of the leading banks, for example Barclays Bank, are utilizing NVQs (national vocational qualifications) in management or customer service to ensure that employees continue their professional development.

An internal marketing programme should be developed with the same rigour and employing the same processes as for external marketing campaigns, including setting objectives, developing a strategy (including segmentation of internal customers), selecting an appropriate marketing mix and evaluating the success of the programme. In each of the various target markets it is essential to identify individuals who are 'supporters', 'neutrals' and 'opposers' in order to develop specific marketing mixes for each group.

Internal marketing is of great significance to service providers because they are offering a highly intangible product. Service providers are highly dependent on their staff to deliver the desired level of customer service, consequently internal marketing is as important for service firms as is external marketing. Internal marketing plays a key role in implementing marketing plans. This is discussed in Chapter 2.

MARKETING IN PRACTICE

First National – Brand-new culture

When Abbey National acquired First National Bank in 1995, the published objective was 'to provide 10 per cent of Abbey National's profits'. Laudable enough – but not terribly inspiring. Without a stronger mission for First National, staff were losing their sense of belonging. In a survey, staff were more likely to see themselves as part of Abbey National or their own specialist division than with First National. Nevertheless, the organization did

---

expand to achieve the Abbey National objective through organic growth and a series of acquisitions, the most recent being three companies from Lombard at the end of 1998. Although this all added up to good news for the business it only added to the lack of identity and unity internally. Initially, First National was seen as a conglomerate of disparate businesses, and staff within the new businesses did not feel integrated. As one member of staff commented, 'there are so many different companies and cultures, it's hard to know where everything fits in'. Another said: 'People need to be aware we all work for the same organization'.

United we stand

The finance industry is notoriously competitive, and it became clear that the lack of cohesion and direction was holding us back. The only way forward was to align people behind a challenging yet commonly-shared goal. Many organizations have not yet realized the value of having their people share a common goal or vision for the future. Those that do often fail to secure the very support they seek from their people. Why? Because the vision is issued as a top-down edict that does not address people's questions and concerns. To avoid this common pitfall, First National asked the Marketing and Communications Agency (MCA) to carry out a strategic review of the company's communication including extensive research which helped to shape the business strategy. The research revealed a gap between the aims of the Board and what people actually understood, and highlighted a number of actions needed:

- Develop a strong brand;

- Align effort around a motivating objective;

- Re-engineer the organization to integrate newly acquired businesses into the whole;

- Introduce a communication strategy to unify the restructured business.

Source: 'Brand new culture' Financial World *May 1999 p24*

Summary

Developing superior relationships with various stakeholder groups is a means by which companies can gain competitive advantage. Customers are obviously a key group with which to develop successful relationships. However, it is also imperative to build good working relationships with suppliers, distributors, franchises and, most importantly, employees.

Companies are recognizing that the cost of acquiring new customers far exceeds that of retaining existing ones. This has led to companies adopting the practices of relationship marketing. This was originally thought to be only relevant in the B2B markets, however it is increasingly being recognized that it is of equal importance in B2C markets. Relationship marketing should not necessarily be applied equally to all customers. Customers vary in terms of the level of service they require and importantly their contribution to company profitability. A key aspect of relationship marketing is in the identification of profitable customers (the old adage that 80% of revenue comes from 20% of customers) and the development of strategies to retain their loyalty. Companies must then have processes in place to monitor retention levels and the success of their relationship marketing activities.

Developing successful relationships, often long term, with other partners in the marketing chain can contribute to competitive advantage and prove beneficial for all partners. The use of agencies and consultancies is increasing, as many companies are now concentrating on their core business and are subcontracting non-core work. It is essential that partners/agencies have clear objectives and guidelines on working practices that will lead to mutually beneficial relationships.

It is increasingly been recognized that successful internal relationships between a firm and its employees are a prerequisite to successful external relationships. Without motivated and satisfied staff it is difficult to see how they can satisfy external customers. Companies are adopting the principles of external marketing and applying them to the internal marketplace. The organizational structure will have a major impact on the organizational culture and the nature of the internal relationships.

References

Easden J (1999) Brand New Culture, *Financial World*, May p24

Christopher M, Payne A & Ballantyne (1994), cited in Wilson M S & Gilligan C (1997) *Strategic Marketing Management*, 2nd edition, CIM Butterworth Heinemann, Oxford

De Souza (1999) Rules of Attraction, *Financial World*, February pp28-31

Dibb, Simkin, Pride & Ferrell (1997) *Marketing Financial Services*, 2nd edition, Butterworth Heinemann, Oxford

Ennew C, Watkins T, Wright M (eds.) (1995) *Marketing Financial Services*, 2nd edition, Butterworth Heinemann, Oxford

Grönroos (1991) The marketing strategy continuum, towards a marketing concept for the 1990s, *Management Decision*, Vol. 29, no 1, pp7-13

Kotler P (2000) *Marketing Management*, The Millennium Edition, Prentice-Hall

Kotler P, Armstrong G, Saunders J & Wong V (1999) *Principles of Marketing*, 2nd European edition, Prentice Hall Europe

Murphy J (1996) Customer loyalty: happy customers add directly to the bottom line, *Financial Times Mastering Management series*, 1 November

Payne A, Christopher M, Clark M & Peck H (1999) *Relationship Marketing – Winning and Keeping Customers*, Butterworth Heinemann-CIM, Oxford

Porter M (1980) *Competitive Strategy*, Free Press, New York.

Worsam M (1998) *Marketing Operations Workbook*, CIM Butterworth Heinemann

Part 4

CASE STUDIES

Introduction

While this case study is presented after a chapter on relationship marketing, the content of the case includes many topics which are covered in this text book, ranging from marketing strategy, the use of the Internet in marketing, relationship marketing, B2B marketing, the process 'P' of the marketing mix etc. Students should therefore consider 'JAL: building an e-business' as an integrative case for the textbook.

Japan Airlines (JAL): Building an e-business

Note: This case study is based on successful implementation of leading e-business technology by IBM, which has been endorsed by the client, Japan Airlines.

The Goal	NEAR-TERM: To establish closer and stronger customer relationships.
	LONG-TERM: To increase customer retention rate and to stimulate travel volume.
The Organization	The largest airline in Asia, JAL employs nearly 20,000 people worldwide and operates in 109 airports in 30 countries. In 1999, JAL carried nearly 33 million passengers.
The results	*'We have found the Internet to be an outstanding medium for establishing deeper connections with our customers...One of the outstanding characteristics of the Internet is speedy communication. We consider this ability to conduct speedy communication to be our most trusted weapon.'*

After launching its Web site in 1995, JAL soon began exploring the opportunity to launch e-commerce services via the Web. A key business driver of JAL's e-business strategy was the desire to position itself at the leading edge of e-commerce to gain first-mover advantage. A more specific goal was to use Web-based e-commerce as a means of further developing its domestic travel business. Its first initiative was to develop a Web-based ticket information and reservation system that allows customers to make, confirm and cancel reservations, as well as to view information on flight schedules, space availability, and arrival and departure information.

JAL's Web-based services have been widely adopted by its customer base, with the number of customers making Internet-based reservations doubling every year. At present, JAL estimates that Internet-based reservations account for more than 10 percent of its total reservations. JAL has reaped a wide range of business results from its e-business initiatives, including an increase in both domestic and international revenues and substantially improved customer satisfaction.

Key Goals of JAL's e-business Evolution

In aggressively pursuing e-business opportunities, JAL seeks to solidify its customer relationships. As Tomohiro Nishihata, JAL's Director of e-Business, Product Planning, explains, JAL's goal has been to engage its customers by stimulating interactivity. 'From the beginning, we have intended not simply to deliver information to our customers, but to be interactively connected with them,' says Nishihata. 'We see personalization technology and targeted communications as an important future tool in our attempts to attract customers and to strengthen our interaction with them.'

In addition to forging closer bonds with customers, e-business technology is also seen by JAL as a strategic marketing tool. Specifically, JAL sees a strong opportunity to leverage the information gained through its various Web programs as a means of attracting and keeping 'high-value' customers. Nishihata views JAL's Cyberflash – an e-mail messaging service that targets JAL's frequent-flyer programme members – as an excellent example of this. 'Ultimately, our goal is to increase the number and the quality of our JAL Mileage Bank membership base,' says Nishihata. 'We have been able to do this by using our messaging programs to promote new services.' JAL has also leveraged its e-mail program to strengthen its service development effort by channelling customer suggestions into new services.

JAL's Recent and Current e-business Initiatives

JAL's most recent initiative, JAL Online, is a B2B e-commerce solution targeted to domestic businesses whose services extend beyond flight reservations to include hotel services and the ability to pay via a corporate credit card. Introduced in June 1999 and now on its second version, JAL Online has been adopted by more than 1,000 companies in Japan.

In late 1999, JAL introduced its 'i-mode' service, which allows customers to use a cellular telephone to make, confirm or cancel their reservations – or to buy tickets via a credit card. Nishihata views JAL's primary motivation in introducing its i-mode service as the desire to offer its customers higher levels of convenience. 'Under one scenario, we see our customers mixing their mobile telephones with their home PC,' says Nishihata. 'For example, they may use i-mode to confirm or cancel the reservations they have made on their home PC.' Nishihata reports that the number of customers buying tickets via i-mode has more than doubled in the first half of 2000, an adoption rate he calls 'very significant.'

Usage of JAL's Web-based Services

Since their introduction in 1996, JAL's Web-based services have been widely adopted by its customer base, with the number of customers making Internet-based reservations doubling every year. 'Based on what we've seen so far, we expect this rate of adoption to continue in 2000,' says Nishihata. 'At present, we estimate that Internet-based reservations account for more than 10 percent of our total reservations.' He adds that when other usage of information services such as checking flight schedules and mileage are taken into account, the JAL site generally receives more than 500,000 hits daily.

Overview of the JAL's Business Results Achieved

Business Process Area	Nature of Benefit	Description or Metric
Customer service	Strengthened relationship	Increased customer satisfaction Increased customer retention
Strategic marketing	Increased revenue	Increased domestic and international traffic
Customer service	Improved efficiency	More efficient, lower cost customer communications

Source: JAL and IDC

Business Results

JAL reports a high degree of acceptance of its Web-based reservation solution, with over ten per cent of its direct reservations (i.e., 5 per cent of its overall reservation volume) made online. From April 2000 to July 2000, the number of online reservations increased 50 per cent. As usage of JAL's Web-based reservation platform has grown, so has the resulting range of business results it has achieved. Among the most direct benefits derived from its Web-based reservation system is an increase in both domestic and international revenues. Nishihata expects the growth of JAL's Internet-based revenues to further accelerate as Internet usage and e-commerce becomes more widely accepted. Nishihata also believes that JAL's online initiatives have strengthened its customer relationships. 'We have found the Internet to be an outstanding medium for establishing deeper connections with our customers, most notably the 500,000 members of JAL Mileage Bank, our frequent-flyer program.' JAL has sought to deepen its customer relations by providing information and special programs such as discounts via its e-mail service. Nishihata notes that for JAL the Internet has greatly simplified the communications process in general, a factor on which it plans to capitalize.

In addition to more frequent communication with its half-a-million JAL Mileage Bank members, JAL plans to provide more targeted information content. 'We absolutely plan to add personalization to our customer communication capabilities,' says Nishihata. 'We are entering upon a new phase where we not only expand our channels and improve the quality of our content – but do so in a highly targeted way. By working with IBM, we hope to leverage its expertise in this and other areas at the leading edge of e-business technology.'

The authors are grateful to IBM for permission to use this material.

- Identify the key services that JAL delivers over the Internet.

- JALs e-business initiative supports marketing activity in the following areas: marketing strategy, relationship marketing and marketing communications. Compare and contrast the effectiveness of these three areas of marketing activity pre- and post- the use of e-business technology.

- Think about the measures that may be used to assess the success of Internet marketing.

Glossary

Benefit segmentation – a form of market segmentation which divides the market according to difference in the benefits sought by the buyer.

Channels of distribution – the system of agencies needed to provide the flow of information, goods and legal title from producer to consumer.

Comprehension – part of the 'perceptual system': new information is compared with the established store of meanings held by the individual, in order to understand and classify the new information.

Cost-per-thousand – used in media planning: calculated by dividing the cost of advertising by the numbers in the audience; it is normally based upon circulation or readership.

Decision-making unit (DMU) – the group of people that may influence purchase decisions; the concept can apply in all marketing circumstances, but has been most associated with industrial marketing.

Demographics – population characteristics; in marketing those factors studied include age, sex, family size and education; some writers now use the term to include social class.

Desk research – research using extant material, i.e. that already available.

Group discussion – an informal meeting convened by a company or agency with eight or ten consumers to elicit their views about a product or advertisement.

Hierarchy-of-effects – a model of the buying process which suggests that buyers move through set sequences from awareness to purchase; has received most comment as a model of the advertising process.

Innovators – the first buyers to be attracted to a new product; it is they who begin the adoption process.

Lifestyle segmentation – the subdivision of a market based upon lifestyles, as measured by activities, interests, opinions and values.

Market development – a strategy for obtaining growth by attracting new market segments.

Market penetration – a strategy for obtaining growth by increasing market share with the same product and no change in target market.

Market research – the collection and analysis of data to provide a description of market characteristics; a part of 'marketing research'.

Market segmentation – the subdivision of a market into parts that are relatively homogenous, so that separate and distinctive marketing plans can be prepared for each segment; it is one way of clearly identifying target markets.

Marketing concept – the view of marketing's role in an organization which emphasizes the need to understand and to anticipate consumer requirements as a basis for all decisions that may affect the market.

Marketing mix – the composite of plans made by an organization dealing with products, prices, promotion and distribution.

Marketing research – research undertaken into an area of marketing planning and operations.

Primary data – information specially collected in a marketing research study, not previously available and not normally published.

Product development – a strategy for obtaining growth by changing (developing) the product to be offered.

Product life cycle – stages in the market acceptance of a product; it can be analysed at the level of the product class, the product form or at the level of the individual brand.

Product manager – an individual given responsibility for the overall planning of a product's success.

Product portfolio analysis – a method of plotting all of a company's brands against their market growth rates and market shares.

Promotion mix – the composite promotional plan, i.e. the personal and non-personal (e.g. advertising) means of communication to be employed.

Relationship marketing/management – the development of long-term relationships with customers, suppliers and organizational staff for each product/service offer. This is achieved through maximizing full economic value to each of these three interest groups by minimizing the full economic costs to those groups.

Secondary data – published data used in marketing research – government statistics are a major source.

Segment base/segment variable – the base or variable chosen for a market segmentation study e.g. a demographic variable such as age.

Test marketing – limited marketing operations on an experimental basis; three purposes have been identified: (1) pilot launch; (2) projectable test launch; (3) market testing.

Undifferentiated marketing – a strategy which treats all consumers as being homogenous; sometimes termed 'market aggregation'.

INDEX

D

X

Z